SPECTROSCOPIC

TECHNIQUES

FOR

**FAR INFRA-RED,
SUBMILLIMETRE AND MILLIMETRE WAVES**

Editor

D. H. MARTIN

*Queen Mary College
University of London*

1967

NORTH-HOLLAND PUBLISHING COMPANY - AMSTERDAM

CHEMISTRY

Library of Congress Catalog Card Number 67–20013

Publishers:

NORTH-HOLLAND PUBLISHING COMPANY – AMSTERDAM

Sole distributors for U.S.A. and Canada:

INTERSCIENCE PUBLISHERS, *a division of*

JOHN WILEY & SONS, INC. – NEW YORK

PRINTED IN THE NETHERLANDS

Contents

530

CHAPTER 4

DETECTORS

by E. H. PUTLEY and D. H. MARTIN

CHAPTER 5

HARMONIC GENERATORS AND SEMICONDUCTOR DETECTORS

by J. G. BAKER

CHAPTER 6

COHERENT SOURCES USING ELECTRON BEAMS

by P. N. ROBSON

CHAPTER 7

TECHNIQUES OF PROPAGATION AT MILLIMETRE AND SUBMILLIMETRE WAVELENGTHS

by D. J. KROON and J. M. VAN NIEUWLAND

Preface

This is a book of techniques for that part of the spectrum which lies between microwaves and the infra-red, that is from about 5 cm^{-1} (or 2 mm wavelength) to 200 cm^{-1} (50 μm). Methods of spectrometry here have improved over the last few years and with this has come a multiplication of applications of importance in solid-state and chemical physics. This book has been designed first to help a reader to assess the capabilities of the several tried and complementary techniques of this region, and to anticipate technical developments, and secondly to assist spectroscopists in setting up suitable instrumentation and in using it to best advantage.

D. H. MARTIN

CHAPTER 1

SPECTROMETRY BETWEEN 3 cm^{-1} AND 200 cm^{-1}

BY

D. H. MARTIN

Dept. of Physics, Queen Mary College, London

1. Introduction

Exploratory spectroscopic studies in the region between 0.05 and 3 mm in wavelength began more than 50 years ago but progress has been greatly impeded by the lack of suitable bright sources so that the development of spectroscopy here has lagged well behind that in other parts of the spectrum. The realisation that simple solids, as well as molecular materials, should exhibit a wide variety of important spectra at these frequencies has recently given impetus to the attempts of spectroscopists to extend the ranges of infra-red and microwave techniques into this part of the spectrum and also to develop new methods. As a result, there is in use here a wider variety of technique than in any other part of the spectrum. The purpose of this introductory chapter is to examine the general considerations involved in assessing the relative merits of the main spectroscopic methods whose details are treated at greater length in subsequent chapters. In addition, the newly developed submillimetre lasers, which find no place in the other chapters, are briefly described, and the chapter finishes with a survey of commercially available equipment.

The range of interest is from roughly 3 mm to 0.05 mm in wavelength, i.e. 3.3 cm^{-1} to 200 cm^{-1} in wave-number (see fig. 1.1). There is no single name in general use for this part of the spectrum, because, as noted above,

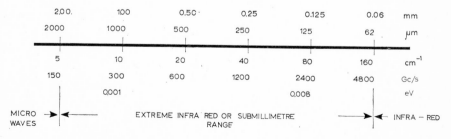

Fig. 1.1.

no one experimental technique at present meets all requirements. The term "millimetric", or "low-millimetric", covers techniques which are extensions of microwave methods, with electron-beam sources, harmonic generators, wave-guides, etc., to wavelengths down to 1 mm. "Submillimetric" refers to the use of similar techniques at wavelengths less than 1 mm. The term "far infra-red" is employed when the techniques in use resemble those of the near infra-red and visible regions, i.e. with broad-band hot-body sources and "optical" devices such as mirrors, diffraction-gratings, interferometers. With both approaches there are difficulties and distinctly new techniques will evolve eventually for much of this spectral region, as convenient and tuneable coherent sources become available and call for methods of handling the radiation with greater precision and flexibility. This is because the wavelengths here are such that components of convenient size for fabrication and manipulation must have dimensions measuring several wavelengths, i.e. neither very much greater than the wavelength as in precision optical methods nor about the same as the wavelength as in microwave methods. Special components of such dimensions are being actively studied and have been called "quasi-optical".

In making a choice from these techniques for a particular application several major considerations must be weighed against each other, including in particular the spectral resolution required, the range of frequency to be scanned, the time available for recording, the ease of operation, and expense or availability of components. The three main methods in present use are diffraction-grating spectrometry, Fourier-transform spectrometry using interferometers, and methods based on the generation of harmonics of microwave sources. The first (ch. 3) is the simplest and least expensive and up to now the most widely used but, though it meets most needs above $100\,\mathrm{cm^{-1}}$, the available power from broad-band hot-body sources decreases drastically as the wavelength increases and this severely limits the attainable resolutions and rates of scan; below $30\,\mathrm{cm^{-1}}$ cooled detectors (ch. 4) might be necessary. The second method (ch. 2) makes more efficient use of source-power, and is therefore faster and can give better resolution; it is well adapted to covering wide spectral ranges from $3\,\mathrm{cm^{-1}}$ to $400\,\mathrm{cm^{-1}}$, but it requires more sophisticated and expensive equipment and, being a comparatively new technique, still needs experienced operators. The last (ch. 5) gives very high resolution since it uses a coherent source and it has been widely used at wavelengths exceeding 1 mm; but the available power falls rapidly with decreasing wavelength and it is still a specialists's technique at wavelengths below 1 mm; the highest frequency reached so far with this method is about $25\,\mathrm{cm^{-1}}$

(0.4 mm). It is not suited to continuous scanning over wide ranges of frequency. The broad principles of these major techniques, as well as details of operation and performance, are given in their respective chapters. In the following section we shall concentrate on those aspects which determine the relative merits of the three methods.

The main concern of this book is with the techniques and not with the interpretation of spectra. We should, however, mention some of the phenomena which are being investigated in the far infra-red and millimetre regions. These include several collective, or large-scale, motions of electrons and ions in crystals as well as atomic and molecular excitations. For pure rotational spectra of molecules this part of the spectrum offers an advantage over the microwave region in that small molecules, with low moments of inertia, can be studied so that molecular distortions, collisions, and interactions might be investigated with simple molecules. Various intra-molecular motions of larger molecules, such as the hindered rotation of one part of a molecule with respect to another and the vibrational motions of heavy atoms in complexes or organo-metallic compounds, can produce far infrared spectra (see e.g. Spectrochimica Acta **19** (1963)) and so too can bending motions of hydrogen bonds. The large-scale or skeletal vibrations of large molecules and polymers are of low frequency and so too are the vibrational modes of crystals which have been widely studied in considerable detail by far infra-red spectroscopy (see MARTIN [1965]). Some electronic tran-

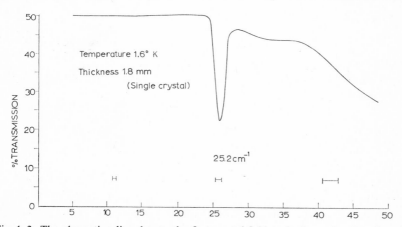

Fig. 1.2. The absorption line due to the first crystal-field excitations of cerium ions in cerium magnesium nitrate. This spectrum was recorded with a grating spectrometer and a cooled indium antimonide detector in a total time of about 120 minutes, at a signal-to-noise ratio of about 50 and at the resolutions indicated on the figure. (By courtesy of Mr. E. Ellis.)

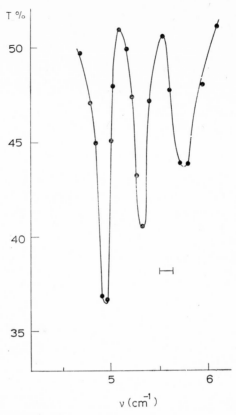

Fig. 1.3. The transmission spectrum of a 3 mm thick sample of $(NH_4)_2 Pt Cl_6$ doped with Ir (Ir: Pt 1:5). The spectrum is believed to be due to excitations of pairs of neighbouring Ir ions coupled by exchange interactions, and it provides a measure of the coupling. This spectrum was recorded with a grating instrument and a cooled indium antimonide detector in a recording time of 40 minutes, at a signal-to-noise ratio of about 20 and at a resolution of 0.15 cm^{-1} as shown in the figure. The sample was at 4 °K. (By courtesy of Mr. M. Platt.)

sitions within ions in crystals fall in the far infra-red; the crystal-field splittings of the ground-states of ions of the transition-elements and the rare-earths, for example, are under investigation (fig. 1.2). Exchange interactions between magnetic ions have been studied both by the excitation of spinwaves in ordered magnetic solids (e.g. fig. 2.10, and SIEVERS and TINKHAM [1961]) and by inducing changes in the relative orientations of the moments of coupled pairs of ions isolated in diamagnetic crystals (fig. 1.3). Other examples of far infra-red electronic spectra in solids are the cyclotron resonance spectra of semiconductors especially those with carriers of very low effective masses (e.g. PALIK and STEVENSON [1963]) and the reflection spectra of superconductors at photon energies close to the energy gap which separates the correlated pairs of superconducting electrons from the continuous energy spectrum of normal electrons (e.g. RICHARDS and TINKHAM [1960]).

The energy of a photon in the far infra-red is equal to kT at a temperature below room temperature – 200 cm^{-1} corresponds to 287 °K. Far infra-red spectra are consequently sensitive to changes in temperature in this range. For excited states of molecules or for internal electronic excitations of ions in crystals, the fractional population of a state of energy E_i at thermal equilibrium is

$$\frac{\exp\left(-E_i/kT\right)}{Z}$$

where the partition function, Z, is

$$\sum_s \exp\left(-E_s/kT\right),$$

a sum over all states s. The strength of an absorption line due to a transition between states i and j is determined as a difference between induced absorption and emission and therefore varies with temperature as the difference in the populations of the initial and final states, i.e. as

$$\frac{\exp\left(-E_i/kT\right)}{Z}\{1 - \exp\left((E_i-E_j)/kT\right)\}.$$

If i is the ground-state and energies are measured from $E_i = 0$, the strength of the transition at $hv = E_i - E_j$ varies as

$$\frac{1}{Z}\{1 - \exp\left(-hv/kT\right)\}$$

and if j lies much lower than any other state this reduces to

$$\{1 - \exp\left(-hv/kT\right)\}/\{1 + \exp\left(-hv/kT\right)\}.$$

Thus, as the temperature is increased from zero to $kT = hv$, for example, the absorption strength falls to about $\frac{1}{2}$, and at $kT = 4hv$ it has fallen to less than 1/10. If there are other low-lying states the intensity will clearly fall more rapidly still as the ground-state is depopulated by transitions to these states. Most electronic spectra in the far infra-red are due to magnetic-dipole transitions and are therefore relatively weak and a temperature such that $kT \lesssim hv$ is therefore normally required for electronic spectra.

For the strong electric-dipole rotational transitions of dipolar molecules, on the other hand, clear far infra-red and millimetre-wave spectra can be obtained even at room-temperature in spite of this effect. All states within $\sim 10kT$ of the ground-state are significantly populated and transitions from all these states will be observable. Allowing for the $(2J+1)$ degeneracy of a rotational state of quantum number J it is a straight forward matter to show that the strongest lines will usually be those for which $hv \simeq kT$.

Loss of absorption intensity resulting from a near equalisation of the populations of the initial and final states does not apply to spectra due to boson-like excitations in solids, for example phonons (lattice vibrational waves) and magnons (spin-waves). Such excitations are not limited in number; a further quantum of lattice vibrational energy can always be added no matter how many are already present. It is true that such spectra can be interpreted in terms of excitations of a fixed number of harmonic oscillators but the levels of an harmonic oscillator are equally spaced and transitions between all pairs of these levels contribute to the spectral line; when the variation of oscillator strength with quantum number is taken into account it is straightforwardly shown that the total absorption strength is independent of temperature. This is in accord with the fact that phonon spectra can be observed at room temperature without large loss of total absorption strength relative to that at low temperatures (fig. 1.4).

A second consideration which leads to a need for low temperatures is that of the breadths of spectral lines. The lifetimes of excited states are determined by the availability of de-excitation processes in which the excitation energy is carried away in some other form. For excited states of solids with energies in the far infra-red region the lattice vibrations in particular represent capacious sinks into which the excitation energy can be transferred by single-quantum transitions because phonons have energies spreading through the far infra-red. (Few lattice vibrations are excited *directly* by incident photons as a result of selection rules requiring an excited phonon to have a transverse dipole moment and a wavelength as well as a frequency equal to the incident phonon's. Otherwise the far infra-red would be blacked out in solids by the absorption due to lattice vibrations.) The transition strengths for de-excitation processes are usually enhanced by the presence of lattice vibrations already thermally excited in the crystal which distort the crystal and therefore relax some of the selection rules arising from the symmetry of the undistorted crystal. This introduces a dependence on temperature of the line-breadths, for example that illustrated in fig. 1.4. There is therefore considerable interest in measurements of line-breadths,

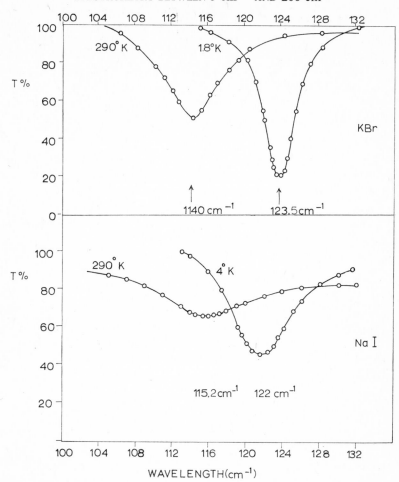

Fig. 1.4. Transmission spectra of thin (about 1 μm) films of KBr and NaI at room temperature and at liquid helium temperature. The absorption lines are due to the excitation of longwave optical lattice vibrations. The spectra were recorded with a grating spectrometer and a Golay detector (at room temperature), at signal-to-noise ratio of about 50, a scanning rate of 1 cm^{-1} per min and at a resolution of 1 cm^{-1}. (By courtesy of Mr. R. P. Lowndes.)

and low-temperatures are desirable for this reason. For gases it is the time between molecular collisions which determines the life-times of excited states and thence the spectral line-breadths. This is temperature-dependent but the pressure is also relevant and extremely narrow lines can be obtained at room temperature if the pressure is sufficiently low (see, for example, figs. 5.25–5.29).

Cryostats for far infra-red investigations at temperatures down to 1 °K require no special cryogenic techniques. For relatively low resolution work the optical design can be simplified considerably by the use of the light-pipes which are convenient for many purposes in the far infra-red (OHLMAN and TINKHAM [1958]). Suitable cryostats are illustrated in figs. 4.4 and 3.10. For high resolution work with millimetre waves, guides and cavities like those used for conventional microwave work can be constructed but higher losses must be expected (see, for example, fig. 5.30 and chapter 7).

2. Optical considerations in assessing a spectrometric method

The spectral information about a sample which can be determined from a given recorded spectrum, or "spectrogram", is limited by the signal-to-noise ratio and by the instrumental resolution at which it was recorded, or, some-times, by the effective sampling interval along the frequency scale which might be greater than the instrumental resolution when a spectrum is re-corded rapidly. These quantities are interdependent because an improvement in signal-to-noise ratio can always be obtained at the cost of a reduction in resolution, by adjustment of the instrument or, alternatively, by "smoothing" the noise on a spectrum already recorded. We must take care to make com-parisons between the performances of different spectrometric methods under properly comparable conditions. If the noise power spectrum is "white" – i.e. independent of frequency – the use of a detector system with an overall response time τ (including the influence of the restricted bandwidth of the amplifier and of the smoothing circuits in the output stages – ch. 4) will suppress the components with frequencies exceeding $\omega\tau \sim 1$ and conse-quently reduces the root-mean-square noise fluctuation on the signal in proportion to $\tau^{\frac{1}{2}}$. This reduction in the uncertainty of the true signal in-tensity reflects, of course, the fact that a time proportional to and about equal to τ is taken in each independent measurement (see below). In ex-periments involving the study of ordinary materials with laboratory samples the dominant noise usually derives from the detector. In some circumstances (e.g. in an observation of a planet through the atmosphere) signal fluctua-tions from other noise sources might dominate that due to the detector, and the noise-spectrum might be far from white; the detector's response-time would still influence the final signal-to-noise ratio but not in proportion to $\tau^{\frac{1}{2}}$.

First we examine the significance of detector response times and sampling intervals in order to compare spectra which are recorded as continuous (if sometimes noisy) lines and those recorded as point-by-point plots. The grating in a dispersion spectrometer is usually driven continuously and produces a spectrum of the first kind; interferometers might also give continuous spectrograms if the Fourier transform of the interferogram is obtained by analogue computations, but most often the interferogram is recorded in digital form at regularly spaced sampling intervals and the computation is made by a digital computer so that the final spectrum is presented as a point-by-point plot; an harmonic generator might be used to give a spectrum in the form of a continuous line if the spectrum falls within the very narrow spectral range which can be covered by electronic tuning of the klystron source, but for a wider range a point-by-point method might be used with mechanical tuning of the klystron cavity. At first sight it might seem that a continuous spectrogram gives more complete information but this view would neglect the fact that any two points in a continuous spectrogram which are recorded at times separated by less than the characteristic response time of the detector system are by no means independent. Any attempt to correct for this by mathematical means results in a reduction in the signal-to-noise ratio, which fact can be seen as follows. If $G'(t)$ is the intensity recorded in the spectrogram as a function of time and $G(t)$ that which would have been given by a hypothetical detector which responded instantaneously, then at any instant

$$\frac{dG'}{dt} = \frac{(G-G')}{\tau}$$

where τ is the time-constant characterising the response of the overall detector system. When there is noise on the record of $G'(t)$ only a mean value for dG'/dt over some time interval Δt can be determined. Use of the relation

$$\frac{\Delta G'}{\Delta t} = \frac{(G-G')}{\tau}, \quad \text{or} \quad (G-G') = \Delta G' \frac{\tau}{\Delta t}$$

would then serve to refine the $G'(t)$ so that it corresponds to the new effective sampling interval Δt. However, the fractional uncertainty in $G(t)$ will clearly be greater than that in $G'(t)$ if Δt is less than τ. There could, therefore, be no reduction in the effective sampling interval, by computation, without an increase in the noise level. Moreover, this increase in noise would be greater than that which would result from a modification of the detector's circuitry to give an actual reduction in the detector response time since the latter is only in proportion to the square root of the detector time-constant. Thus, while the relation above might be used with $\Delta t = \tau$ to correct for some of the distortion of the spectrum which results from the fact that the detector takes time to respond, there can be no useful reduction in the effective sampling interval below a value equal to the increment in frequency which is scanned in a time equal to the time-constant τ. When a spectrum is recorded point-by-point, a time at least equal to τ would be spent on each point, and so the maximum effective rate of scan would be one sampling interval (here the separation of successive points) per time-constant, just as it is for continuous recording.

There are other instrumental contributions to the spectral resolution of a spectrogram which might dominate that due to the effective sampling interval. In the cases of the dispersion and interferometric methods based on broad-band sources these arise from limitations on the accuracy with which an instrument can separate or code signals of differing wavelengths; in the case of the methods based on harmonic generation the instrumental limit is the instability in frequency of the fundamental source over the time required to record a point in the spectrum and measure the frequency. In the latter case this limiting resolving power is high, usually well exceeding 10^4, and this might be greater than a particular experiment demands so that a rate of recording might be chosen which is high enough for the effective sampling interval to set the limit to the resolution achieved. For the methods using broad-band sources, however, the instrumental resolution can be varied at will by instrumental adjustments (see below) and, since an adjustment which reduces the resolving power increases the signal-to-noise ratio, the instrumental resolving power is usually chosen to be as low as will meet the needs of the experiment in hand. The effective sampling interval will also be chosen to fall within this required resolution, of course; it will, in fact, usually be made several times smaller than the instrumental resolution because the corrections referred to above, which correct distortions of the spectrum due to the response time of the detector, will not then be necessary, except when intensity measurements of high accuracy are required, because the change $\Delta G'$ occurring in the interval τ could not be large. The noise can subsequently be averaged, to that appropriate to a sampling interval equal to the resolution, by computation or much more easily "by eye" on inspection of the spectrogram.

The resolving powers which can be obtained at specified signal-to-noise levels with dispersion and interferometric spectrometers can most easily be discussed in terms of a record like that shown in fig. 1.5a which represents

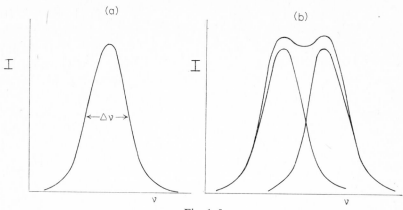

Fig. 1.5

the spectrum which would be produced by a grating spectrometer, or by an interferometric spectrometer, if the source were monochromatic or, equivalently, if a sample having an extremely narrow absorption line were mounted in front of a broad-band source. This spectrum shows a peak which is centred at the frequency of emission or of absorption but it has a non-zero width arising from deficiencies of the spectrometer. Such a curve is normally roughly Gaussian and can be characterised by its width at half-height, Δv, which provides the quantitative measure of the instrumental resolution. The ratio $\Delta v/v$ (which is equal to the corresponding ratio in terms of wavelength, $\Delta \lambda/\lambda$) is the *fractional resolution* and its reciprocal $v/\Delta v$ is the *resolving power*.

With a grating instrument, a curve like that in fig. 1.5a would be obtained by recording the intensity at the exit slit of the monochromator as a function of the angular setting of the grating and by calibrating the angular setting in terms of infra-red frequency using the grating equation (see fig. 3.2)

$$n\lambda = 2d \cos \alpha \cos \theta.$$

The non-zero width of the spectral line results from two major factors. First, the grating equation strictly indicates only the direction of maximum constructive interference; for a grating of finite width, i.e. for a finite number of secondary sources, the diffracted beam is most intense in this direction but is not strictly confined to it. It diverges over an angle which can be regarded as arising from diffraction at the aperture presented by the full area of the grating. As is well-known, the associated *diffraction-limited resolving power* of a grating in first order is equal to the number of lines on the grating or to the number of half-wavelengths in the projection of the width of the grating onto the direction of the incident or diffracted beam. Secondly, the widths of the entrance and exit slits of a grating monochromator contribute to the instrumental resolution. With non-zero slit widths a collimator cannot perfectly collimate the beam which is incident on the grating, and the condenser cannot illuminate the exit slit exclusively with the radiation diffracted by the grating into a particular direction. The resulting resolving power is shown in ch. 3 to be equal to about F/s where F is the focal length of the collimator and condenser, and s is the width of the entrance and exit slits. Aberrations in the optical system have a negligible effect on resolution at these long wavelengths.

With a two-beam interferometric spectrometer a curve like that in fig. 1.5a would be produced as a Fourier transform of an apodised interferogram (ch. 2). A monochromatic source in a two-beam interferometer would produce a sinusoidal variation of the intensity of the central spot of the interference pattern when the moveable reflector is displaced at a constant velocity. In practice, of course, the sinusoidal interferogram is of finite length, equal to the maximum path difference between the two beams, and this is the origin of the finite resolution. If the mirror movement is repeated a large number of times, as in the periodic methods, a Fourier analysis of the interferogram can clearly contain only harmonics of the repeat frequency, i.e. the Fourier components will be separated by an infra-red frequency equal to $1/2d$ (cm^{-1}) where $2d$ is the maximum path-difference corresponding to the full displacement, d cm, of the reflector. The frequency of the monochromatic source cannot be determined more closely than this. Equivalently, in aperiodic methods where only a single, slow, mirror movement is made, a truncated Fourier integral is taken (ch. 2) and a monochromatic source would produce a spectrum like that in fig. 1.5a with a width $1/2d$ (cm^{-1}) for the finite interferogram of length $2d$. The resolving power is thus equal to the number of half-wavelengths in the distance d. The widths of the entrance and exit slits can also affect the performance of an interferometer but this proves to be a much less restrictive consideration than the slit-width limitation for a grating spectrometer because the directions of rays in an interferometer are not essentially associated with the separation of different wavelengths as they are in an instrument based on spectral dispersion. The limit to the resolving power set by this consideration is $2(F/s)^2$ (see fig. 2.4) rather than the (F/s) for the grating spectrometer.

Thus, the resolving powers of both grating and interferometric spectrometers are determined by two factors; the first the diffraction or interference limit, and secondly the effects of non-zero slit-widths. As far as the first limitation is concerned there is little to choose between the dispersion and interferometric methods. In each case this limiting resolving power is equal to the number of half-wavelengths in a distance equal to the dimension of that part of the instrument which involves the greatest mechanical precision – the projected width of the grating in one case and the displacement of the moveable mirror in the other. There would be a considerable increase in the size and complexity of either instrument, beyond what is most convenient in practice, if this dimension were to exceed 5–10 cm. Most operating instruments fall in this range and would therefore have diffraction or interference-limited resolutions in the range 0.1–0.05 cm^{-1}. The important difference between the two methods is that, with slits wide enough to give an acceptable signal-to-noise ratio, the slit-width limitation overrides this interference limit for grating instruments but not with interferometers. With an interferometer based on a collimator and condenser with focal length about 30 cm, slit-widths near 1 cm can be used at all frequencies below 200 cm^{-1}, without reducing the resolution below the 0.1 cm^{-1} interference limit for a maximum path difference of 5 cm (and without loss of signal due to inability to condense the radiation sufficiently to bring it within the receptor areas of the detectors now in use in the far infra-red). In contrast, slits as wide as 1 cm in a grating spectrometer incorporating mirrors of similar focal length would set the slit-width limited resolving power at only $F/s = 30$, well below the diffraction limit. Alternatively, if the slit-widths were reduced to 0.3 cm and 0.03 cm at 10 cm^{-1} and 100 cm^{-1} respectively, the slit-width limit would be about the same as the diffraction-limit, but there would be a loss, by $\times 10$ and $\times 10^3$ respectively, in the signal strength. There is, moreover, another way in which an interferometer offers an advantage over the dispersion methods. This appears when the times required to obtain the spectrum at a given noise level are considered. With a grating spectrometer using a single detector the radiation leaving the exit slit at any instant is restricted in infra-red frequency to one resolution interval; almost all of the radiation passing through the monochromator when a broad-band source is in use falls on the jaws of the exit slit where the information it carries is lost. With an interferometer there is no dispersion and all of the radiation from the source falls on the detector throughout the full recording time; the Fourier components representing separate resolution-intervals are separated *subsequently*, together with noise on each within its resolution interval, in computing the Fourier transform. The consequence of this difference is that the noise in the latter case is effectively averaged over the full recording time for every resolution interval whereas in the former case it is averaged only over the time taken for the spectrometer to scan one resolution interval. Thus, for an interferometer to show the same absolute noise level on the final spectrum as a grating spectrometer, the time taken to record the whole interferogram need only be in principle equal to that taken in recording a single resolution interval with the grating instrument. The ratio of the time taken to record the spectrum with the grating instrument to that required to record the interferogram with the interferometer is therefore equal to the number of resolution-intervals required in the spectrum; this is because, whereas the spectral range of interest can be covered selectively with the grating instrument, the full interferogram, which would allow the computation of the whole spectrum from zero to the maximum frequency, must be recorded with the interferometer, no matter how restricted the range of interest (there is a possibility that the use of sharp band-pass filters might in the future reduce this limitation – ch. 2, section 4.2).

We can illustrate the improvements in performance which interferometers should offer over grating instruments according to these elementary optical considerations with a few examples. First consider instruments of moderate size, based on collimators and condensing mirrors with a 30 cm focal length and with f/4 apertures (the power in such an aperture, from slits of width and height about 1 cm, can be condensed into the areas of most thermal detectors – a few mm square – without serious loss). We should consider separately the performances near the extremes of the far infra-red, at 10 cm^{-1} and 100 cm^{-1}. At 10 cm^{-1}, a grating spectrometer with a mercury arc lamp as source and a cooled detector can give a spectrum with a resolution of 0.2 cm^{-1} at a signal-to-noise ratio of about 25 and at a rate of scan of about 0.1 cm^{-1} per min – say 100 min to record the spectrum from 10 to 20 cm^{-1} (see fig. 1.3). For this the resolving power is $F/s = (10/0.2)$ so that the slit-width would be 0.6 cm. Now an interferometer of similar size would operate with entrance and exit slit-widths near 1 cm and the signal intensity at each frequency would therefore be larger by the factor $(0.6)^{-2}$. The noise level in the final spectrum would be the same as that in the grating's spectrum if the whole interferogram were recorded in the time taken to scan one resolution-interval with the grating spectrometer, i.e. 2 min. This would be impracticably and unnecessarily fast, and a longer time – say 15 min – would no doubt be taken with a consequent reduction in the noise, *if it is white*, by the factor $(2/15)^{\frac{1}{2}}$. The comparative performances for a spectrum from 10–20 cm^{-1} are thus:

Grating spectrometer; 100 min at a signal-to-noise ratio of 25 for a resolution of 0.2 cm^{-1}.

Interferometer; 15 min at a signal-to-noise ratio of 200 for a resolution of 0.2 cm^{-1}.

If the cooled detector were replaced by a room-temperature detector, with a signal-to-noise ratio say 20 times inferior, the recording times would have to be increased by a factor $(20)^2$ in order to record a similar spectrogram and would clearly be impossibly long. At the other end of the far infra-red, at 100 cm^{-1}, resolving powers of about 100, i.e. resolutions of 1 cm^{-1}, can be obtained at signal-to-noise ratios of about 50 using moderately large grating instruments with the best room temperature detectors and at scanning rates of about 1 cm^{-1} per min (ch. 3). A similar argument to that above then leads to the following comparative performances for the running times required to record a spectrum over the range 75 cm^{-1} to 150 cm^{-1}:

Grating spectrometer; 75 min at a signal-to-noise ratio of 50 for a resolution of 1 cm^{-1}.

Interferometer; 15 min at a signal-to-noise ratio of about 2000 for a resolution of 1 cm^{-1}.

A more effective use of the interferometer might be to sacrifice this high signal-to-noise ratio for a greater resolution. If the maximum path difference were increased by $\times 10$ to give a resolution of 0.1 cm^{-1} in the same running time, the signal power would be shared among 10 times as many Fourier components but the noise on each would be unchanged. We would have therefore:

Interferometer; 15 min at a signal-to-noise ratio of 200 for a resolution of 0.1 cm^{-1}.

It should be stressed that the performances quoted above for the interferometer are not the working performances of actual interferometers, but ideal values, relative to those of working grating instruments assuming a white noise spectrum on the detector output. Too few details of the performances of working interferometers have been published to allow generalisations to be made – it is still a relatively new technique. Figure 2.4 in chapter 2 records a spectrum obtained with an interferometer and a cooled detector in 50 minutes and shows a signal-to-noise ratio of the order of 30 and a resolution of 0.2 cm^{-1} from 18 cm^{-1} to 85 cm^{-1}. This performance falls somewhat short of those derived above but shows a considerable improvement over that of grating instruments of comparable size (see KNEUBUHL et al. [1966] for the performance data of a much larger grating instrument). As spectroscopists gain experience in avoiding the sources of distortion in interferometric spectra (see the following section and chapter 2) they can look forward to performances in this range. We have remarked above that the superiority of the interferometric method over grating spectrometry is less the more restricted the spectral range of interest, and is greater the wider the range to be covered. This is because the recording time required, with an interferometer, to give a spectrum at a given resolution and signal-to-noise ratio does not depend, in principle, on how wide a spectral range is to be covered. The detector must respond quickly enough, of course, to record the Fourier component associated with the maximum frequency of interest (or, equivalently, to allow the accumulation a sufficient number of sampling points in a digital record) but the time over which the noise on each Fourier component is effectively averaged in computing the final spectrum is the full recording time; consequently the response time of the detector system can be reduced, by adjusting the bandwidth or smoothing circuit in the detector system, without changing the noise level in the spectrum. There are, of course, limitations to the range covered by an interferometer; there are the "optical" limitations associated with the precision required of the optical components and with finding beam dividers which cover an adequate range efficiently (ch. 2, fig. 2.12) but probably more important is the time taken in computing the Fourier transform which increases rapidly with the number of sampling points (ch. 2, section 4.2) and also the increasing numerical precision to which each digital reading must be recorded.

If brighter sources were available, there would be no great difficulty in constructing and operating two-beam interferometers with mirror movements somewhat larger than the 10 cm or so currently used but severe problems would be met if attempts were made to provide the precision and length (10^2–10^3 cm) required for a resolution exceeding 1 in 10^4 in the far infra-red. Multiple-beam interferometers, such as the Fabry-Perot, could provide a high resolution with a smaller plate separation, but, though like two-beam interferometers they are free of the severe slit-width limitations of grating spectrometers, they share the other weakness of the dispersion methods that only one resolution-interval is incident on the detector at a time. (Fabry-Perot interferometers have, however, recently been used as monochromators in the far infra-red at fairly low resolutions, by ULRICH et al. [1963], and as resonant cavities in conjunction with microwave harmonics by VALKENBURG and DERR [1966].) Even if much better broad-band sources become available so that the resolutions attainable with the "optical" methods can be pushed beyond the present limits of 1 in 10^2 to 10^3, it is unlikely that they will ever be used to provide resolutions beyond 1 in 10^4.

For very high resolution, methods based on monochromatic sources are more promising. The use of diodes of various kinds to generate harmonics of the outputs of microwave klystrons is already a well established technique up to frequencies near 10 cm^{-1} and in the hands of experts this approach has been pushed to 25 cm^{-1} (ch. 5). Here the limiting resolving power is set by the stability of the fundamental frequency during a measurement and can exceed 10^5 without elaborate control circuits. The signal strength from such a source falls rapidly above 10 cm^{-1} as the harmonic number increases and the best detection methods are required to obtain useful results.

The high coherence of such a source can bring with it optical problems arising from the interference effects which are produced when a coherent beam is partially reflected or scattered by discontinuities or obstacles in the optical path – including the sample and its holder. In the microwave region the use of wave-guides, resonant cavities, and the other components of microwave circuits, provides a means of controlling such effects systematically, but conventional wave-guide systems, when scaled down for millimetre and submillimetre wavelengths become excessively attenuating and at frequencies above 10 cm^{-1} over-moded arrangements will be necessary (ch. 7). Optimum solutions to this problem are not yet known. The use of light-pipes is possible but care must be taken to reduce, by tapering and by avoiding discontinuities whenever possible, any reflections from the ends of pipes, windows, etc. because, with the frequency defined to 1 in 10^5 at 10 cm^{-1}, reflection from discontinuities as far as 10^3 cm apart would give clear interference effects which would lead to spurious variations in the signal strength reaching the detector if the frequency were varied by 10^{-3} cm^{-1} or more in an attempt to record a spectrum. On the fundamental side of the harmonic generator such effects can be controlled by the tuning adjustments of conventional microwave techniques but this is a tedious process. This is but one of the reasons why the use of highly coherent sources for scanning wide ranges of frequency is difficult. The high coherence of a klystron source derives from the precision of the resonance of its cavity and this sets limits to the range of frequency over which a single klystron can be tuned. Electronic tuning is restricted to very narrow ranges but mechanical distortion of the cavity can be used to give up to ±5% variation in frequency between $\frac{1}{2}$-power points. Several klystrons are therefore necessary to give continuous spectral coverage but fewer are needed the higher the harmonics in use. A ±5% tuning range is in principle enough to give a continuous coverage with a single klystron above the frequency of the tenth harmonic because the span covered by one harmonic overlaps that of the next. At the higher harmonic frequencies (above, say, 16 cm^{-1}), the low intensity also exaggerates the difficulties of covering a wide spectral range in reasonable times.

It is perhaps too soon for much use yet to have been made in spectroscopy of the newly developed millimetre and submillimetre backward-wave oscillators (ch. 6) and the far infra-red lasers (section 4). Both are highly coherent and their use would not avoid the optical problems discussed above, but, either alone or in conjunction with multiplier and mixer diodes, they might soon make more power available for high resolution spectroscopy through the submillimetre range.

3. Choice of spectrometric method

The main questions which arise in choosing between alternative spectrometric methods for the range 3–200 cm^{-1} will be raised in this section but the other chapters of the book give the detailed information on which a choise must be based. It is, of course, not always possible to arrive at a clear-cut preference because many of the considerations involved are difficult to quantify and it is often difficult to anticipate the demands which a projected investigation will make of the apparatus to be used. Unfortunately the more versatile and powerful an instrument the more expensive it usually is and the less easy it often is to use even for experiments which would be within the capability of simpler and cheaper instruments.

We can note first that, as a consequence of the low energy available, no spectra taken by the methods based on the generation of harmonics of a microwave source (ch. 5) have at present been reported for frequencies above about 25 cm^{-1} and the only experiments of this kind reported for frequencies above about 10 cm^{-1} have been precision determinations of the frequencies of very narrow absorption lines of low pressure gases at room temperature, for which scanning over very narrow spectral ranges only is required. The newly-developed submillimetre oscillators (ch. 6) and lasers (section 4) have not yet been used for spectroscopy as such and the lasers, being fixed in frequency, might be limited to magnetic resonance spectroscopy or other special applications. At present, therefore, an experimenter should plan to do high-resolution spectroscopy above 10 cm^{-1} only if much of his interest and attention can be devoted to the technique itself. For work below 10 cm^{-1} high resolution techniques have been more widely applied (ch. 5) and specially designed microwave equipment is available commercially (section 5). Even here, where the signal strength is good, these methods are not well-suited to scanning a wide range of frequency continuously, for the reasons outlined at the end of the preceding section and for some purposes the continuously scanning grating and interferometric methods based on broad-band sources might be preferable even though the shortage of power from available broad-band sources limits the attainable resolution to about 0.15 cm^{-1} between 3 cm^{-1} and 10 cm^{-1}, even with cooled detectors, as illustrated by figs. 1.3 and 2.10.

Turning now to the other end of the range of interest in this book, that is to about 200 cm^{-1}, we reach the domain in which grating spectrometry is well-established. Grating instruments to give resolutions of about 1 cm^{-1} at rates of scan near 1 cm^{-1}/min and using room-temperature detectors can be fairly easily designed and constructed (ch. 3); better performances can be achieved with larger instruments and cooled detectors. Commercial instruments are also available (ch. 3 and section 5) which, with several automatic changes of gratings and filters, give spectra from about 30 cm^{-1} to about 1000 cm^{-1}. With an interferometer, to compete with the resolutions which the grating instruments offer near 1000 cm^{-1}, the necessary number of sampling points in the interferogram (and the precision with which they must be recorded) would be so great that a large and fast computer for the Fourier transform computations would be essential and the running time so long that the cost would be prohibitive for most purposes.

It is between 10 cm^{-1} and 400 cm^{-1} that the grating and interferometric methods compete. It can be said immediately that the interferometric method is optically superior for the reasons examined at length in the preceeding section of this chapter. It can give higher resolutions in shorter running times and at higher signal-to-noise ratios than the grating method. Its prime intrinsic disadvantage is that the spectrum has to be derived by computation from an interferogram which demands that a suitable computer, or access to one, be available. There are a number of operational difficulties (in addition to risks of occasional punching and computing errors) which can introduce false features into a computed spectrum and the performances of interferometric spectrometers fall some way short of the theoretical expectations, relative to grating spectrometers, outlined in the preceding section. The nature of the difficulties can be illustrated as follows. Suppose that the source intensity is not perfectly stable but shows a periodic variation with an amplitude equal, say, to 1% of the total signal strength. In the case of a spectrum produced by a grating instrument this would cause a variation which, at 1%, would normally fall within the noise level and pass unnoticed. On the other hand, in the case of an interferometer which is being used to give a spectrum with a resolving power of 100 or more, this 1 % variation would be of the same order of magnitude as the amplitude of a single Fourier component and, if the frequency of the periodic variation fell within the range covered by the Fourier analysis it would be mistaken for modulation due to interference and a strong but spurious absorption (or emission) band would appear in the spectrum. Movements of mirrors or beam splitters, or other instabilities in the optical system, or small variations in the sensitivity of the detector system, can clearly have similar consequences. The variations need not be sustained throughout the record to have a significant effect – a damped oscillation would transform as a broadened spectral line. More generally we can conclude that noisy *modulations* of the total signal strength which fall in the range of frequency over which the Fourier analysis is made will produce strong noise on the final spectrum. The range of frequency involved is up to the value R/T where R is the resolving power at the maximum infra-red frequency and T is the time taken to record the interferogram once; for aperiodic interferometers this would usually be of the order $(200/6000)$ cycles per second, i.e. 33 seconds per cycle, and for periodic interferometers usually in the audio-frequency range (and at harmonics of the repeat frequency of the reciprocating mechanical motion of the moving mirror!). Freedom from these sources of irreproducibility in the spectra obtained by an interferometric instrument requires that the instrument be well designed and constructed and also carefully used. As designs become more foolproof and correct methods of operation better, and more widely, understood the potential of interferometry will be more fully realised.

Noise fluctuations which are added to the signal in the course of the detection but which have a power spectrum which is independent of frequency are *better* handled by the interferometric methods – as shown for "white" noise in the preceding section. However, excess low-frequency noise can be more serious for the interferometric method than for a grating spectrometer, relatively speaking. For example, additional low-frequency noise on a grating spectrogram would not greatly reduce the ability to resolve a doublet or to measure a line-breadth if this excess noise had a characteristic period equal to the time taken to scan several resolution intervals – though it would confuse an attempt to detect weak absorption lines. Similar noise on an interferogram could transform into excess noise at the low frequency end of the spectrum, within the resolution interval, and at this end of the spectrum, therefore, the interferometer would not be as advantageous as the calculation based on white-noise would suggest. On the other hand (as pointed out in ch. 2), the interferometric method reduces the uncertainty in absolute intensity arising from *slow* zero-level drifts because this gives Fourier components only at the extreme low frequency end of the spectrum, which is normally of little interest.

A great advantage of the interferometric method is the wide range of frequency which can be covered without the need to change optical components (ch. 2). With a grating instrument the diffraction grating, and/or a combination of filters, must be changed at least every octave and usually about twice every octave if optimum signal intensity is required (ch. 3). In commercial grating spectrometers the changing of gratings and filters is effected automatically of course, but the necessary equipment brings with it additional expense and usually some loss of flexibility in the application of the spectrometer to complicated sampling situations. The interferometric method is not at present as free from impediments to continuous frequency coverage as is possible in principle, because the beam dividers in use work well only over limited spectral ranges or have several dips in efficiency (fig. 2.12).

The computing requirements for an interferometer are detailed in ch. 2. To fully realise the high resolutions possible access to a large digital machine is essential. A main disadvantage of this, of course, is the expense but the delay in obtaining the spectrum which it implies poses additional problems when the investigation in hand is one requiring constant modification of the experiment in the light of the spectroscopic measurements, or when a fault in the instrument is being corrected. In these circumstances the gain in recording speed offered by the interferometric method is at least in part lost. Small special purpose computers which can be attached to the instrument are now available (section 5), and others are being developed. These make it possible to exploit the fast recording times of interferometers but to reach the highest resolving powers within their power requires a fast, large capacity, computer.

The summary below (table 1.1) provides a broad indication of the capabilities of typical working instruments but the other chapters of this book should be consulted for detailed data and the qualifications to which the data are subject. The data below are mainly drawn from published spectra of water vapour for which there is little or no loss of signal power in the sampling apparatus and in continuous background absorption in the sample itself. In experiments in which there is such a loss, it can adversely influence the time taken to record a spectrum at a given resolution and signal-to-noise ratio because, if the signal intensity is reduced by a factor p, the recording time must be increased by p^2 to reduce the noise by the same factor. A similar consideration applies to variations in the minimum detectable signal

TABLE 1.1

Range (cm⁻¹)	Method	Resolution (cm⁻¹)	Signal-to-noise ratio	Time for one resolution interval (min)	Time for total range (min)	Comments
3–10	Harmonic generation	$<10^{-5}$	$>10^2$			Scanning is difficult.
	Interferometer	0.1	40	–	200	Cold detector (see fig. 2.10).
	Grating	0.15	20	5	400	Cold detector (see fig. 1.3).
10–25	Harmonic generation	$<10^{-5}$	10^2–1	1		(see fig. 5.59).
10–50	Grating	1.0	50	2	120	Cold detector (see fig. 1.2).
10–100	Interferometer	0.2	>30	–	100	Cold detector (see fig. 2.8).
25–100	Grating	0.5	50	0.3	120	Room-temperature detector (see fig. 3.12).
30–400	Interferometer	2.0	>140	–	160	Room-temperature detector. From literature of Grubb Parsons Ltd., and R.I.I.C. Co.
	Grating	2.0	35	1	120	Room temperature detector, double-beam instrument. From literature of Beckman Instruments Corp.

from one detector to another. There is a difference of about ×20 between the best room temperature detectors and the best detectors operating in liquid helium (ch. 4) and even among detectors of a given type there can be variations almost as large as this. The recording times quoted in the table allow for the need to take a background spectrum as well as a sample spectrum (except with double-beam instruments) but they do not include the computation times for the interferometric instruments.

When faced with making a choice of spectrometric method it is, of course, necessary to assess the resolution and signal-to-noise ratios required for the investigations envisaged. The resolution clearly influences the extent to which the intrinsic breadth of a spectral line can be determined and also the extent to which a doublet structure can be resolved (see fig. 1.5(b)). The Rayleigh criterion defines the resolution of an instrument to be equal to the separation of two equally strong, narrow, lines for which the recorded spectrum would show a doublet structure in which the minimum in intensity at the centre is 81% of the maxima in intensity. This would clearly give roughly the same result as the definition we have used earlier which is that the resolution is equal to the breadth at half-height of the spectrum recorded for a single narrow (monochromatic) line. The quantitative significance of the Rayleigh criterion in the present connection, however, is rather obscure, because it derives from the form of the diffraction image of a point source, whereas, in the far infra-red, dispersion spectrometers are slit-width limited and interferograms are apodised. It is, moreover, more sensitive to details of the slit-function and apodisation functions than the definition we prefer. Though the instrumental resolution is clearly relevant to line-breadth measurements and the resolving of fine-structures, it cannot be considered separately from signal-to-noise ratio. This is particularly obvious in the case of resolving fine-structure because, if the signal-to-noise ratio were, say, 500, a doublet structure would be clearly established even if the minimum at the centre were only 1% below the maxima. That signal-to-noise ratio is relevant also when measuring line-breadths is made clear by the fact that, if there is no noise on a spectrogram and if the slit-function or apodisation-function of the instrument is known, the intrinsic line-breadth can be determined by computational analysis of the spectrogram no matter what the instrumental resolution (provided a functional form can be assumed for the line). ROSSLER [1965] has shown in detail how to do this for Lorentzian spectral lines and Gaussian slit-functions and has tabulated the results. The limit to what can be done in this direction is obviously set by the noise on the spectrogram which results in a greater uncertainty in the derived line-breadth the smaller this breadth relative to the resolution. The optimum balance between signal-to-noise ratio and resolving power – one is increased when the other is decreased – for any particular problem is not obvious. This is particularly so for grating spectrometers because a decrease in resolving power by a factor q brings with it a large increase, as q^2, in the signal-to-noise ratio and also an increase proportional to q in the rate of scan. An inspection of Rossler's results indicates that there would usually be little point in setting the resolution much wider than the line-breadth but that, when signal intensity is low, it might be advantageous to go as far as that. If the intrinsic line-breadth is so wide that a signal-to-noise of, say, 50, can be obtained with a resolution which is, say, $\frac{1}{10}$ of the intrinsic line-breadth, then obviously, the high resolution would be used because it would give a good value directly without computation. (Many materials show spectra which belong to the latter case but all experimenters will know how frequently they become involved in those problems which are beyond – or almost beyond – the best their technique is capable of.) With an interferometer there is much less to be gained in signal-to-noise ratio on reducing the resolution – the technique makes more efficient use of signal power in the first place. Consequently the optimum choice for the resolution is usually somewhat higher than the intrinsic line-breadth to be measured. A method of computing the spectrum from an interferogram using Hilbert transforms (SAKAI and VANASSE [1966]) has recently been explored as a method of obtaining a better resolution than that obtained by Fourier transformation; this is done, of course, at the expense of a decrease in signal-to-noise ratio and only a limited useful up-grading of resolving power can be expected.

4. Submillimetre lasers

The recent discoveries (CROCKER et al. [1964]) of the laser oscillations initiated by pulsed electrical discharges through various gases have transformed the source situation in the submillimetre region. A large number of frequencies have been found at which such oscillations can with line-breadths exceeding 1 in 10^5, and in view of the fact that a fairly small number of gases have so far been investigated, it seems clear that there will soon be available fairly simple and robust pulsed sources with peak-powers at least at the fractional watt level, providing coherent submillimetre radiation at a large number of fixed frequencies throughout the spectrum from the near infra-red through to the microwave region. The impact on submillimetre spectroscopy would be great and immediate if it were not for the fact that there is as yet no prospect of varying the frequencies so as to provide the possibility of scanning. Nevertheless, the laser sources will no doubt be used for magnetic resonance spectroscopy, where there is no need to vary the frequency, and for other special applications. Most of the existing lasers are pulsed, without outputs lasting several microseconds. Various considerations involving the electrical supply (a discharge from a ~ 0.1 μF capacitor charged to ~ 25 kV) and conditions in the active gas, limit the repetition rate typically to a few pulses per second. Recently continuous wave operation has been achieved in a submillimetre laser oscillator with an output power at the milliwatt

TABLE 1.2

Wavelength (mm)	Peak power (W)	Gas	Reference
0.047251	0.08	Water vapour	MATHIAS and
0.047469	0.06		CROCKER [1964]
0.047693	0.04		
0.048677	0.07		
0.055077	0.06		
0.057660	0.02		
0.067177	0.01		
0.12624	1	Dimethylamine	MATHIAS et al.
0.12875	1		[1965]
0.13095	1		
0.13503	0.2		
0.18190	0.1	Deuterium +	
0.19008	0.1	bromine cyanide	
0.19483	0.02		
0.20453	0.04		
0.21114	0.04	Dimethylamine	
0.30994	0.4		
0.31108	0.7		
0.33683	7		
0.37280	0.1		
0.3108	3	Cyanic compounds	STEFFEN et al.
0.3365	10		[1966]
0.5382	0.5		
0.7735	0.5		

level (GEBBIE [1966]). The design of submillimetre lasers, particularly in regard to reducing the lengths of the discharge tubes of the early models which were several metres long, is developing continually, and so too are the gases being used. We shall, therefore, simply illustrate in the table above (table 1.2), some of the current performance data and references. No truly spectroscopic use has yet been made of lasers (except in as much as the excited states and species involved in the stimulated transitions are themselves the subject of study and dispute). Recently the first commercial submillimetre gas lasers have become available (section 5).

5. Availability of instruments and components

Most of the published spectra of the far infra-red and low millimetre regions
have been obtained with instruments made to the designs and in the machine-
shops of their users. This situation is changing as instruments and components become commercially available. Generally speaking details of commercial sources of equipment have not been given in the other chapters of
this book in order that they might be listed together in this section with an
overall warning that no list could be complete, if only because new and
improved instruments are continually being developed and offered for sale.
The lists below are offered, therefore, as a fairly full survey of what is
available but may not be complete, particularly with regard to suppliers.

Millimetre-wave components

TRG Inc., Massachusetts, and Philips Electrical Co., Eindhoven, have a full
range of microwave components for wavelengths down to 1.36 mm (220
Gc/s) including wave-guides, frequency meters, directional couplers, attenuators, etc.

ADTEC (Advanced Technology Corporation), Maryland, and FXR Inc.,
New York, produce millimetre wave diodes for detection (e.g. in radiometers) and for harmonic generation for use down to 1.2 mm wavelength
(down to 0.5 mm in development).

Millimetre-wave sources

Electron-beam sources of millimetre-waves are manufactured by:
    CSF (Compagnie Generale de Telegraphie Sans Fils), Paris, who produce
        submillimetre, as well as millimetre, backward-wave oscillators
    Elliot Co. Ltd., Borehamwood, London
    Litton Industries, California
    Amperex Electronic Corp., New York
    Varian Associates, California
    Sperry Rand Corp., Florida
    Hughes Research Labs., California
    Oki Electric Co. Ltd., Tokyo.

Lasers

Submillimetre lasers are produced commercially by G. and E. Bradley,
London.

Grating spectrometers

Complete double-beam grating spectrometers, using room-temperature Golay detectors in most cases, and designed for the range from 30 cm^{-1} to 400 cm^{-1} (and, with special arrangements, to 1000 cm^{-1}) are produced by:

Grubb Parsons, Newcastle-upon-Tyne
Perkin-Elmer Corp., Connecticut
Beckman Instruments, Inc., California
Hitachi, Ltd., Japan
Japan Spectroscopic Co. Ltd., Japan.

Gratings for the far infra-red have been manufactured for sale by:

Bausch and Lamb Optical Co., Rochester
Perkin-Elmer Corp., Connecticut
Ferrand Optical Co., Bronx, New York.

Interferometric spectrometers

Michelson interferometers for use from 10 cm^{-1} to 500 cm^{-1}, with Golay detectors and punched-card or paper tape output facilities are produced by:

Grubb Parsons, Newcastle-upon-Tyne
Research and Industrial Instruments Co., London
A small Fourier transform computer for use with an interferometer is also offered by Research and Industrial Instruments, and a computing service for customers' interferograms is provided by Grubb Parsons.

Components

Mercury-arc lamps in fused quartz envelopes and suitable as far infra-red sources are made by most manufacturers of street-lamps etc., including the following companies:

Hanau, Hanovia, Philips, A.E.I., Mazda, General Electric.

Golay detectors are produced by:

Unicam Instruments, Cambridge, England
Epply Laboratory Inc., Newport.

Germanium bolometric detectors and cryostats by:

Texas Instruments Inc., Texas.

Indium antimonide photoconductive detectors and cryostats by:

Mullard Ltd., London.

Low noise amplifiers for use with detectors are supplied by:

Princeton Applied Research Corp., New Jersey
(Several manufacturers offer lock-in amplifiers suitable for use with a low-noise preamplifier).

Metal mesh and grids suitable for far infra-red polarisers, filters and beam dividers are produced by:

Buckbee Mears Co., Minnesota
Ratozzi and May, Frankfurt.

References

A. CROCKER, H. A. GEBBIE, M. F. KIMMIT and L. E. S. MATHIAS, Nature **201** (1964) 250.
H. A. GEBBIE, 1966, private communication.
F. K. KNEUBÜHL, J. F. MOSER and H. STEFFEN, J. Opt. Soc. Am. **56** (1966) 760.
D. H. MARTIN, Advances in Physics **14** (1965) 39.
L. E. S. MATHIAS and A. CROCKER, Phys. Letters **13** (1964) 35.
L. E. S. MATHIAS, A. CROCKER and M. S. WILLS, Electronics Letters **1** (1965) 45.
R. C. OHLMAN, P. L. RICHARDS and M. TINKHAM, J. Opt. Soc. Am. **48** (1958) 531.
E. D. PALIK and J. R. STEVENSON, Phys. Rev. **130** (1963) 1344.
P. L. RICHARDS and M. TINKHAM, Phys. Rev. **119** (1960) 575.
A. RÖSLER, Infra-red Physics **5** (1965) 51.
A. SAKAI and G. A. VANASE, J. Opt. Soc. Am. **56** (1966) 17.
A. J. SIEVERS and M. TINKHAM, Phys. Rev. **124** (1960) 321 and **129** (1960) 1995.
H. STEFFEN, J. STEFFEN, J. F. MOSER and F. K. KNEUBÜHL, Phys. Letters **20** (1966) 20; **21** (1966) 425.
R. ULRICH, K. F. RENK and L. GENZEL, IEEE Trans. MTT. **11** (1963) 363.
E. P. VALKENBURG and V. E. DERR, Proc. IEE **54**, 493.

CHAPTER 2

FOURIER TRANSFORM SPECTROSCOPY

BY

P. L. RICHARDS

*Bell Telephone Laboratories Incorporated,
Murray Hill, New Jersey, USA*

1. Introduction

Perhaps the most frequently encountered problem in far infrared (sub-millimeter) spectroscopy is the measurement of the optical properties of a material over a wide range of frequencies. The traditional approach to this problem has been to use a mercury arc lamp as a continuum source and a diffraction grating monochromator to scan the spectral region of interest (ch. 3). In recent years, however, Fourier transform spectroscopy with a two-beam interferometer has become a competitive technique. When high resolution is required, or when a wide spectral range is to be explored, Fourier transform spectroscopy is usually the more effective method.

The principles of the method of Fourier spectroscopy date back at least 60 years to the pioneering work of MICHELSON [1902]. He discovered that the interference pattern from a two-beam interferometer, as a function of the path difference between the two beams, is the Fourier transform of the light illuminating the interferometer. By observing these interference patterns, Michelson was able to measure such quantities as spectral line width, doublet separation, etc. Two factors seriously restricted the usefulness of his method. Since Michelson observed the fringes visually, he could not measure the absolute intensity of the interference pattern as a function of path difference; he could only estimate the relative visibility of fringes. Such restricted information permits unambiguous analysis of only those spectra with a center of symmetry, such as a single symmetrical line or symmetrical doublet. The second limitation on Michelson's work was the absence of adequate computing facilities to perform the Fourier analysis for complicated spectra. He did, however, make some use of a small mechanical Fourier analyzer to construct visibility curves of known spectra. The subsequent development of optical detectors and electrical data recording techniques soon overcame the measuring difficulties encountered by Michelson, but only during the past decade have digital or analog computing techniques advanced sufficiently to make Fourier transform spectroscopy a practical technique for complicated spectra.

2. Theory

There have been a number of excellent papers written on the theory of Fourier transform spectroscopy (STRONG and VANASSE [1959], JACQUINOT [1960], CONNES [1961] and GENZEL [1960]). The review of the theory which follows, therefore, will emphasize only those aspects which seem to be most important in practice for the far infrared. If a two beam interferometer is illuminated with monochromatic light of intensity S_0, the interference pattern, or interferogram $I(\Delta)$, as a function of the path difference Δ between the two beams, has the form

$$I(\Delta) = S_0(1 + \cos 2\pi v\Delta), \tag{2.1}$$

where the frequency, v, is measured in (length)$^{-1}$. For arbitrary spectral input, $S(v)$,

$$I(\Delta) = \int_0^\infty S(v) \left[1 + \cos 2\pi v\Delta\right] dv$$

$$= \tfrac{1}{2}I(0) + \int_0^\infty S(v) \cos 2\pi v\Delta \, dv, \tag{2.2}$$

where $I(0)$ is the intensity at zero path difference. Application of the Fourier integral theorem for the even function $I(\Delta)$ gives us the desired spectrum,

$$S(v) = 4 \int_0^\infty \left[I(\Delta) - \tfrac{1}{2}I(0)\right] \cos 2\pi v\Delta \, d\Delta, \tag{2.3}$$

in terms of the measured quantity, $I(\Delta)$. This is the fundamental relation of Fourier transform spectroscopy. The interferogram is measured as a function of path difference, and the spectrum is computed from eq. (2.3) by analog or digital means.

In practice, of course, the interferogram cannot be measured to infinite values of Δ; there must be an experimentally determined cut-off at $\Delta_{\max}$ of the integral in eq. (2.3). It is this cut-off which limits the resolution in Fourier transform spectroscopy. The approximate spectrum $S_c(v)$, which is then obtained, can be examined by substituting eq. (2.2) into the truncated integral (2.3)

$$S_c(v) = 4 \int_0^{\Delta_{\max}} \left[\int_0^\infty S(v') \cos 2\pi v'\Delta \, dv'\right] \cos 2\pi v\Delta \, d\Delta. \tag{2.4}$$

Carrying out the integration over Δ,

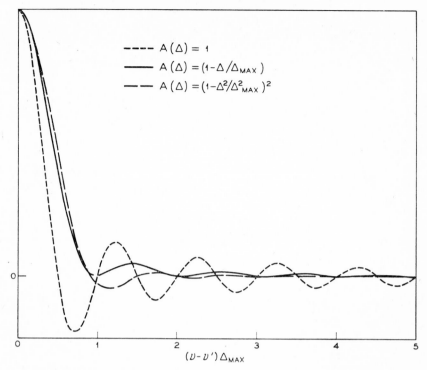

Fig. 2.1. Typical instrumental functions $R(v, v', \Delta_{max})$ available from Fourier transform spectroscopy by using various apodization functions $A(\Delta)$. See eq. (2.7) for explanation of the curves.

$$S_c(v) = \int_0^\infty S(v')R(v, v', \Delta_{max})\, dv', \tag{2.5}$$

where

$$R = \left[\frac{\sin 2\pi(v-v')\Delta_{max}}{2\pi(v-v')\Delta_{max}} + \frac{\sin 2\pi(v+v')\Delta_{max}}{2\pi(v+v')\Delta_{max}}\right] 2\Delta_{max}. \tag{2.6}$$

The computed spectrum, $S_c(v)$, is thus the convolution of the actual spectrum $S(v')$ with the instrumental function R. For example, if $S(v')$ is a single spectral line of unit strength at $v' = v_0$ whose width is much less than $1/\Delta_{max}$, then $S_c(v)$ is simply the instrumental function $R(v, v_0, \Delta_{max})$.

If, for all frequencies of interest, $v' \gg 1/\Delta_{max}$, then the second term in R can be neglected and the instrumental function becomes $R = 2\Delta_{max}[\sin 2\pi(v-v')\Delta_{max}]/2\pi(v-v')\Delta_{max}$. This function, which is plotted in fig. 2.1, has width at half its height of $\delta v \simeq 0.7/\Delta_{max}$, so that the smallest frequency interval resolved is approximately the reciprocal of Δ_{max}. The assumption of $v' \gg 1/\Delta_{max}$, which was used to simplify the form of R, is therefore valid if the resolving power $v/\delta v$ is large in the spectral region of interest.

The subsidiary maxima of the instrumental function are frequently troublesome. They arise from the sharp cut-off at Δ_{max} and can consequently be reduced by removing the discontinuity at that point. The process of introducing a smooth cut-off function $A(\Delta)$ into the truncated integral (2.3) to give

$$S_c(v) = 4 \int_0^{\Delta_{max}} [I(\Delta) - \tfrac{1}{2}I(0)]A(\Delta) \cos 2\pi v\Delta \, d\Delta \qquad (2.7)$$

is called apodization and has been investigated by many authors (STRONG and VANASSE [1959], CONNES [1961], GEBBIE [1960], PARSHIN [1962], VANASSE [1962], LOWENSTEIN [1963], and FILLER [1964]). To illustrate the procedure, we show in fig. 2.1 the instrumental functions computed from eq. (2.7) for several apodizing functions $A(\Delta)$. In each case the shape is improved relative to the unapodised function (curve (a)) at the cost of a spread in the central maximum. For linear apodization with $A(\Delta) = 1 - \Delta/\Delta_{max}$ (curve (b)), the instrumental function has the Rayleigh form

$$R = \Delta_{max}[\sin \pi(v-v')\Delta_{max}]^2/[\pi(v-v')\Delta_{max}]^2 \, .$$

In this case Rayleigh's criterion for resolution may be used to state that two lines separated by the frequency interval $\delta v = 1/\Delta_{max}$ are resolved. That is, for any two spectral elements to be resolved, their respective contributions to the interferogram must be out of phase by at least 2π before the maximum path difference is reached. For apodization according to $A(\Delta) = (1 - \Delta^2/\Delta^2_{max})^2$ we obtain the instrumental function

$$1.066 \, \Delta_{max}[2\pi(v-v')\Delta_{max}]^{-\frac{5}{2}}J_{\frac{5}{2}}[2\pi(v-v')\Delta_{max}]$$

as drawn in fig. 2.1 (CONNES [1961]). This shows that further improvement results when an apodizing function with no discontinuities in slope at $\Delta = 0$ or $\Delta = \Delta_{max}$ is used.

In order for apodization to have an appreciable effect, there must be spectral elements which are unresolved, or barely resolved. These can be narrow lines, sharp edges, or simply noise. In practice, apodization is useful for cleaning up noisy spectra and for judging the significance of structure near strong narrow lines. It is often useful for this purpose to compare both apodized and unapodized spectra. Though there has been considerable interest in the details of different apodization functions, these differences are not often significant in practice. When in doubt about the effect of the instrumental function on the measured spectrum, it is usually better to recompute the doubtful region of the spectrum with a different (preferably higher) resolution than to use a different apodization function.

There is one case in which the instrumental function of Fourier spectroscopy can cause very serious distortion of the computed spectrum. The derivation of eq. (2.3) assumed that $I(\Delta)$ was an even function. For this to be true, a precise experimental identification must be made of the $\Delta = 0$ point on the interferogram. The result of an error of Δ_0 in the zero path difference point is an interferogram,

$$I(\Delta) = \tfrac{1}{2}I(\Delta_0) + \int_0^\infty S(v) \cos 2\pi v(\Delta - \Delta_0)\, dv, \qquad (2.8)$$

which is no longer an even function of Δ. If eq. (2.3) is used to compute a spectrum from (2.8), then $S_c(v)$ is the convolution of the true spectrum $S(v')$ with the new instrumental function

$$R = \cos\left(2\pi v'\Delta_0\right) \left[\frac{\sin 2\pi(v-v')\Delta_{max}}{2\pi(v-v')\Delta_{max}}\right] 2\Delta_{max} +$$

$$+ \sin\left(2\pi v'\Delta_0\right) \left[\frac{1-\cos 2\pi(v-v')\Delta_{max}}{2\pi(v-v')\Delta_{max}}\right] 2\Delta_{max}. \qquad (2.9)$$

The assumption of large resolving power has again been used to neglect terms in $v+v'$. If the frequencies of interest are low enough (or Δ_0 small enough) that $v'\Delta_0 \ll 1$, then R has its usual form. At higher frequencies, however, the second term in (2.9) will become important. It is an odd function of $(v-v')$ so that the computed spectrum $S_c(v)$ for a symmetric spectral line will be asymmetric. The effects of a phase error, described here for unapodized spectra, are similar for all types of apodization (CONNES [1961]). As an example we show in fig. 2.2 a linearly apodized instrumental function with phase error $\Delta_0 v = 0.015$, and, in fig. 2.3, the effect of such an instrumental function on a spectrum, taken from the work of LOWENSTEIN [1963]. The small phase error seriously distorts the spectrum, even causing it to go negative at high frequencies. Negative spectra of this type were disturbing features of early results of Fourier transform spectroscopy.

The best way to avoid distortion of computed spectra due to phase errors is to eliminate Δ_0 by precise phase adjustment, or to measure Δ_0 and intro-

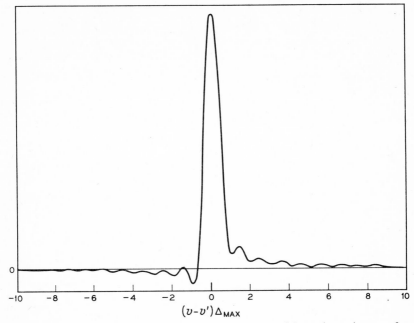

Fig. 2.2. Linearly apodized instrumental function computed from the cosine transform eq. (2.3) with a phase error $\Delta_0 = 0.015/\nu'$ (LOWENSTEIN [1963]).

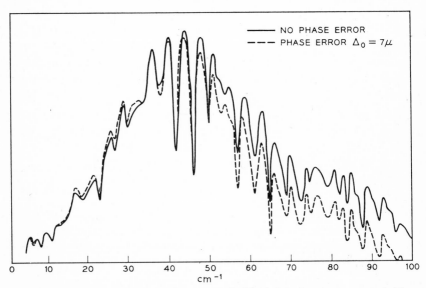

Fig. 2.3. The effect of a 7μ phase error on a typical far infrared spectrum computed from the cosine transform eq. (2.3) (LOWENSTEIN [1963]).

duce a compensating correction into the spectrum computation (LOWEN-STEIN [1963]). In some cases, especially at high frequencies or when precise intensity measurements are required, however, the phase correction cannot be made with sufficient accuracy. It is then desirable to measure the inter-ferogram for an equal distance on each side of $\Delta = 0$ and to compute the spectrum from the full Fourier transform

$$S(v) = 2 \int_{-\infty}^{\infty} [I(\Delta) - \tfrac{1}{2}I(\Delta_0)] \, e^{i2\pi v \Delta} \, d\Delta \qquad (2.10)$$

in place of eq. (2.3). The interpretation of the complex spectrum $S(v)$ be-comes clear if we substitute (2.8) into (2.10) and carry out the integration for the simple case of $\Delta_{max} = \infty$ (that is, assuming that all features of $S(v)$ are fully resolved). The resulting complex spectrum is

$$S(v) = P(v) + iQ(v) = S(v) \cos 2\pi v \Delta_0 - iS(v) \sin 2\pi v \Delta_0. \qquad (2.11)$$

The desired real spectrum is recovered, and the unknown phase error Δ_0 is eliminated, by computing the modulus $| S(v) | = [P^2(v) + Q^2(v)]^{\frac{1}{2}}$ of the com-plex spectrum. The instrumental function for this spectrum is just the abso-lute value or modulus of the usual function. The linearly apodized instrumen-tal function is unchanged by this procedure since for it $| R | = R$.

Because of the absence of phase error distortions, the technique of mea-suring the interferogram for equal distances on either side of $\Delta = 0$ and using the modulus of the full Fourier transform (2.10) is useful when the intensity must be known exactly. A second advantage of the method is that it helps to average out the effect of any experimental asymmetry of the inter-ferogram due to lack of flatness or poor alignment of interferometer com-ponents.

LOWENSTEIN [1963] has pointed out that a phase error which is small compared with $1/v_{max}$ can be corrected by integrating the complex Fourier transform (2.10) from $\Delta \approx 0$ to $\Delta = \Delta_{max}$. In this case, however, the instru-mental function is much less desirable since the width of the central maxi-mum is doubled and there is more weight in the wings than when the integration is carried over $-\Delta_{max} \le \Delta \le \Delta_{max}$.

The ultimate limit for the resolution available from an interferometer with finite aperture has been given by JACQUINOT [1960]. If the limiting aperture subtends a solid angle $\Omega = \pi\theta^2$ at a collimating mirror as is shown in fig. 2.4, an extremal off-axis ray through the interferometer has a path difference $1/\cos \theta \sim 1 + \Omega/2\pi$ times that of an axial ray. The spread in values, $\delta\Delta/\Delta$, of path difference corresponds to a spread in frequency of $\delta v/v = \delta\Delta/\Delta =$

$\Omega/2\pi$, thus limiting the resolving power to values less than $v/\delta v = 2\pi/\Omega$. This limitation is rarely of practical importance in the far infrared since resolving powers up to 10000 can be obtained, for example, with 12 cm dia. optics if the limiting aperture is a Golay detector.

Another effect of the finite aperture is that the mean path difference for

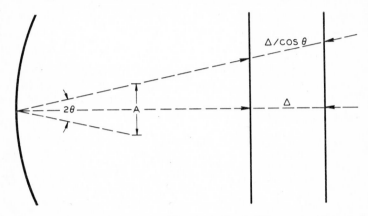

Fig. 2.4. An illustration of how a spread in values of path difference is obtained when the collimating mirror is illuminated with light from a finite aperture A.

all rays passing through the interferometer is $1/\cos\theta = 1+\Omega/4\pi$ times that of an axial ray. Thus, if the axial path difference is used in the computation of the spectrum, the frequencies of all spectral elements are overestimated by the factor $1+\Omega/4\pi$. This frequency correction must be applied even when the resolving power is substantially below the theoretical limit.

3. Advantages of Fourier transform spectroscopy

In an energy starved region of the electromagnetic spectrum like the far infrared or, more generally, for any weak-source experiment, Fourier spectroscopy has several advantages over the more conventional techniques using diffraction gratings or prisms as dispersion devices. In many cases these advantages outweigh the difficulties involved in performing the computation of the spectrum.

One major advantage of Fourier transform spectroscopy over dispersion spectroscopy arises because it is not necessary to use narrow slits to obtain high resolution. For a given resolution, the width of the slits of a monochromator are restricted by the finite dispersion available from practical gratings.

Thus, except for very large instruments, resolution is obtained at the cost of not filling the large infrared detectors currently available.

An interferometer designed to be used for Fourier spectroscopy in the far infrared can easily be made large enough that the resolution is limited by the maximum path difference used. Therefore, to double the resolution of a given spectrum, it is necessary to double Δ_{max}, and so to double the measuring time. By contrast, for a dispersion monochromator, the entrance and exit slits must be halved so that the signal intensity is reduced by a factor of four and, assuming that the noise is random, it therefore takes 16 times as long to obtain a given spectrum with double the resolution and the same signal-to-noise ratio.

FELLGETT [1958] has pointed out a second major advantage over dispersion spectroscopy which depends on the fact that spectroscopy is detector-noise limited in the far infrared. With an interferometer, the whole spectral range of interest is incident on the detector at one time, rather than a single resolution width as is the case with a monochromator. Assuming otherwise comparable efficiency, the interferometer can obtain the whole spectral region of interest in the time taken by the monochromator to obtain one resolution width. This so-called multiplex advantage is particularly important when searching a wide region of the spectrum at high resolution.

A third advantage of interference spectroscopy is that there is no requirement for a complicated system of filters such as that required to reject unwanted orders of diffraction in a grating monochromator. A cut-off at high frequencies must be made when the Fourier transformation is done by digital computer, as will be discussed later, but with a grating instrument a filter combination with sharp cut-off characteristics is required at least for every octave covered (ch. 3, section 3.3).

The major disadvantage of Fourier transform spectroscopy, is, of course, that the spectrum is not measured directly. An interferogram is measured from which the spectrum must be computed. There are various approaches to Fourier transform spectroscopy which differ primarily in the way in which the computation problem is solved.

4. Methods of Fourier transformation

As has been pointed out by GENZEL [1960] there are two experimental approaches to Fourier transform spectroscopy, the periodic and the aperiodic. We will discuss first the advantages and difficulties of the periodic method and then consider aperiodic spectroscopy with digital Fourier transformation, which is the more widely used technique.

4.1. PERIODIC METHOD

When we examine the analysis problem posed by Fourier spectroscopy, it is tempting to vary the path difference $\varDelta$ rapidly enough in time that the characteristic frequencies in the interferogram lie in the audio range. When this is done, an audio-frequency band-pass filter can be used to perform the Fourier analysis. The signal-to-noise ratio obtained from currently available

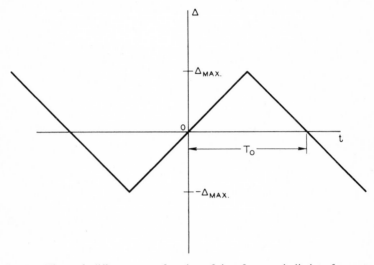

Fig. 2.5. The path difference as a function of time for a periodic interferometer.

detectors is much too low to permit gathering useful far infrared data in a single rapid scan of the interferogram, so $\varDelta$ must be varied periodically. It is most useful to vary $\varDelta$ with the constant-velocity saw-tooth motion shown in fig. 2.5. The examples of typical far infrared interferograms in fig. 2.6 show that $I(\varDelta)$ is least sensitive to errors in $\varDelta$ at $\varDelta_{max}$ where, for well resolved spectra, $I(\varDelta)$ is nearly constant. Since the turning points of the interferometer can never be perfectly sharp, they are, therefore, best chosen to be at $\pm \varDelta_{max}$.

The mathematical analysis of Fourier spectroscopy presented in section 2 is more appropriate for the aperiodic method since we assumed that $I(\varDelta) = \frac{1}{2}I(0)$ for $\varDelta > \varDelta_{max}$, rather than that $I(\varDelta)$ repeats itself periodically. In the following discussion of periodic Fourier spectroscopy the analogous analysis for the latter case will be developed (GENZEL [1960], GENZEL and WEBER [1958], HAPP and GENZEL [1961]).

It is convenient to make the linear dependence of path difference on time explicit, $\varDelta = \alpha t$, so that the interferogram (2.2) becomes

$$I(t) = \int_0^\infty S(v)\,[1+\cos 2\pi v\alpha t]\,\mathrm{d}v, \qquad (2.12)$$

for $-\tfrac{1}{2}T_0 \le t \le \tfrac{1}{2}T_0$. In order to express the periodicity of the interferogram in time with period $T_0 = 1/f_0$, we expand (2.12) in a Fourier series,

$$I(t) = \int_0^\infty S(v)\left[B_0(v\Delta_{\max}) + \sum_{n=1}^\infty B_n(v\Delta_{\max})\cos\left(2\pi nf_0 t\right)\right]\mathrm{d}v. \qquad (2.13)$$

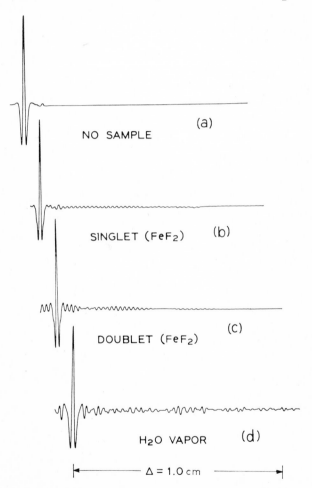

(a)

NO SAMPLE

SINGLET (FeF₂) (b)

DOUBLET (FeF₂) (c)

H₂O VAPOR (d)

$\longmapsto$ —— $\Delta = 1.0\,\mathrm{cm}$ —— $\longrightarrow$

Fig. 2.6. Examples of interferograms measured with a Michelson interferometer for various types of spectra. Curve (a) is the interferogram of a mercury arc lamp. Curves (b) and (c) show interferograms for antiferromagnetic resonance in FeF_2. Curve (d) is an interferogram for H_2O vapor. In all cases, filters were introduced which cut the spectra off at $100\ \mathrm{cm}^{-1}$.

The interferogram as a function of time is a series of harmonics of the fundamental interferogram repetition frequency f_0. If an audio bandpass filter is tuned to mf_0, where m is an integer, and if the filter is narrow enough to reject $(m \pm 1)f_0$, the rectified signal will be

$$S_c(v_m) = \frac{2}{\pi} \int_0^\infty S(v) B_m(v \Delta_{max}) \, dv . \tag{2.14}$$

Equation (2.14) is analogous to eq. (2.5) with the frequency $v_m = m/2\Delta_{max}$, which is associated with the index m, playing the role of v'. We see that the spectrum $S_c(v_m)$ computed by this analog technique at the optical frequency v_m is just the convolution of the actual spectrum $S(v)$ with the instrumental function $B_m(v \Delta_{max})$. By the usual Fourier series expansion,

$$
\begin{aligned}
B_m(v \Delta_{max}) &= \frac{1}{T_0} \int_{-\frac{1}{2}T_0}^{+\frac{1}{2}T_0} [1 + \cos 2\pi v \alpha t] \cos 2\pi n f_0 t \, dt \\
&= \frac{2v(-1)^m \sin 2\pi v \Delta_{max}}{2\pi(v^2 - v_m^2)\Delta_{max}} .
\end{aligned}
\tag{2.15}
$$

This expression for $B_m(v \Delta_{max})$ is identical with eq. (2.6) for $B(v, v', \Delta_{max})$ if we restrict the continuous variable v' to the discrete values $v_m = m/2\Delta_{max}$.

Since the instrumental function is the same for periodic and aperiodic Fourier spectroscopy, computed spectra differ only in that $S_c(v)$ is a continuous function, while $S_c(v_m)$ has values only at the discrete frequencies v_m. The information contained in the two computed spectra is the same, however, since the points $v_m = m/2\Delta_{max}$ are spaced slightly closer than the resolution width, $\delta v \simeq 0.7/\Delta_{max}$ for an unapodized spectrum.

Apodization of a periodic interferogram is entirely analogous to the aperiodic case, though again the mathematical description is formally different. The apodization can be performed by a shutter or amplifier gain adjustment coupled to the interferometer drive. The apodization function, like the interferogram, is then an even periodic function of time which can be expressed as a Fourier series,

$$C(t) = C_0 + \sum_{k=1}^\infty C_k \cos 2\pi k f_0 t . \tag{2.16}$$

The apodized instrumental function can be computed by inserting $C(t)$ into the integral in eq. (2.15). The result of modulating the interferogram with the apodizing function $C(t)$ which is periodic with frequency f_0 is, not surprisingly, to produce sidebands on the instrumental function separated from v_m by multiples of $1/2\Delta_{max} = f_0/c$ where c is the velocity of light. For the simple case of the apodization function $C(t) = C_0 + C_1 \cos 2\pi f_0 t$ there are only two sidebands,

$$B_m^{\text{apodized}}(v\Delta_{max}) = B_m C_0 + \tfrac{1}{2} C_1 (B_{m-1} + B_{m+1}). \tag{2.17}$$

The troublesome subsidiary maxima of the instrumental function can be almost completely eliminated by an optimum choice of the strength of this single pair of sidebands (HAPP and GENZEL [1961]).

In the analysis of the instrumental function for periodic Fourier spectroscopy, we have assumed that the audio band-pass filter lets through only the frequency mf_0, and is narrow enough to reject $(m+1)f_0$. In practice, a lock-in or phase sensitive detector is usually used as the filter and then the audio frequency bandwidth is just the reciprocal of the electronic time constant used. Thus, in order to obtain the instrumental function and resolution described above, a time constant must be used which is long compared with T_0, the repetition period of the interferogram. Alternatively we may say that a time constant of at least this length is needed so that the d.c. output signal will not show a pulse each time the interferometer passes the sharp peak in the interferogram at $\Delta = 0$ (see fig. 2.4). The effect of too short a time constant is to allow sideband frequencies to contribute to the output, and thus to modify the apodization and, ultimately, to widen the instrumental function.

In summary, in the periodic method of Fourier spectroscopy, the path difference of the two beam interferometer is varied with the saw-tooth motion of period $2T_0$ shown in fig. 2.3. (Note that the interferogram, an even function of Δ, has the period T_0.) Each resolution width of the spectrum then appears as an audio frequency harmonic of the fundamental frequency $f_0 = 1/T_0$. The spectrum is recovered by passing the signal from the far infrared detector through an amplifier, with bandwidth $< f_0$, which is tuned to each harmonic in turn (or through several amplifiers simultaneously, each tuned to a separate harmonic).

There are technical problems associated with each stage of the measurement which must be overcome before a successful periodic Fourier spectrometer can be built. The construction of an adequate periodic drive is perhaps the most difficult. Several successful interferometers have been built with a Δ_{max} of a few cm, and a T_0 of a few seconds, in which the saw-tooth motion is derived from a cam (GENZEL and WEBER [1958], HAPP and GENZEL [1961], BARKER and TINKHAM [1961]). In each case the operation is limited to frequencies lower than $\sim 100 \text{ cm}^{-1}$ because of mechanical inaccuracies.

When T_0 is several seconds, the bandwidth requirements necessitate the use of phase sensitive detectors for the spectrum analysis. The provision of an accurate phase reference from the interferometer then becomes a major mechanical problem. Unless the signal applied to the synchronous rectification stage of the amplifier is accurately symmetrical with respect to the $\Delta = 0$ point, phase errors of the type discussed in section 2 will result. Since it is usually necessary to make far infrared measurements over a range of frequencies, there must be a different relationship between the reference frequency and the interferometer drive rate for each far-infrared frequency $v_m = m/2\Delta_{max}$ of interest.

Two solutions to this problem have been used. Genzel and co-workers have built periodic interferometers which sweep frequency v_m continuously by keeping m fixed and varying Δ_{max}. This technique has the feature of automatically decreasing the interval resolved as the frequency decreases so that constant resolving power is maintained. The phase-reference signal for the amplifier, of fixed frequency mf_0, can be derived from an electrical cam rotating with the cam of the mechanical drive. The variable amplitude reciprocating motion of the interferometer mirror is derived from the cam by a mechanism carefully designed to preserve the symmetry of the reference signal about $\Delta = 0$. Periodic interferometers constructed in this way have proved to be practical far infrared and millimeter-wave spectrometers. Because elaborate filtering is not needed, they are more reliable in spectral purity than the diffraction grating monochromator. The mechanical difficulties associated with a large Δ_{max}, however, limit them to relatively low resolution service.

Spectrometers of this type do not make use of the multiplex advantage of Fourier spectroscopy because they sample only one harmonic in the interferogram at a time. A periodic Fourier spectrometer has been constructed (ALVES and TINKHAM [1965]) which simultaneously amplifies and detects a hundred harmonic frequencies v_m. In this approach, a hundred phase-reference signals are derived directly from the interferometer motion, one for each m value of interest, and Δ_{max} is kept constant. The simultaneous observation of one hundred frequencies gives this spectrometer a large multiplex advantage over a grating monochromator.

Existing periodic Fourier spectrometers have generally been of the lamellar grating type (see section 5). This choice can be criticized from the point of view that the moving parts are unnecessarily massive. If a Michelson interferometer of relatively small size were used, then the mass of the moving parts could be kept down to a few hundred gram. This change would simplify the construction of the rapidly reciprocating types of interferometers and would, perhaps, allow other solutions to the drive problem than the cams that are currently used. It might then be possible to increase Δ_{max} so as to obtain better resolution than is currently possible with periodic instruments, and to decrease T_0 to be able to use time constants as short as detector noise will permit. Also, an increase in mechanical precision by a factor of 2 or 3 over present instruments would permit use of the periodic method up to frequencies at which commercial dispersion spectrometers perform adequately for most experiments.

These comments should demonstrate that, though currently existing designs of periodic interferometers are either difficult to construct or are limited in speed, resolution and range, there is scope for improvement.

4.2. APERIODIC METHOD

The most widely used method of Fourier transform spectroscopy at the present time is to record the interferogram once, slowly enough to average the noise to an acceptable value, and to compute the spectrum on a general purpose digital computer. In this aperiodic method, which was proposed by FELLGETT [1958] and first used in the far infrared by GEBBIE and VANASSE [1956] the interferogram is sampled at small uniform intervals of path difference and the Fourier integral (2.3) is approximated by a sum for computational purposes.

An obvious advantage of this technique over periodic Fourier spectroscopy is that the interferometer moves slowly and so is relatively easy to construct. The major disadvantage is the delay usually associated with using a large computer. The experimenter may have to wait hours, or even days, to learn the result of varying an experimental parameter. Against this must be set the anicillary advantages of having a computer available because it is very convenient, for example, to be able to compute and plot ratios of spectra, attenuation constants, and strengths of absorption lines. Considering all of the techniques currently available, digital Fourier transformation of interferograms from aperiodic interferometers is currently the most effective method of doing high resolution spectroscopy in the far infrared.

The fact that data are acquired only at intervals of Δ has several consequences which must be examined. The sampling theorem of information theory (GOLDMAN [1953]) tells us that in order to obtain all of the information in the spectrum from $0 < v < v_{max}$ it is necessary to sample $I(\Delta)$ at intervals of $\Delta = \frac{1}{2}v_{max}$. The computed spectrum will then contain, at the frequency v, "false energy" of frequencies

$$(2n v_{max} - v) \quad \text{and} \quad (2(n-1)v_{max} + v) \quad \text{where } n = 1, 2, 3, \dots . \quad (2.18)$$

In effect, the whole electromagnetic spectrum is folded accordion fashion on to the region $0 < v < v_{max}$. (Here we have a one-dimensional analog of the reduced-zone scheme in the Brillouin zone theory of solids.) In order to obtain an unambiguous spectrum, it is necessary to use filters to isolate one of these folds of the spectrum. It is usual to cut the spectrum to zero at v_{max} and

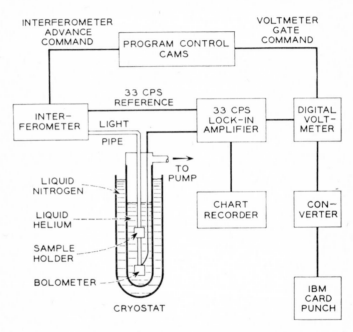

Fig. 2.7. Block diagram of an interferometric spectrometer including cryostat for measuring transmittance at low temperatures.

keep it zero for all higher frequencies, thus studying the first fold, $0 < v < v_{max}$. The required filtering is not as difficult as the removal of unwanted orders of diffraction from a grating, since v_{max} can be chosen to be arbitrarily far away from any spectral feature of interest. In principle it is possible to isolate and study any fold of frequency range $(n-1)v_{max} < v < n v_{max}$, though the filtering becomes more difficult.

In order for digital Fourier analysis to be a practical technique, it is necessary to transmit the data to the computer efficiently. As an example of one way in which this can be done, a complete system (RICHARDS [1964a]) designed for far infrared measurements of solids is shown in fig. 2.7. This system samples the interferogram automatically and records the data in digital form on punched cards. The optical energy from the interferometer is conveyed by a light pipe into a cryostat, through the sample, and to a doped germanium bolometer detector (see ch. 4, section 5.5). The detector signal is amplified by a 33 cps lock-in amplifier and fed to a digital voltmeter whose output is coupled to a card punch. The choice of punched cards rather than paper tape was made to be compatible with the available computer. Either will serve adequately, though the cards are more convenient when it proves necessary to edit the interferogram data. The amplifier output is also displayed on a chart recorder for visual examination.

In order to maximize the duty cycle of the measurements, the interferometer is moved rapidly between points and is stopped long enough to average the noise at the points where data are needed. This is accomplished by a rather involved system of cams, gears, and magnetic clutch which advances the interferometer and gates the digital voltmeter. Typical timing cycles are a one sec gate time repeated every 3 sec, a 10 sec gate time repeated every 15 sec, and a 20 sec gate time repeated every 30 sec. The fastest cycle can generally be used at frequencies higher than 10 cm^{-1} unless the interferometer efficiency is low, or the sample blocks too much of the beam.

An alternative procedure is to drive the interferometer continuously. The gate time of the digital voltmeter must then be very short compared with the time required to move between sampling points in order to avoid distorting the data. The effects of noise can be minimized if an amplifier time constant approximately equal to the time between points is used. In addition to its averaging effect on noise, such a time constant attenuates the higher Fourier components (spectral frequencies) in the interferogram. The required cutoff of the spectrum at v_{max} can thus be accomplished by electronic rather than by optical filtering. By the use of multiple RC networks, this electronic cutoff can be made advantageously sharp. The phases of the higher frequency components in the interferogram are shifted by the time constant, so electronic filtering should only be used when recording $I(\Delta)$ for equal distances on either side of $\Delta = 0$, and computing the full Fourier transform.

If use is being made of the multiplex advantage to examine a wide spectral range, then the data recording system must have a large dynamic range. As an example consider the spectrum shown in fig. 2.8. Many lines, especially at the two ends of the spectrum where the optical signal was weak, had an integrated area of less than 0.1 per cent of the area under the un-normalized spectrum. Thus, the contribution of these lines to the interferogram was never greater than 0.1 per cent of the peak at $\Delta = 0$. If the interferogram

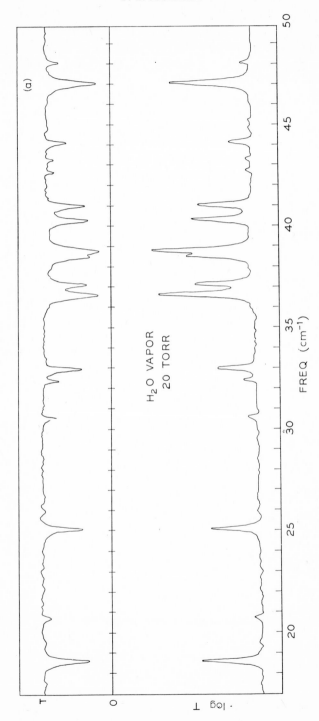

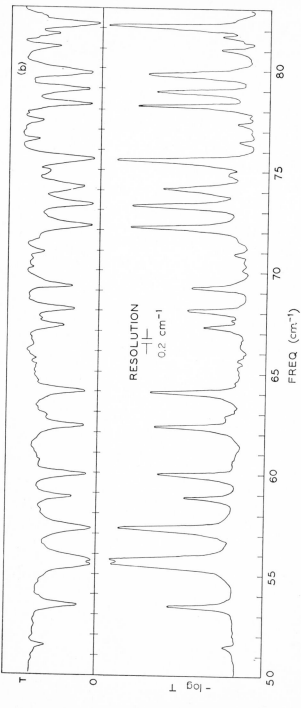

Fig. 2.8. Transmittance T and absorption coefficient $-\log T$ of a 1.5 m path of H_2O vapor at a pressure of 20 Torr measured using a Michelson interferometer. The data shown here were obtained by drawing a smooth curve through the computed points which were at intervals of 0.1 cm^{-1}. The measured frequencies should be reduced by $1.45 \times 10^{-4} \nu$ to correct for the effects of finite instrumental aperture.

were recorded on a typical chart recorder with a dead space equal to 0.1 to 0.2 per cent of full scale, or on a digital system with only three significant figures, these lines would be lost.

The sensitivity of the data recording system to small changes in the interferogram must be maintained, even when such changes are apparently obscured by noise. Very narrow lines often appear in computed spectra whose contribution to the interferogram cannot be seen by eye. It is also important that the linearity of the system be adequate to accurately record the shape of the peak in the interferogram at $\Delta = 0$. Errors in the height of this peak affect the over-all level of the spectrum.

In the system described here, the data are recorded on punched cards in the form of 5 or 6 digit numbers, and are fed into an IBM 7094 computer along with a program deck, which instructs the computer to count the number of points to get N, to average the last ten points to obtain a representative value of $\langle I(\Delta_{max}) \rangle$, and to subtract $\langle I(\Delta_{max}) \rangle$ from each value of $I(\Delta)$ to obtain $F_n = I(\Delta_n) - \langle I(\Delta_{max}) \rangle$. The raw (unapodized) spectrum,

$$S_1(\nu_m) = F_0 + 2 \sum_{n=1}^{N} F_n \cos \frac{nm\pi}{N}, \qquad (2.19)$$

and a linearly apodized spectrum,

$$S_2(\nu_m) = F_0 + 2 \sum_{n=1}^{N} \left(1 - \frac{n}{N}\right) F_n \cos \frac{nm\pi}{N}, \qquad (2.20)$$

are then computed for the range of frequencies (values of m) required by the program deck. Because the computations (2.19) and (2.20) can be interleaved, it takes only slightly longer to do both than it does to compute either separately. With the most useful program decks a second spectrum, which usually corresponds to a normalization with the sample out of the beam, is also computed. Useful quantities such as the ratio between the two spectra, the negative logarithm of the ratio (absorption coefficient), and a running sum of the absorption coefficient data to facilitate estimates of line intensities can then be computed. The results are tabulated and plotted by the computer printout. The convenient form in which the data are obtained is one of the major advantages of numerical Fourier transformation. Examples of measured interferograms, $I(\Delta)$ are given in fig. 2.6 and of computed spectra in figs. 2.8, 2.9 and 2.10 (RICHARDS [1964a]).

Neglecting constant factors, the truncated sum over F_n in eq. (2.19) approximates the integrated interferogram of eq. (2.3) by a series of steps out to $\Delta_{max}(n = N)$ and thereafter by a straight line. We use $\langle I(\Delta_{max}) \rangle$ for the

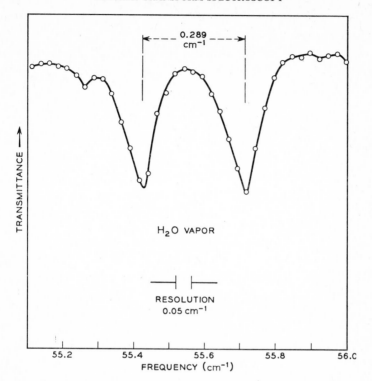

Fig. 2.9. Transmittance of a 1.5 m path of H_2O vapor at a pressure of 2 Torr measured using a Michelson interferometer. The measured frequencies should be reduced by $1.45 \times 10^{-4}\nu$ to correct for the effects of finite instrumental aperture.

value of the straight line in eqs. (2.19) and (2.20) rather than $\frac{1}{2}I(0)$ as would be expected from eq. (2.3) for two reasons. The first is that any unmodulated energy will displace the experimental zero line so that $\frac{1}{2}I(0)$ cannot be measured directly. If Δ_{max} is large enough to resolve the spectrum, as is the case for fig. 2.6(a), (b) and (c), but not (d), the integral term in eq. (2.2) is negligible, so $I(\Delta_{max}) = \frac{1}{2}I(0)$. Also, in the presence of any experimental drift, the use of $\frac{1}{2}I(0)$, which is then different from $\langle I(\Delta_{max})\rangle$, would introduce a step discontinuity in the approximate interferogram at Δ_{max} which would distort the spectrum. If the interferogram were recorded on both sides of $\Delta = 0$, the base line should be chosen so as to pass through the data at both $\pm\Delta_{max}$. In general, because of instrumental drift, this base line would then have a finite slope.

It is interesting to note that instrumental drift is less serious in Fourier transform spectroscopy than in single beam spectroscopy with a monochro-

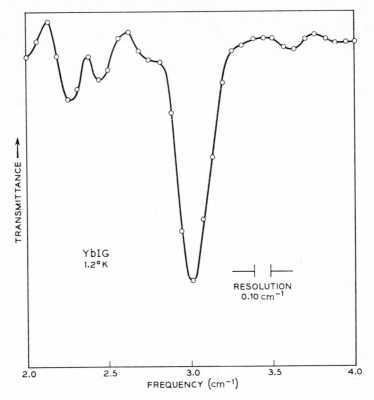

Fig. 2.10. Zero-field ferrimagnetic resonance in a 1 cm thick powder sample of ytterbium iron garnet at 1.2°K, measured using a lamellar grating interferometer. Frequency corrections due to finite instrumental aperture are negligible here, but a reduction of $2.17 \times 10^{-4}\nu$ must be made because of the separation of the entrance and exit slits of the lamellar grating interferometer.

mator since, using the above-mentioned precautions, it usually corresponds to such low frequency Fourier components that appreciable distortion of the spectrum occurs only below the lowest frequencies of interest. It is therefore possible to obtain reliable transmission values from the ratios of two spectra measured at different times, even when there is some drift. A drift in sensitivity will change the effective form of the apodization function slightly, but this is not usually observable.

The expense of computing the final spectra is a factor which cannot generally be neglected when digital Fourier computation is used. With modern computors, however, the cost is rarely prohibitive. For example, the linearly apodized data shown in fig. 2.8, along with an equal amount of unapodized data, were computed in 0.12 hours on an IBM 7094. To double the resolution over the whole spectrum would increase the computing time by about a factor of four since twice as many Fourier sums would be needed, each with twice as many terms. It would also have taken about four times as long to compute the same spectrum if the interferogram were measured equally on either side of $\Delta = 0$ and no phase information obtained so that the full Fourier transform (2.10) was required. This saving in computing time, especially important for high resolution spectra, is perhaps the major advantage of using experimentally determined phase information in the computation.

For a constant number of computed spectral points, the computing time rises linearly with v_{max}, so that cost may become prohibitive at near infrared frequencies. For example, an interferometer (GEBBIE et al. [1962]) designed to rival the best resolution available from gratings at 10^4 cm^{-1} required Δ_{max} ~ 30 cm. If the sampling interval is such that $v_{max} = 10^4$ cm^{-1}, then the computer program described above would require ~ 0.4 hours on an IBM 7094 to compute one resolution width of the spectrum and its normalization. An examination of eq. (2.18) indicates one way in which this cost can be reduced. In general only a small part of the region $0 < v < 10^4$ cm^{-1} is actually needed at such high resolution. If v_{max} is chosen so that the region of interest is closely bracketed by $(n-1)v_{max}$ and nv_{max} where n is an integer, and if the spectrum outside this range is cut to zero by appropriate filtering, then the spectrum will be recovered by the relatively coarse sampling at intervals $\Delta = 1/(2v_{max})$ as if it lay in the interval $0 < v < v_{max}$. The number of interferogram data points, and thus the computing cost, are reduced by the factor n in this procedure which is known as aliasing. Aliasing succeeds because, for a given Δ_{max}, the amount of information in the spectral region of width δv is the same, no matter where it is located. The computing time required to recover it should therefore be the same.

The optical filtering problem is a major obstacle to the efficient use of aliasing in the near infrared. Using a narrow bandpass electronic filter would be a useful technique in this case. The fact that the filtering is never sharp, so that the spectrum cannot be used close to nv_{max}, makes it unimportant that the instrumental function is slightly modified near nv_{max} by the aliasing procedure (PARSHIN [1963]).

If the range over which a Fourier transform spectrometer is to be used extends to conventional infrared frequencies, then precautions must be taken to maintain adequate mechanical precision. An advantage of digital Fourier transformation is that data are required only at specific values of Δ which can themselves be precisely located with an interferometric technique. It is thus not necessary to use a high quality lead screw. The data of figs. 2.8–2.10 show that the lead screw from a commercial traveling microscope stage is adequate at frequencies lower than 100 cm^{-1}. At higher frequencies it is customary to use a Moiré fringe system to locate the points where data are to be obtained (GEBBIE [1960], GUILD [1960]).

At the present time, aperiodic interferometers with digital Fourier transformation are capable of producing good quality spectra relatively rapidly. To do this they make use of all three advantages over dispersion spectroscopy mentioned in section 3. Detectors are fully illuminated even at high resolution, all parts of the desired spectrum are measured simultaneously with reasonably good efficiency, and filtering, though still required, is simpler than with diffraction gratings. The only major disadvantage of the method is that its use is limited to laboratories with rapid access to adequate digital computors. A small special purpose digital computor with adequate speed, which has been designed for use with Fourier transform spectroscopy, may help to extend the general usefulness of the method (FUJITA et al. [1965]).

4.3. ANALOG FOURIER TRANSFORMATION WITH APERIODIC INTERFEROMETERS

The underlying idea behind all *periodic* Fourier spectrometers discussed in section 4.1 is the convenience and economy of analog computation of the spectrum. Much of this convenience might be gained with an *aperiodic* interferometer by a technique which we may call analog Fourier transformation of interferograms from aperiodic interferometers. One such technique is now being developed commercially (by Block Associates and by Research and Industrial Instruments Co.). The interferogram is sampled at uniform intervals of Δ during a single pass of the interferometer, which is slow enough to average the noise to an acceptable value. This information is digitalized and stored in a magnetic core memory. The memory is then swept rapidly and periodically so as to provide a signal that is periodic in time, and this is played back through a narrow-band audio amplifier.

In order to retain all of the information in the memory, the rate of scanning of the memory must be greater than the rate of scanning the original interferogram, by an amount equal to the bandwidth of the audio amplifier times the total time required to record the interferogram. The amplifier bandwidth then accepts only one frequency mf_0. The spectrum is obtained by tuning the analyzing amplifier at the rate of f_0 cycles per period of the interferogram. The sampling interval of the interferogram required to retain all spectral information up to some cut-off frequence ν_{max} is the same as for the aperiodic method described in the preceding section. Approximating the interferogram by a step function before *analog* computation of the spectrum multiplies the spectrum by $\sin(\pi v/2v_{max})/(\pi v/2v_{max})$. This factor is relatively unimportant over the region of interest, $v \le v_{max}$.

A variation of this technique which has proved useful in the near infra-red is to tape record the interferogram, join the tape into a loop, and play it back at a higher speed. The large speed-up generally required for the far infrared can be obtained by re-recording the tape several times. A method intermediate between periodic Fourier spectroscopy and the periodic analysis of an aperiodically recorded interferogram may be useful in cases of such poor signal-to-noise ratio that the tape speed-up required would be too large. The interferogram could be tape recorded periodically at relatively slow rate, for example, by reversing a lead screw interferometer drive. The total time for recording data would be determined by the noise. A moderate speed-up would then permit analog analysis of the spectrum. For example, a commercial audio spectrum analyser with a 2 cps bandwidth coupled with a tape speed-up by a factor of 32, which is available without re-recording, would analyze the periodic output of an interferometer with $T_0 = 16$ sec.

The advantage of using a stored interferogram in the methods discussed above is that the actual interferometer motion can be slowed to the point where its construction is greatly simplified, and the multiplex advantage is maintained since data from the whole spectrum are recorded simultaneously. The time required to process the spectrum must not, of course, be neglected. It is equal to the time required to record the interferogram times the number of resolution widths of interest, divided by the speed-up factor.

5. Types of interferometer

In principle, any two beam interferometer will serve for Fourier transform spectroscopy. Two types, however, have proved thus far to be the most useful in the far infrared. These are the lamellar grating interferometer first used by STRONG and VANASSE [1958] and the Michelson interferometer first used in the far infrared by GEBBIE [1960]. In this section, lamellar grating and Michelson interferometers constructed by the author will be used as examples. An attempt will be made to emphasize those features which are generally important for interferometers of each type. These interferometers are used in the aperiodic mode so provisions have been made to cut the spectrum off at v_{max}. Adequate filtering was obtained for values of $v_{max} \lesssim 200$

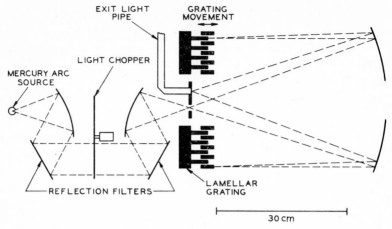

Fig. 2.11. The far infrared lamellar grating interferometer used by the author.

cm^{-1} with 10 mils of black polyethylene and one or two reflections from wire mesh filters (ch. 3). Both interferometers were designed for solid state physics investigations in which high magnetic fields and temperatures in the liquid helium range are usually necessary. Consequently, light pipes were used which allow a substantial simplification of cryogenic systems. The light is focused into the 1.1 cm diameter light pipe with an area-solid angle product of at least 0.5 sterad cm^2 so as to fully fill the indium-doped germanium bolometer detector.

5.1. LAMELLAR GRATING INTERFEROMETER

The lamellar grating interferometer shown in fig. 2.11 was designed so that it can be converted into a diffraction grating monochromator by lifting out the lamellar grating plates and inserting a dispersion grating mount in their place. Similarly, existing large grating monochromators can usually be converted for use as lamellar grating interferometers. Radiation from the mercury arc source is reflected from two filters before entering the interferometer proper and being collimated by the 30 cm diam. paraboloid. When it reaches the lamellar grating, which is used in zero order, half of the radiation reflects off the fronts and half off of the backs of the grooves so that there is a path difference between the two halves of the beam equal to twice the groove depth. The front lamellar grating plate, which appears as a discrete set of slats in the cross section shown in fig. 2.11, is mounted on three ball bushings and is driven by a micrometer screw so that the path difference is continuously variable over the range -0.5 cm $\leq \Delta \leq 10$ cm. The lamellar grating plates, which have a grating constant of $d = 1.9$ cm, were made of stress relieved aluminum slats cemented together with Epoxy resin and ground flat on their front faces. A better procedure would be to machine them from solid aluminum or steel.

As is discussed by STRONG and VANASSE [1960] the zeroth order of diffraction from the lamellar grating is modulated as $\cos^2 \pi v \Delta$ when Δ is varied, and all other even orders are missing. The odd orders of diffraction are modulated as $\sin^2 \pi v \Delta$. If the entrance and exit slits are wide enough to accept the first or higher orders of diffraction, then there will be some cancellation and

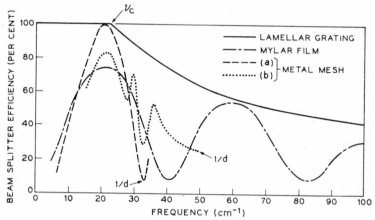

Fig. 2.12. Comparison of the beam splitting efficiencies for the lamellar grating interferometer and the Michelson interferometer with various types of beam splitters. The beam splitters shown are a 3 mil Mylar polyester film and electrodeposited metal mesh at normal incidence (a), and at a 45° angle of incidence (b). The frequency at which cancellation begins to occur in the lamellar grating interferometer, and the frequencies at which the wavelength equals the grating constants of the metal mesh, are marked as v_c and $1/d$, respectively. These curves give the relative efficiencies of the different instruments assuming the vignetting and reflection losses to be similar.

the efficiency of the interferometer will suffer. The illumination in the first order is $(2/\pi)^2$ times that in the zeroth order so it makes little difference, at any given frequency, whether the slits are closed to reject the first order, or the cancellation is allowed to take place. Since we are usually interested in a spectrum over a wide range, however, it is preferable to leave the slits wide open so as to have maximum efficiency at the longer wavelengths where there is no cancellation. Used in this manner, a lamellar grating interferometer has an efficiency approaching 100 per cent at frequencies below $v_c = f/sd$ where the cancellation begins. Here f is the focal length of the collimating mirror, d is the grating constant, and s is the slit width. For the present instrument with its circular slits, the efficiency falls off with frequency as shown in fig. 2.12. Because of the reduced efficiency beyond v_c the lamellar grating plates were not designed to have the precision achieved by STRONG and VANASSE [1960]. Mechanical inaccuracies limit their use to frequencies below ~ 100 cm^{-1}.

The increasing output with increasing frequency from a mercury arc more than makes up for the decreasing interferometer efficiency beyond v_c, so that the characteristic mercury arc lamp spectrum, when measured with the lamellar grating interferometer, has a broad flat maximum between 25 and 70 cm^{-1} which rolls off at higher and lower frequencies. As will be discussed more fully in section 6, the performance of this interferometer was generally satisfactory, and was especially noteworthy in the range from 3 to 20 cm^{-1}.

Since the loss of efficiency beyond v_c is the fundamental limitation of a lamellar grating interferometer, it is useful to consider how to maximize $v_c = f/sd$. For instruments with the same area-solid angle product, f/s can be increased only by using larger mirrors and gratings. Thirty cm, however, seems to be about as large as is practical. If some factor such as detector size limits the area-solid angle product to less than 0.5 sterad cm^3, v_c will be proportionally larger. It is practical to decrease the grating space, d, somewhat from our value of 1.9 cm. With $d = 1$ cm, v_c would be 45 cm^{-1} giving very good performance out to ~ 200 cm^{-1}. Aside from practical difficulties of construction, decreasing d much further will adversely affect resolution at long wavelengths. This effect can be estimated by considering the familiar case of a TE$_{0,1}$ mode in a microwave waveguide. An electromagnetic wave propagating between two parallel conducting planes separated by $\frac{1}{2}d$, and polarized parallel to the planes, will have its phase velocity increased by the factor $[1-(vd)^{-2}]^{-\frac{1}{2}}$. The other polarization is unaffected. The effective Δ for the two polarizations will differ by five per cent for $d = 1$ cm and $v = 3$ cm^{-1}. This limits the resolution to ~ 0.1 cm^{-1} for unpolarized radiation.

5.2. MICHELSON INTERFEROMETER

The most useful alternative to the lamellar grating interferometer described above is called a Michelson interferometer, though it is more properly a Tyman-Green interferometer since it uses collimated light. We have built the very simple Michelson interferometer shown in fig. 2.13, and have used it extensively in the far infrared. The evacuable tank in which both interferometers are used is designed so that the mirror alignment is adjustable from the outside, and the path difference is made variable over -0.5 cm $\leq \Delta \leq$ 20 cm by mounting one flat mirror on a precision traveling microscope stage.

In a Michelson interferometer, the diameter of the collimating mirrors is determined only by the Jacquinot limit discussed in section 2, rather than by a need to keep the ratio f/s large as must be done in dispersive systems. Because of the desirability of using existing mirrors which were larger than necessary, the paraboloids used in the Michelson interferometer have diameters and focal lengths of 23 cm. The angle of acceptance of the light pipe and detector, however, limits the optical system to an effective $f/1.3$ aperture, giving an area-solid angle product of ~ 0.64 sterad cm^2, and 18 cm diameter collimating mirrors. The large over-all size of the Michelson interferometer

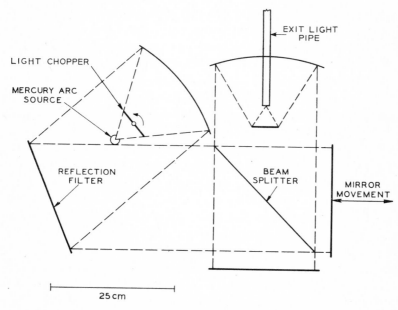

Fig. 2.13. The far-infrared Michelson interferometer used by the author.

reduces frequency corrections due to finite aperture, and allows us to use the particularly simple optical system shown in fig. 2.13. We are limited, however, to beam splitter materials which are available in relatively large areas.

The weakest link in the far-infrared Michelson interferometer is the beam splitter. A membrane with reflectance R, and transmittance T, each equal to 0.5 would be an ideal beam splitter. In practice, the best one can do is to use dielectric reflection from a film, or metallic reflection from a wire screen. The most commonly used film is Mylar polyester because it is readily available and has a reasonably high dielectric constant. We have measured T and R

at a 45° angle of incidence for a 3 mil mylar beam splitter. The product TR which, when compared with the ideal value of $TR = 0.25$, gives the beam splitter efficiency, is plotted in fig. 2.12. It is clear that such a beam splitter is most useful for frequencies close to the first interference maximum – its efficiency being better than 50 per cent over a factor of 3 in frequency. The increasing absorption with frequency, which causes the decrease in the height of the interference maxima, is compensated for by the fact that thinner beam splitters are used at higher frequencies. The beam splitter is usually chosen so that ν_{max} lies at the first interference pattern minimum to aid in cutting the spectrum to zero at that point. One useful feature of Mylar is that when it is stretched across a hoop and baked for a few hours at 130–160°C, crystal growth takes place which equalizes the tension in the film and improves its flatness. This is especially important when working at frequencies higher than $100 \ cm^{-1}$. A distinctive feature of Michelson interferometry with Mylar beam splitters is that the mercury arc spectrum drops rapidly due to the rapid fall in beam splitter efficiency at frequencies below $\sim \frac{1}{5} \nu_{max}$. It would, of course, be desirable to use films with higher dielectric constants to extend the usable range of frequencies. Some improvement can be obtained by evaporating the proper thickness of germanium on a Mylar or polyethylene beam splitter. If this is done, a compensating plate must then be used. At present, part of the multiplex advantage is lost because of the bandwidth limitations of the beam splitter. As will be discussed more fully in section 6, our Michelson interferometer using Mylar beam splitters gave very good results, especially at frequencies above $20 \ cm^{-1}$.

Another type of beam splitter is the metal mesh used by RENK and GENZEL [1962] for interference filters. The estimate shown in fig. 2.12(a) of the efficiency of a typical metal mesh beam splitter was obtained by scaling Renk and Genzel's transmittance measurements made at normal incidence to a lower frequency to facilitate comparisons with the other beam splitters, and by approximating TR by $T(1-T)$, that is, by neglecting the small amount of absorption in the metal. For frequencies below $\sim 1/d$, where d is the grating constant of the mesh, the metal mesh has a higher peak efficiency than the Mylar film, but is useful over a slightly smaller frequency range. Measurements (GENZEL [1965]) of the reflectance and transmittance of mesh at a 45° angle of incidence show complicated polarization dependent interference effects, especially for frequencies higher than $\sim \frac{1}{2}d$, but beam splitting efficiency roughly similar to that for normal incidence occurs at lower frequencies, as is shown in fig. 2.12. The efficiency of a metal mesh beam splitter is a sensitive function of the dimensions of the mesh and, for the case of non-normal incidence, of its orientation with respect to the plane of incidence. The examples shown in fig. 2.12, however, are probably representative of what can be obtained for frequencies below $\sim 1/d$. For frequencies above $\sim 1/d$, however, it is not possible to estimate beam splitter efficiency from transmittance and reflectance measurements because the beam splitting action comes partly from wave front division, as with a lamellar grating interferometer.

With currently available beam splitting materials the Michelson interferometer is slightly less efficient than a big lamellar grating interferometer over most of the far infrared region. Since, however, it is somewhat easier to construct, especially with sufficient precision to work at conventional infrared frequencies, it is the more widely used design. The Michelson interferometer would also have the advantage for periodic use that its flat movable mirror can be made much lighter than a lamellar grating plate.

6. Performances of interferometers and conclusion

The work which has been done on the methods of Fourier transform spectroscopy can only be justified by its promise as a practical spectroscopic tool which *actually performs* better than the diffraction grating monochromator under practical experimental conditions. Though the theoretical advantages outlined in section 2 appear to be very important, very few data have been published showing direct comparisons with other types of instruments. Consequently our conclusions will have to be limited to general comments based on typical results of the various techniques.

At their present state of development, periodic interferometers have limited resolution, but good radiation purity compared with grating spectrometers. They are therefore well adapted to absolute measurements of far infrared optical properties at moderate resolution. They are convenient to use since the data are obtained immediately from the analog Fourier analysis. For typical results see the measurements of the transmission and reflection from metal mesh by GENZEL [1964].

The most impressive features of aperiodic Fourier transform spectroscopy with digital Fourier transformation is the speed with which high resolution spectra are obtained for a very wide spectral range. Because of this speed, good results can be obtained with extremely weak signals such as are encountered from the mercury arc at frequencies less than 10 cm^{-1}.

As a demonstration of the performance of an aperiodic Michelson interferometer we show, in fig. 2.8, curves of the transmittance, T, and the absorption coefficient, $-\log T$, for a 1.5 meter path through water vapor at a pressure of 20 Torr. The water vapor and normalization runs were each recorded over $0 \leq \Delta \leq 5$ cm in 50 min, integrating each point for a one second gate time, and using a one mil Mylar beam splitter with $\nu_{max} = 100$ cm^{-1}. The linear apodization used gives a resolution width equal to $1/\Delta_{max}$ $= 0.2$ cm^{-1}. This is verified by the 0.29 cm^{-1} water vapor splitting at ~ 55 cm^{-1}. Higher resolution spectra at this pressure did not sharpen the lines appreciably, indicating that they were pressure broadened to widths of $\sim$ 0.3 cm^{-1}. To demonstrate the full resolution available with the Michelson interferometer, water vapor at 2 Torr was measured out to $\Delta_{max} = 20$ cm and the transmittance shown in fig. 2.9, was computed in the vicinity of the ~ 55 cm^{-1} splitting. Measurements as a function of pressure indicate that the width seen is still influenced by pressure broadening, but the doublet is almost completely separated. Water vapor spectra have been measured on grating monochromators with comparable resolution to that shown in fig. 2.8, but they were recorded much more slowly and show considerable effects of false energy (YAROSLAVSKI and STANEVICH [1959]).

These measurements were made with the Michelson interferometer in one of its most useful ranges. The power available from the lamp is large enough above ~ 20 cm^{-1} that a given Mylar beam splitter could be used over more than a factor of four in frequency. At lower frequencies, where beam splitter inefficiency cannot be tolerated, sweeping the frequency range from 3 to 20 cm^{-1} would require several changes of beam splitter. It is preferable, therefore, to use a lamellar grating interferometer similar to the one discussed in section 5 which has an efficiency approaching 100 per cent in this range. As an example of the performance of this lamellar grating interferometer we show in fig. 2.10 the transmittance of a one cm thick powder specimen of ytterbium iron garnet at 1.2°K. The spectrum (RICHARDS [1963, 1964b]), which shows a zero-field ferrimagnetic resonance at 3.0 cm^{-1}, was measured over $0 \leq \Delta \leq 10$ cm using a 20 sec gate time and $\nu_{max} = 20$ cm^{-1}. The apodized resolution of 0.10 cm^{-1} is comparable to the natural line width. The signal-to-noise ratio deteriorates rapidly below ~ 3 cm^{-1} because of the rapid decrease in power from the lamp, but is better than 40 for 4 cm$^{-1} < \nu < 15$ cm^{-1}. This spectrum demonstrates the feasibility of doing reasonably high resolution infrared spectroscopy in a frequency range which overlaps with that of commercial microwave oscillators.

The best available evidence that absorption coefficients can be measured with high accuracy by the method of aperiodic Fourier spectroscopy comes from the work of GUSH and BOSOMWORTH [1965] on the absorption of compressed gases. These authors take precautions to maintain precise linearity between radiation power input and detector voltage, and make use of eq. (2.10) to compute the spectrum from interferograms recorded for equal distances on either side of $\Delta = 0$. Agreement with data obtained using dispersion grating techniques, and the repeatability of their data with different experimental parameters indicates an absolute accuracy of the order of one per cent.

Mention should also be made of the technique used by CHAMBERLIN [1963] et al. and by BELL [1965] for measuring index of refraction. Their work was done using digital computation of aperiodic interferograms, but could, in principle, be done with a periodic spectrometer using two phase sensitive detectors in quadrature. When a partially transparent material of thickness t and index n is placed in one arm of a Michelson interferometer, an extra path difference equal to $\Delta_0 = 2(n-1)t$ is introduced. In general, there will be some dispersion so that Δ_0 will be a function of v. An average value of $\langle \Delta_0 \rangle$ and thus of $\langle n \rangle$ can be obtained directly by observing the shift of the peak in the interferogram when the material is inserted. The frequency dependent index can be computed from the equation

$$n(v) = 1 + \frac{1}{2t} \tan^{-1} \frac{Q(v)}{P(v)}, \qquad (2.21)$$

which follows directly from eq. (2.11) if $P(v)$ and $Q(v)$ are the real and imaginary parts of the complex spectrum computed from (2.10). The correct branch of the inverse tangent function is obtained by inspection of the average index $\langle n \rangle$ and the form of the spectrum $|S(v)| = [P^2(v) + Q^2(v)]^{\frac{1}{2}}$ over which it is averaged. This technique promises to be useful, for example, in the study of the optical phonons in solids.

In addition to the topics already mentioned, studies have been made of optical phonon absorption in solids (SUTHERLAND [1963]), absorption by molecules trapped in clathrate compounds (BURGIEL et al. [1965]), ferrimagnetic, anti-ferromagnetic, spin, and cyclotron resonance in solids (RICHARDS [1963, 1964b], BURGIEL and HEBEL [1965], RICHARDS and SMITH [1964]), fluorescence from solids (ARCHBOLD and GEBBIE [1962]), optical properties of gas plasmas (LLEWELLYN-JONES and BROWN [1964]), rotational and vibrational spectra of gases (SUTHERLAND [1963]) and many other systems.

The number of physical and chemical problems for which far infrared Fourier transform spectroscopy has been used is thus growing rapidly. An explosive increase might be anticipated now that interferometers have become commercially available (ch. 1, section 5).

References

R. V. ALVES and M. TINKHAM, private communication.

E. ARCHBOLD and H. A. GEBBIE, Proc. Phys. Soc. **80** (1962) 793.

A. S. BARKER Jr. and M. TINKHAM, Bull. Am. Phys. Soc. **6** (1961) 112.

E. E. BELL, Proc. Conf. Photographic and Spectroscopic Optics, Tokyo and Kyoto, Jap. J. Appl. Phys. **4** Suppl. 1 (1965) 412.

J. C. BURGIEL and L. C. HEBEL, Phys. Rev. **140** (1965) A925.

J. C. BURGIEL, P. L. RICHARDS and H. MEYER, J. Chem. Phys. **43** (1965) 4291.

J. E. CHAMBERLIN, J. E. GIBBS and H. A. GEBBIE, Nature **198** (1963) 874.

J. CONNES, Rev. optique **40** (1961) 45, 116, 171 and 231.

P. FELLGETT, J. Phys. Radium **19** (1958) 187 and 273.

A. S. FILLER, J. Opt. Soc. Am. **54** (1964) 762.

S. FUJITA, H. YOSHINAGA, K. CHIBA, K. NAKANO, S. YOSHIDA and H. SUGIMORI, Proc. Conf. Photographic and Spectroscopic Optics, Tokyo and Kyoto, Jap. J. Appl. Phys. **4** Suppl. 1 (1965) 429.

H. A. GEBBIE, N.P.L. Symposium on Interferometry (H. M. Stationary Office, London, 1960) p. 423.

H. A. GEBBIE, K. J. HABELL and S. P. MIDDLETON, Proc. Conf. on Optical Instruments and Techniques (Chapman and Hall, London, 1962) p. 43.

H. A. GEBBIE and G. A. VANASSE, Nature **178** (1956) 432.

L. GENZEL, J. Mol. Spectroscopy **4** (1960) 241.

L. GENZEL, Proc. Conf. Photographic and Spectroscopic Optics, Tokyo and Kyoto, Jap. J. Appl. Phys. **4** Suppl. 1 (1965) 353.

L. GENZEL and R. WEBER, Z. angew. Phys. **10** (1958) 127, 195.

S. GOLDMAN, Information Theory (Prentice-Hall, Inc., Englewood Cliffs, New Jersey, 1953) p. 67.

J. GUILD, Diffraction Gratings as Measuring Scales (London, Oxford University Press, 1960).

H. P. GUSH and D. R. BOSOMWORTH, Can J. Phys. **43** (1965) 729, 751.

H. HAPP and L. GENZEL, Infrared Phys. **1** (1961) 39.

P. JACQUINOT, Rep. Prog. Phys. **23** (1960) 267.

D. T. LLEWELLYN-JONES and S. C. BROWN, 1964 Annual Meeting, Plasma Physics Div., Am. Phys. Soc.

E. V. LOWENSTEIN, Appl. Optics **2** (1963) 491.

A. A. MICHELSON, Light Waves and their Uses (Univ. of Chicago Press, 1902).

P. F. PARSHIN, Opt. i Spektroskopia **13** (1962) 740. (Engl. transl. Opt. Spektry. **13** (1962) 418).

P. F. PARSHIN, Opt. i Spektroskopia **14** (1963) 388 (Engl. transl. Opt. Spektry. **14** (1963) 207).

R. F. RENK and L. GENZEL, Appl. Optics **1** (1962) 643.

P. L. RICHARDS, J. Appl. Phys. **34** (1963) 1237.

P. L. RICHARDS, J. Opt. Soc. Am. **54** (1964a) 1474.

P. L. RICHARDS, J. Appl. Phys. **35** (1964b) 850.

P. L. RICHARDS and G. E. SMITH, Rev. Sci. Inst. **35** (1964) 1535.

J. D. STRONG, J. Opt. Soc. Am. **47** (1957) 354.

J. D. STRONG and G. A. VANASSE, J. Phys. Radium **19** (1958) 192.

J. D. STRONG and G. A. VANASSE, J. Opt. Soc. Am. **49** (1959) 844.

J. STRONG and G. A. VANASSE, J. Opt. Soc. Am. **50** (1960) 113.

G. SUTHERLAND, Pure Appl. Chem. **1** (1963) 33.

N. G. YAROSLAVSKI and A. E. STANEVICH, Opt. i Spektroskopia **5** (1958) 384 and Opt. i Spektroskopia **7** (1959) 626 (Engl. transl. Opt. Spectry. **7** (1959) 380).

G. A. VANASSE, J. Opt. Soc. Am. **52** (1962) 472.

CHAPTER 3

GRATING SPECTROSCOPY

BY

G. R. WILKINSON

Kings College

AND

D. H. MARTIN

Queen Mary College, University of London

1. Introduction

Grating spectroscopy was the first of the modern far infrared techniques to be introduced and up to now it has been much the most fruitful. The method is essentially the same as that in wide use in the near and middle infra-red and some recent sophisticated instruments have been designed to operate from wavelengths of a few microns to well into the far infra-red. Different components of the technique provide the major experimental difficulties, however, as the method is extended to longer wavelengths, and it is the special considerations which apply to the region from about 50 μm (200 cm^{-1}) out to 2 mm (5 cm^{-1}) with which we are concerned in this chapter.

A grating spectrometer comprises four main parts. There is a broad-band source; a monochromator which provides a nearly monochromatic beam at its exit slit and which contains the dispersive grating unit and various filters; the sample holder or cell which frequently includes a cryostat for work at liquid nitrogen or liquid helium temperatures; and, lastly, a detector (which might also be at the temperature of liquid helium) and its recorder. In this chapter these main components will be examined in turn and a few examples of complete spectrometers will be described and discussed. A section is included on the important question of testing resolution and spectral purity and of calibration.

2. Sources

A broad-band source is required for grating spectrometry. Mercury arc lamps of the kinds used for street lighting have been widely used; among the commercial types which have been reported as satisfactory far infra-red sources are Hanau Q400, G.E. A.H. 4, Philips H.P.K. 125W, A.E.I. MBL/D. Each of these has a wattage in the range 125–250 W and the arc runs at several atmospheres pressure in a fused quartz tube of length a few cm and of width about 1 cm. If the lamp is supplied with an outer glass envelope it must be removed because glass is strongly absorbing over much of the far infra-red. Measurements of the effective black-body temperatures of these sources give values of about 4000–5000 °K for frequencies below 50 cm^{-1} and a large decrease to less than 1000 °K above 100 cm^{-1} (HADNI et al. [1963], PAPOULAR [1964]). The reason for this drop in effective temperature is that the radiation comes mainly from the arc at the long-wave end while at the short-wave end the signal is from the hot envelope because the fused quartz is opaque above about 70 cm^{-1}. For this reason the long-wave signal may be modulated if the power supply is a.c.*

Above 100 cm^{-1}, where the arc lamps function merely as hot quartz rods, other hot-body sources such as the globar can be brighter. The rising black-body curve compensates, however, for the decreasing effective temperature and, unless the highest possible resolution at the short-wave end of our range is required, the provision of an alternative source in a spectrometer may be more trouble than it is worth.

In most spectrometers the arc lamp is enclosed in a water-cooled tube with a slit about 1 cm wide to provide the effective source. A mechanical shutter or chopper is used to interrupt the beam from the source at a frequency to which the detector's amplifier responds selectively (chapter 4). In this way the detector can distinguish between the signal and the thermal radiation from other parts of the spectrometer which, being unfiltered by the mono-chromator, can be at least comparable with the signal itself particularly when a cold detector is in use. This shutter should be on the source side of the monochromator in order that the thermal radiation from its blades should not reach the detector unfiltered. Simple rotating toothed discs are usually employed. The chopper unit is usually fitted with a pea-lamp and photo-diode, mounted on opposite sides of the chopper blades, to provide a signal as a phase-reference for the detector amplifier (chapter 4).

A hot-body source radiates very weakly in the far infra-red and the con-sequent shortage of signal power is the dominant problem to be faced in far infra-red grating spectroscopy. The development of a source more selective than a hot-body in the spectral distribution of its radiation (though still broad-band) would improve techniques greatly.

---

* These lamps also emit ultra-violet radiation and the usual precautions are required to prevent damage to eyes and skin.

3. Monochromators

3.1 OPTICAL DESIGN AND PERFORMANCE

The most widely used monochromator for the far infra-red is of the Czerny-Turner type illustrated in fig. 3.1. The system is self correcting as far as spherical aberations are concerned and spherical mirrors can be used. The Fastie-Ebert modification also shown in the figure, in which a single mirror replaces the pair, offers slightly less freedom of choice of optical path but has the advantage that mounting is very simple. The third type shown in the figure, the Littrow mounting, involves the use of a single off-axis para-

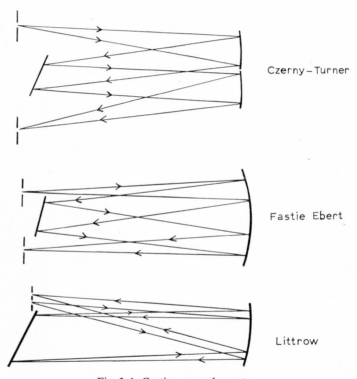

Czerny–Turner

Fastie Ebert

Littrow

Fig. 3.1. Grating monochromators.

bolic reflector. It has few advantages over the Czerny Turner system apart from taking up rather less space, and in view of the cost of the paraboloid it is rarely used except in some commercial far infra-red spectrometers.

The optical theory of a grating spectrometer has been given by DALY and SUTHERLAND [1949] and by STRONG [1949]. We are interested here in how the attainable resolution is influenced by the dimensions of the mono-chromator. If the entrance slit (height l, width s) is fully illuminated with radiation at a spectral brightness B_v, and if ϕ is the solid angle subtended at the entrance slit by the illuminated area of the grating (and collimator), then the power at the frequency v collected by the grating is proportional to $B_v \phi l s$. The power falling on the exit slit (also of height l and width s) is therefore proportional to $(R_v B_v \phi l s^2 / D_v F)$ where D_v is the angular dispersion of the grating, F is the focal length of the condenser mirror, and $(1 - R_v)$ is the fraction of the power entering the collimator which is absorbed at the reflecting surfaces or in the filters or is diffracted into orders other than that of interest. The slit-width limit to the attainable resolution is proportional to $s/D_v F$ (see below) and so we can say that, for slits set at widths to give a specified signal strength at the exit slit, the slit-width limited resolutions of several monochromators would depend on their dimensions and on B_v, inversely as $(R_v B_v \phi l D_v F)^{\frac{1}{2}}$. For high resolution, therefore, each of these parameters should be as large as practicable.

If the source is a hot-body, B_v increases linearly with temperature in the far infra-red. The improvement in resolution resulting from an increase in temperature might be less than as $T^{\frac{1}{2}}$, however, because a reduction in R_v might result if, in order to maintain spectral purity in the face of the increase as T^4 in the *short*-wave radiation from the source, the filtering had to be more severe. The brightness of available sources is discussed in section 2. The upper limit to ϕ is normally set by the solid angle over which the detec-tor will accept signal power and by its window size. The same considerations limit l (aberration effects are not normally important in the far infra-red). Most detectors, when their associated condensing optics are optimised, have maximum useful ϕ-values which correspond to f-numbers of about $f/4$, and to maximum useful slit heights of about 1–2 cm. An increase in F, keeping ϕ con-stant, results in an improvement in resolution as $F^{\frac{1}{2}}$, but increasing F at constant ϕ brings a rapid increase in the size and inconvenience of the spectrometer. A popular compromise has been to use gratings about 10 cm $\times$ 10 cm in size and collimators with focal lengths about 40 cm, but a few larger instruments have been built to give better resolution. Lastly there is D_v, but for a given v this depends neither on the grating size nor on order number (see below).

The concept of spectral resolution has been discussed in chapter 1, sec-tion 2. For a grating spectrometer, the slit-width limited resolution can be deduced as follows from the grating equation (for first order)

$$\frac{\lambda}{d} = \cos(\alpha_i - \theta) + \cos(\alpha_0 + \theta),$$

where λ is the wavelength, d is the grating spacing, θ the angle between the grating and the monochromator axis, and α_i, α_0 are the angles of incidence and diffraction relative to that axis (see fig. 3.2). If α_i and α_0 vary by δ_i and δ_0 representing the non-zero slit widths, we have

$$\frac{\delta\lambda}{d} = -\sin(\alpha_i-\theta)\,\delta_i - \sin(\alpha_0+\theta)\,\delta_0.$$

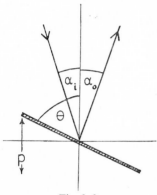

Fig. 3.2.

If we put $\delta_i = 0$ and consider the variation of $\delta\lambda$ as δ_0 changes from $+\delta$ to $-\delta$, where 2δ is the angular width of the exit slit, we should be deducing the spectral spread of the energy emerging from the exit slit and deriving from the central strip of the entrance slit. This is illustrated in fig. 3.3(a). Similarly if we put $\delta_i = \delta$ and let δ_0 range from $+\delta$ to $-\delta$ as before, we should be considering the spectral spread of the energy deriving from the outer strip of the entrance slit. The results of doing this for all strips in the entrance slit are included in fig. 3.3(a), and are transferred to fig. 3.3(b)

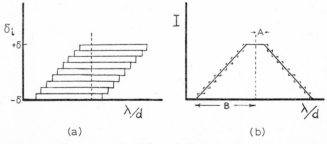

(a)   (b)

Fig. 3.3. (a) The spread in wavelength of the radiation contributed by successive strips of the entrance slit to the signal emerging from the exit slit of a monochromator. (b) Slit-function of a monochromator.

to give a spectral distribution for the energy emerging from the exit slit and deriving from the whole of the entrance slit. This trapezoidal "slit function" has a full width $2B = 4\delta \cos\alpha \sin\theta$ and a width at the top $2A = 4\delta \sin\alpha \cos\theta$. The spectral resolution, $\Delta\lambda$, can be defined as the width of the slit-function at half-height, i.e.

$$\frac{\Delta\lambda}{d} = A + B = 2\delta(\cos\alpha \sin\theta + \sin\alpha \cos\theta) = 2\delta \sin(\alpha + \theta).$$

The angular width of the slit is equal to $(s/F)\cos\alpha$ so that

$$\frac{\Delta\lambda}{d} = \frac{s}{F} \cos\alpha \sin(\alpha + \theta)$$

and the *fractional* resolution is

$$\frac{\Delta\lambda}{\lambda} = \frac{\Delta v}{v} = \frac{s}{F} \frac{\cos\alpha \sin(\alpha + \theta)}{2 \cos\alpha \cos\theta} = \frac{\sin(\alpha + \theta)}{\cos\theta} \frac{s}{2F}$$

$$\text{i.e.} \ \frac{\Delta\lambda}{\lambda} = \frac{\Delta v}{v} \simeq \frac{s}{F}$$

since $\alpha \sim 10°$ and $\theta \sim 70°$.

We have here considered resolution in terms of the spread in wavelength of the energy emerging from the monochromator for a fixed setting of the grating, θ, and with a broad-band source uniformly filling the entrance slit. Instead we might have taken the entrance slit to be filled with *monochromatic* light and then rotated the grating and computed the width of the intensity-versus-θ peak. This could then be converted into an apparent wavelength spread using the grating equation above. The same result would have been obtained.

We can refer back now to the first part of this section to note that the fractional resolution of a monochromator of fixed dimensions, for a specified signal output, varies in proportion to $(B_v D_v)^{-\frac{1}{2}}$. A black body has a brightness which varies as v^2 and, by differentiation of the grating equation (with $\alpha_i = \alpha_0$) we have

$$D_v = \frac{d\theta}{d\lambda} = \frac{-1}{2d \cos\alpha \sin\theta} = \frac{-1}{\lambda \tan\theta} \ \text{i.e.} \propto v.$$

The frequency dependence of the fractional resolution would therefore be as $v^{-\frac{3}{2}}$ for a black-body source. In the far infra-red the effective black-body source temperature is not constant, however (section 2), and the frequency dependence of B_v is less rapid than as v^2. If it were as $\sim v$, the fractional resolution would vary as $\sim v^{-1}$ and so the resolution expressed in cm^{-1} would be independent of frequency. This is very roughly the situation in practice. With a large spectrometer or with a good cold detector, the attainable resolution is about 0.2 cm^{-1} throughout the far infra-red; with a spectrometer of moderate size and with a good room temperature detector the attainable resolution is roughly 1 cm^{-1} (but see section 4 for the relevance of signal-to-noise ratios and scanning rates to these figures).

We should remark that the slit-width is but one of several distinct factors which can limit the resolution of a grating spectrometer, but it is normally the dominant one. Aberrations in the optical components and defects in the gratings are not normally of any significance at these long wavelengths but the diffraction limit of the grating might be. The grating limit to the *fractional* resolution is 1 in N where N is the number of lines on the grating. The resolution itself (in cm^{-1}) is equal to the reciprocal of the distance $2\,L\cos\theta\cos\alpha$, where L is the width of the grating, i.e. about twice the distance p in fig. 3.2. At blaze, θ is about 70° and $\alpha \sim 10°$, and so the resolution in cm^{-1} is $\sim 1/L$ with L in cm. The grating limits in most far infrared spectrometers are thus ~ 0.1 cm^{-1} throughout the range. This is beyond the best reported resolutions, but only just (section 8). If available sources could be improved in brightness by an order of magnitude the grating limit and not the slitwidth or energy limit could thus be the dominant one.

3.2. GRATINGS

The dominant consideration in designing a grating for the far infra-red is to use as much as possible of the radiation available from the source. To this end the gratings in use tend to be fairly large, commonly about 10×10 cm^2 and in some cases as much as 35×35 cm^2. For the same reason they are normally echelette gratings, that is to say reflection gratings with grooves having a saw-tooth profile as illustrated in fig. 3.4. Though the angle of

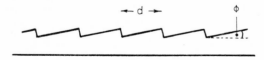

Fig. 3.4. Echellette grating.

diffraction for each order of any grating is determined by the groove spacing and not the groove shape, the distribution of the incident energy among the several orders *is* determined by the grooves' profile. The special merit of the echelette profile is that the incident power at a given wavelength tends to be concentrated into a single order. The theory of diffraction by an echelette grating, using certain assumptions known as the scalar approximation, has been presented by MADDEN and STRONG [1958]. This shows that the order into which incident power of a given wavelength is mainly concentrated is that whose angle of diffraction lies closest to specular reflection from the long faces of the grooves. This is illustrated in fig. 3.5 in terms of the "grating

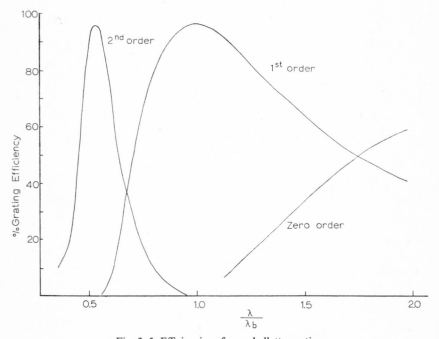

Fig. 3.5. Efficiencies of an echellette grating.

efficiency" which is the fraction of the incident power at each wavelength diffracted into the order in question. The grating is said to be "blazed" for the wavelength, λ_b, at the peak of the first order efficiency curve, which is close to the wavelength for which the grating angle θ is that for specular reflection from the long faces of the grooves. Figure 3.5 shows that for wavelengths near λ_b most of the incident power falls into the first order and very little falls into the second (and higher) orders. As the wavelength increases beyond λ_b an increasing fraction of the incident power falls into the "zero order", i.e. is diffracted without dispersion as if specularly reflected from the plane of the grating. Efficient use of the available source power is therefore made when a grating is used from $\frac{2}{3}$ to $\frac{3}{2}\lambda_b$. The grating equation for the nth order is

$$\frac{n\lambda}{d} = 2 \cos\alpha \cos\theta$$

(see fig. 3.2; $\alpha_i = \alpha_0$). At the grating angle for which radiation of wavelength λ in first order reaches the detector, radiation of wavelength λ/n in n^{th} order will also reach it. If the grating efficiency were plotted against grating angle θ, rather than against λ as in fig. 3.5, the peaks of the several orders (except zero order) would all fall near the blaze setting of the grating, at which $\theta = (\frac{1}{2}\pi - \phi)$ (but would be narrower the higher the order number and in the limit of very short wavelengths would correspond to specular reflection from the long faces of the grooves). For this reason it might be best when very high spectral purity is required to use a grating over a range restricted to the long-wave side of its blaze peak because highly efficient filters would be required to remove the second and higher orders close to the blaze setting (see the following section).

The "scalar approximation" suppresses some of the effects to which the imposition of proper boundary conditions at the surface of the grating would lead; in particular it cannot predict the observed fact that echelette gratings distribute the incident energy among the diffraction orders slightly differently for beams polarised perpendicularly to and parallel to the grooves. A full theory is extremely complicated (see STROKE [1962]). The scalar approximation is more nearly correct as the wavelength becomes small compared with the groove spacing. Most far infrared gratings have been ruled with a shallow groove angle (fig. 3.4) between 10° and 20°, and so the wavelength in first order is decidedly less than the groove spacing and the results of scalar theory for grating efficiency might be expected to be roughly correct (and recent measurements have confirmed this – M. Kimmit, private communication).

Gratings for the far infra-red have recently become available commercially (chapter 1, section 5) and have been ruled successfully in the machine shops of several laboratories. Great dimensional precision is not essential for these long waves. The main problems are those of maintaining a good echellette groove-profile while removing the appreciable quantity of material from each groove. For the longer wavelengths aluminium alloy or brass blanks are cut with steel tools on a planing or milling machine. For wavelengths below about 150 μm, i.e. for more than about 40 grooves to the cm, greater care and better tools are required. Tool wear can be reduced by cutting the grooves in a soft "solder" alloy mounted on a backing plate. Plastic or resin replicas can be taken from a metal master grating and, after being aluminised, perform quite as well as the original. The series of gratings required to cover a wide spectral range should follow a geometric series of groove spacings because each covers a range of about $\times 2$ in frequency. For example, the following series:

$$\text{lines/cm: } 7.5, \ 15, \ 30, \ 60, \ 120$$

would cover the range from roughly $5 \ \text{cm}^{-1}$ to $240 \ \text{cm}^{-1}$ since α is normally $\sim 10°$ and $\phi \sim 20°$ and so $\lambda_b \sim d$ or $\nu_b \sim N \ \text{cm}^{-1}$ for N lines to the cm.

3.3. FILTERS

Owing to the extremely low intensity of the far infra-red radiation from hot-body sources a major experimental problem is encountered in trying adequately to separate this small signal from the more intense radiation at shorter wavelengths. The process of filtering separates roughly into two stages. The first involves the removal of the radiation at near infra-red and shorter wavelengths. Though this radiation is many orders of magnitude more intense than the far infra-red component there is no great problem in removing it by absorption filters. For work at wavelengths exceeding 50 μm $(200 \ \text{cm}^{-1})$ this bulk filtering is commonly achieved by transmission through a thin (~ 0.1 mm) sheet of black polyethylene and a disc of crystal quartz, which can be 2 mm thick for $\lambda > 100$ μm $(100 \ \text{cm}^{-1})$ but which should be thinner than this if the shortest wavelength of interest approaches the strong cut-off in the quartz at about 40 μm $(250 \ \text{cm}^{-1})$ shown in fig. 3.6. The second stage of filtering is that which removes the radiation which would fall in the second and third orders of the dispersing grating (or in the third and fourth if the grating is being used in second order). This is a more difficult problem because a filter with a sharp cut-off is required if high spectral purity is to be obtained without serious loss of signal power in the range of interest. A variety of reflection and transmission filters have been used to this end and are described below. (Although ionic crystals exhibit a strong dispersion associated with optical lattice vibrations in the far infra-red, prisms have not been used to separate the orders of a grating – in the manner familiar in the near infra-red – because strong absorption is associated with this dispersion over a wide range of frequency as a result of multi-phonon processes – MARTIN [1965].)

Generally speaking, transmission filters are more convenient because their orientation is not critical, they are easily interchanged and do not complicate the optical path of the instrument. Two types have recently been introduced. The first uses the absorptive properties of a number of inorganic compounds which are dispersed in powdered form in polyethylene sheets (YAMADA et al. [1962], MANLEY and WILLIAMS [1965]). Some examples are included in fig. 3.6. To fabricate such filters the powdered compounds can be mixed with

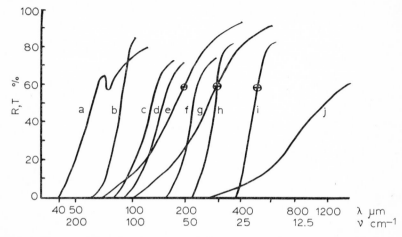

Fig. 3.6. Characteristics of various transmission and reflection filters referred to in the text. (a) Transmission through 1 mm crystal quartz. (b), (c) and (d) Transmission through polyethylene containing various mixed powders (b) $Cu_2O + W_2O_3$, (c) $Al_2O_3 + Cr_2O_3 + NaCl$, and (d) $Al_2O_3 + Cr_2O_3 + K_2CrO_4$. (e) and (g) Transmission through polyethylene gratings; $d = \lambda$ at points marked $\oplus$. (f) Transmission through powdered mixtures of $TlI + TlCl + WO_3 + Cu_2O$ dispersed in polyethylene. (h) and (i) Reflection from metal meshes with $a/d = 0.4$; $d = \frac{1}{2}\lambda$ at points marked $\oplus$. (j) Transmission through 5 mm of CaF_2.

high-density polyethylene powder and then heated to melt the polyethylene. The resulting pill can then be rolled or pressed at a temperature sufficient to soften the polyethylene. The second type of transmission filter uses the scattering and diffracting properties of a polyethylene sheet whose surface bears an impression of the rulings of a grating (MOLLER and MCKNIGHT [1963]). For wavelengths decidedly greater than the groove spacing there is no scattering and no diffraction of the beam, and little absorption, but radiation of shorter wavelength is scattered or diffracted out of the beam by reflection or refraction. Such a filter is fabricated by pressing the polyethylene sheet on to the face of a heated grating made by cutting symmetrical 90° grooves in a metal blank. The transmission characteristics of such filters have a common shape when plotted against λ/d, where d is the spacing of the grooves, and filters of this kind can be designed to provide a cut-off at any desired wavelength in the extreme-infra-red. The common characteristic is included in fig. 3.6. In applications where very high spectral purity is required, crystals of alkali halides a few mm thick can be used as transmission filters because they absorb extremely strongly over a wide spectral range (see the curve for CaF_2 in fig. 3.6). There is, however, also a serious loss of power in the range of interest. (If such crystals are used at 4 °K a much sharper cut-off is obtained – MARTIN [1965].)

These transmission filters are easy to make and to use but their cut-offs are not very sharp. Best results are obtained, as far as spectral purity is concerned, if a main dispersion grating is used to cover a range to the long-wave side of the peak in its first order blaze and if a transmission filter is introduced which already attenuates appreciably at the blaze wavelength, at which the second order efficiency of the grating is low (see fig. 3.5). As the transmission of the filter increases with increasing wavelength the first order efficiency of the grating decreases, so that the net effect is a fairly flat overall characteristic with an overall efficiency in the region of 30–40% over a fairly wide range, from about 1.1 to 2.0 times the blaze wavelength.

The need for adequate filtering is illustrated by the following considerations. In the far infra-red $hv \ll kT$ where T is the source temperature, and the frequency-dependence of the black-body emission relation reduces to

$$E_v \, dv \propto v^2 \, dv,$$

where $E_v \, dv$ is the energy in the spectral interval dv. The energy in a given *fractional* bandwith therefore varies as v^3 i.e. with order number, n, as n^3. Thus, in order to keep the second order energy in the output from a mono-chromator to less than 8% of the first order output, the ratio of the overall transmission of the system for the second and first order signals must be less than 1%; for third order radiation the ratio would be less than 0.3%.

The transmission filters already described can give spectral purities of about 95% or better, provided, as we have remarked above, care is taken in choosing the range over which the main dispersion grating is used, and in selecting the cut-off frequency of the filter. It is always prudent, however, to test the spectral purity of a monochromator (see below) and one or another of the filters described below may be required in addition to, or as an alternative to, the convenient transmission filters already described.

There are four kinds of reflection filter in use. The simplest is a metal mirror with an abraded surface (a "scatter plate"). Such a reflector behaves specularly for wavelengths greater than the widths and depths of the abrasions but scatters shorter wavelengths out of the beam. The cut-off wavelength can be varied to some extent by varying the coarseness of the grinding powder used in the abrasion. Carborundum of grade 120, used on an aluminium alloy reflector, gives a cut-off at about 150 μm (67 cm^{-1}) (BLOOR et al. [1961]). For a cut-off at a longer wavelength, suitable abraded reflectors would be difficult to make and it is easier to cut grooves in the surface of a metal plate to make a reflection grating. Such a grating is set so as to reflect the wavelengths of interest in zero order and scatters or diffracts the short-wave power out of the beam. It would have about twice as many lines to the cm as the main grating with which it is to be used. This use of a grating in zero order as a filter was first suggested by WHITE [1947] and has been discussed by HADNI [1963] and PALMER [1963]. Their special virtue is their high reflectivity above cut-off, well above 90%, so that as many as four reflections can be used to give a sharper cut-off without serious loss of power in the pass band (but with some complication in the optical path, of course). Their performance depends in a complicated way on groove-shape, orientation, and angle of reflection (near normal reflection is thought to be best) and they can also show subsidiary reflection maxima at wavelengths just below the nominal cut-off so that, again, it would be prudent to test for spectral purity. The most recently introduced reflection filters, particularly applicable at longer wavelengths, are metallic wire meshes which transmit or scatter short waves and specularly reflect long waves (MITSUISHI et al. [1963]; RENK and GENZEL [1961]). These probably have the sharpest cut-offs of the filters in present use. When plotted against λ/d, where d is the mesh spacing, the transmission characteristic is the same for all meshes with the same a/d ratio, where a is the wire diameter. The characteristic for a/d about 0.4 and an angle of incidence of 15°, is included in fig. 3.6. These meshes can be constructed from simple "wire-cloth" for longer wavelengths, and from electro-formed meshes (ch. 1, section 5) for the short-wave end of our range. The last type of reflection filter to be described is the oldest and was used by Rubens and others in the very early experiments in far infra-red spectroscopy. These are the "restrahlen reflectors" which make use of the fact that an ionic crystal exhibits a high reflectivity over a band of frequencies near the frequency of each optical mode of lattice vibration. Simple diatomic ionic crystals such as the alkali halides and the alkaline earth difluorides have but a single restrahlen reflection and two or more reflections from such crystals provides a good filtering action. NaCl has been used for the range 45–65 μm, KBr for 65–100 μm and the mixture of thallium salts known as KRS 5 for 100–200 μm (e.g. FARMER and KEY [1965]) and if KCl and CsBr are used in addition to these, the range from 45 μm (222 cm^{-1}) to 200 μm

(50cm^{-1}) can be covered with a crystal reflectivity nowhere less than 80 %. Single crystals are not essential for restrahlen plates because plates made of pressed or bonded powders can be almost as highly reflecting (JONES et al. [1964]).

In summary, in designing a spectrometer provision should be made for the insertion of a set of transmission filters and it is wise to include provision for at least two changeable reflection filters set near normal incidence.

Several methods have been used for testing spectral purity. The simplest is to take a test sample which has a strong absorption line in the first order spectrum of the grating, and which transmits well at the wavelengths cor-

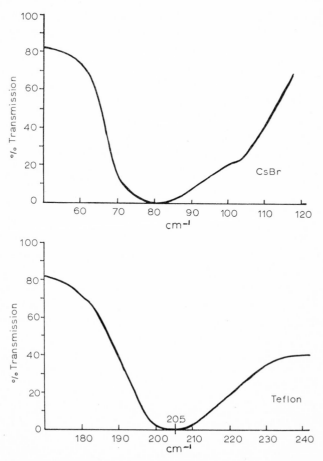

Fig. 3.7. Tests of spectral purity at 80 cm⁻¹ and 205 cm⁻¹ using a CsBr mull in Nujol and a thin sheet of teflon (after records obtained with the Beckman IR.11 and the Perkin-Elmer 301 spectrometers respectively).

responding to the second and third orders. The test sample is made sufficiently thick to absorb more than, say, 99.9% at the absorption line. Any power transmitted at the grating setting corresponding to this line can then be attributed to spectral impurity. Two examples are shown in fig. 3.7. That the sample is sufficiently thick can be determined by measurements on thinner samples and will also be indicated by a flat top to the absorption peak. An alternative method of testing spectral purity is to record the spectrum of a gas with a simple and known rotation spectrum, such as NH_3 or HCl, and then to make a careful search for absorption lines showing up in second and higher orders and lying between the expected first order lines (BLOOR et al. [1961]). The tests for spectral purity should particularly be made close to the peak of the blaze, if spectra are to be recorded through this peak, since it is here that the grating efficiencies are greatest for all orders (section 3.2).

Using the methods described in this section spectral purities exceeding 99% at 50 μm (200 cm^{-1}) and 95% at 200 μm (50 cm^{-1}) can be achieved. At wavelengths greater than 300 μm it might be difficult to maintain as high a purity as this without significant loss of first order radiation. The use of an InSb detector helps here, however, because its sensitivity falls rapidly with decreasing wavelength below about 200 μm (ch. 4).

Finally mention should be made of perhaps the most effective, but also the most elaborate, method of filtering for the far-infra-red (BELL et al. [1962]). This involves the reflection of the beam from a lamellar reflector like that used in interferometry (chapter 2, section 5.1). Part of the beam is reflected from a stationary set of lamellae and the rest from a moving set. The latter suffers a Doppler shift in frequency and so, when the two reflected beams are recombined, there result beats, or amplitude modulation. The beat frequency varies with the infra-red frequency; in particular the beat frequency is quite different for the several orders coming from the diffraction grating at a given setting. By tuning the detector amplifier to the appropriate beat frequency the several orders are perfectly separated. The function of the lamellar reflector is the same as in the interferometer of chapter 2, section 5.1, but is here used as part of a dispersion spectrometer which has the advantages and disadvantages of such instruments compared with interferometric spectrometers (chapter 1).

In the short-wave infra-red and the visible region, sophisticated band-pass filters are available which are based on interference effects in multi-layer structures of dielectric films. Recently the use of such filters has been extended as far as the 10–20 μm region. It is probable that methods will be found in the future for fabricating interference filters suitable for the far-infra-red. Simple narrow-band Fabry-Perot filters have already been constructed from metal mesh reflectors (ULRICH et al. [1963]).

3.4. POLARIZERS ETC.

For a full study of anisotropic crystals it is essential to use linearly polarized infra-red radiation, so that absorption and reflection spectra may be recorded with the electric vector of the radiation along the different principal crystal axes. There are several methods of producing polarized radiation in the far infra-red region. Perhaps the simplest to make is the type that depends upon the selective reflection at the Brewster angle, i.e. the angle for which tan θ = n where n is the refractive index. A transmission polarizer may be constructed from a stack of taut polyethylene sheets ($n = 1.46$) at 55.5° to the beam (MITSUISHI et al. [1960]). Alternatively mylar, or polyethylene terephthalate ($n = 2.65$) can be used at 69.5°. About 12 or more films are required to produce satisfactory results. It is an advantage if films of several thicknesses are selected and mounted with varying spaces between them so as to reduce the effect of troublesome interference fringes. Polarized radiation can also be obtained by reflection from silicon surfaces ($n = 3.4$) at an angle of 75°. Because of the high refractive index two reflections are sufficient to give 95% polarisation.

Perhaps the most satisfactory and most easily used polarizer for the far-infra-red is that based on the polarization produced on transmission through a wire grid. With a spacing d, a polarisation $\sim 98\%$ can be expected for $\lambda > 3d$ (LARSEN [1962]). Grids consisting of gold strips on a mylar base, with up to 1000 lines to the inch, have been made (Buckbey Meers Inc.) and make good polarizers for wavelengths greater than about 100 μm i.e. for frequencies less than 100 cm^{-1}. Grid polarizers might also be produced by shadowing the grooves of a transparent plastic replica of a diffraction grating with an evaporated metal (HASS et al. [1965]).

It should be noted that the grating and reflection filters in any grating spectrometer may partially polarize the radiation and mistakes can occur in measuring the absorption or reflection spectra of single anisotropic crystals or polymers if this is not recognised.

Other optical components which have recently been constructed and tested in the very far infra-red are retarder or quarter-wave plates of quartz and an isolator which, making use of Faraday rotation near to a cyclotron resonance frequency, passes plane polarized radiation in one direction only (RICHARDS and SMITH [1965], PALIK [1965]).

3.5. SOME MECHANICAL DESIGN CONSIDERATIONS

The first decision that has to be made in designing the structure of a grating spectrometer is whether to evacuate it or to rely on flushing with dry air. Absorption due to the excitation of the pure rotation spectrum of atmospheric water vapour is extremely intense and evacuation is the most effective way of eliminating it even though it may increase the complexity and cost of the spectrometer to some extent. In view of the comparatively low resolution that can be achieved in the far infra-red, it is only necessary to reach a pressure within the range of any good rotary pump. If the spectrometer is not evacuable, and present commercial far infra-red grating spectrometers are not, then it must be flushed continuously with dry air both during and long before use. An activated alumina drier is convenient for this purpose, especially the form that uses two columns one of which regenerates whilst the other circulates, but it requires a small compressor capable of providing air at a pressure of about 60 lb/square inch. Alumina dried air still contains sufficient water vapour to give appreciable absorption and unless a double beam system is used it is not really satisfactory (see fig. 3.14).

Possibly the simplest vacuum arrangement which is compatible with the Fastie-Ebert or Czerny-Turner monochromators is the one illustrated in fig. 3.8. The optical components of the monochromator are mounted on a

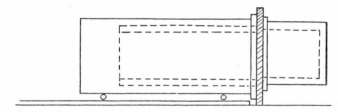

Fig. 3.8. A monochromator and source unit (broken lines) mounted from a vertical face-plate (shaded) can be enclosed by vacuum tanks as illustrated.

rigid base plate which is supported by a vertical face plate. A cylindrical tank, closed at one end, encloses the system and the rim at the open end seals directly on to the face plate with an O-ring. The tank can be easily removed if it is mounted on rollers running in a track. The system, particularly the detector, should be well isolated from vacuum pump vibration. It is an advantage if the sample compartment can be separated by vacuum windows from the rest of the spectrometer so as to reduce the repumping time on changing specimens or so as to allow spectra to be recorded with the sample chamber flushed with dry air instead of being evacuated (particularly useful when using liquid samples). Quartz crystal discs, polyethylene discs or thin mylar sheets make suitable windows and can be sealed with O-rings.

It is highly desirable that the spectrum should be recorded against a scale linear in frequency. There are several methods of achieving this by arranging for the grating to be rotated in such a way that the spectrum is scanned at a constant rate in cm^{-1} sec^{-1} when the drive shaft is rotated at a constant rate. A carefully shaped cam can be used to rotate the lever arm

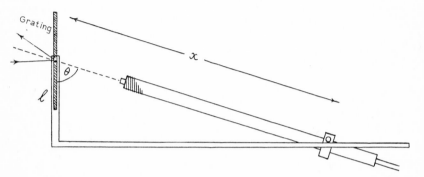

Fig. 3.9. A "secant-drive" mechanism. The long arm is held in contact with the nut on the lead-screw by a spring but slides with respect to it as it moves along the screw.

attached to the grating table; if several gratings are used it is a comparatively easy matter to mount an appropriate cam for each. Alternatively a "secant drive" of the kind illustrated in fig. 3.9 can be constructed. From the grating equation for first order (see section 3.2)

$$v \propto \sec\theta$$

and from fig. 3.9:

$$\sec\theta = \frac{x}{l}.$$

Hence

$$v \propto x,$$

so that a constant rate of rotation of the lead screw gives a uniform rate of scan in cm^{-1} sec^{-1}. The shaft for the grating lead screw rotates slowly and can be passed through a simple O-ring seal in the face-plate.

Slit mechanisms in the far infra-red need not be of high mechanical precision because operating slit-widths are usually greater than 1 mm. It is convenient if the left hand jaws of both slits are linked together and move in opposition to the right hand jaws, similarly linked together, so that the centres of the slits are stationary. The plate to which each jaw is fixed can be arranged to move in a low friction guide provided by two ball bearings in a V-groove and can be driven by an arm pivoted at a point midway between the slits and linked to a nut on a fine pitched screw. The driving shaft passes through the face-plate of the monochromator so that the slit-width can be adjusted from outside the vacuum enclosure and a counter can be attached to the shaft to indicate the slit width.

Electrical leads into the vacuum compartment can be readily made by simple ceramic pin seals or by cable sockets sealed by small O-rings. Electrical breakdown might occur at supply leads when the pressure in the tank reaches 1 mm Hg but this is readily prevented by setting the terminals in paraffin wax.

Automatic filter changing can be readily arranged using small electric motors controlled by switches and relays working from the grating drive.

4. Detection and recording

Chapter 4 is devoted to the detectors and associated amplifiers which are useful for the far infra-red and for millimetre-waves. In this section we shall consider how the various operational parameters of a detector influence the recording of spectra by grating spectrometers.

The resolution, the time taken to record a spectrum, and the signal-to-noise ratio of the recorded spectrum are interrelated quantities. The operating conditions chosen for a spectrometer will normally represent a compromise between the desire for high resolution, that for high signal-to-noise, and that for fast scanning rates. With a given detector the signal-to-noise ratio can be improved by increasing the time-constant of the smoothing circuit in the output stage of the amplifier. The detector then requires longer to respond adequately to a given change in signal intensity and so the rate of scan of the spectrum must be reduced proportionately. A rate of scan of about 1 resolution interval in 3 or 4 response times is often acceptable in exploratory studies but if accurate measurements of the peak intensities of strong sharp lines are required this could be too fast because the detector has time to register only about 90 % of the true change in intensity occurring in a resolution interval.

We can determine the interrelation of these three quantities as follows. The signal intensity falling on the detector is proportional to the square of the entrance and exit slit-width and therefore to the square of the resolution Δv (section 3.1); the noise on the record is inversely proportional to the square root of the response time of the detector system, τ (chapter 4). Thus the signal-to-noise ratio

$$\left(\frac{S}{N}\right) \propto (\Delta v)^2 \, \tau^{\frac{1}{2}}.$$

But the rate of scan of the spectrum, $R \, \text{cm}^{-1} \, \text{sec}^{-1}$, is proportional to $\Delta v/\tau$ for a specified acceptable distortion and so we have

$$\left(\frac{S}{N}\right) \propto (\Delta v)^2 \left(\frac{\Delta v}{R}\right)^{\frac{1}{2}} = \frac{(\Delta v)^{\frac{5}{2}}}{R^{\frac{1}{2}}}$$

so that, for a given detector and monochromator, variations in resolution, in rate of scanning and in signal-to-noise ratio must conform to

$$\left(\frac{S}{N}\right)^2 \frac{R}{(\Delta v)^5} = \text{constant}$$

and it is within this condition that the optimum compromise must be sought. It reveals a rapid variation of signal-to-noise ratio and/or recording rate with resolution. The figures quoted in section 6 indicate that, with a good far infra-red spectrometer used in conjunction with a Golay detector operating at room temperature, for $(S/N) = 50$ and $\Delta v = 0.5 \, \text{cm}^{-1}$, R is about $0.025 \, \text{cm}^{-1} \, \text{sec}^{-1}$. The constant in this case is therefore about 60. Double-beam commercial instruments have values between 1 and 3.

The constant factor above also indicates how the performance of a spectrometer should change with an improved detector performance or with loss of signal power, e.g. by continuous background absorption in a sample, or in passing through a cryostat, etc. A detector operating in liquid helium can have a signal-to-noise ratio at least 20 times better than the best detectors operating at room temperature, giving an increase by $\times 400$ in scanning rate for a given resolution and signal-to-noise ratio. Or, for a given scanning rate, this increase in detector performance would give an improved resolution by about a factor $\times 3.5$. A loss of 50% of the signal power would lead to a decrease in the scanning rate for a given resolution and signal-to-noise ratio by a factor $\times 4$, but only a small change in resolution at a given rate of scan.

Double-beam methods of spectrophotometry like those which are usual in the grating spectrometers used in the nearer infra-red (which give directly a record of the *fractional* transmission or reflection of a sample) are used in the commercially available far infra-red spectrometers (see section 6). Most other far infra-red spectrometers which have been described in the literature are single beam instruments. Apart from the increased cost and elaboration of a double-beam system there might arise special difficulties when samples at low temperatures are being investigated (and low temperatures are frequently required in far infra-red spectroscopy for the reasons considered in chapter 1, section 1). These difficulties arise with the optical null methods usually used in the conventional infra-red. In these a chopping unit is required after the sample, as well as before it, so that the thermal emission by the sample is chopped. Consequently, unless there happens to be an equal thermal emission by components in the path of the reference beam, including the optical null attenuator, the sample's transmission or reflection spectrum will be distorted, and for low sample temperatures probably overwhelmed, by the thermal emission effects. MINAMI et al [1965] describe a double-chopping system which avoids these problems. The Savitzky-Halford method in which the sample beam and reference beam signals are electronically ratioed is free from this difficulty because no chopper system is required after the sample – the detector "sees" both the sample path and the reference path continuously. In its simplest form this method uses in each of the reference and sample beams only half the optical aperture which could be used in single-beam operation. We have noted above that a reduction by $\times \frac{1}{2}$ in the signal intensity results in an increase by $\times 4$ in the recording time for a given signal-to-noise ratio and resolution; a double-beam method which reduces the signal intensity by $\times \frac{1}{2}$ therefore takes twice as much recording time as would single-beam recording of sample and background spectrograms successively. Nevertheless, the time saved in having the ratioing and recording performed in a single step and the reduction in the effects of drifts in source intensity and amplifier gain might make the double-beaming worthwhile. If the source optics and associated filters can be duplicated for sample and reference beams – as they are in the PE 301 spectrometer described in section 6 – the Savitzky-Halford method does not result in the $\times \frac{1}{2}$ reduction in signal intensity.

5. Sampling techniques

GASES. In the case of inert and harmless gases the simplest procedure, at least for a vacuum instrument, is to introduce them into the whole spectrometer at a sufficient pressure to give absorption of the required intensity. This applies particularly to water vapour, of course, which is widely used for calibration. For this purpose the saturation vapour pressure at room temperature (15 mm Hg), in a path of about 1 m, gives an adequate spectrum and unless a calibration of the highest precision is required, the water vapour can be in air. Gas cells for the conventional infra-red are available commercially, and usually have path lengths of 10 to 20 cm. If fitted with suitable windows for the far infra-red, e.g. 1 mm of high density polyethylene or crystal quartz, or thin mylar, they are suitable for many purposes. When it is necessary to avoid pressure broadening, low pressure and a long path-length must be used. Several types of multipass cell are available for the conventional infra-red but a multipass cell for the far infra-red should be designed to match the larger apertures ($f/2$ to $f/5$) of spectrometers in this region and the cross-section of the beam at a focus may be several mm across.

A difficulty to be overcome in studying gases in the far infra-red region is associated with the removal of water vapour from the gas under investigation. This may be done by condensation by a refrigerant and careful refractionation or by drying agents; it may sometimes be necessary to place P_2O_5 containers in the gas cell to remove the last traces of water vapour.

If it is required to heat the gas cell (e.g. to increase the vapour pressure) flexible heating tapes can be wrapped around the cell; and for cooling (e.g. to reduce the intensity of hot bands) the cell can be packed round by solid CO_2 in a suitably shaped container of expanded polystyrene.

LIQUIDS. Variable path liquid cells are commercially available with quartz or high density polyethylene windows and most are suitable for far infra-red work provided they do not have to be placed in the evacuated chamber of the spectrometer. Suitable organic solvents which have little or no absorption in 1 mm path in the far infra-red include carbon tetrachloride, hexane, carbon disulphide, chloroform, benzene and dioxane.

SOLIDS. Weak absorption spectra (such as the vibrational spectra of non-dipolar molecular solids or electronic spectra due to magnetic-dipole transitions) can be investigated in transmission, with sample thicknesses in the range from a few tenths of 1 mm to a few mm. If single crystals are available, or if polycrystalline aggregates having a fairly high packing factor can be formed by pressing, this range of sample thickness poses no particular difficulties. If neither of these forms is possible, spectra might be obtained using a powder sample dispersed in liquid paraffin (Nujol) as a mull, or compacted with a binder such as paraffin wax or polyethylene pressed in a heated press. If the dielectric constant of the material is high, however, it must be borne in mind that effects due to scattering might be present in the spectra recorded with dispersed powder samples.

Materials with strong absorption spectra (such as the vibrational spectra of polar crystals) can be studied in transmission only with very thin samples. Single crystals of many materials can be polished, with care, to thicknesses below 0.1 mm, i.e. 100 μm, but single crystal samples with thicknesses below, say, 10 μm cannot be prepared in this way, at least not with diameters of a few mm or more, as is required in the far infrared. Transmission studies have been made of the intense absorptions due to the lattice vibrations in many simple ionic compounds using evaporated films with thicknesses down to 1 μm and less. Not all materials will form films by evaporation, however. A few spectra of strongly absorbing materials have been obtained with finely powdered samples as described above but it should be noted that such samples may give spurious results in the far infra-red because the wavelength can be comparable with, or larger than, the particle size; with materials having strong resonances this can lead to strong scattering effects and electrical de-polarisation effects which can shift the frequencies at which strong absorption occurs. Evaporated films of materials which do not have cubic crystal sym-metry, though continuous, might also be subject to spurious effects of these kinds because the micro-crystallites will not be dielectrically isotropic.

Mainly because of the difficulties encountered in preparing samples of strongly absorbing materials for study by transmission there have recently been developed methods for analysing the reflection spectra of solids to give the frequency dependence of the real and imaginary parts of the dielectric constants (MARTIN [1965]). Sample discs with diameters of about 1 cm or more are required for this (samples of smaller diameter can be studied in transmission using conical light pipes to condense the radiation beam down to the size of the sample; the resulting beam would be spread over too wide an angle of divergence to be useful for reflection spectra however).

Vibrational spectra of solids can be studied at room temperature but there is frequently an appreciable sharpening of the absorption lines on reducing the temperature to 100 °K or less. Electronic spectra in the far infra-red are very much weaker at room temperature than at low temperatures because the upper and lower states involved in the transitions are more nearly equally populated at the higher temperature (chapter 1, section 1). For studies of solids in the far infrared, sample cryostats for liquid helium and liquid nitrogen are therefore frequently required. When a detector cooled by liquid helium is being used the simplest arrangement is to use a single cryostat for both sample and detector, making use of glass dewar vessels. The detector cryostat in figure 4 of chapter 4, for example, is easily modified to incor-porate a sample holder into the light pipe, as illustrated in fig. 3.10(a). In order to obtain a background spectrogram with which to compare the sample spectrogram, the sample can be moved to one side using a coupling rod which passes through an O-ring seal in the top-plate of the cryostat. If the range of temperature over which the sample is to be studied is wide a heater can be incorporated in the sample chamber but a sufficiently long light-pipe and dewar vessel must be used so that the sample can be mounted well above the detector. To allow the sample to reach a low temperature the copper plate in which it is mounted should be connected to the outer casing of the sample-holder with copper braid, and a filter window to remove most of the heat radiation from the top of the dewar should be mounted at the entrance to the sample chamber (e.g. 1 mm crystal quartz and thin black polyethylene).

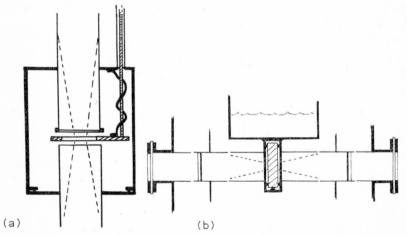

(a)   (b)

Fig. 3.10(a). A sample holder mounted in a light-pipe. (b) A sample carriage (shaded) attached to the helium can in a metal cryostat. The carriage can be moved into and out of the beam, which is guided by the segmented light-pipe, by a rod which passes through an O-ring seal in the wall of the cryostat and which can be disengaged from the carriage after the adjustment is made.
In both (a) and (b) thermal contact between the sample holder and the refrigerant is through copper braiding (shown in (a) but not in (b)). The broken lines indicate conical light pipes which can be introduced when the available samples are small.

If a room temperature detector is in use, or if there are reasons for separating sample and detector cryostats, it is probably more convenient to use a metal cryostat for the sample rather than one based on glass dewars. A suitable optical arrangement is illustrated in fig. 3.10(b). The radiation is guided through and out of the cryostat by short lengths of light-pipe attached to the outer case and to the radiation shields. Windows serving as heat shields must be included if the sample is to reach temperatures in the liquid helium range. In such a light-pipe system the beam from the monochromator is focussed at the outer window of the cryostat rather than at the sample and this reduces considerably the sizes of the windows in the outer case and heat-shields. The radiation leaving the cryostat at the end of the light-pipe system does not constitute a true optical focus but, if the diameter of the light-pipe is about equal to that of the focussed image at the entrance to the cryostat, the emergent beam is much the same as that leaving a focus. It can be treated as such if further optical operations are required following the cryostat so that, for example, double-beam photometric methods would be possible. The simplest arrangement, however, and one which leaves the greatest room for any apparatus which provides an environment for the sample (e.g. magnetic fields, high pressure, illumination, or etc.) is to have the sample directly in front of the detector. The radiation can then be condensed directly on to the detector after leaving the cryostat; most simply with a conical light-pipe.

Cryostats similar to that just described for liquid helium can, of course, be used for work at liquid nitrogen temperatures, with considerable simplification due to the fact that a radiation shield is not essential. It is even possible to work with a continuous cupro-nickel light-pipe, of length about 20 cm, passing straight through a bath of liquid nitrogen contained in a box made of expanded polystyrene lined with a resin or with a polyethylene bag.

The use of light-pipes (see OHLMAN et al. [1958]) provides solutions to many problems in sampling.

6. Spectrometers

An ideal instrument would combine high flexibility in its optical performance and sampling facilities with a wide range of automatic programs (filter changes, etc.) and with ratio recording using a double-beam system. However, such an instrument would be extremely complicated and very expensive and a compromise is usually found which best fits the kind of problem to be investigated with the spectrometer. Careful consideration must be given to the required signal-to-noise ratio, resolution and scanning time, and to the needs for easy sample-changing and for space to provide the desired sample environment (magnetic fields, high pressure, illumination, etc.). For gases and for solids at low temperatures a resolution better than 1 cm^{-1} is desirable, whereas for liquids, and for many exploratory studies of solid state spectra,

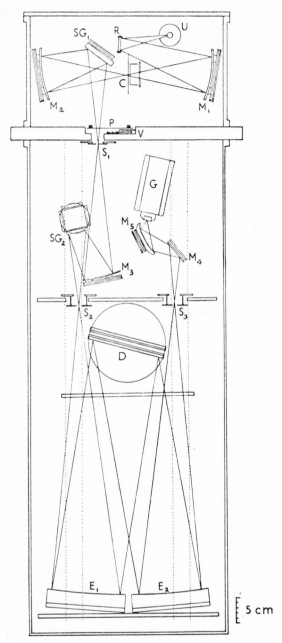

Fig. 3.11. A high performance vacuum spectrometer.

a resolution poorer than 2 cm^{-1} might be adequate. The first calls for a high resolution instrument and probably for a large sample space which is best met by providing open access to the output beam of the monochromator. The second requires a low resolution monochromator but with automatic recording and several scanning programs.

Several far infra-red spectrometers which have been designed to meet these varying demands have been described in the literature. We have included several references to these in the list at the end of the chapter (marked with an asterisk *).

To illustrate some design features of far infra-red spectrometers, two typical instruments will now be described in more detail. Firstly, a high performance vacuum grating spectrometer and secondly a commercial double beam spectrometer.

The optical layout of a vacuum spectrometer constructed at Kings College, London, is shown in fig. 3.11. It is based on a Czerny-Turner monochromator. The source U is an 80 W high pressure mercury arc lamp with quartz envelope (GEC MB/U with glass envelope removed) of dimensions 12×30 mm^2. The lamp housing is water cooled. Radiation from the source is reflected by the interchangeable filter R whose segments include restrahlen plates, scatter gratings and reflection meshes. The spherical concave mirror M_1 (radius of curvature 210 mm) forms an inverted reduced image of U at the sampling point C. The beam is chopped at 11 cycles/sec., either in front of the sample as shown or in front of the source U. M_2 produces an erect image of U at S_1, after reflection from the filter SG_1. Transmission filters may be inserted before the fore slit S_1. These are absorption filters or polyethylene transmission echelletes of the kinds described in section 3.3. A concave mirror M_3 ($R = 262$ mm) images the fore slit S_1 at the entrance slit S_2 of the monochromator after reflection from the interchangeable filter SG_2.

The monochromator has two square mirrors 15×15 cm^2 with focal length 558 mm, i.e. $f/3.5$. To cover the range 10 cm^{-1} to 240 cm^{-1} four gratings with blaze angle 20° are used. The approximate ranges are as follows:

15 lines/cm	10– 30 cm^{-1}
30 lines/cm	30– 60 cm^{-1}
60 lines/cm	60–120 cm^{-1}
120 lines/cm	120–240 cm^{-1}.

In each case the gratings can be used beyond the blaze angle so that there is considerable overlap in coverage.

Two gratings are mounted vertically, back to back, on a table driven by a 6″ diameter phosphor-bronze worm gear. M_5 is an off-axis ellipsoidal mirror which focuses the radiation on to a Golay cell, G, with a quartz window which is transparent below 240 cm^{-1}.

Alternatively, the radiation can be deflected from the spectrometer, by rotating mirror M_4 through 90° so as to direct the beam through a quartz-window in the vacuum tank, to a cooled detector and also to the sample should the associated apparatus be too large for the usual sampling point at C.

The optics in the source unit are readily rearranged so that reflection studies can be carried out. In this case M_1 is replaced by two spherical concave mirrors. The sample remains at C, a plane mirror is inserted before S, and the beam is chopped in front of the source U.

The monochromator is rigidly attached to a vertical 1″ thick face plate by four $1\frac{1}{4}$″ diameter stainless steel tubes. At the other ends of the tubes is fixed a 15″ disc of duralumin which carries the monochromator mirrors E_1 and E_2. The whole is enclosed by a 15″ diameter cylinder of welded steel with $\frac{3}{16}$″ walls which runs on a track and seals with an O-ring on to the face plate. The source unit is enclosed by a separate tank which also seals with an O-ring to the face-plate. V in the diagram is an isolation valve which is used when samples are changed. The worm gear of the grating mount runs on a shaft which passes through a seal in the face plate to a geared synchronous motor unit outside the vacuum and carries a revolution counter. The total error due to irregular tooth profile and pitch circle run out amount to no more than 0.0002″ which gives rise to an error of less than 0.03 cm^{-1} at 100 cm^{-1}.

The slit assembly is a separate unit easily detached from the main framework. A $2\frac{1}{2}$″ lead screw and nut are coupled with a pin and slot to an 8″ lever which is pivoted midway between the entrance and exit slits. The left hand jaws of each slit are rigidly coupled together and sprung on to the edge of the 8″ lever $1\frac{1}{2}$″ from the fulcrum. The right hand jaws of each slit are similarly coupled so that when the centre lever is moved the slit width changes in such a way that the image of the entrance slit fills the exit slit for all slit widths. It has been shown by Fastie that the wavelength errors at the end of a straight slit due to astigmatism in the Ebert system is given by $dv = vl/8F$ where l is the straight slit length and F the focal length of the Ebert mirrors. In this instrument this amounts to about 0.02 cm^{-1} at 200 cm^{-1} and is even less at 25 cm^{-1}. Hence curved slits are not necessary.

The reflection and transmission filters are on motor driven shafts and can be changed automatically. The vacuum need only be broken once, to change one pair of monochromator gratings for another, during a full scan over the range 10 to 240 cm^{-1}.

The optics in the source unit can be readily rearranged to permit transmission or reflection studies to be made. In either case up to three samples can be attached to a sample holder at C which can be cooled to 80 °K. By moving the holder vertically each sample can be investiged consecutively. Cell windows are not necessary providing a liquid nitrogen cooled finger is present in the small tank to avoid condensation on to the sample when it is at low temperature.

Typical instrument performance parameters with a Golay detector are: a scanning rate of 1.5 cm^{-1}/minute for a resolution of 0.5 cm^{-1} and a signal-to-noise ratio of 50 to 1. Part of the pure rotational spectrum of water vapour, between 50 and 75 cm^{-1}, as recorded with the spectrometer, is shown in fig. 3.12. The two absorption peaks near 55 cm^{-1}, which are just resolved, are spaced by 0.26 cm^{-1}.

We now turn to the Perkin-Elmer 301 spectrometer, illustrated in fig. 3.13, as an example of a commercial double beam instrument. The instru-

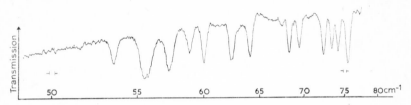

Fig. 3.12. The transmission spectrum of water vapour between 50 and 77 cm^{-1} as recorded by the spectrometer of fig. 3.11.

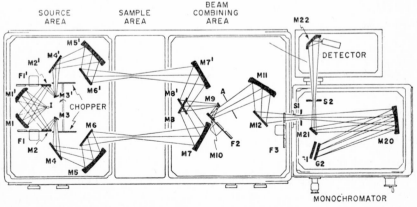

Fig. 3.13. A double-beam spectrometer (P.E.301).

ment has $f/3.8$ optics, and can be used over the range 40–600 cm^{-1}, with four gratings blazed at 444, 333, 222, 89 and 60 cm^{-1}. It uses the Halford-Savitzky double-beam photometric system to give direct fractional transmission spectra. The method is flexible as far as the changing of gratings and filters is concerned and avoids difficulties due to thermal radiation from the sample and its holder (section 4). The sample and reference beams are separately derived from the source and are chopped 90° of phase with each other. After the sampling areas, they arrive at the toroidal mirrors M7 and M7′ which direct the beams to an aperture-splitting mirror assembly. This serves to combine the two beams in the same vertical plane, but only the top and bottom halves of each beam respectively are utilised. M9 is a field mirror which forms an image of the pupil of the system, which is the grating, at the aperture-splitting mirrors. This ensures uniform illumination of the grating by each of the beams. The monochromator is of conventional Littrow design with a 21° off-axis parabolic mirror. Two 68.6 mm gratings are mounted back to back and are easily removed and replaced by the other pair. The grating drive incorporates a cosecant bar system (c.f. fig. 3.9) to give a scan linear in wavenumber. Each grating may be rotated through 38°. The slit mechanisms permit a slit opening from 0 to 10 mm. An off-axis ellipsoidal mirror focusses the light from the exit slit on to the Golay pneumatic detector which has a 3/16″ diamond window. The 6 : 1 reduction in image size ensures that there is little loss in beam energy. There are reflection filters at M2 and M2′ and at M10, and a transmission filter at F3; at each of these positions there are several alternative filters mounted on a wheel and any can be brought into the optical path by setting the corresponding knob on the control panel.

The instrument is not evacuated but is flushed with dry air. The effectiveness of the air drying and of double beaming is illustrated by fig. 3.14 which shows water vapour spectra obtained in the region of the very strong 203 cm^{-1} absorption band. The spectra show successively the results for a) single beam undried, b) single beam after $\frac{1}{2}$ hour purging, c) single beam after 4 hours purging, d) double beam after one hour purging.

The sampling compartment can be isolated from the rest of the system when changing samples to reduced the re-introduction of water-vapour into the system. There is 5″ between the centre of the sample beam and the floor of the sampling compartment, and the floor space is 7″ × 17″. This is sufficient room for most solid, liquid and gas cells and for small sample cryostats but, being at a point in the middle of the system's optics, these would have to be designed so as not to change the optical paths. Being constructed on the

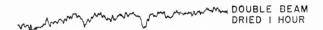

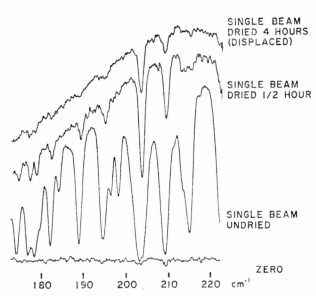

Fig. 3.14. Spectrograms illustrating the reduction of absorption by atmospheric water vapour by drying (for the P.E.301 spectrometer).

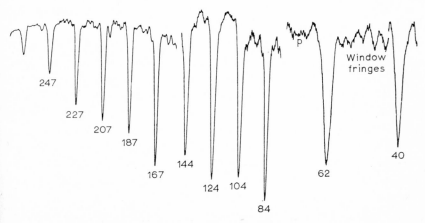

Fig. 3.15. The pure rotation absorption spectrum of HCl vapour at 100 mm Hg pressure and with a 10 cm path. Recorded in 30 minutes with a P.E.301 spectrometer (see the table at the end of the chapter for accurate frequencies for these lines).

modular system there would be a possibility, should the sample apparatus be large or complicated, of introducing the sample between the monochromator and the detector unit but it would then be necessary to operate the spectrometer as a single beam instrument when extremely good purging of water vapour would be necessary (c.f. fig. 3.14).

To illustrate the resolution, signal-to-noise ratio, and scanning times possible with this instrument fig. 3.15 shows the rotational spectrum of HCl vapour recorded with it in a total time of 30 minutes, i.e. at a rate of about 1.4 cm^{-1} sec^{-1}. The resolution appears to be about 4 cm^{-1} and the signal-to-noise ratio about 30 to 1 over most of the range.

Performances similar to those quoted here for the P.E. 301 can be obtained with other commercially available spectrometers (see chapter 1, section 5).

7. Assessment of performance including calibration

To characterise the performance of a spectrometer requires a determination of the spectral resolution attainable at various frequencies in its range, at specified signal-to-noise ratios and specified rates of scan. In addition some indication is required of the uncertainty in the measured intensity due to the presence of scattered radiation and to imperfect filtering, but this question has been considered in section 3.3.

Spectral resolution (chapter 1, section 2) can be directly measured if a nearly monochromatic source is available or if a sample with very sharp absorption lines can be used. In either of these cases the resolution is the apparent breadth (in cm^{-1}) at the half-height points of the spectral line recorded by the spectrometer (when plotting the intensity of emission or the coefficient of absorption respectively). The emission lines of a far infrared gas laser (chapter 1, section 4) or of a harmonic generator (chapter 5) would be ideal for this but a method requiring less specialised equipment is to use a gas sample having strong absorption lines at a pressure sufficiently low for the collision broadening to be much less than the resolution (as could be checked by making measurement at several pressures). Simple dipolar molecular gases such as HCl and HCN are well suited to this application (cf. fig. 3.15).

An alternative and equivalent method of assessing resolution is more frequently adopted however. Use is made of a sample having a pair of sharp absorption lines of roughly equal strength and separated in frequency by about the resolution interval. The slit-widths are adjusted so that the pair of lines roughly conform to the Rayleigh criterion according to which two lines separated by the resolution interval would give a minimum in the intensity between the lines equal to 0.81 of the intensities at the line maxima. The resolution at other settings of the slits is then determined, provided the entrance slit remains uniformly illuminated, since it is in proportion to the slit-widths (section 3.1). The width above which the image of the source fails to fill the entrance slit uniformly can be deduced by plotting a signal intensity against the square of the slit-width which should be linear if the entrance and exit slits are ganged together so as to have equal widths. A number of common gases have rotational spectra which provide suitable pairs of lines. Each pure rotation line of NH_3 – except the lowest – is an inversion doublet with a spacing of about 1.3 cm^{-1}. HCN and N_2O have pure rotation lines at nearly constant spacings of 3.0 cm^{-1} and 0.8 cm^{-1} respectively. The numerous lines in a spectrum of water vapour provide several pairs suitable for assessing resolution (see fig. 3.16).

The measured resolution should be in at least approximate accord, of course, with that which can be computed along the lines given in section 3.1. The resolution intervals marked on published spectra are frequently values obtained by calculation rather than by measurement. If the collimator and the condenser mirrors in a spectrometer are poorly adjusted so that they do not have foci at the entrance and exit slits respectively the measured resolution will be poorer than it should be; the observed resolution can thus be used to test the alignment of the optics.

The resolution is determined by the width of the entrance and exit slits and not by the detector's properties. There would however, be little point in attempting to obtain such a high resolution that the slit-width limited signal become too low to give a useful signal-to-noise ratio. Normally the resolution of interest will be one that is obtained with a signal-to-noise ratio in the range 20 to 100 – the former would be appropriate if the main interest were in a good resolution of strong lines and the latter if it were important to observe weak lines. The signal-to-noise ratio at a given slit-width can always be improved by increasing the response time of the detector but this reduces the rate at which the spectrum can be scanned, as examined in section 3.1. The slow scanning rates necessary in the far infra-red pose one of the major difficulties of spectroscopy in this region and so it is generally expedient to determine the fastest acceptable scanning rate for each application. This is done directly by recording part of a spectrum at several scanning speeds for a fixed detector time-constant to find that corresponding to the greatest acceptable distortion of the spectrum. (A rate equal to one resolution interval in, say, 3 or 4 detector time-constants gives the detector sufficient time

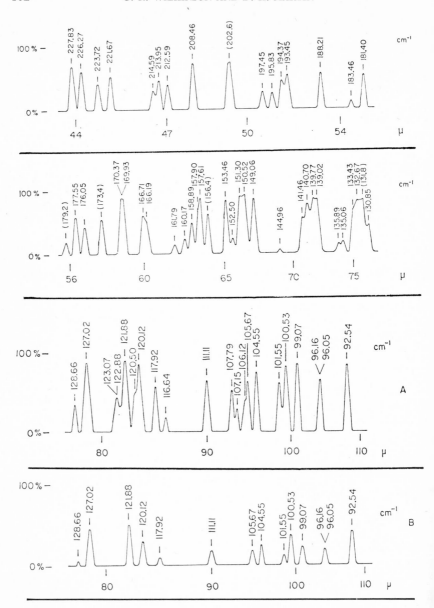

Fig. 3.16. (Cont. on next page.)

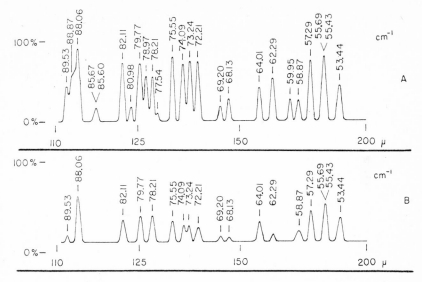

Fig. 3.16. The pure rotation spectrum of water vapour between 44 and 200 μm (by courtesy of the Perkin-Elmer Company). Between 80 and 200 μm two records are given, A and B, for different water vapour contents. The frequencies assigned to the lines are computed from near infra-red and microwave data; high resolution measurements on several water-vapour lines indicate that these values should be correct to at least ± 0.1 cm^{-1} for low-pressure vapour. For water vapour frequencies between 200 and 2000 μm see the table at the end of this chapter.

to record only about 90% of the intensity change occurring within a resolution interval and can shift the frequency of the recorded peak intensity by about one quarter of a resolution interval.)

A grating spectrometer can be calibrated by measurement of the dimensions of the monochromator and grating but it is easier, over most of the far infra-red, to use known frequencies for the rotation spectra of simple gases, including water vapour. The tables which follow, and fig. 3.16, list the rotational frequencies (in cm^{-1}) for a number of such gases. We have calculated those for HCl, HBr, DBr, HI, CO, HCN, N_2O and NH_3 using the rotational and distortion constants implied by the observed microwave and near infra-red spectra of these gases. Only for a few lines have far infra-red measurements of sufficient resolution to test these figures to the accuracy quoted been made (by harmonic generation – see chapter 5). The frequencies for water vapour have been deduced from assignments of near infra-red lines by BENEDICT et al. [1952, 1957].

Hydrogen iodide

$J'' \to J'$	HI	$J'' \to J'$	HI
$0 \to 1$	12.8520(0)	$7 \to 8$	102.41(5)
$1 \to 2$	25.6992(2)	$8 \to 9$	115.09(6)
$2 \to 3$	38.536(9)	$9 \to 10$	127.73(4)
$3 \to 4$	51.360(3)	$10 \to 11$	140.32(4)
$4 \to 5$	64.164(5)	$11 \to 12$	152.86(2)
$5 \to 6$	76.945(0)	$12 \to 13$	165.34(4)
$6 \to 7$	89.69(7)		

Deuterium bromide

$J'' \to J'$	DBr[79]	DBr[81]
$0 \to 1$	8.49605(0)	8.49083(6)
$1 \to 2$	16.9899(8)	16.9795(5)
$2 \to 3$	25.4796(6)	25.4640(3)
$3 \to 4$	33.963(0)	33.942(1)
$4 \to 5$	42.437(8)	42.411(8)
$5 \to 6$	50.902(0)	50.870(8)
$6 \to 7$	59.353(6)	59.317(2)
$7 \to 8$	67.790(2)	67.748(8)
$8 \to 9$	76.21(0)	76.16(3)
$9 \to 10$	84.61(1)	84.55(9)
$10 \to 11$	92.99(0)	92.93(4)
$11 \to 12$	101.34(7)	101.28(5)
$12 \to 13$	109.67(8)	109.61(1)
$13 \to 14$	117.98(2)	117.91(0)
$14 \to 15$	126.25(6)	126.18(0)

Hydrogen bromide

$J'' \to J'$	HBr[79]	HBr[81]
$0 \to 1$	16.7003(6)	16.6951(6)
$1 \to 2$	33.3924(7)	33.3820(8)
$2 \to 3$	50.0680(7)	50.0524(9)
$3 \to 4$	66.718(9)	66.698(2)
$4 \to 5$	83.336(8)	83.310(9)
$5 \to 6$	99.913(5)	99.882(5)
$6 \to 7$	116.440(9)	116.404(8)
$7 \to 8$	132.910(7)	132.869(6)
$8 \to 9$	149.315(0)	149.268(8)
$9 \to 10$	165.64(6)	165.59(5)
$10 \to 11$	181.89(5)	181.83(9)
$11 \to 12$	198.05(4)	197.99(3)
$12 \to 13$	214.11(5)	214.05(0)
$13 \to 14$	230.07(2)	230.00(2)
$14 \to 15$	245.91(5)	245.84(0)
$15 \to 16$	261.63(7)	261.55(8)

Hydrogen chloride

$J'' \rightarrow J'$	HCl^{35}	HCl^{37}
$0 \rightarrow 1$	20.878(2)	20.846(8)
$1 \rightarrow 2$	41.743(7)	41.681(0)
$2 \rightarrow 3$	62.583(9)	62.489(9)
$3 \rightarrow 4$	83.386(1)	83.260(8)
$4 \rightarrow 5$	104.137(7)	103.981(3)
$5 \rightarrow 6$	124.82(6)	124.63(9)
$6 \rightarrow 7$	145.43(9)	145.22(1)
$7 \rightarrow 8$	165.96(3)	165.71(4)
$8 \rightarrow 9$	186.38(7)	186.10(8)
$9 \rightarrow 10$	206.69(8)	206.38(8)
$10 \rightarrow 11$	226.88(3)	226.54(3)
$11 \rightarrow 12$	246.93(0)	246.56(0)
$12 \rightarrow 13$	266.82(8)	266.42(9)
$13 \rightarrow 14$	286.56(4)	286.13(6)
$14 \rightarrow 15$	306.12(7)	305.66(9)

Carbon monoxide

$J'' \rightarrow J'$		$J'' \rightarrow J'$	
$0 \rightarrow 1$	3.84503	$20 \rightarrow 21$	80.5196(9)
$1 \rightarrow 2$	7.68992(0)	$21 \rightarrow 22$	84.3308(3)
$2 \rightarrow 3$	11.53451(3)	$22 \rightarrow 23$	88.138(7)
$3 \rightarrow 4$	15.37866(6)	$23 \rightarrow 24$	91.943(3)
$4 \rightarrow 5$	19.2222(3)	$24 \rightarrow 25$	95.7444(4)
$5 \rightarrow 6$	23.0650(6)	$25 \rightarrow 26$	99.541(7)
$6 \rightarrow 7$	27.9070(1)	$26 \rightarrow 27$	103.335(3)
$7 \rightarrow 8$	30.7479(3)	$27 \rightarrow 28$	107.124(9)
$8 \rightarrow 9$	34.5876(9)	$28 \rightarrow 29$	110.910(4)
$9 \rightarrow 10$	38.4261(0)	$29 \rightarrow 30$	114.691(7)
$10 \rightarrow 11$	42.2630(7)	$30 \rightarrow 31$	118.468(7)
$11 \rightarrow 12$	46.0984(1)	$31 \rightarrow 32$	122.241(0)
$12 \rightarrow 13$	49.9319(8)	$32 \rightarrow 33$	126.008(6)
$13 \rightarrow 14$	53.7636(6)	$33 \rightarrow 34$	129.771(5)
$14 \rightarrow 15$	57.5932(9)	$34 \rightarrow 35$	133.529(5)
$15 \rightarrow 16$	61.4207(1)	$35 \rightarrow 36$	138.282(2)
$16 \rightarrow 17$	65.2457(8)	$36 \rightarrow 37$	141.029(7)
$17 \rightarrow 18$	69.0683(6)	$37 \rightarrow 38$	144.771(9)
$18 \rightarrow 19$	72.8883(0)	$38 \rightarrow 39$	148.508(4)
$19 \rightarrow 20$	76.7054(8)	$39 \rightarrow 40$	152.239(3)
		$40 \rightarrow 41$	155.964(4)

Hydrogen cyanide

$J'' \to J'$		$J'' \to J'$	
0 → 1	2.95643(1)	22 → 23	67.856(5)
1 → 2	5.91279(3)	23 → 24	70.793(6)
2 → 3	8.86901(4)	24 → 25	73.729(1)
3 → 4	11.82502(6)	25 → 26	76.662(9)
4 → 5	14.78075(8)	26 → 27	79.594(8)
5 → 6	17.73614(1)	27 → 28	82.524(8)
6 → 7	20.6911(0)	28 → 29	85.452(9)
7 → 8	23.6455(8)	29 → 30	88.379(0)
8 → 9	26.5994(9)	30 → 31	91.303(0)
9 → 10	29.5527(8)	31 → 32	94.224(8)
10 → 11	32.5053(6)	32 → 33	97.144(4)
11 → 12	35.4571(8)	33 → 34	100.061(7)
12 → 13	38.4081(6)	34 → 35	102.976(7)
13 → 14	41.3582(3)	35 → 36	105.889(2)
14 → 15	44.3073(2)	36 → 37	108.79(9)
15 → 16	47.2553(7)	37 → 38	111.70(6)
16 → 17	50.202(3)	38 → 39	114.61(1)
17 → 18	53.148(0)	39 → 40	117.51(3)
18 → 19	56.092(5)	40 → 41	120.41(3)
19 → 20	59.035(7)	41 → 42	123.30(9)
20 → 21	61.977(4)	42 → 43	126.20(3)
21 → 22	64.917(7)	43 → 44	129.09(3)

Nitrous oxide

$J'' \to J'$		$J'' \to J'$	
0 → 1	0.838021(5)	26 → 27	22.6125(3)
1 → 2	1.670387(2)	27 → 28	23.4489(3)
2 → 3	2.51404(7)	28 → 29	24.2852(1)
3 → 4	3.35204(3)	29 → 30	25.1213(6)
4 → 5	4.19002(2)	30 → 31	25.9573(9)
5 → 6	5.02797(9)	31 → 32	26.7932(9)
6 → 7	5.86591(0)	32 → 33	27.6290(4)
7 → 8	6.70381(2)	33 → 34	28.4646(5)
8 → 9	7.54167(9)	34 → 35	29.3001(2)
9 → 10	8.37950(7)	35 → 36	30.1354(4)
10 → 11	9.21729(3)	36 → 37	30.9706(0)
11 → 12	10.05503(1)	37 → 38	31.8056(1)
12 → 13	10.89271(8)	38 → 39	32.6404(5)
13 → 14	11.73034(9)	39 → 40	33.4751(3)
14 → 15	12.56792(0)	40 → 41	34.3096(3)
15 → 16	13.40542(7)	41 → 42	35.1439(6)
16 → 17	14.24286(5)	42 → 43	35.9781(1)
17 → 18	15.08023(0)	43 → 44	36.812(1)
18 → 19	15.91751(8)	44 → 45	37.645(8)
19 → 20	16.75472(4)	45 → 46	38.479(4)
20 → 21	17.59184(5)	46 → 47	39.312(8)
21 → 22	18.4288(8)	47 → 48	40.146(0)
22 → 23	19.2658(1)	48 → 49	40.979(0)
23 → 24	20.1026(5)	49 → 50	41.811(7)
24 → 25	20.9393(9)	50 → 51	42.644(3)
25 → 26	21.7760(1)	51 → 52	43.476(6)

Ammonia

K	J →	0	1	2	3	4	5	6	7	8	9	10	11
0*	a → s	19.097											
	s → a		40.524	58.826	80.061	98.356	119.259	137.520	157.974	176.150	196.060	214.077	233.374
1	a → s		38.975	58.828	78.632	98.365	118.007	137.536	156.932	176.173	195.238	214.107	232.759
	s → a		40.537	60.342	80.080	99.733	119.283	138.712	158.002	177.135	196.094	214.859	233.413
2	a → s			58.835	78.649	98.392	118.044	137.584	156.990	176.242	195.318	214.197	232.859
	s → a			60.389	80.135	99.796	119.354	138.792	158.090	177.230	196.196	214.969	233.531
3*	a → s				78.676	98.436	118.105	137.663	157.083	176.358	195.442	214.356	233.010
	s → a				80.230	99.904	119.475	138.923	158.237	177.386	196.374	215.142	233.742
4	a → s					98.495	118.189	137.770	157.220	176.513	195.631	214.554	233.259
	s → a					100.057	119.645	139.112	158.440	177.611	196.607	215.410	234.001
5	a → s						118.292	137.906	157.386	176.713	195.863	214.817	233.554
	s → a						119.868	139.358	158.708	177.901	196.919	215.745	234.358
6*	a → s							138.063	157.585	176.952	196.142	215.137	233.914
	s → a							139.665	159.041	178.260	197.304	216.155	234.796
7	a → s								157.810	177.225	196.465	215.507	234.330
	s → a								159.444	178.693	197.767	216.649	235.322
8	a → s									177.530	196.826	215.925	234.805
	s → a									179.204	198.312	217.227	235.933
9	a → s										197.220	216.386	235.331
	s → a										198.944	217.896	236.639
10	a → s											216.880	235.902
	s → a											218.664	237.446
11	a → s												236.507
	s → a												238.363

* Denotes the strong lines corresponding to transitions from $\varLambda$-levels. Line frequencies in wavenumbers (cm^{-1}).

Water vapour

Assignment		Assignment	
$2_2 \rightarrow 3_{-2}$	6.12	$3_3 \rightarrow 3_{-1}$	36.59
$4_0 \rightarrow 5_{-4}$	10.86	$0_0 \rightarrow 1_0$	37.13
$3_1 \rightarrow 4_{-1}$	12.67	$2_1 \rightarrow 3_{-1}$	39.45
$5_5 \rightarrow 6_1$	14.65	$5_3 \rightarrow 6_{-1}$	38.63
$6_5 \rightarrow 7_3$	14.74	$3_{-1} \rightarrow 3_2$	38.8
$3_3 \rightarrow 4_{-1}$	14.98	$7_5 \rightarrow 8_2$	38.8
$5_4 \rightarrow 6_2$	15.60	$4_{-2} \rightarrow 4_0$	40.25
$4_1 \rightarrow 5_0$	15.83	$2_0 \rightarrow 2_2$	40.98
$1_{-1} \rightarrow 1_1$	18.58	$6_3 \rightarrow 7_1$	42.56
$4_3 \rightarrow$ ^{r}	20.63	$5_1 \rightarrow 6_{-3}$	44.13
$2_{-2} \rightarrow 2_0$	25.11	$5_3 \rightarrow 5_{-1}$	47.05
$3_1 \rightarrow 4_0$	30.48	$5_2 \rightarrow 6_0$	51.12
$4_2 \rightarrow 5_{-2}$	32.26	For higher frequencies	
$1_0 \rightarrow 2_{-2}$	32.93	see figure 3.16.	

For the relative strengths of these lines see fig. 2.8.

References

E. E. BELL, M. E. VANCE, P. B. BURNSIDE and R F. ROWNTREE, Spectrochim. Acta **18** (1962) 1393.

W. S. BENEDICT, Mem. Soc. Roy. Sci. Liege, Vol. Hors Ser. **2** (1957) 18.

W. S. BENEDICT, H. H. CLAASSEN and J. H. SHAW, J. Res. Nat. Bur. Standards **49** (1952) 91.

*D. BLOOR, Spectrochim. Acta **21** (1965) 595.

*D. BLOOR, T. J. DEAN, G. O. JONES, D. H. MARTIN, P. A. MAWER and C. H. PERRY, Proc. Roy. Soc. **A260** (1961) 510.

E. F. DALY and G. B. B. M. SUTHERLAND, Proc. Phys. Soc. **A62** (1949) 205.

*C. B. FARMER and P. J. KEY, Appl. Optics **4** (1965) 1051.

*L. GENZEL and W. ECKHARDT, Z. Phys. **139** (1954) 579.

A. HADNI, Spectrochim. Acta **19** (1963) 793.

A. HADNI, E. DECAMPS and J. MUNIER, Rev. Opt. **42** (1963) 584.

M. HASS, M. O'HARA and LIEKHARDT, J. Opt. Soc. Am. **55** (1965) and Appl. Optics **4** (1965) 1027.

G. O. JONES, D. H. MARTIN, P. A. MAWER and C. H. PERRY, Proc. Roy. Soc. **A261** (1961) 10.

T. LARSEN, I.R.E. Trans. on M.T.T. **10** (1962) 191.

R. P. MADDEN and J. STRONG, Appendix P in: Concepts in Classical Optics (J. Strong, Freeman and Co., San Francisco and London, 1958).

T. R. MANLEY and D. A. WILLIAMS, Spectrochim. Acta **21** (1965) 737.

D. H. MARTIN, Advances in Physics **14** (1965) 39.

*T. K. MCCUBBIN, R. P. GROSSO and J. D. MANGUS, Appl. Optics **1** (1962) 431.

S. MINAMI, H. YOSHINAGA and K. MATSUNAGA, Appl. Optics **4** (1965) 1137.

A. MITSUISHI, Y. YAMADA, S. FUJITA and H. YOSHINAGA, J. Opt. Soc. Am. **50** (1960) 433.

A. MITSUISHI, Y. OTSUKA, S. FUJITA and H. YOSHINAGA, Japan J. Appl. Phys. **2** (1963) 574.

K. D. MÖLLER and R. V. MCKNIGHT, J. Opt. Soc. Am. **53** (1963) 760 (and see W. G. ROTH-SCHILD, J. Opt. Soc. Am. **54** (1964) 20).

*K. D. MÖLLER, V. P. TOMASELLI, L. R. SHUKE and B. K. MCKENNA, J. Opt. Soc. Am. **55** (1965) 1233.

*NOLT and A. J. SIEVERS, J. Opt. Soc. Am. **55** (1965) 1586.

R. C. OHLMAN, P. L. RICHARDS and M. TINKHAM, J. Opt. Soc. Am. **42** (1958) 531.

*R. C. OHLMAN and M. TINKHAM, Phys. Rev. 123 (1961) 425.

E. D. PALIK, Appl. Optics 4 (1965) 1017.

C. H. PALMER, J. Opt. Soc. Am. 53 (1963) 1005.

R. PAPOULAR, Infrared Physics 4 (1964) 137.

K. F. RENK and L. GENZEL, Appl. Optics 1 (1961) 643.

P. L. RICHARDS and G. E. SMITH, Rev. Sci. Instr. 35 (1964) 1535.

*D. W. ROBINSON, J. Opt. Soc. Am. 49 (1959) 966.

G. W. STROKE, J. Opt. Soc. Am. 52 (1962) 1324 and Physics Letters 5 (1963) 45.

J. STRONG, J. Opt. Soc. Am. 39 (1949) 320.

R. ULRICH, K. F. RENK and L. GENZEL, I.E.E.E. Trans. on M.T.T. 11 (1963) 363.

Y. YAMADA, A. MITSUISHI and H. YOSHINAGA, J. Opt. Soc. Am. 52 (1962) 17.

*H. YOSHINAGA, S. MINAMI, I. MAKINO, I. IWAHASHI, M. INABA and K. MATSUMOTO, Appl. Optics 3 (1964) 1425.

* References in which complete spectrometers are described.

CHAPTER 4

DETECTORS

E. H. PUTLEY

Royal Radar Establishment, Malvern, England

AND

D. H. MARTIN

Queen Mary College, University of London, London, England

1. Introduction

The part of the spectrum with which we are concerned involves detection techniques similar both to those used in the near infrared and to those used in the microwave region. There are photoconductive detectors, using one or another of several extrinsic effects in InSb or Ge, for use from the short wavelength end to beyond 1 cm, and point-contact crystal rectifiers have been used in video and superheterodyne systems from the long-wave end down to less than 0.5 mm. In addition to these there are a number of widely used thermal detectors which in principle respond throughout the spectrum. These detectors are described in sections 2–5 of this chapter and their relative merits are discussed in section 7 following an examination, in section 6, of the properties of the low-noise amplifiers which are essential parts of most detector systems. Finally, section 8 has been added at the proof stage to cover recently reported developments.

2. The performance of an ideal detector

Considerable thought has been given to defining figures of merit for comparing the performance of infra-red detectors (JONES [1959]) but these figures of merit depend upon certain assumptions concerning the mode of operation of the detector which are not applicable to many of the submillimetre detectors. The performance of these detectors will be described here by considering four quantities; the voltage responsivity,

$$r = \Delta V / \Delta P \qquad (4.1)$$

where ΔV is the change in output voltage from the detector produced by a change ΔP in the submillimetre power incident on it; the noise equivalent power (n.e.p.), P_N, defined as the power from the signal source required to give a voltage output equal to the root mean square (r.m.s.) noise voltage output; the response time τ, and the band of the spectrum to which the detector responds.

In determining the noise equivalent power three sources of noise must be considered. First, the detector will receive black-body radiation from its surroundings and the intensity of this radiation will fluctuate. The r.m.s. fluctuation in the power absorbed by the detector ΔP_B can be calculated from the black-body distribution, the geometrical configuration and spectral response of the detector (LEWIS [1947], PUTLEY [1964a and b]). Corresponding to ΔP_B, there will be an r.m.s. noise voltage in the detector output given by

$$\Delta V_B = r \Delta P_B. \tag{4.2}$$

The second source of noise is the detector itself. Electrical, and in some cases thermal, fluctuations in the detector element will produce an r.m.s. noise voltage ΔV_D. Some contribution to this voltage may be due to contact or surface effects which in principle could be eliminated by perfect design. Even if these were eliminated, the Johnson noise would remain, so that ΔV_D is certainly not less than the Johnson noise voltage. The third source of noise is that produced by the amplifier which amplifies the output from the detector prior to recording or display; the total amplifier noise can be expressed as an equivalent r.m.s. voltage at the amplifier input, ΔV_A.

The total r.m.s. noise voltage ΔV_T referred to the input of the amplifier is then

$$\Delta V_T^2 = \Delta V_B^2 + \Delta V_D^2 + \Delta V_A^2. \tag{4.3}$$

Since ΔV_B is produced by a fluctuation that is independent of the detector or its amplifier, an ideal detector will be defined as one in which

$$\Delta V_B^2 \gg \Delta V_D^2 + \Delta V_A^2 \tag{4.4}$$

so that the noise equivalent power, P_N, is

$$P_N = \Delta P_B. \tag{4.5}$$

First we consider a thermal detector, such as a bolometer, which responds to the whole range of the spectrum. If this is placed in thermal equilibrium in a black-body enclosure at a temperature T, integrating the black-body distribution over the entire spectrum to give ΔP_B and hence P_N shows that

$$P_N = 4(\sigma k)^{\frac{1}{2}} T^{\frac{5}{2}} (AB)^{\frac{1}{2}} \tag{4.6}$$

(SMITH et al. [1957]). Here σ is Stefan's constant, k Boltzmann's constant, A the area of the detector and B the bandwith of the amplifier. Putting

$A = 1$ cm^2, $B = 1$ c/s, and $T = 300$ °K gives

$$P_N = 5.5 \times 10^{-11} \text{ W}. \qquad (4.7)$$

The most sensitive submillimetre detectors operate at liquid helium temperature. The amount of background radiation received from the immediate surroundings of the detector at helium temperature will be negligible compared with the radiation received through the optical system of the detector from the room temperature surroundings. This is limited by the field of view of the optics and by the presence of cooled filters in front of the detector or by the spectral response of the detector itself. If it is assumed that only radiation between two frequencies v_1 and v_2, emanating from a small solid angle α in a direction making an angle θ with the normal to the detector's surface, contributes to the room-temperature background and that the detector absorbs completely all radiation between these limits, then the following expressions can be derived for P_N (PUTLEY [1964a]):

$$P_N = 2.77 \times 10^{-18} T^{\frac{5}{2}} \{\alpha \cos\theta \cdot AB[J_4(x_1) - J_4(x_2)]\}^{\frac{1}{2}}, \qquad (4.8)$$

$$P_N = 3.99 \times 10^{-18} \frac{T^{\frac{3}{2}}}{\lambda} \{\alpha \cos\theta \cdot AB[J_2(x_1) - J_2(x_2)]\}^{\frac{1}{2}}. \qquad (4.9)$$

Eq. (4.8) applies to detectors whose response is proportional to the energy received while (4.9) applies to those in which the response is proportional to the number of quanta absorbed. T is the temperature of the background, not that of the detector. λ is the wavelength in cm, A the area in cm^2 and B the amplifier bandwidth in c/s. $x = hv/kT$ and $J_n(x)$ is a function tabulated by ROGERS and POWELL [1958]:

$$J_n(x) = \int_0^x \frac{x^n e^x}{(e^x - 1)^2} dx.$$

For a detector responding only over a narrow bandwith, $\Delta x \ll x$, (4.8) and (4.9) both reduce to

$$P_N = 3.99 \times 10^{-18} \frac{T^{\frac{3}{2}}}{\lambda} \{\alpha \cos\theta \cdot AB \cdot \Delta x\}^{\frac{1}{2}}. \qquad (4.10)$$

For a numerical example, consider an energy detector which responds to all wavelengths longer than 100 μm and has an effective field of view of $\frac{1}{5}$ steradian. Then applying eq. (4.8) gives, with $A = 1$ cm^2 and $B = 1$ c/s

$$P_N = 3.64 \times 10^{-13} \text{ W}. \qquad (4.11)$$

This example corresponds to the broad band InSb sub-millimetre detector discussed in section 4.1. As a second example suppose the detector responded only over a bandwidth of 10% centred at 500 μm. Then from eq. (4.10)

$$P_N = 1.84 \times 10^{-14} \text{ W}. \tag{4.12}$$

These performances of thermal detectors are to be compared with that of an ideal radio-frequency receiver, e.g. a superheterodyne receiver operating at frequency v as discussed in ch. 5, section 3.6. In this case

$$P_N \sim kT(B_i B_0)^{\frac{1}{2}} \quad \text{(when } hv \ll kT) \tag{4.13}$$

if B_i is the bandwidth of the intermediate frequency amplifier and B_0 that of the final detector stage. Again putting $B_i = B_0 = 1$ c/s and $T = 300$ °K,

$$P_N = 4 \times 10^{-21} \text{ W} \tag{4.14}$$

to be compared with e.g. (4.7). The principal factor responsible for this large difference is that for the superheterodyne receiver only fluctuations on signals with frequencies within a bandwidth $\sim B_i$ contribute to the noise but for the infra-red thermal detector the whole infra-red spectrum contributes fluctuations.

If $hv > kT$ we need a different expression because (4.13) then corresponds to less than one quantum received during the length of time devoted to an observation, i.e. B_0^{-1}. An approximate expression for the noise equivalent power of an ideal detector when $hv \gg kT$ is that indicating one quantum received in B_0^{-1} sec, i.e.

$$P_N \sim hvB_0 \quad (hv \gg kT). \tag{4.15}$$

A more exact calculation (GELINAS and GENOUD [1959]) introduces a factor between 1 and 10 on the right hand side, the value depending on the precise definitions of P_N and B, but (4.15) is adequate for the present discussion.

We have plotted the P_N given by equations (4.13) and (4.15) in fig. 4.1 for a range of background temperatures between 300 °K and 1.5 °K. In the submillimetre region of the spectrum $hv \sim kT$ and neither relation is accurate. A more complete calculation (MCLEAN and PUTLEY [1965]) shows, however, that the curves in fig. 4.1 give a fair indication of the magnitudes of the n.e.p. for ideal receivers.

A comparison of equations (4.7), (4.11) and (4.12) with equation (4.14) and fig. 4.1 shows that an ideal superheterodyne receiver has a much lower n.e.p. than an ideal thermal detector. We shall see, however, that practical photoconductive and bolometric detectors approach the ideal limits quite

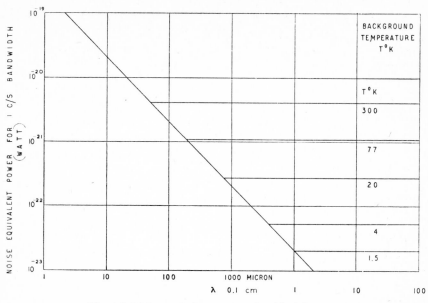

Fig. 4.1. Noise equivalent power of an ideal detector.

closely but existing microwave receivers in the submillimetre region do not. Also it should be noted that a superheterodyne receiver will detect only over a spectral bandwidth equal to twice the bandwidth of the intermediate frequency amplifier and for the purposes of eq. (4.14) this was taken to be only 1 c/s.

3. Point-contact detectors *

It has been known for some time that point-contact detectors based on the rectifying property of a metal-semiconductor junction, as used at microwave frequencies, can be used at wavelengths between 1.0 and 0.1 mm (HAPP et al. [1957]). Spectra obtained using this type of detector in a video system in conjunction with a harmonic generator source have been published in a series of papers by Gordy and his colleagues (BURRUS and GORDY [1954]), the most recent results being obtained at a wavelength of 0.43 mm (JONES and GORDY [1964]). Point-contact detectors have also been used in superheterodyne systems down to 1 mm (MEREDITH and WARNER [1963]; COHN et al. [1963]) and recently at 0.5 mm (BAUER et al. [1966]).

* See ch. 5 for a more detailed discussion of crystal detectors.

The performance of a point-contact detector falls as the wavelength is reduced at a rate determined by the product RC of the capacity of the junction and of the spreading resistance of the semiconductor under the rectifying contact. Assuming that the capacity is made as small as practicable, the semiconductor with the highest conductivity should give the best results at the shortest wavelengths so that, for material of comparable purity, the semiconductor with the highest mobility should be the best. Thus germanium should be superior to silicon and some III–V compounds superior to germanium. This conclusion is borne out by experience. The performance of silicon detectors starts to deteriorate at about 3 cm while that of recent germanium detectors does not fall off until the wavelength falls to 5 mm. Below this wavelength superior results are obtained with GaAs and the performance of this material should not fall until the wavelength falls below 1 mm. Theoretically the performance obtainable with InSb should be superior to all these materials, but attempts to produce satisfactory rectifying point-contacts with this material have been disappointing. Failure due to technological difficulties of this kind are very real with this type of device.

MEREDITH and WARNER [1963] have measured the performances of several video receivers at 2 mm and 1 mm wavelengths, based on G.E.C. VX 3352 germanium rectifier crystals. They obtained a n.e.p. for a 1c/s output bandwidth of 2.5×10^{-11} W at 2 mm and 4×10^{-9} W at 1 mm. A rectifier's performance should fall off at a rate of 6 dB per octave at high frequencies due to intrinsic capacities and resistances but the rate found here is 22 dB. The additional loss is attributable to losses in the 1 mm waveguide mount which might be reduced to some extent by mounting the rectifier in over-size waveguide or using an optical system to condense the radiation on the detector.

MEREDITH and WARNER [1963] also constructed and tested superheterodyne receivers, based on the same crystals. At 2 mm they obtained an n.e.p. for a 1 c/s output bandwith of 7×10^{-15} W with an input (I.F.) bandwidth of 60 Mc/s. This corresponds to 20 dB relative to the ideal value – eq. (4.13). More recently BAUER et al. [1966] and COHN et al. [1963], have used gallium arsenide crystals in superheterodyne receivers operating at a signal wavelength of 0.5 mm (600 Gc/s). The superheterodyne action involved mixing with the second harmonic of a local 300 Gc/s oscillator. A noise-figure of about 33 dB relative to the ideal value (eq. (4.13)) was achieved with an intermediate frequency of 2–4 Gc/s, an I.F. bandwith of 1.6 Gc/s, and an output smoothing time-constant equal to 10 sec. This corresponds to an n.e.p. of about 10^{-13} W for a 1 c/s output bandwith. (See also section 8.)

4. Photoconductive detectors

A number of photoconductive processes are now known which are excited by submillimetre radiation (PUTLEY [1964b]) and sensitive, fast, detectors have been based on them. These detectors operate at temperatures in the liquid helium range.

The energy of a 100 μm photon is sufficiently high to ionize the shallowest impurity centres in Ge. Extrinsic photoconductivity has therefore been observed in the infra-red out to about 120 μm in Ge doped with Sb (FRAY and OLIVER [1959]) and with B (SHENKER et al. [1964]) or Ga (MOORE and SHENKER [1965]). These detectors operate at 4 °K and specific detectivities* better than 2×10^{11} cm cps$^{\frac{1}{2}}$ W^{-1} have been measured at 100 μm. For the best results the concentration of the principal impurity should be between 10^{14} and 10^{15} cm^{-3} while the concentration of compensating impurities should be as small as possible, being about 10^{12} cm^{-3} in the best available material. One might expect these conditions to be satisfied most easily with B as the principal impurity, but SHENKER et al. report obtaining better results with Ga.

Since the impurity ionization energy is related to the effective mass of the free carrier, the ionization energy of hydrogenic impurities in low-mass semiconductors such as n-type InSb should be smaller, and the limiting wavelengths of detection longer. Unfortunately, a large radius for the orbit of an electron attached to an impurity centre also goes with a low mass and the critical impurity concentration at which overlap occurs decreases. With Ge a concentration of about 10^{17} cm^{-3} is required for overlap and it is easy to prepare material with a sufficiently low concentration to avoid this difficulty. With InSb, however, the corresponding critical concentration is about 10^{13} cm^{-3}, and since the purest available InSb still contains at best 10^{14} cm^{-3} impurities, overlap occurs and its behaviour is metallic even at low temperatures.

Simple extrinsic photoionization photoconductivity has not been observed, therefore, beyond the long-wave threshold of the doped Ge detectors. However, a number of photoconductive effects associated with *free* carriers, which can occur out to wavelengths of at least 1 cm, have been discovered in studies of InSb and Ge and have been applied in detectors. In semiconductors with high mobilities the coupling between the free carrier electrons and

---

* The specific detectivity is the reciprocal of the noise equivalent power for a detector of 1 cm² area. It is a convenient term only for detectors for which the n.e.p. varies as (area)$^{\frac{1}{2}}$, which does not apply to the majority of the detectors considered in this chapter.

the lattice is weak at low temperatures with the result that, when the electrons steadily absorb energy from an applied field (and steadily pass it on to the lattice) the mean electron energy rises appreciably above its thermal equilibrium value. If the electron-electron interactions are strong the distribution of energy amongst the electrons will correspond to a thermal distribution for some temperature T_e higher than T the lattice temperature. The measured conductivity will therefore correspond to T_e rather than to T whereas the measured sample temperature (the lattice temperature) will still be T. Hot electron effects of this kind are most readily observed as marked deviations from Ohm's law for applied d.c. fields ~ 1–10 V/cm. If the electron heating is caused by direct free carrier absorption of incident radiation the effects appear as a form of photoconductivity.

At a high frequency ω such that the displacement current is large compared with the conduction current, the free carriers absorb radiation with an absorption coefficient, α, which is proportional to the conductivity, σ,

$$\sigma = \sigma_d(1+\omega^2\tau_e^2)^{-1},$$

where σ_d is the conductivity at zero frequency and τ_e the electron scattering time. α thus decreases as λ^2 for frequencies exceeding the characteristic value given by $\omega\tau_e = 1$. For pure Ge this characteristic frequency corresponds to $\lambda \sim 1$ cm and for pure n-type InSb it corresponds to $\lambda \sim 1$ mm. The absorption at higher frequencies can be enhanced by applying a strong magnetic field to induce cyclotron resonance. At the resonance frequency the absorption should rise to a value comparable with the low frequency free-carrier value so that photoconductivity should appear over the narrow frequency range determined by the line width of the cyclotron resonance.

In InSb, with $\omega\tau_e \sim 1$ for $\lambda \sim 1$ mm, significant hot electron photoconductivity is observed from a wavelength of about 200 μm, rising to a maximum value at about 1 mm and continuing at approximately this level until the wavelength is increased to at least 1 cm. The application of a magnetic field of up to about 9 kG enhances the effect without introducing any marked resonant effects (see section 4.1) and it was under these conditions that the effect was first observed in this material (PUTLEY [1960, 1961]). When a larger magnetic field is applied the photo-effect is greatly enhanced at shorter wavelengths, peaking at approximately the cyclotron resonance wavelengths (section 4.2). In Ge, with $\omega\tau_e \sim 1$ for $\lambda \sim 1$ cm, hot electron photoconductivity can be induced in the millimetre region through the resonant effect (GOODWIN and JONES [1961]) and it was under these conditions that such effects were first observed (ZEIGER et al. [1959]).

Highly effective submillimetre detectors have been based on these mechanisms in InSb and they will be described in more detail in the next two sub-sections. Suitable elements of InSb (and cryostats for them) have recently become commercially available (ch. 1, section 5).

4.1. InSb DETECTOR IN SMALL OR ZERO MAGNETIC FIELDS

The characteristics of hot electron photoconductivity have been discussed by KOGAN [1962] and by ROLLIN [1961]. Simplified expressions for the responsivity and the time-constant of a detector based on this effect can be obtained from Kogan's results:

$$r = a\beta V/v\sigma \qquad (4.16)$$

$$\tau = \frac{2}{3}\frac{k}{e}\beta\frac{dT}{d\mu}. \qquad (4.17)$$

In these expressions V is the d.c. voltage applied to the detector, v its volume, σ its electrical conductivity, μ the electron mobility, and a is the fraction of the incident signal power absorbed by the detector. β is a coefficient measuring the extent of the deviation from Ohm's law and is defined by

$$\beta = \frac{1}{\sigma}\frac{d\sigma}{d(E^2)} \qquad (4.18)$$

where E is the electric field. At small values of E,

$$\sigma = \sigma_0(1+\beta E^2) \qquad (4.19)$$

where σ_0 is the conductivity at zero electric field.

The quantities appearing in equations (4.16), (4.17) can all be determined by measuring the current-voltage characteristics of the detector over a range of temperature near the operating temperature. Thus the performance to be expected at a wavelength ~ 1 mm can be calculated and compared with observed results. With no magnetic field there is good agreement (PUTLEY [1964c, 1965]).

Quite apart from cyclotron resonance effects (considered in section 4.2) the presence of a magnetic field modifies considerably the behaviour of pure n-type InSb. The magnetic freeze-out effect (SLADEK [1958]) reduces the free electron concentration and in addition to this the magneto-resistance effect reduces the mobility and β. Thus μ, σ and β are all changed. In assessing the consequences for r and τ, through equations (4.16) and (4.17), it should be noted that the acceptable value of V will depend on σ and so, too, will the fractional power absorbed by the detector, a. The nett effects have been considered by PUTLEY [1964b]. For fields up to 6–7 kG the responsivity, r, should increase and the time-constant, τ, should decrease, and these findings are confirmed by observation.

The responsivity and time-constant of such a detector are recorded in figs. 4.2 and 4.3 (PUTLEY [1965]). The In Sb element is fabricated from material containing about 5×10^{13} cm^{-3} free electrons and best results are obtained with material having a mobility greater than 5×10^5 cm^2 V^{-1} s^{-1} at 77 °K. The size of the element is about $5 \times 2 \times 2$ mm, its surfaces are lightly ground and contacts are attached at the ends using indium solder. Fig. 4.2 shows the dependence of responsivity upon wavelength and induction, while fig. 4.3 shows the dependence of the response time upon magnetic induction and

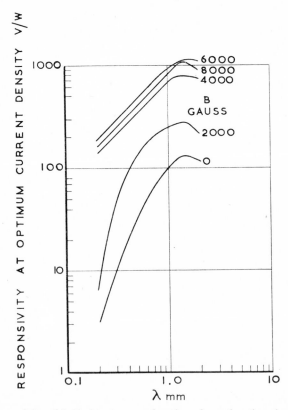

Fig. 4.2. Responsivity of InSb detector as a function of wavelength and magnetic induction (PUTLEY [1963]).

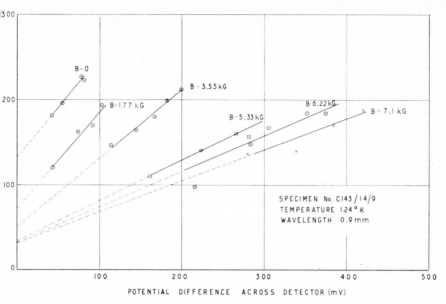

Fig. 4.3. Response time of InSb detector as a function of magnetic induction and electric field (PUTLEY [1964b]).

electric field; at 1.8 °K for fig. 4.2 and 1.24 °K for fig. 4.3. The resistance of such an element at 1.8 °K changes from about 100 Ω in zero field to 1000–10000 Ω in a field of 6–7 kG.

InSb elements have been used in two kinds of detector system. In the first a magnetic field is used to enhance the responsivity, as indicated above. The major source of noise then proves to be in the amplifier (see section 6) and, taking a noise-equivalent resistance of about 100 Ω, the n.e.p. implied by a responsivity of 1000 V/W (fig. 4.2) is about 10^{-11} W for a 1c/s output bandwidth. In the second (KINCH and ROLLIN [1963]) no magnetic field is applied but a transformer is used to amplify the output of the detector. Step-up ratios of × 100 are possible (section 6) which more than compensate for the smaller responsivity and a n.e.p. of 10^{-12} W for a 1 c/s output bandwidth is attainable. The use of the transformer greatly increases the response time, however, from $\sim 10^{-7}$ sec for the element operated in a magnetic field to $\gtrsim 10^{-4}$ sec with a transformer. The simultaneous use of magnetic field and step-up transformer would be of little advantage because the resistance of the element is relatively high in the magnetic field (section 6).

A cryostat suitable for an InSb detector is shown in fig. 4.4. The element is mounted inside a small superconducting solenoid wound with niobium

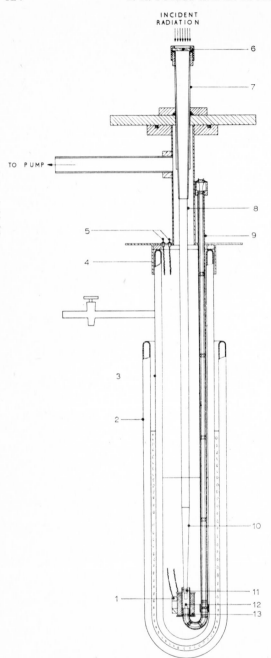

1. Quenching magnet.
2. Outer nitrogen dewar.
3. Inner dewar containing helium at 1.5 °K.
4. Dewar cap.
5. Leads to magnet and solenoid.
6. Polyethylene seal.
7. Copper tapered light pipe.
8. Cupro-nickel light pipe.
9. Screening tube containing low-capacity leads from detector.
10. Tapered copper light pipe.
11. Cooled filter.
12. Indium antimonide detector.
13. Superconducting niobium solenoid.

Fig. 4.4. Cryostat for a cooled detector (PUTLEY [1963]).

wire, providing inductions up to about 8 kG. For the second type of detector described in the preceding paragraph this solenoid would be replaced by the transformer. The incident radiation is conducted on to the detector via the long, straight, cupro-nickel light pipe and the electro-formed tapered pipe. This is terminated by a cooled filter which prevents the shorter infra-red radiation from the warmer parts of the apparatus reaching the detector (e.g. a layer of black polyethylene and a 1 mm plate of crystal quartz – see ch. 3). Unlike the cooled thermal detectors described in section 5, there is no reason why the detector element should not be immersed in the liquid helium, especially when the temperature of operation is below the super-fluid transition so that there is no bubbling.

4.2. InSb DETECTORS IN LARGE MAGNETIC FIELDS

When a magnetic induction greater than about 8 kG is induced in InSb, the broad-band response described in section 4.1 is replaced by a response peaked near the cyclotron resonance wavelength. Typical results are shown in fig. 4.5, which shows how the resonance wavelength varies with magnetic field. The effect cannot be observed near 50 μm because it is swamped by the strong absorption band due to lattice vibrations but it may be observed on either side of it. The work of BROWN and KIMMITT [1963, 1965] and the theoretical studies of HASEGAWA and HOWARD [1961] indicate that the transi-

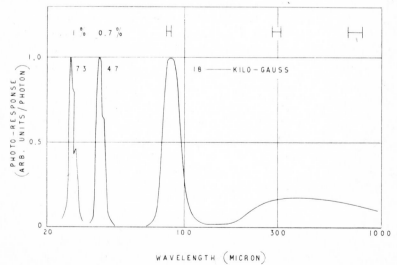

Fig. 4.5. Performance of tunable InSb detector (BROWN and KIMMT [1965]).

tion responsible for the absorption will be from the ground state of the frozen out impurity levels (SLADEK [1958]) to an excited state representing cyclotron resonance of an electron still attached to an impurity centre. This excited state is higher than the lowest Landau level of the conduction band so that the excited electron is easily transferred to the conduction band. The resonance energy differs slightly from the cyclotron energy.

This detector can be used in a cryostat similar to that shown in fig. 4.4 but with the niobium coil replaced by a niobium-zirconium one. With a field of 58 kG the detector operates at 32 μm and the wavelength increases approximately inversely to the field as this is reduced. When operated at 4 °K the bandwith is about 5–10% and at 100 μm wavelength the noise equivalent power is about 10^{-11} W. This is comparable with that of a doped Ge detector (section 4, introduction) with whose range it overlaps. One advantage of this detector is that its resistance is relatively low so that it is easy to incorporate it in circuits which will not dampen its short time constant (10^{-7}–10^{-6} sec). Also its response is narrow-band so that its use simplifies the problem of filtering which is often troublesome in far infra-red grating spectroscopy (ch. 3).

5. Thermal detectors

A thermal detector is one in which the incident radiation heats the receiving element and the change in temperature is determined as the measure of the incident power. The principal thermal detectors used in the submillimetre region will be described in this section. The big advantage of the thermal detectors is that they respond over a very wide range of the spectrum. They have high detectivities but may be unsuitable for use with pulsed sources, as in plasma spectroscopy, because their time constants usually exceed about 1 msec (but see also section 8). The most widely used submillimetre detector is the Golay cell (section 5.1) which operates at room temperature. To improve significantly on the sensitivity of the Golay cell requires a detector operating at low temperature, and the other thermal detectors described here are bolometers operating at liquid helium temperatures.

5.1. THE GOLAY CELL

This is a pneumatic detector (GOLAY [1947]) which is commercially available (ch. 1, section 5). The absorbed radiation heats up gas, normally xenon, enclosed in a small cavity. One wall of the cavity is formed by a flexible membrane which is distorted by the changes in pressure of the gas when heated by the radiation. The outside of the membrane forms a mirror which reflects a beam of light onto a photoemissive cell so that the absorption of the radiation produces an electric signal by deflection of the light beam.

The incident radiation heats the xenon indirectly being absorbed first by an aluminium film in the cell which is adjusted to have an impedance matching that of free space so that the absorption is practically independent of wavelength from the ultra-violet to mm wavelengths. Unfortunately no window material is available which is transparent over the whole of this range and the spectral response of a particular cell will therefore be determined mainly by its window. For the submillimetre region crystal quartz windows are usually used, or diamond windows if the region below 50 μm wavelength is also to be covered. The long wave limit is determined by the diameter of the window aperture, and can be at least 5 mm. Near the cut-off wavelength the performance will cease to be independent of wavelength and may show resonance effects.

Two big advantages of the Golay cell are that it operates at room temperature and that it is readily available from manufacturers (ch. 1, section 5). A noise-equivalent-power of about 10^{-10} W is quoted for these detectors for an output bandwidth of 1 c/s, and performances at or close to the quoted values can be obtained in practice without excessive precautions. This is remarkably close to the limit for an ideal thermal detector at room temperature (eq. (4.7)). The response time is about 15 msec. A few cells tend to be microphonic and some respond less well in the far infra-red than in the near infra-red (where they are normally tested by the manufacturer) and in bad cases replacement is the most effective cure. Some models of the Golay cell operate perfectly well in vacuum.

Compared with the cooled bolometers and photoconductive detectors the Golay cell is up to two orders of magnitude less sensitive and is relatively slow. For many spectroscopic purposes it may be adequate, however (ch. 1, sections 2 and 3).

5.2. COOLED BOLOMETERS

A bolometer is constructed from a material with a high temperature coefficient of resistance, α. It is arranged so that when the absorption of radiation causes its temperature to rise the resulting change in resistance can be observed by a suitable bridge and amplifier.

The performance of a bolometer (SMITH et al. [1957], JONES [1953]), can be expressed by the following equations for the responsivity r and time constant τ, in which a is the fraction of incident signal absorbed,

$$r = a\ \alpha V/(G-\alpha Q) \tag{4.20}$$

$$\tau = C/(G-\alpha Q). \tag{4.21}$$

These are valid for incident radiation which is chopped at an angular frequency ω such that $\omega\tau < 1$. V is the voltage applied to the bolometer and Q the electrical power dissipated in it. C is the thermal capacity of the element and G the thermal conductance coupling the bolometer to the constant temperature bath to which it is attached. These relations show that for a high responsivity α must be large and G small; but a small G means a long τ unless C is also kept small. Thus the element must be made as small and light as is consistent with efficient absorption of the radiation or ease of manufacture.

Cooling a bolometer will improve its performance because, in addition to reducing noise, cooling to helium temperatures reduces considerably the thermal capacity of the element and very large values of α can be obtained with superconductors and with semiconductors. Two semiconducting and a superconducting bolometer are described in the following sections. The main features of a suitable cryostat have already been described in section 4.1 (fig. 4.4). For thermal detectors it is necessary to operate the receiving element in a high vacuum in order to maintain adequate thermal isolation from the thermal sink. For this reason the light-pipe assembly must be vacuum-tight, and the main problem here is in sealing the detector housing at the cold end. This can be done using a low-melting-point alloy solder or alternatively – if repeated demounting is anticipated – a thin polyethylene gasket tightly clamped between lapped brass plates, as shown in fig. 4.6. It may not be necessary to incorporate a diffusion pump in the system because the liquid helium will maintain a high vacuum provided the system is leak free. A mechanical pump to remove the air before cooling is all that is essential.

5.3. GERMANIUM BOLOMETERS

A very sensitive Ge bolometer has been developed using similar material to that used for Ge thermometers. In Ge doped with a concentration $\sim 10^{16}-10^{17}$ cm^{-3} of shallow impurities a marked bolometric effect is observed at liquid helium temperatures, especially at wavelengths beyond the

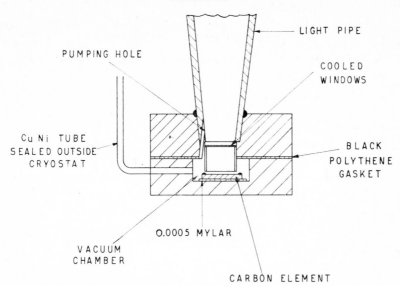

Fig. 4.6. Section of a carbon bolometer assembly (P. Porteous, private communication) illustrating the mounting of a cooled thermal detector. The detector is here supported on the mylar film; alternatively a thermal detector might be supported by its electrical leads only. The leads must be thermally anchored to the heat sink (e.g. by winding a few cm round a metal pin and glueing) but a few cm of unattached (unglued) fine-gauge lead may be required between the detector element and the thermal sink to achieve an appropriate response time. The vacuum seal is here a polyethylene gasket; alternatively it could be a gold-wire O-ring.

photoconductivity cut-off wavelength (the photoconductive effect is weak since the impurity concentration is high enough for overlap to occur – section 4). Pure Ge is transparent to sub-millimetre radiation and it appears that the impurity carriers are responsible for absorbing the radiation. Unlike the InSb hot-electron detector (section 4) the carriers in this heavily doped Ge are tightly coupled to the lattice and the energy absorbed by them raises the temperature of the whole specimen. It appears that to achieve a high temperature coefficient of resistance the correct concentration of compensating impurities is required, but no systematic study of the effect of this on the performance has yet been reported. Suitable samples are available commercially (ch. 1, section 5).

Germanium bolometers have been described by LOW [1961] and by RICHARDS [1964]. The impurities used are Ga or In. Plates, about 4×4 mm and 0.1–0.2 mm thick, have copper leads (~ 40 s.w.g.) attached using In solder. The element is supported by its leads which are thermally attached to a heat sink and the thermal time constant can be varied by adjusting their length. A response time of about 1 ms and a noise-equivalent-power of better than 10^{-11} W, for a 1 c/s output bandwith, can be obtained (section 6), i.e. more than an order of magnitude better than the Golay detector. A typical resistance for one of these detectors is about 200 kΩ, and currents in the range 5 to 50 μA are used.

The Ge bolometer thus compares favourably with the InSb detectors in the range 200 μm–600 μm. At shorter wavelengths it might be preferred because the decrease in free carrier absorption can be corrected by coating with a 'black' material – this is not permissible in the case of the photo-conductive InSb detectors in which the free carriers must do the absorbing. The bolometer cannot compete with the InSb detectors in applications where high speed of response is important.

5.4. Carbon bolometers

Certain types of commercial carbon resistors have a very large temperature coefficient of resistance below 20 °K. These have been used for some time as resistance thermometers (CLEMENT and QUINNELL [1952]) and they can also be used to make a sensitive bolometer (BOYLE and RODGERS [1959], RICHARDS and TINKHAM [1960]).

Fig. 4.7 shows a carbon bolometer assembly designed by Porteous (private communication). The element was cut from a 2 W 56 ohm Allen-Bradley resistor, in the form of a plate about $8 \times 4 \times 0.3$ mm. Leads were attached by first plating a strip, about 1.5 mm wide, at each end with indium. Small blobs of indium were then formed on the ends of 47 s.w.g. copper wires and these blobs were united with the indium strips by cold welding. The element was then glued down and insulated from the brass base of the detector capsule by a sheet of 0.0005 inch mylar. The capsule is vacuum sealed with a polyethylene gasket and evacuated. The detector is operated below the He λ-point (2.17 °K), to improve the responsivity and to eliminate noise due to bubbling helium.

This detector has a noise-equivalent-power of about 3×10^{-11} W for an output bandwidth of 1 c/s and has a time constant of about 1 ms and a resist-ance of about 100 kΩ. This type of detector is fairly easy to construct and requires materials that are readily available. It is less sensitive than the germanium bolometer described above, but it offers a clear gain in detec-tivity over the Golay cell. It has a very high responsivity ($\sim 2 \times 10^4$ V/W) which is offset by a correspondingly high noise.

5.5. SUPERCONDUCTING BOLOMETERS

Superconductors undergo the transition from normal to superconducting behaviour in a temperature range which may be as small as 0.001 °K, though the transition width depends both on the material and on the method of fabrication of the sample. Consequently, near their transition temperatures, samples of superconductors have a higher value of α than any other material and they were used to construct the first cooled bolometers. ANDREWS et al. [1946] and FUSON [1948] used niobium nitride but more recently bolometers using tin have been described by MARTIN and BLOOR [1961].

The sensitive element of Martin and Bloor's bolometer is an evaporated film of tin, dimensions 3 mm × 2 mm × 2 μm thick, deposited on a 3 μm thick mica substrate and with a resistance of about 10 Ω. This element is supported from a split brass cylinder by nylon threads 10 μm in diameter and 0.5 mm long. Electrical contact is obtained by evaporating Pb over the edges of the element, the nylon threads and the faces of the brass block. Since Pb becomes a superconductor at 7.3 °K it will provide perfect electrical contact at the transition temperature of tin (3.7 °K). The method of mounting keeps the thermal conductance to the brass block as small as possible thus ensuring a high responsivity.

Martin and Bloor obtained a noise-equivalent-power of about 3×10^{-12} W (with $\tau \sim 0.05$ sec) and a responsivity of about 10^3 V/W using a step-up transformer in the liquid helium (section 6). This does not represent the limit attainable with this type of detector since no attempt was made to "black" the detector and it is estimated that only 1 % of the incident power was absorbed. Moreover, the dominant noise source was the amplifier, and better performance would be obtained with the amplifiers now available (section 6). Its main disadvantage is that it requires precise automatic temperature control, an accuracy of 10^{-5} °K being required. Now that easily operated semiconducting bolometers and the InSb detectors are available it is not widely used, but it remains potentially the most sensitive of the thermal detectors, having a high value of the ratio r^2/R_d (eq. (4.33)).

6. Amplifiers for use with detectors

The cooled detectors described in the preceding sections have responsivities which are in the range 10^3 to 10^4 V/W and they may be used to record incident signal powers of 10^{-10} W or less. The output signals are therefore typically of the order 10^{-6} to 10^{-7} V or less and must clearly be amplified if they are to be recorded or displayed. Care is required in designing and constructing the amplifier if signals at these levels are not to be submerged in noise originating in the amplifier itself. The performances of detectors cannot be assessed without reference to the performances of amplifiers.

For low-noise amplification a tube with a high transconductance is required. The STC 3A/167M, the Philips 7090, the G.E. 7588 and the RCA nuvistor tubes have been used successfully. The noise characteristics of some transistors (e.g. the T.I. 2 N 930 and 2 N 918, the Fairchild 2 N 3117 and BC 154) and of some field-effect transistors (e.g. the T.I. 2 N 2500 and Fairchild 3277) now rival those of the best vacuum tubes in appropriate conditions. They may be preferred in some circumstances because they are less prone to microphonic disturbances. Such a tube or transistor can be incorporated in a simple broad-band first stage using wire-wound or metal film resistors and with good electrical screening from outside interference (the manufacturers will normally recommend suitable circuit designs). In some circumstances performance is improved by spring mounting and by enclosure in a μ-metal box. Battery supplies are sometimes used but well-designed power supplies should also be satisfactory. Non-microphonic input cable may be advantageous if the first stage cannot be located close to the detector and the input cable is subject to some vibration.

It is customary to modulate the incident signal by mounting a rotating or reciprocating shutter right in front of the source in the optical system or, in the case of a klystron, by modulating its electrical supplies. The signal then alternates, at ω_s say, which differentiates it from the power reaching the detector from other parts of the apparatus (and this can be appreciable with cooled detectors). "Chopping" in this way also serves to avoid the drifting problems associated with d.c. amplifiers and to translate the frequency at which amplification is required away from the band about zero-frequency where all amplifiers are particularly noisy. Most vacuum tubes and transistors generate "flicker" noise which is characterised by a power spectrum which decreases roughly inversely as the frequency. This noise exceeds other types of noise, with flatter power spectra, below a frequency which varies from one type to another but which lies in the range 10^2–10^4 c/s for most tubes of interest here. It is therefore desirable to have a chopping frequency as high as practicable, preferably above this flicker noise region. Limits will be set by the speed of response of the detector (its output falls when $\omega_s \tau \gtrsim 1$) or, in the case of fast detectors, by mechanical considerations at the chopper. In practice, chopping frequencies vary from about 10 c/s for use with slow thermal detectors up to 2 kc/s for mechanical shutters, and tens of kc/s for electrically modulated sources, when used with fast detectors. This is, therefore, the range of frequency over which the noise characteristics of amplifiers are of interest. (In some special applications of millimetre and far infra-red techniques the source is pulsed, e.g. studies of pulsed plasmas, and then wide-band amplifiers are required.)

The noise originating within a vacuum tube amplifier can be expressed as an equivalent r.m.s. noise voltage, e_A, at the *input*, obtained by dividing the amplifier's contribution to the r.m.s. noise voltage at the output by the gain of the amplifier. e_A will vary with the bandwidth of the amplifier B, normally in proportion to $B^{\frac{1}{2}}$ for not too broad a B as a result of the fact that B is generally controlled by parts of the circuit which contribute negligible noise. It is then useful to introduce, as a measure of the noise quality of an amplifier which does not depend on B, the noise-equivalent-resistance R_A which is defined by

$$e_A^2 = 4kTBR_A \qquad (4.22)$$

and is thus the resistance whose Johnson noise in bandwidth B is equal to e_A. Amplifier noise is not white and so R_A must be regarded as a frequency dependent quantity (but independent of B so long as B is reasonably small). The noise generated in a *vacuum tube* amplifier would not be expected to vary much with the impedance in the input circuit until that reaches a sufficiently large value for the grid currents to produce significant noise voltages. The noise-figure of such an amplifier can therefore be calculated with the aid of the equivalent circuit diagram shown in fig. 4.7. E is an e.m.f.

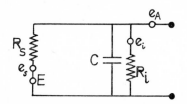

Fig. 4.7. Equivalent input circuit for noise calculations.

representing the signal; R_s the source resistance and e_s the noise e.m.f. originating in the source; R_i is the input resistance of the amplifier and e_i the Johnson noise e.m.f. for R_i. The noise-figure of an amplifier is defined as the power (i.e. mean *square* voltage) noise-to-signal ratio at the amplifier's output divided by that at the source. Now, for a voltage gain G, and neglecting C,

signal-to-noise ratio (power) at source: E^2/e_s^2,

signal power at output: $G^2\{ER_i/(R_i+R_s)\}^2$,

noise power at output: $G^2 \left\{ e_A^2 + e_i^2 \dfrac{R_s^2}{(R_s+R_i)^2} + e_s^2 \dfrac{R_i^2}{(R_s+R_i)^2} \right\}$.

Hence, the noise-figure of the amplifier, NF, is given by

$$NF = 1 + \frac{e_i^2}{e_s^2} \frac{R_s^2}{R_i^2} + \frac{e_A^2}{e_s^2} \frac{(R_s+R_i)^2}{R_i^2}; \qquad (4.23)$$

e_i^2 is equal to $4kTR_iB$ and e_A^2 is $4kTR_AB$ (as above). e_s^2 is at least equal to the Johnson noise associated with R_s at the temperature of the source T_s, but there will also be other kinds of noise in a detector (current noise, background radiation noise, etc.) which might be significant. We shall represent e_s^2 by $4\alpha kT_sR_sB$ where $\alpha > 1$. We then obtain

$$NF = 1 + \frac{T}{\alpha T_s} \left\{ \frac{R_s}{R_i} + \frac{R_A}{R_s} \left(1 + \frac{R_s}{R_i} \right)^2 \right\}. \qquad (4.24)$$

We have used this relation to draw fig. 4.8, which shows the way in which the NF depends on a room-temperature source resistance ($\alpha = 1$) and on frequency (through the frequency dependence of R_A). In constructing the figure we have taken R_i to be 10 MΩ (see below) and R_A to fall inversely as the frequency (flicker noise) from 100 kΩ at 10 c/s to 10 kΩ at 100 c/s and then to approach a constant value of 2 kΩ at higher frequencies.

At a given frequency there is clearly an optimum source resistance at which the NF is a minimum. For low-noise amplifiers $R_A \ll R_i$ and so eq. (4.24) reduces to the following forms for values of the source resistance much greater than the optimum value, and much smaller, respectively,

$$NF = 1 + \frac{T}{\alpha T_s} \frac{R_A}{R_s} \quad \text{for} \quad R_s \ll (R_A R_i)^{\frac{1}{2}} \qquad (4.25)$$

and

$$NF = 1 + \frac{T}{\alpha T_s} \frac{R_s}{R_i} \quad \text{for} \quad R_s \gg (R_A R_i)^{\frac{1}{2}} \qquad (4.26)$$

In designing a detector various thermal and optical considerations may limit the choice of resistance for the detector element. However, a transformer can sometimes be used (see below) to transform the source resistance to an optimum value, without changing the signal-to-noise ratio associated with the detector, and so it is worthwhile to find the value of R_s which minimises the NF given by eq. (4.24). This proves to be:

$$R_s^0 = (R_A R_i^2/(R_i + R_A))^{\frac{1}{2}} \simeq (R_A R_i)^{\frac{1}{2}} \qquad (4.27)$$

i.e. the geometric mean of R_A and R_i, and this is independent of the value taken by $T/\alpha T_s$. The variation of this optimum value with frequency is drawn in fig. 4.7 as a dotted line and is (when $R_i \gg R_A$)

$$NF^0 \simeq 1 + \frac{T}{\alpha T_s} 2 \left(\frac{R_A}{R_i}\right)^{\frac{1}{2}}. \qquad (4.28)$$

This points to the desirability of having as low a value for (R_A/R_i) as possible.

Measurements on *vacuum tube* amplifiers give results which follow this

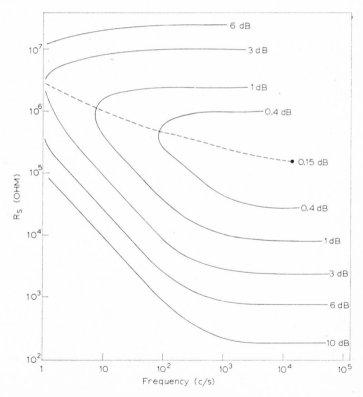

Fig. 4.8. The noise-figure of an amplifier as a function of frequency and source resistance (at 300 °K) as calculated in the text.

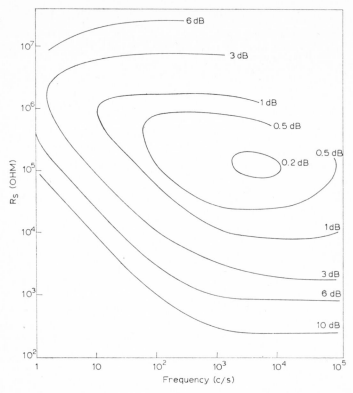

Fig. 4.9. The measured noise-figure of an amplifier with a nuvistor tube in the first stage. (after the data for a PAR Type A amplifier from Princeton Applied Research Corp.).

general pattern, confirming that an amplifier's noise property can be summarised by specifying values for R_A and R_i. For example, the observed data recorded in fig. 4.9 for a low-noise amplifier (ch. 1, section 5) bear a close resemblance to fig. 4.8. Inclusion of the input capacity (C in fig. 4.7) would close the loops in fig. 4.8 like those in fig. 4.9.

It is fairly straightforward to make rough determinations of R_A and R_i for any amplifier provided R_A is small compared with R_i. Mean square output voltages are recorded for a series of resistors connected across the input terminals. These give a straight line when plotted against the resistance and the negative intercept on the resistance axis measures R_A (see eq. (4.25)). (This method could give erroneous results if the amplifier were designed for fast pulse signals because the changing RC value of the input circuit could then change the effective bandwidth.)

Most of the submillimetre detectors described earlier in this chapter operate at temperatures in the liquid helium range. The optimum source resistance (eq. (4.27)) is *independent* of the temperature of the source and of α but the associated optimum noise-figure is not (eq. (4.28)). Equation (4.28) indicates that an amplifier with an optimum noise-figure of 0.5 dB for a source at room-temperature would have an optimum noise-figure of 11 dB when used with a source at the reduced temperature $\alpha T_s = 3\,^\circ K$. If cooled detectors are to be used, therefore, it would clearly be an advantage to have amplifiers with noise-figures well below 0.5 dB (the noise-figure usually quoted for an amplifier is that appropriate for a room-temperature source).

To this end low-noise tubes (see the beginning of this section) would be individually selected and used in circuits well screened from acoustic and vibrational, as well as electrical, interference. Operating conditions should also be optimised – operating at an anode current lower than that specified for normal operation usually reduces flicker-noise and grid-currents significantly. The latter can make an important contribution to noise when a cooled detector of very high resistance is involved. With a source resistance of, say, 100 kΩ, a r.m.s. fluctuation in the grid-current as low as 10^{-13} A would give a noise-voltage of 10^{-8} V which would be more than twice the Johnson noise of the source if it were at less than 3 °K. This noise would not be included in the R_A determined by the method mentioned above.

It is currently possible to achieve noise-performances at the following levels:

R_A: 50 Ω in broad-band use up to 10 Mc/s
           250   Ω at 2 kc/s (i.e. 0.002 μV in 1 c/s bandwidth)
           1 kΩ at 200 c/s (0.004 μV in 1 c/s)
           5 kΩ at 30 c/s (0.01 μV in 1 c/s).

Recently parametric amplifiers using varactor diodes have been developed (BIARD [1963]) which avoid the flicker-noise responsible for the rise in R_A with decreasing frequency which is apparent in the data quoted above. With these amplifiers, R_A can be kept below 1 kΩ down to frequencies as low as 1 c/s. Flicker-noise can also be avoided, even with slow detectors, by passing an alternating current through the detector, rather than a direct current (MARTIN and BLOOR [1961]). The main amplification then takes place at the frequency of this a.c. which provides a carrier for amplitude-modulation by the response of the detector to the incident radiation signal, chopped at a lower frequency. The values quoted above for R_A can be obtained with input impedances of several MΩ. Thus for the optimum source resistance, noise-figures below 0.2 dB can be obtained for a source at room temperature (eq. (4.28)). For a cold source, at 1 °K say, which contributes only Johnson noise, this same optimum noise-figure corresponds to ~10 dB (eq. (4.28)).

Some of the transistors introduced in recent years can be used in the construction amplifiers which approach quite closely the noise performances of the best vacuum-tube amplifiers provided the operating conditions are carefully chosen. They are relatively free from microphonic disturbances and are more readily powered by battery sources and so might be preferable in some experiments. The input impedance and noise-equivalent resistance for a transistor tend to vary with source-resistance and supply voltages and currents, and more data are required for transistors than for vacuum-tube amplifiers if an optimum circuit design for a particular application is to be determined but these data are normally provided by the manufacturers. With N-P-N diffused planar silicon transistors, such as the Texas Instruments 2N930 and the Fairchild 2N3117, optimised noise-equivalent resistances of 1.6 kΩ for a 10 kΩ source impedance and of 6 kΩ for a 100 kΩ source-impedance, have been measured at 1 kc/s and with an input impedance of about 400 kΩ (PLATT and PUPLETT [1965]), i.e. $NF \sim 0.65$ and 1.0 dB respectively for the source at room temperature (eq. (4.24)). These compare favourably with the noise-figures quoted above for vacuum tube amplifiers with similar source impedances. The flicker-noise region in currently available transistors tends to set in below about 1 kc/s, however, rather than at about 100 c/s for nuvistor tubes. Field-effect transistors have been recently introduced which provide low-noise performances at high input impedances, in excess of 10 MΩ, and at high source impedances in excess of 100 kΩ. At a source impedance of 500 kΩ a noise-figure of less than 0.5 dB is quoted for a Texas Instruments 2N2500 field effect transistor at frequencies above 1 kc/s.

It is seen above that the best noise-figures for vacuum tube amplifiers are obtained with source resistances of order 100 kΩ and for transistor amplifiers with source resistances ranging upwards from 10 kΩ. Some of the detectors described earlier do have resistances which fall in the desirable range but others do not. To cut a detector element to such a size and thickness that its resistance matches a given amplifier, could seriously reduce its responsivity. For example, the indium antimonide detectors described in section 4.1 have resistances of about 10 Ω in the absence of a large magnetic field. Increasing the resistance by reducing the thickness of the sample would reduce considerably the fractional absorption of the incident beam. However, for this, and other low resistance detectors, the use of a step-up transformer can permit the detector element to be matched to the amplifier to achieve the optimum noise-figure. Consider the circuit in fig. 4.10a containing a transformer with primary and secondary inductances L_p and L_s and turns ratio $n = (L_s/L_p)^{\frac{1}{2}}$. R_d is the detector resistance and R_L is a resistance representing the total losses in the windings and core which can be determined by measuring the Q-factor of the secondary inductance, equal to $\omega L_s/R_L$. E represents the signal e.m.f.. Application of Thevenin's theorem at the points AA gives the equivalent circuit shown in fig. 4.10b. If C, which will include the stray winding capacity of L_s, is adjusted to resonate with L, another application of Thevenin's theorem at the points BB gives the equivalent circuit in fig. 4.10c. The use of a transformer to couple

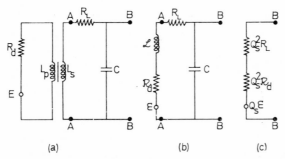

Fig. 4.10. Equivalent circuits for amplification by transformer. $\mathscr{E} = n_d E$; $\mathscr{R}_d = n_d^2 R_d$;
$\mathscr{L} = L_s - n_d^2 L_p$; $Q_s = \omega \mathscr{L}/(\mathscr{R}_d + R_L)$; $n_d^2 = n^2/(1 + R_d^2/\omega^2 L_p^2)$.

a detector to an amplifier is thus equivalent to the direct coupling of a source of e.m.f.. $Q_s \mathscr{E}$ and resistance $(Q_s^2 R_L + Q_s^2 \mathscr{R}_d)$ (see the caption to fig. 4.10) and this equivalence extends to Johnson noise voltages provided the resistance $Q_s^2 \mathscr{R}_d$ is treated as being at the detector temperature T_d and $Q_s^2 R_L$ at T_L the temperature of R_L. If the detector noise exceeds the Johnson noise by a factor α then the power noise-to-signal ratio at the detector itself is proportional to $\alpha R_d T_d/E^2$ while that at the equivalent source is proportional to

$$\frac{Q_s^2(\alpha \mathscr{R}_d T_d + R_L T_T)}{Q_s^2 \mathscr{E}^2} = \frac{\alpha R_d T_d}{E^2} + \frac{R_L T_L}{n_d^2 E^2}.$$

Thus the noise-figure for the transformer stage is

$$NF = 1 + \frac{R_L T_L}{\alpha \mathscr{R}_d T_d}. \tag{4.29}$$

We show below that the second term can be made negligible. We can there-fore achieve conditions corresponding to the optimum noise-figure of an amplifier by using a transformer to make $Q_s^2 \mathscr{R}_d$ equal to the amplifier's optimum source resistance. At chopping frequencies exceeding 200 c/s the commercially available powdered metal cores made for high grade filter coils etc. meet these requirements. Inductances between 750 mH and 5 H can be obtained with coils wound on toroidal cores with outside dimensions less than 2 cm height $\times 7$ cm diameter. For $L_s = 1$ H, $R_d = 10\ \Omega$ and putting $Q_s^2 \mathscr{R}_d$ equal to $10^5\ \Omega$, to match it to the optimum source resistance for an amplifier (see fig. 4.9 and eq. (4.27)) the relations in the caption to fig. 4.10 lead to a turns-ratio $n = 10^2$ and $Q_s = 17$, for a chopping fre-quency of 1 kc/s. At higher frequencies, or with higher L_s, the matching condition gives rise to a smaller Q_s, i.e. a broader banded system. If a highly tuned system is acceptable (i.e. a slow response time) much smaller induct-ances are required. For example, matching can be achieved at 1 kc/s with $L_s = 20$ mH, but then $Q_s = 100$ and $n_d \simeq 1$ with $n \simeq 10^2$ and $\omega L_p \simeq 10^{-2}$ (so that, in this limit, the performance is nearly the same as would be ob-tained by connecting L_s and C directly in series with the detector, without transformer action at all – see fig. 4.10c). Powdered metal cores have per-meabilities up to ~ 140 which may be too small to achieve the optimum matching for frequencies below about 200 c/s and then strip-wound cores would be necessary.

For a cooled detector we must have $R_L T_L < \alpha \mathscr{R}_d T_d$ if the noise-figure for the transformer stage is to be less than 3 dB, where T_d and T_L are the temper-atures of the detector and the transformer (eq. (4.29)). In the first case con-sidered in the previous paragraph we had $Q_s = 17$ which, when compared with a Q-factor for a free inductor of about 280 at 1 kc/s and at room temperature, indicates $R_L \simeq \frac{1}{16}\mathscr{R}_d$. Thus the noise-figure for the transformer amplification would, in this case, exceed 3 dB for a $10\ \Omega$ bolometer at $2\ ^\circ$K unless the total detector noise should be 10 times greater than the Johnson noise contribution, or unless the transformer should be cooled so that R_L and T_L are greatly reduced. There are other reasons why cooling the trans-former may be desirable when a cooled detector is being used. To keep thermal losses low it is customary to use leads having electrical resistances of $10–30\ \Omega$ to connect room temperature apparatus to that at liquid helium temperature. If such a lead were used to couple a cooled detector to a trans-former at room temperature its resistance would be comparable with the detector resistance and over most of its length it would be at a much higher temperature. It would therefore be the dominant noise-source. If the transformer is cooled with the detector this problem does not arise, and, moreover, it is then possible to use a simple but highly effective super-conducting screen round the transformer to eliminate outside electrical and magnetic interference. In these ways it can be arranged that no great loss of signal-to-noise ratio should result from the transformer amplification stage. Cooled transformers have been used in conjunction with a super-conducting bolometer (MARTIN and BLOOR [1961]) and with indium anti-monide detectors (e.g. KINCH and ROLLIN [1963]).

A low-noise pre-amplifier, such as those discussed above, is followed in an overall detector system, by an amplifier tuned to the frequency at which the incident radiation is modulated or chopped and by a rectification stage to produce a d.c. signal which can be recorded. Commonly a smoothing circuit is introduced just prior to the recorder to further reduce noise fluctuations in the d.c. output. The amplifier could be tuned in conventional ways using resonant circuits or selective feed-back and the rectification could be effected with diodes. It is usual, however, to make use of methods of phase-sensitive detection which have some of the advantages of the techniques of coherent detection discussed in ch. 5, section 3.6. That is to say, a switching circuit is used to reverse the output of the amplifier (which need be only very broadly tuned) at the chopping or modulating frequency. The signal com-ponent in the input then produces a d.c. component in the output whereas all noise components, which have frequencies differing from the chopping frequency and its odd harmonics, contribute only alternating components in the output and these can be suppressed by smoothing circuits. If the drive signal for the switching circuit is derived directly from the modulating unit or chopper (e.g. by mounting a pea-lamp and photo-diode on opposite sides of the shutter blades) the system cannot drift out of tune. Amplifers with phase-sensitive detection circuits have been described, for example, by WILLIAMS [1965], and are available commercially – they are sometimes called lock-in, homodyne, or synchronous amplifiers.

Whatever method is used, there is a relation between the overall response time of the system and the effective bandwidth for noise calculations. With phase-sensitive detection an input noise component of frequency $v_m \pm v_d$, where v_m is the chopping or modulation frequency, contributes a component at v_d to the output. This is attenuated by the smoothing network by a factor $(1 + 4\pi^2 v_d^2/\tau_s^2)^{-\frac{1}{2}}$ relative to the d.c. component, where τ_s is the time-constant of the smoothing network. The 3 dB point occurs at $v_d = 1/2\pi\tau_s$ which cor-responds to input frequencies $v_m \pm 1/2\pi\tau_s$ and so the effective bandwidth for noise calculations is $B \simeq 1/\pi\tau_s$. With a simple tuned amplifier, of bandwidth

B_A centred at v_m the corresponding relation can be found analysing the results of suddenly switching on an input signal of frequency v_m. The amplifier passes only those Fourier components which fall within its bandwidth and there results an output at v_m whose amplitude increases with a time-constant τ_r which is related to the bandwidth by $B_A = 1/2\pi\tau_r$. If, before recording, the output is rectified, by a square-law device say, a noise component of frequency $v_m \pm v_d$ will mix with the signal, if this is well above noise, to give a component at v_d and this can then be further reduced by smoothing circuits. But, as for the phase-sensitive detection, the effective bandwidth is now $B \simeq 1/\pi\tau_s$ if $\tau_s > \tau_r$. In each case, therefore, the reduction of a noise bandwidth can be achieved only at the expense of an increase in the response time of the system. (See SMITH [1951] for a full discussion.)

7. Comparison and summary of the performances of detectors

We are now in a position to consider the performances of the several detectors described in preceding sections. They are summarised in the table. A detector which has a responsivity r, eq. (4.1), a resistance R_d, and which generates a noise power which is greater by a factor α than the Johnson noise appropriate to R_d at the detector temperature T_d, shows a signal-to-noise power ratio equal to

$$\frac{r^2 a^2 P^2}{4\alpha k T_d R_d B} \tag{4.30}$$

where P is the signal power incident on the detector, of which a fraction "a" is absorbed, and B is the amplifier bandwith. If F_A is the amplifier noise-figure appropriate to a source resistance equal to R_d, then the *overall* signal-to-noise power for a detector directly coupled to the amplifier is

$$\frac{r^2 a^2 P^2}{4\alpha k T_d R_d B F_A}. \tag{4.31}$$

If a transformer, with noise-figure F_T, is used to transform the detector resistance to the value corresponding to the smallest amplifier noise-figure, F_A^0, the overall signal-to-noise power ratio is

$$\frac{r^2 a^2 P^2}{4\alpha k T_d R_d B F_T F_A^0}. \tag{4.32}$$

The "minimum detectable power", or "noise-equivalent power", n.e.p., defined as that incident power which gives an overall signal-to-noise ratio equal to unity, is thus

$$\text{n.e.p.} = \frac{(4kT_d\alpha R_d BF)^{\frac{1}{2}}}{ra} \tag{4.33}$$

where $F = F_A$ or $F_T F_A{}^0$ respectively for the two cases cited above. Formulae for F_A, $F_A{}^0$ and F_T are given in eqs. (4.24), (4.28) and eq. (4.29), in terms of α, R_d, the noise-equivalent resistance of amplifier, R_A, and R_i its input resistance.

The noise cannot be less than the Johnson noise and α therefore exceeds 1. Calculation (PUTLEY [1964a]) shows that the radiation noise discussed in section 2 in connection with ultimate sensitivities should be negligible compared with Johnson noise unless R_d is less than $300\,\Omega$ and r is at least $1000\,\text{V/W}$ – it will not normally be significant. Fluctuations in the temperature of a detector element occur due to thermodynamic fluctuations in the exchange of heat with the thermal sink to which it is linked and these contribute noise which is commonly of similar magnitude to the Johnson noise. With semiconducting detectors, particularly the carbon bolometers, there may also be "current noise" arising from the flow of current. The two kinds of noise are absent when no current flows through the detector element, and in this way they can be distinguished from the Johnson noise experimentally. For most of the thermal and photoconductive detectors described in this chapter α lies between 2 and 6.

In addition to the n.e.p., the responsivity, the intrinsic response time, τ, and the receptive area, are important specifications for a detector. They are included in the data presented in table 4.1.

We should draw attention to some sources of ambiguity in comparing and specifying the performances of detectors. First, the n.e.p. figures quoted by some authors refer to *absorbed* power rather than, as here, to the power *incident* on the detector. This happens when the n.e.p. is determined indirectly through eq. (4.33) (using a responsivity measured by recording the resistance of the detector as a function of the ohmic power dissipated in it by the current passing through it) but neglecting "a" in the equation. The absorptivities of detectors range from well in excess of 50% for a carbon bolometer to less than 5% for a metallic superconducting bolometer. A similar ambiguity may arise, when a detector in a cryostat is involved, in connection with the loss of signal power in the cryostat's light pipes, or at the windows in radiation shields. This loss is commonly about 50% and there may also be some limiting of the useful aperture. The table quotes the n.e.p. for the power at the detector rather than that at the cryostat's window.

TABLE 4.1

Detector	Area (mm^2)	Operating temperature $(°K)$	n.e.p. for 1 c/s bandwidth (W)	Responsivity (V/W)	Detector's response time (sec)	Operating wavelength and remarks
Ideal superheterodyne	—	300	4×10^{-21}	—	—	$\lambda > 1$ mm
Meredith and Warner superhet.	—	300	7×10^{-15}	—	10^{-9}	$\lambda = 2$ mm (response time determined by receiving bandwidth)
Meredith and Warner video receiver	—	300	2.5×10^{-11}	—	10^{-9}	$\lambda = 2$ mm
	—	300	4×10^{-9}	—	10^{-9}	$\lambda = 1$ mm
Ideal thermal receiver	100	300	5.5×10^{-11}	—	—	Background at 300 °K
	100	1.5	9.8×10^{-17}	—	—	Background at 1.5 °K
	100	1.5	3.6×10^{-13}	—	—	300 °K background for $\lambda > 100$ μm
	100	1.5	1.8×10^{-14}	—	—	300 °K background for 10% bandwidth at 500 μm
Golay detector	15	300	10^{-10}	$\sim 10^5$	10^{-2}	$\lambda < 5$ mm
Carbon bolometer	20	2.1	3×10^{-11}	2.1×10^4	10^{-3}	Operates over whole sub-mm band
Germanium bolometer	15	2.1	3×10^{-12}	4.5×10^3	10^{-3}	Near infra-red to several mm

Detector						Comments
Superconducting tin bolometer	6	3.7	1×10^{-12}	10^3	10^{-2}	Covers whole of sub-mm band
Ideal photoconductive detector	100	1.5	6.5×10^{-13} 6.5×10^{-14} 1.8×10^{-14}	—	—	$\lambda = 100\ \mu m$ $\left\{\vphantom{}\right.$ 300 °K background for $\lambda = 1000\ \mu m$ $\left.\vphantom{}\right\}$ $\lambda > 100\ \mu m$ $\lambda = 500\ \mu m$; 300 °K background over a 10% bandwidth
InSb wide-band detector with magnetic field	5	1.5	2×10^{-11} 1×10^{-11} 5×10^{-12}	200 500 1000	2×10^{-7}	$\lambda = 200\ \mu m$ $\lambda = 500\ \mu m$ $\lambda = 1000\ \mu m$
InSb detector, zero magnetic field, cooled input transformer	15	1.8	5×10^{-13}	300	10^{-4}	$\lambda = 300\ \mu m$-8 mm (response time determined by the transformer)
Tuned InSb detector	25	4	8×10^{-12} 5×10^{-11}	—	$\sim 10^{-6}$–10^{-7}	$\lambda = 150\ \mu m$, bandwidth 15% $\lambda = 26\ \mu m$, bandwidth 8%
Ge cyclotron resonance detector	2	4	2×10^{-12}	$\sim 10^6$	5×10^{-9}	$\lambda = 8$ mm
Boron-doped Ge photoconductor	15	4	2×10^{-12}	—	10^{-7}	From $\lambda = 30\ \mu m$ to 135 μm

Secondly the n.e.p. figures quoted by some authors would be appropriate if a noiseless amplifier were available, but in practice many detectors are amplifier-noise limited (see below). The table gives data which takes account of amplifier noise at the chopping frequencies used. Finally, it should be noticed that the quoted n.e.p.'s in the table refer to an overall effective bandwidth of 1 c/s, i.e. an overall system response time of about $\frac{1}{3}$ sec (section 6). It is not the performance which can be obtained at the quoted detector response time. The n.e.p. of a detector-system normally varies roughly inversely as the square root of the overall response time of the system (eq. (4.33) and section 6). For applications where the detection of extremely weak signals is more important than speed of response, a narrow bandwidth or long circuit time-constants would be employed and a very short detector response time is of no advantage. In fact it would normally be advantageous, when possible, to design the detector to have as large a time-constant as is consistent with a chopping frequency outside the flicker noise region (section 6) because in this way a larger r would normally result (eqs. (4.20) and (4.21)). The time-constants of the bolometer detectors, which can readily be adjusted by varying the thermal conductances to the thermal sinks, are in the range 10^{-2}–10^{-3} sec for this reason. The time-constants of the photoconductive detectors are not easily adjusted independently of the other important material properties, and it is not easy to obtain increased responsivities by increasing their time-constants. The detector response time *is* of importance in applications where short pulsed signals are to be detected by the detector, because it must be less than the shortest pulse to be resolved. For pulses less than 1 msec the bolometric detectors would need to be redesigned for shorter τ with resultant decreases in responsivities below those quoted in the table. The photoconductive detectors on the other hand resolve 1 μsec pulses, when used with a wide-band amplifier, at the full responsivity quoted in the table.

We shall now briefly consider the thermal and photoconductive detectors described in this chapter in turn.

For the germanium bolometer detectors described in section 5.3, R_d ranges from about $2 \times 10^4 \, \Omega$ at 2.15 °K to about $2 \times 10^5 \, \Omega$ at 1.2 °K. The time-constants of the bolometers are $\sim 5 \times 10^{-3}$ sec indicating that we should take R_A equal to 2 kΩ, as would be appropriate for a chopping frequency of 100 c/s (section 6). Eq. (4.25) then gives an amplifier noise-figure of $1 + 10/\alpha$ for operation at 2.15 °K and eq. (4.28) gives a noise-figure of $1 + 5/\alpha$ for operation at 1.2 °K. If α should be as large as 5 we should expect the amplifier noise to dominate at 2.15 °K but detector noise will be important at 1.2 °K.

Experimental findings are in accord with this; LOW's [1961] detector was amplifier limited at 2.15 °K but other workers have found detector noise exceeding the amplifier noise at 1.2 °K. The n.e.p. and responsivity for 2.15 °K are given in the table; for 1.2 °K the responsivity may increase by about ×4 giving some improvement in n.e.p.

For the zero field indium antimonide detectors described in section 4.1 we have $R_d = 10\,\Omega$ at 1.8 °K, which permits the use of a transformer with $n \simeq 100$ (section 6). The detector is fast in its response and the chopping frequency can be as high as 1 kc/s for which $R_A = 500\,\Omega$ is appropriate. Eq. (4.28) indicates a noise-figure equal to $1 + 3/\alpha$, so that, with $\alpha = 4$, the detector noise exceeds the amplifier noise, and the device is detector limited (KINCH and ROLLIN [1963]) if the transformer itself has a low noise-figure and matches optimally. Similar conclusions would apply to the super-conducting bolometer described in section 5.3 which has a similar resistance and responsivity. The n.e.p. quoted in the table was amplifier limited, however, since R_A was 100 kΩ in the experiments of MARTIN and BLOOR [1961].

For the indium antimonide detector in a magnetic field, described in sections 4.1 and 4.2, eq. (4.25) gives an amplifier noise-figure of about $1 + 25/\alpha$ when $R_A = 500\ \Omega$ is used, as appropriate for a chopping frequency of 1 kc/s. This detector is therefore severely amplifier-limited and considerable improvement in the already good n.e.p. would result if quieter amplification were possible. The time-constant of this detector is extremely short and it can be used to detect incident signals in the form of pulses of short duration. The detector resistance must be sufficiently low in such an application to give an adequately short time-constant for the input circuit and on this point too the indium antimonide detector with applied field meets the requirements, having a relatively low resistance (1 kΩ–10 kΩ). If the stray capacitance in the input circuits can be kept below 100 pF, pulses as short as 10^{-6} sec can be resolved. R_A can be as low as 100 Ω for high frequency or pulse application (section 6) and the n.e.p. per 1 c/s bandwidth quoted in the table is for this value. Large magnetic fields are required to operate the InSb detector at wavelengths less than 150 μm and here the use of a doped germanium photoconductive detector (section 4) might be more convenient.

In conclusion we can summarise the relative merits of the detectors discussed in this chapter as follows. The Golay detector has been much the most widely used detector from wavelengths below 25 μm to beyond 2 mm, and the crystal video detector from wavelengths exceeding 3 cm down to 1 mm. Both are commercially available and operate at room temperature with a minimum of ancillary equipment. Over the spectral range of interest in this book however, say from 50 μm to 2 mm, they frequently fail to meet the needs of spectroscopists (ch. 1). This arises from the very low brightness of spectroscopic sources there, and also from the rapid decrease in the detectivities of crystal video detectors as the wavelength falls below 2 mm (section 3). The Golay detector approaches the ultimate limit of sensitivity (section 2) for a wide-band thermal detector at room temperature, and in order to improve significantly on its performance it is necessary to reduce detector noise either by having a detector with a limited spectral range of response or by using a cooled detector. Superheterodyne receivers (section 3) have narrow bands of spectral response and at wavelengths above about 0.5 mm such detectors have n.e.p.'s superior to those of cooled photo-conductive and thermal detectors. However, their extremely narrow bands of spectral response would make them less useful than cooled detectors except in very high resolution applications, and they are relatively elaborate. They have not yet been used for much spectroscopy. Of the cooled detectors the InSb antimonide detector with transformer (section 4.1) offers the best sensitivity at wavelengths exceeding about 300 μm, up to at least 8 mm, and for most spectroscopic purposes the relatively low response time resulting from the use of a transformer is no disadvantage. The germanium bolometer (section 5.3) would be an alternative in this range and would be preferable at wavelengths below about 200–300 μm where the indium antimonide is less absorbing and where the germanium can be blackened. The superconducting bolometer (section 5.5) is much less simple than either of these because very close temperature control is required; but it is as sensitive and probably offers the best prospect of improving further on the n.e.p. of cooled detectors. There is little now to recommend the carbon bolometer (section 5.4) other than the immediate availability of suitable material. Where highspeed response is required, the InSb detector with a magnetic field (section 4.1) is the most effective detector at wavelengths through the submillimeter region and out to about 2 mm, beyond which a superheterodyne receiver may be superior. For wavelengths less than 100 μm the fast indium antimonide detector requires very large fields and the doped germanium photo-conductive detectors (section 4) might be preferable.

8. Recently reported work

Attention must be drawn to three recent developments. First, the current-voltage characteristics of superconducting Josephson tunneling junctions have been found to respond to radiation in the mm range and GRIMES et al. [1966] have shown that detectors with noise equivalent powers at 1 mm wavelength of 5×10^{-13} W per 1 c/s bandwith can be constructed with In-In and Nb-Nb point contact junctions of this kind. Moreover their response is extremely fast, probably with response times less than 1 nsec, and extends to submillimetre wavelengths for which the photon energy is several times as large as the superconducting energy gap.

Secondly, the development of submillimetre lasers (ch. 1, sections 5 and 6) means that heterodyne techniques of detection are assuming greater importance at shorter wavelengths. Photoconductive and thermal detectors can be used in heterodyne systems (ARAMS et al. [1966]). The response times of some bulk detectors are not as short as those of point-contact crystal detectors but for some applications, such as mm wave radiometers, this is not important. PUTLEY [1966a] has shown that the InSb photoconductive detector described in section 4.1 could be used in a superheterodyne system which is more sensitive at 1 mm than any other available at this wavelength and experimental confirmation has been obtained by WORT [1966] who obtained a noise-equivalent power per 1 c/s bandwidth somewhere between 10^{-17} and 10^{-18} W. Recent experiments by GEBBIE et al. [1967] have shown that both the InSb detector and the pyroelectric detector mentioned in the following paragraph may be used in a heterodyne system at 337 μm, using a CN laser as a local oscillator.

Thirdly, with the development of submillimeter lasers, there has grown a requirement for detectors offering short response times, robustness, and ease of operation rather than an extremely low noise equivalent power. Promising results have been obtained with pyroelectric thermal detectors of triglycine sulphate. This material absorbs well in the sub-mm region and fairly robust detectors have been constructed which need no cooling and which respond rapidly enough to resolve the pulsed output ($\sim$5 μsec) from a 337 μm CN laser and from water vapour lasers at 28 and 120 μm. The n.e.p. obtainable is still somewhat poor compared with that of the (much slower) Golay cell, but this should be improved with further development (PUTLEY [1966b], LUDLOW et al. [1967]).

150   E. H. PUTLEY AND D. H. MARTIN

Acknowledgements

We are very grateful to Mr. J. Ludlow and Mr. M. Platt for very helpful discussions on the material of this chapter.

References

D. R. ANDREWS, R. M. MILTON and W. J. DESORBO, J. Opt. Soc. Am. **36** (1946) 518.
F. ARAMS, C. ALLEN, B. PEYTON and E. SARD, Proc. I.E.E.E. **54** (1966) 612.
R. J. BAUER, M. COHN, J. M. COTTON and R. F. PACKARD, Proc. I.E.E.E. **54** (1966) 595.
J. R. BIARD, Proc. I.E.E.E. **51** (1963) 298.
W. S. BOYLE and K. F. RODGERS, J. Opt. Soc. Am. **49** (1959) 66.
M. A. C. S. BROWN and M. F. KIMMITT, Brit. Comm. and Electronics **10** (1963) 608.
M. A. C. S. BROWN and M. F. KIMMITT, Infrared Physics **5** (1965) 93.
C. A. BURRUS and W. GORDY, Phys. Rev. **93** (1954) 897.
J. R. CLEMENT and E. H. QUINNELL, Rev. Sci. Instrum. **23** (1952) 213.
M. COHN, F. L. WENTWORTH and J. C. WILTSE, Proc. I.E.E.E. **51** (1963) 1227.
S. J. FRAY and J. F. C. OLIVER, J. Sci. Instrum. **36** (1959) 195.
N. FUSON, J. Opt. Soc. Am. **38** (1948) 845.
D. G. GALLOWAY and C. W. TOLBERT, Rev. Sci. Instrum. **35** (1964) 628.
H. A. GEBBIE, N. W. B. STONE, E. H. PUTLEY and N. SHAW (1967) to be published.
R. W. GELINAS and R. H. GENOUD, Rand Corporation Report P-1697 (1959).
M. J. E. GOLAY, Rev. Sci. Instrum. **18** (1947) 357.
D. W. GOODWIN and R. H. JONES, J. Appl. Phys. **32** (1961) 2056.
C. C. GRIMES, P. L. RICHARDS and S. SHAPIRO, Phys. Rev. Letters **17** (1966) 431.
H. HAPP, W. ECKHARDT, L. GENZEL, G. SPERLING and R. WEBER, Z. Naturforsch **12a** (1957) 522.
H. HASEGAWA and R. E. HOWARD, J. Phys. Chem. Solid **21** (1961) 179.
G. JONES and W. GORDY, Phys. Rev. **135** (1964) A295.
R. C. JONES, J. Opt. Soc. Am. **43** (1953) 1.
R. C. JONES, Proc. I.R.E. **47** (1959) 1495.
M. A. KINCH and B. V. ROLLIN, Brit. J. Appl. Phys. **14** (1963) 672.
SH. M. KOGAN, Fiz. Tverd. Tela **4** (1962) 1891 (Eng. transl. Sov. Phys. Solid State **4** (1963) 1386).
W. B. LEWIS, Proc. Phys. Soc. **59** (1947) 34.
F. J. LOW, J. Opt. Soc. Am. **51** (1961) 1300.
J. LUDLOW, W. H. MITCHELL, E. H. PUTLEY and N. SHAW (1967) to be published.
D. H. MARTIN and D. BLOOR, Cryogenics **1** (1961) 159.
T. P. MCLEAN and E. H. PUTLEY, R.R.E. Journal (April 1965) 5.
R. MEREDITH and F. L. WARNER, I.E.E.E. Trans. MTT-11 (1963) 397.
W. J. MOORE and H. SHENKER, Infrared Physics **5** (1965) 99.
M. PLATT and P. PUPLETT, private communication (1965).
E. H. PUTLEY, Proc. Phys. Soc. **76** (1960) 802.
E. H. PUTLEY, J. Phys. Chem. Solids, **22** (1961) 241.
E. H. PUTLEY, Proc. I.E.E.E. **51** (1963) 1412.
E. H. PUTLEY, Infrared Physics **4** (1964a) 1.
E. H. PUTLEY, Phys. Stat. Solids **6** (1964b) 571.
E. H. PUTLEY, Hot electron effects and photoconductivity in InSb; in: Physique des Semiconducteurs, ed. M. Hulin (Dunod, Paris, 1964c) p. 443.

E. H. PUTLEY, Appl. Opt. **4** (1965) 649.

E. H. PUTLEY, Proc. I.E.E.E. **54** (1966a) 1096.

E. H. PUTLEY, J. Sci. Instrum. **43** (1966b) 857.

P. L. RICHARDS, J. Opt. Soc. Am. **54** (1964) 1474.

P. L. RICHARDS and M. TINKHAM, Phys. Rev. **119** (1960) 575.

W. M. ROGERS and R. L. POWELL, Tables of Transport Integrals, National Bureau of Standards Circular 595 (July 1958).

B. V. ROLLIN, Proc. Phys. Soc. **77** (1961) 1102.

H. SHENKER, W. J. MOORE and E. M. SWIGGARD, J. Appl. Phys. **35** (1964) 2965.

R. J. SLADEK, J. Phys. Chem. Solids **5** (1958) 157.

R. A. SMITH, Proc. I.E.E. **98**, part 4 (1951) 43.

R. A. SMITH, F. E. JONES and R. P. CHASMAR, The Detection and Measurement of Infra-red Radiation (Clarendon Press, Oxford, 1957) Ch. III.

R. J. STRAIN and P. D. COLEMAN, I.E.E.E. Trans. MTT-11 (1963) 434.

P. WILLIAMS, J. Sci. Instrum. **42** (1965) 474.

A. WORT, private communication (1966).

H. J. ZEIGER, C. J. RAUCH and M. E. BEHRNDT, J. Phys. Chem. Solids **8** (1959) 496.

CHAPTER 5

HARMONIC GENERATORS
AND SEMICONDUCTOR DETECTORS

BY

J. G. BAKER

Schuster Laboratory, University of Manchester

Introduction

Harmonic generation is the most widely used technique in the presently thriving field of millimetre wave spectroscopy and until recently was the only means of producing coherent radiation at short millimetre and sub-millimetre wavelengths. Although this range is now also reached by electronic oscillators (ch. 6) and by far infra-red lasers (ch. 1) the harmonic generator is as yet unsurpassed as a broadband spectroscopic source of high resolution. For example a harmonic generator driven by a carcinotron oscillator that is itself tuneable over the range of 8 mm to 12 mm wavelength can produce useful power at all wavelengths from an upper limit of 6 mm to a lower limit in the 0.75–1 mm region. Throughout this range of almost a decade, a frequency stability of better than 1 in 10^6 can easily be maintained, making high resolution spectroscopy a matter of routine. In addition the harmonic generation process makes it possible to count these high frequencies in terms of an accurately known radio frequency, thus substituting a precise measurement of frequency for the more troublesome and less accurate process of measuring the wavelength.

Work on the harmonic generation of longer millimetre wavelengths by means of microwave rectifier diodes started at the Massachussets Institute of Technology as long ago as 1945, but the credit for the development of this work into a sustained and determined attack on the problems of generating submillimetre wavelengths must go to Gordy. He and his co-workers at Duke University tried many methods of fabricating and mounting these diodes, and in 1954 brought out an "open-guide" type of mounting (KING and GORDY [1954]) that has remained essentially unchanged ever since. With this, power at submillimetre wavelengths was detected for the first time, and improvements in the diode by Ohl and Burrus combined with the use of shorter wavelength microwave oscillators have together culminated in measurements at 0.43 mm wavelength (JONES and GORDY [1964]). Other semiconductor sources of millimetre wavelengths have appeared since 1960 but their performance has not been nearly so good. Tunnel diodes used as fundamental oscillators can generate microwatts of power at 3 mm, whilst varactor diodes used as harmonic generators have produced milliwatts at 2 mm, but both devices show as yet little prospect of submillimetre wave generation. Even the very successful Gunn effect and avalanche diode sources that have recently been developed operate only at longer millimetre wavelengths.

A completely different approach to the problem, by Froome, has yielded much more promising results. This work grew out of his observation in 1946 that "cold cathode" discharges such as a mercury arc produce a very high cathodic electron density, and that this density responds to rapid changes in the arc current without an apparent time lag. Between 1957 and 1962 he developed a submillimetre wave source (FROOME [1960]) that uses an arc between platinum electrodes in high pressure argon gas as the non-linear multiplying element of a microwave harmonic generator. This has produced detectable power at 0.3 mm, the twenty-ninth harmonic of his fundamental source, and represents both the shortest wavelength and highest harmonic reached up to the present time by any harmonic generation technique. Another harmonic generating device that is capable of withstanding similar and even greater microwave drive powers is the ferrite multiplier. Unfortunately its efficiency as a harmonic generator is much lower than might be expected on elementary theoretical grounds, and no submillimetre wave measurements have been reported up to the present.

Despite the considerable attention that has been paid over the years to the harmonic generation of millimetre wavelengths, the complementary problem of their detection has until recently been neglected. Semiconductor detectors in particular show a notoriously erratic performance, which makes comparisons between the results of different experimenters rather unreliable. Meredith and Warner have carried out a study of various detector materials (MEREDITH et al. [1964]) and obtained an encouraging measure of agreement between theory and experiment. A survey of presently available devices by BURRUS [1966] shows that at last detector design can be called a science rather than an art.

Harmonic generators have been used in several laboratories for spectroscopic studies of gases and of solids in the low millimetre range; some measurements on gases have also been made at submillimetre wavelengths. The use of the several devices mentioned in this introduction will form the subject of this chapter, together with a description of the spectroscopic techniques involved.

1. Properties of semiconductor junctions

An understanding of the processes involved at a rectifying semiconductor junction is an essential preliminary to any thorough discussion of the semi-conductor devices to be described later in this chapter. The detailed investigations that have been made of these processes and of transistor action in the past ten years have thrown a great deal of light on the mechanism of harmonic generation, and have resulted both in improved and in new milli-metre wave sources. A brief survey of the band theory of semiconductors and of junctions between them is given here; more detailed treatments appear in many books on diodes and transistors (SIMPSON and RICHARDS [1962], MOLL [1964]).

In a crystal the outer valence electrons of the atoms which combine to form the lattice can in principle wander freely through the crystal without being definitely attached to any one atom. The quantised states of motion of such electrons have energies which are closely spaced in an energy level diagram, forming almost continuous bands of permissible energy separated by gaps of inadmissible energy, which correspond to states of motion of the valence electrons that are not permitted. It is the size of the gap between the highest occupied state and the lowest unoccupied state, at zero absolute temperature, which determines whether a solid is to be a metal, a semicon-ductor or an insulator (fig. 5.1).

In a metal the highest occupied state lies within a band, and a small

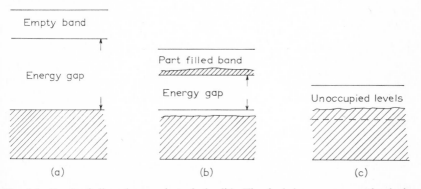

Fig. 5.1. Bands of allowed energy in typical solids. The shaded areas represent levels that are almost completely filled by electrons; the clear areas represent levels that are almost empty at room temperature. The boundary between these two areas is not sharp, and is represented here by a wavy line.

electric field can change the states of motion of the uppermost electrons to produce a current. In a good insulator, such as diamond or ice, the valence electrons fill all the states up to the top of a band, and the energy gap is of the order of several electron volts of energy. Electrons would have to be heated to tens of thousands of degrees or accelerated by an electric field of many thousands of volts per centimetre before they could change their states of motion by jumping this gap, and so at room temperature the electrons of an insulator do not take part in normal electrical conduction. The unique feature of a semiconductor crystal is that in it the energy gap is rather small, ranging from perhaps 0.5 to 1.5 eV. Even at room temperature a small proportion of the valence electrons have acquired enough energy to jump this gap, and the proportion increases rapidly with temperature. An electron in the upper, part-filled band, known as the conduction band, can move freely under the influence of small electric fields. At the same time the electrons in the lower, almost full band, known as the valence band, also become mobile by virtue of the unoccupied states left in this band. In effect, a valence electron jumps into the "hole" left in one atomic shell, a second electron then jumps into the "hole" left by the first, and so on. The net result is that a "hole" moves in a direction opposite to that in which an isolated electron would move, i.e., as if the "hole" were positively charged. All the transport properties of the valence electrons can in fact be described by treating the "holes" as *positively* charged particles with characteristic masses and speeds of their own. Current through a semiconductor is thus carried both by holes in the valence band and by electrons in the conduction band, in the same fashion as it is carried by positive and negative ions in an electrolytic solution.

The semiconductors in most widespread use are silicon and germanium, both elements of Group IV in the Periodic Table, with a diamond-like lattice structure. Recent years have seen the development of many new semiconductor materials, and two of particular interest here are gallium arsenide and indium antimonide. Both are III–V semiconductors, containing equal proportions of a Group III and a Group V element, but with the same average number of valence electrons per atom as silicon and germanium.

The electrical conductivity of a semiconductor rises rapidly with temperature, due to an increase in the number of both conduction electrons and holes. Many of the effects we are looking for could be shown by a pure ("intrinsic") semiconductor of this type, but they would be very strongly temperature dependent. Useful semiconductors are not pure but are doped by the addition of between one and a thousand parts per million of suitable impurities that will produce an excess of either electrons or holes within the material. A Group IV semiconductor might be doped with a Group V element, such as arsenic, antimony or phosphorus, each atom of which has one valence electron more than the atom it replaces; these electrons are pushed into the conduction band to form excess negative charge carriers, i.e. an n-type semiconductor. Similarly doping with a Group III element, such as boron, aluminium or gallium, leads to the production of excess holes in the valence band and a p-type semiconductor. III–V semiconductors are doped by Group II elements (e.g. zinc, copper) or Group VI elements (e.g. tellurium). In quantum mechanical terms, doping produces narrow bands of impurity energy levels within the forbidden energy gap (fig. 5.2).

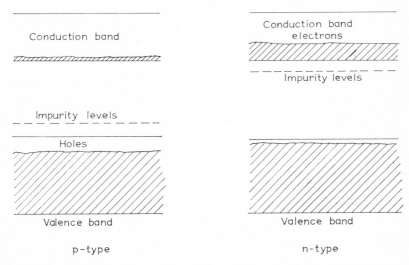

Fig. 5.2. Bands of allowed energy in typical extrinsic semiconductors. The shaded areas represent levels that are almost completely filled by electrons; the clear areas represent levels that are almost empty at room temperature, and so may be considered to be occupied by holes. The boundaries between such areas are not sharp, and are represented here by wavy lines.

These impurity bands lie at a distance of the order of 0.02 eV from the adjacent valence or conduction band, an amount which is less than the average thermal energy of an electron at room temperature, and so the properties of such an "extrinsic" semiconductor depend mainly on the degree of doping and very little on temperature. The excess charge carriers produced by doping, whether electrons or holes, are known as majority carriers of current, and are generally much more numerous than the thermally

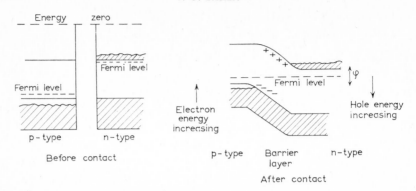

Fig. 5.3. Bands of allowed energy at a p-n junction. The electrical double layer of charge formed at the junction is shown but, for simplicity, energy levels due to impurities and minority carriers have been omitted.

generated carriers which would be present in a pure semiconductor. However a small equilibrium concentration of carriers of the opposite charge to those produced by doping does remain, and these minority carriers play a significant part in conduction at semiconductor junctions.

When p- and n-type semiconductors are brought into contact with each other or with certain metals, the junction acts as a rectifier, passing current in one direction much more easily than in the other. Figure 5.3 shows the pattern of energy levels at a p-n junction before and after contact is made.

The condition for thermodynamic equilibrium after contact is that the Fermi energy levels in the two materials must coincide. This Fermi level represents the statistically weighted mean energy taken up by electrons entering the material, whether they enter the valence or the conduction band. In p-type material it lies close to the valence band, due to the existence of many holes, whilst in n-type material it lies close to the conduction band. In order to align the two Fermi levels there must therefore be a step-like variation in both valence and conduction band energies across the junction. This occurs over a barrier layer of semiconductor of the order of 10^{-5} cm in thickness, which is stripped of both electrons and holes to form an electrical double layer of charge. The high electric field thus produced across the barrier (or depletion) layer repels majority carriers from both sides, but drags minority carriers of the opposite charge across as soon as they enter the layer from either side.

It is possible to derive an expression for the current characteristic of this rectifying junction by making a number of simplifying assumptions. There is always a minority carrier current due to the diffusion, across the junction, of minority carriers that have been generated close to it thermally or by external radiation. In the absence of an external voltage this must be balanced by a majority carrier current due to the small proportion of majority carriers that succeed in mounting the energy step. If this step is of magnitude ϕ eV, the proportion will vary as exp $(-q\phi/kT)$, where q is the numerical value of the electronic charge. Here we assume that the carriers have a Boltzmann energy distribution, an approximation closely followed in practice.

Thus:

Majority carrier current – minority carrier current $= 0$

$$I_M e^{-q\phi/kT} - I_m = 0.$$

Applying an external voltage, V, with polarity such as to make the p-type material more positive (and therefore to *lower* its energy) lowers the energy step to $(\phi - V)$. The majority carrier current increases but the minority carrier current is unaffected. Hence:

Nett current = majority carrier current − minority carrier current

$$= I_M e^{-q(\phi-V)kT} - I_m$$

$$= I_m (e^{qV/kT} - 1). \tag{5.1}$$

The argument used is equally applicable to a voltage of the opposite polarity, and so equation (5.1) represents the rectifying characteristic of a p-n junction (sketched in fig. 5.5). More rigorous theory (SIMPSON and RICHARDS [1962], MOLL [1964]) leads to the same equation, which is found to reproduce the observed low frequency characteristics of junction diodes with considerable accuracy. At microwave and millimetric wavelengths, however, it is necessary to take account of minority carrier storage effects. During forward conduction, when the current is high, large numbers of majority carriers are transferred from one side of the junction to the other, thereby becoming minority carriers. In time they disappear by combining with majority carriers of the opposite polarity, usually after being trapped by a defect in the semiconductor lattice, but the average time for this to take place – the minority carrier lifetime – has been observed to vary from as much as 10^{-3} sec in silicon to as little as 10^{-10} sec in gallium arsenide. These times are distinctly longer than the period of a millimetre wave cycle, and so many of the carriers driven across the junction by such a cycle will return when its polarity reverses, nullifying the rectifying action of the barrier. Junction diodes are little used at the shorter microwave wavelengths for this reason.

Metal to semiconductor junctions show a rather different behaviour (fig.

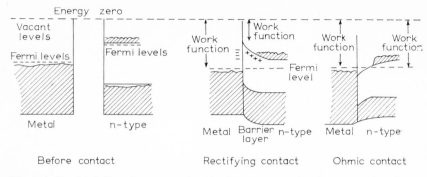

Fig. 5.4. Bands of allowed energy at a junction between a metal and n-type semiconductor. If the work function of the metal exceeds that of the semiconductor a barrier layer is formed within the latter, giving rise to a rectifying contact. If the opposite is true, electrons can pass freely from one side to the other, giving rise to an ohmic contact.

5.4). Because of the different nature of the two materials, a contact potential difference appears between them, corresponding to the difference in energy needed to ionise an electron (the "work functions") from the respective Fermi levels on either side of the junction. This contact potential forms a barrier to the passage of electrons from metal to semiconductor and of majority carriers from semiconductor to metal if it is of the appropriate polarity. It should be noted that a rectifying contact of this kind can form between a metal and either a p-type or an n-type semiconductor; in both cases a depletion layer is formed within the semiconductor as before but not within the metal. In such junctions the role played by minority carriers at p-n junctions is taken by electrons passing from metal to semiconductor; this current is independent of external voltages, which simply raise or lower the semiconductor energy levels and vary the flow of majority carriers in the opposite direction correspondingly. Thus a relation analagous to (5.1) holds, though the coefficient I_m has a different origin. As minority carriers cannot exist within the metal and are not injected into the semiconductor there is no problem of minority carrier storage, and "point contact" diodes of this kind are in universal use at microwave frequencies. Very recently technological improvement in the production and coating of thin epitaxial layers of silicon has led to the appearance of large area metal to semiconductor junction diodes (known as Schottky, or hot carrier diodes) which have the stability and reproducibility of p-n diodes without their carrier storage drawbacks, but these are as yet suitable only for longer millimetre wavelengths.

A further possibility not so far considered is that of a contact potential polarity such that no barrier forms. In this case current can flow freely in either direction whatever the polarity of the external voltage, and the junction is ohmic rather than rectifying. Thus any kind of junction may be produced by choosing the metal and semiconductor appropriately. In practice the situation is not nearly so clear cut; the contact potential for a given semiconductor varies little whatever the metal chosen, a result thought to be due to the formation of surface states of abnormal energy within the semiconductor. Furthermore many of the apparently simple metal to semiconductor junctions to be described in the succeeding pages are made by a "forming" process in which metal atoms enter and dope the bulk semiconductor. The resulting junction consists of an ohmic metal-to-semiconductor contact in series with a p-n junction.

Figure 5.5 illustrates the deviation of a practical small area junction used at millimetre wavelengths from the ideal characteristic. In the direction of forward conduction (current flow from p- to n-) the current rises more slowly than equation (5.1) would suggest, and eventually the characteristic becomes linear rather than continuing to increase exponentially. Both of these features are due to the small contact dimensions, which cause surface effects to

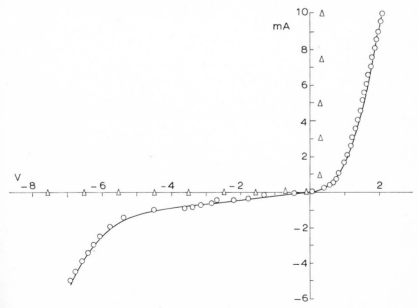

Fig. 5.5. Comparison of the ideal diode characteristic (triangles) given by $I_M = 0.005 \{\exp (qV/kT)—1\}$ with the observed characteristic (circles) of a diode generator of millimetre wavelengths.

dominate. At low forward voltages the characteristic takes the form:

$$I = I_m (e^{\alpha V} - 1) \tag{5.2}$$

in which α is no longer 40 V^{-1} at room temperature as given by equation (5.1); instead it may fall to 20 V^{-1} for germanium or as low as 10 V^{-1} for silicon. As the forward voltage rises the constriction in current flow near the junction causes the appearance of a series or spreading resistance, r_s, within the semiconductor, and much of the applied voltage appears across this rather than across the junction itself. Typical resistances range from tens to hundreds of ohms.

In the reverse conduction direction (current flow from n- to p-) the current should become constant at the small value I_m. In practice it increases appreciably with rise in reverse voltage, due to surface effects that are not yet well understood. When the reverse voltage reaches a value that depends on the degree of doping, the junction breaks down abruptly and passes a current that increases rapidly with little further increase in voltage. This phenomenon of "avalanche breakdown" is characteristic of all semiconductor junctions and is due to electrical breakdown of the thin depletion layer in the very high electric field that is applied to it. The process is analogous to that involved in a gas discharge; carriers accelerated by the field collide with neutral lattice atoms and produce further carriers that are accelerated in their turn to produce still more carriers. The semiconductor lattice is not damaged unless the heat dissipation becomes great enough to cause thermal migration of doping impurities. The slope resistance of the breakdown characteristic depends on how far the carriers generated within the depletion layer penetrate into the bulk semiconductor, but is normally of a similar magnitude to the forward resistance. When the avalanche current becomes large the finite transit time of the carriers across the depletion layer leads to a phase shift that can cause microwave oscillations, and such an avalanche diode has been used to generate millimetre waves.

A further property of reverse biased semiconductor junctions useful at microwave frequencies is that of charge storage. The depletion layer behaves roughly as a parallel plate capacitor, storing the carriers that have been stripped from the atoms within it. The width of this layer, and hence its capacity, varies with reverse voltage, and it is readily shown (SIMPSON and RICHARDS [1962], MOLL [1964]) that this capacitance obeys the relation:

$$C = C_0(1 + V/\phi)^{-n} \tag{5.3}$$

where C_0 represents the capacitance at zero bias voltage, V the numerical value of the reverse voltage applied, and the exponent n varies from $\frac{1}{2}$ to $\frac{1}{3}$ depending on the abruptness of the transition from p-type to n-type semiconductor at the junction. Diodes of this type, known as *varactors*, are in widespread use in parametric amplifiers and centimetre wavelength harmonic generators.

Operating as they do under reverse bias, varactors do not suffer from the effects of minority carrier storage. Indeed it has been found that a certain amount of forward bias operation during the conduction cycle is beneficial, as the capacitance is then varying most rapidly. Equation (5.3) ceases to be applicable when forward current flows, but charge storage is still present. This has been utilised rather ingeniously in the *step recovery diode*, in which the minority carrier lifetime is extended and the rate at which they cross the junction increased by suitably grading the concentration of doping impurity. The majority carriers injected during the forward half cycle return before the reverse half cycle is complete, and, when this supply runs out, the diode snaps off abruptly, reverting to its normal small reverse current. The current waveforms in various kinds of diode are shown in fig. 5.6, and it will be

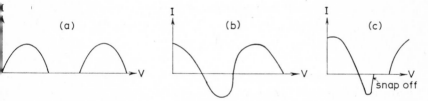

Fig. 5.6. Waveforms of the currents produced in typical diode harmonic generators by a sinusoidally varying voltage, (a) rectifier diode, (b) varactor, (c) step recovery diode.

seen that the jump in the step recovery diode waveform is a richer source of harmonics than that of any other diode. Unfortunately the shortest transition time so far produced is 10^{-10} sec, rather too long to be useful for generating millimetre wavelengths.

As the impurity concentrations rise to relatively high values, say 300–1000 parts per million, the completely new phenomenon of "tunnelling" appears. The depletion layer becomes progressively thinner because less material is needed to provide the charge for the electrical double layer, and the voltage of backward breakdown falls. When the depletion layer thickness is of the order of 10^{-6} cm, quantum mechanical "tunnelling" of the electrons can take place between p-type and n-type material without their having to climb over any intervening energy step. It is only necessary that empty levels

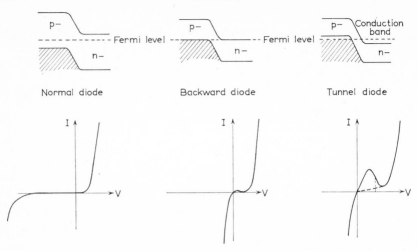

Fig. 5.7. Schematic diagrams of the change in energy levels at the junctions of a number of diodes of a special type, with corresponding current vs. voltage characteristics.

(i.e. holes) at the same energy as those already occupied by the electrons be available on the opposite side of the junction. The condition that the Fermi energy levels be the same at each side of the junction still holds, but these levels have now moved into the adjacent conduction or valence band due to the high concentration of impurities. Figure 5.7 shows the resulting energy level diagram, together with the characteristics of the new kinds of diode that exploit this situation.

The *backward diode*, a recent arrival on the semiconductor scene, behaves in much the same way as a normal diode when forward biased. In the backward direction however, the effect of making the p-type material more negative and the n-type material more positive is to bring electrons in the p-type valence band to the same energy level as empty states in the n-type conduction band. Electrons can then tunnel across the barrier from the p-side to the n-side, and will do so in increasing numbers the more the p-levels are raised. This results in a very rapid increase of current with voltage in the backward direction. If the backward diode characteristic of fig. 5.7 is viewed "in reverse", it appears as a miniature version of the normal diode characteristic, but with a much greater "forward" to "back" resistance ratio. This promises to be very useful for low level detection and mixing, as will be discussed later.

In the case of the *tunnel diode*, electrons are already tunnelling through the barrier before any voltage bias is applied. This tunnel current of course flows in both directions across the junction. With increasing backward voltage the tunnelling rate increases, and the behaviour is like that of a backward diode. But applying a forward voltage causes the tunnelling rate to decrease, and eventually to cease, when the p-type valence band is lowered below the n-type conduction band. At the same time the normal current flow of equation (5.1) is taking place. The sum of these two effects gives the tunnel diode characteristic of fig. 5.7, with a negative slope resistance over a range of small forward bias voltages. If a tunnel diode is put in parallel with a tuned circuit, and forward-biased, it will tend to produce oscillations at the resonant frequency of the circuit. Because of the very low capacitance associated with the small junction, these oscillations can take place at millimetre wavelengths.

A further use of the tunnelling process is in the production of ohmic metal to semiconductor contacts when the contact potential would not normally permit this. By alloying the metal with a small quantity of the same impurity as that used to dope the semiconductor and passing a brief heavy surge of current through the junction, it is possible to dope the semiconductor so heavily that tunnelling takes place at the junction with the metal, no matter what the polarity of the applied voltage. The impurity concentration gradually falls off to that in the normally doped semiconductor as the distance from the original junction increases, but nowhere is there any rectifying junction.

It is apparent from this introduction that a diode rectifier is a rather complicated device, consisting as it does of a nonlinear resistance shunted by a nonlinear capacitance, the whole in series with a spreading resistance. Fortunately it is possible to use simplified electrical equivalent circuits in specific diode applications. In the following sections we shall be considering the use of a diode in turn as (a) a rectifying harmonic generator, (b) a detector, (c) a varactor harmonic generator, and (d) a tunnel or avalanche diode oscillator. The appropriate equivalent circuit appears at the start of each theoretical treatment, and the reasons for each choice will be summarised here.

(a) A rectifying harmonic generator is subjected to a microwave signal of large amplitude which drives it heavily into forward conduction or avalanche breakdown, or both. The average value of the junction resistance is therefore very small, of the order of a few ohms, and it shunts the junction capacitance of perhaps 0.1 pF even at 100 Gc frequency. The effect of the latter, and of any variation in it, may therefore be neglected, and the equivalent circuit consists of a perfect diode in series with the spreading resistance of the real diode.

(b) In diode detection of small millimetre wave signals a situation opposite to that of (a) holds. The junction resistance is large and is at least partly shunted by the junction capacitance. The only simplification possible is that the variation in capacitance over the millimetre wave cycle is negligible, and so the equivalent circuit becomes a nonlinear resistance shunted by a fixed capacitance, together with a series spreading resistance.

(c) A varactor is normally reverse biased, and is driven with little or no excursion into the regions of forward bias and avalanche breakdown. The junction resistance is therefore even larger than in case (b), and is completely shunted by the nonlinear capacitance. The equivalent circuit consists simply of a nonlinear capacitance in series with a fixed spreading resistance.

(d) When oscillating, a diode source of millimetre waves behaves as if the junction resistance were negative. This resistance is still shunted by the varying junction capacitance, but for simplicity the equivalent circuit is taken as a negative resistance shunted by a fixed capacitance, the two in series with a fixed positive spreading resistance.

2. Rectifier diode harmonic generators

In this section we consider the use of a rectifying point contact between a metal and a semiconductor to generate millimetre wavelength harmonics of the signal from a conventional microwave source of frequency f. This is termed the fundamental, whilst the harmonic at frequency nf is termed the nth harmonic. The rectifying contact is mounted within the waveguide carrying the fundamental power, and harmonic power is drawn off through smaller wave-guide whose dimensions are beyond cutoff for the fundamental and unwanted lower harmonics.

Any microwave rectifier must simultaneously generate harmonics of the incident frequency, and these will normally propagate along the fundamental waveguide. A simple harmonic generation circuit consists of such a rectifier followed by a microwave high pass filter to remove the fundamental, and more sophisticated versions of this simple circuit have been used for milli-metre wave generation (WESSEL and STRAIN [1964]). They correspond to the parallel equivalent circuit of fig. 5.15a, in which the diode is shunted across two transmission lines in parallel, one resonant at the fundamental and the other at the harmonic frequency. Though it is mathematically equivalent to the series circuit of fig. 5.15b, the parallel configuration has always per-formed less well as a microwave harmonic generator, and will not be con-

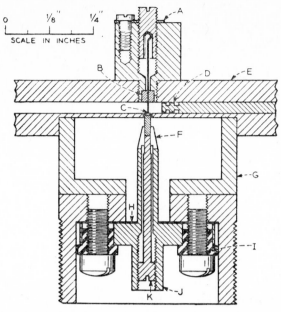

Fig. 5.8. Cross-sectional view of a wave-guide circuit for the generation of higher order harmonic frequencies from a 24 Gc fundamental source. (A) anti-backlash spring, (B) gold alloy contact metal bushing, (C) bombarded silicon crystal, (D) mm-wave tuning piston, (E) mm-wave guide, (F) spring jaw chuck, (G) K-band wave guide, (H) mica washer, (I) nylon bushing, (J) d.c. bias connection, (K) crystal position adjustment (from OHL, BUDENSTEIN and BURRUS [1959]).

sidered further here. In the series configuration, the diode links two completely separate fundamental and harmonic circuits; the microwave equivalent of this is the crossed-guide harmonic generator of figs. 5.8–5.10, in which the fundamental and harmonic waveguides are mounted at right angles and the metal wire forming one side of the point contact passes through the centre of each.

The basic layout of such a harmonic generator has been described a number of times (VAN ES et al. [1960]), the differences between the various generators being largely ones of detail. A 0.5 mm diameter crystal of semiconductor is mounted with its face flush with the broad wall of the harmonic waveguide, and a crimped tungsten whisker about 0.04 mm in diameter makes the rectifying contact and acts as an aerial linking the two waveguides (except in the generator of fig. 5.8, in which the crystal itself is the link). Microwave radiation does not escape along this wire because the crimp and the insulating washer by which it is mounted together act as a microwave

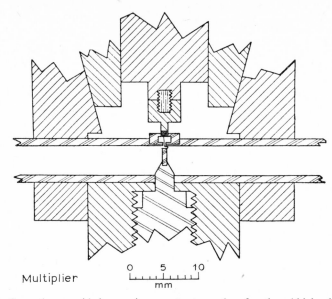

Multiplier

Fig. 5.9. Crossed waveguide harmonic generator to produce fourth and higher harmonics of a 24 Gc fundamental. Contact is made between a silicon crystal in a differential screw mount and a tungsten whisker mounted in a brass post extending across the fundamental waveguide (from KING and GORDY [1954]).

choke and shunt capacitor. This insulation also permits the application of external d.c. bias to the contact. Obstructions and discontinuities in the harmonic waveguide are kept down to an absolute minimum, both crystal and whisker entering through holes only slightly larger than their own dimensions, and in some designs being held in gold or Teflon bushes to assist alignment. In addition the length of coaxial line between the two waveguides must be reduced to about a quarter wavelength at the harmonic desired by milling down the waveguide walls. The exact contact position is set by a coarse adjustment of the whisker mount, whilst the pressure is controlled by moving the crystal at right angles to the harmonic waveguide by a differential screw whose movement should be no more than 0.1 mm per revolution.

The reactive impedance presented by the structure in the fundamental waveguide to the oncoming microwaves may be tuned out, or matched, by a waveguide short circuiting plunger behind the contact and tuning stubs, or an E/H tuner, before it. Very careful matching is necessary only in precision work at one frequency; normally a reasonable match is maintained over a 1–2% frequency variation with readjustment. Matching in the harmonic waveguide is necessarily much simpler, because stubs and sidearms tend

Fig. 5.10. Photograph of the components of the harmonic generator of fig. 5.9. The crystal and its mount are at the left, the whisker, post and nylon holder at the lower centre, and a mm wave tuning stub at the top centre (scale in centimetres).

to excite unwanted modes of harmonics for which the waveguide is very far from cutoff. A short circuiting rod flush with the waveguide is generally satisfactory though silver plating it or shaping it as a reaction plunger (OHL et al. [1959]) does improve the harmonic output somewhat. The guide sizes used are dictated by the fundamental source and harmonic desired; fundamentals from 25 Gc (RG53/U) to 100 Gc (WR10) have been used, and harmonic guide has ranged from the convential 0.86×0.43 mm^2 (RG139/U) and 0.35×0.175 mm^2 to the more unusual 3.7×0.8 mm^2 and 1.0×0.25 mm^2 (OHL et al. [1959]). These extreme ratios result in a lowering of the waveguide characteristic impedance, producing better matching to the harmonic generator at very high frequencies (cf. theory in sub-section 2.1). Such small waveguide sizes are difficult to fabricate and attenuate millimetre waves severely, so that it is customary to taper up the guide to a size approaching that of the fundamental as soon as practicable, despite the fact that it will then support microwave modes other than the dominant TE$_{01}$ mode.

The various components of a 25–100 Gc harmonic generator are shown in fig. 5.10. The setting up of a contact commences with electropolishing and pointing the tungsten whisker by immersing it in a dilute ($\sim$5 per cent) solution of potassium hydroxide and passing current at a few milliamperes, first a.c. and then d.c. through it, making the point of the whisker the cathode. It is occasionally desirable to clean the whisker of its oxide layer by 15 minutes immersion in 25% hydrofluoric acid – the crystal, too, may benefit from an etch of a few seconds – but these precautions are only necessary when the components have been stored for a long period in a humid atmosphere. The whisker is then centred and set up with its tip at one face of the harmonic waveguide, and the crystal wound down by means of the differential screw until contact is made. This contact may be monitored by either d.c. or microwave methods; in the former case by using a high resistance source that limits the current to tens of microamperes and in the latter case by observing the rectified output when microwave power is applied. Usually the first contact is a rather poor source of harmonics, but further movement of the crystal until the force on the contact corresponds to several grams weight will produce a rise in harmonic output, whilst the rectified output tends to fall. From this point on optimisation of a particular harmonic is a matter of trial and error, involving rotation of the crystal or whisker, variation of d.c. bias, and adjustment of the contact pressure and fundamental and harmonic matching devices. It may also be necessary to adjust the length of the whisker, but good broadband results are generally obtained when the crimp in it is close to the face of the fundamental waveguide, possibly because millimetre wavelength radiation is then confined to the harmonic waveguide. The external d.c. bias supply should be readily adjustable in magnitude and polarity, and should include a 500–1000 Ω series resistor to avoid the inadvertent application of a current great enough to destroy both whisker and contact; values up to 15 mA are reasonably safe. Despite the seeming length and complexity of the operations above, the setting up of a satisfactory contact generally involves less than an hour's work, and, once made, such a contact is stable for months or even years except under conditions of gross mechanical shock or electrical overload. During the optimisation process, however, the best harmonic output tends to appear only in brief bursts as the various parameters are adjusted, and it is advisable to use a detector with a response time measured in milliseconds so that these bursts are not missed.

The identification of a particular harmonic can be a troublesome process. Most of the harmonic power tends to be concentrated in the lowest frequency that the harmonic waveguide will pass, and the use of a broad band detector will lead to the optimisation of this lowest harmonic. Higher harmonics may be isolated by means of a high pass filter, consisting of two waveguide taper sections joined at the narrow end, whose dimensions are beyond cutoff for the lower harmonics. It is not really necessary to interpose a section of waveguide beyond cutoff between the tapers because the harmonics beyond cutoff decay at a rate of almost 54.6 dB per wavelength within the filter, and a path length of only 1 mm at this attenuation is sufficient to reduce them to negligible proportions. Filters of this kind are made by electroforming on polished mandrels tapering to an apex angle of 10°–20°. It is customary to taper both waveguide dimensions, though it has been shown sufficient to taper the broad dimension of the waveguide alone (CLOUSER and GORDY [1964]). This process involves the technical difficulty of extracting the mandrel from the finished filter section through rather small holes; two suitable mandrels used by the author have consisted of hard wax (cast in a steel mold) and perspex. Copper is electroplated over an initial conducting layer of fine graphite or silver, and the mandrels extracted by melting the wax or cooling the perspex in liquid nitrogen. Other workers have used polystyrene and stainless steel (BAUER et al. [1966]).

For harmonic numbers (n), approaching double figures, filters become ineffective, and it is necessary to use spectrometric methods. Figure 5.11 shows the output of a harmonic generator after it has passed through a diffraction grating spectrometer (chapter 3); the frequency of the source remains fixed and successive harmonics are focussed on the detector by

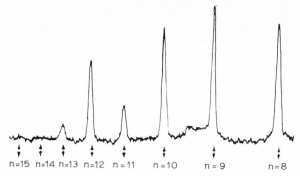

n=15 n=14 n=13 n=12 n=11   n=10   n=9   n=8

Fig. 5.11. Harmonics of a 35 Gc source of power $\frac{1}{2}$–1 W produced by a bombarded silicon harmonic generator, d.c. biased to the "reverse break" in its characteristic. The harmonics are displayed by a reflection grating spectrometer set for maximum sensitivity in the region of 11th–14th harmonics, and using a Golay detector (courtesy of K. D. Froome).

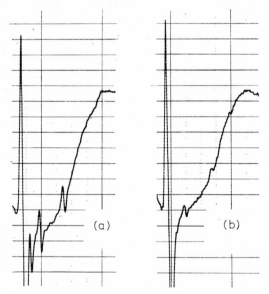

(a)   (b)

Fig. 5.12. Harmonics of a 24 Gc source of power 100 mW produced by a bombarded silicon harmonic generator. The harmonics are displayed as spectral absorption lines of gaseous OCS. In the left-hand diagram the fourth to eighth harmonics are optimised by using reverse d.c. bias; in the right-hand diagram open circuiting the harmonic generator has reduced the amplitude of these but resulted in detectable power at the ninth harmonic.

rotation of the grating. The width of the harmonic lines is set by the resolving power of the grating. Alternatively a gas absorption spectrometer may be used, with the results displayed in fig. 5.12. The theory and practice involved are discussed in detail later in this section, and it suffices here to say that at suitable fundamental frequencies a gas absorption occurs at almost, but not exactly, the frequency of every harmonic of this fundamental. As the fundamental is swept by a small amount, the spectrometer will show a set of absorption lines each of which corresponds to one particular harmonic. The harmonics may be identified by accurate frequency measurement or by counting up from the lowest transmitted by the harmonic waveguide. Figure 5.12 shows how a particular harmonic can be optimised in the presence of others by varying the generator parameters.

Although most semiconductors will give some lower harmonics when used in a harmonic generator of the type described, the selection of a suitable

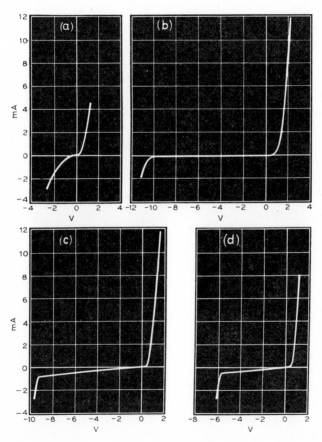

Fig. 5.13. *I–V* characteristics of tungsten-point-contact diodes on 0.023 Ω cm boron-doped silicon, surface treated as follows: (a) chemically etched; (b) carbon bombarded, 40 keV; (c) phosphorus bombarded, 40 keV; (d) phosphorus diffused (from BURRUS [1964])

semiconductor material for this purpose demands reasonable care. Silicon (KING and GORDY [1954]), germanium (MEREDITH and WARNER [1963]) and gallium arsenide (DEES and SHEPPARD [1963], BAUER et al. [1966]) have all been used successfully at millimetre wavelengths, but silicon has so far produced the best results at submillimetre wavelengths (JONES and GORDY [1964], OHL et al. [1959]). In every case high resistivity (0.01–0.02 Ω cm) material is used by contrast to the low resistivity material needed for detectors. The most dramatic results have been obtained from the use of bombarded silicon, first produced by Ohl in 1952 and developed as a harmonic generator by Burrus, Trambarulo and Ohl (OHL et al. [1959]), who succeeded in increasing the available power at 0.78 mm wavelength thirtyfold. This material is made by high temperature bombardment of silicon with 40000 eV positive ions, and its production demands considerable experience in the handling of semiconductors, but it has unfortunately never been made commercially available. Recently Burrus has described a much simpler process of high temperature phosphorus diffusion (BURRUS [1964]) that produces material of as good a performance as bombarded silicon. Figure 5.13 shows that the effect of these treatments on the characteristics of a point contact diode is to raise the backward breakdown voltage and to increase the abruptness of avalanche breakdown. Both of these features tend to increase the harmonic power output, as the theoretical treatment to follow will show. The exact cause of this change in electrical characteristics is not known, but it is believed that a thin n-type layer forms on the surface of the p-type semiconductor. At low frequencies this forms a junction diode of large area, but millimetre wavelengths are confined by the skin effect to a transmission line with an area corresponding to that of the extremely small metal point (BURRUS [1966]). Thus the size of the contact may be determined by the experimenter without affecting its electrical properties.

2.1. THEORY OF HARMONIC GENERATION

It has been shown that a semiconductor harmonic generator can be represented by the equivalent circuits of fig. 5.15, in which contact capacitance is disregarded, because of the very large microwave voltage applied. Let us assume for the moment that this voltage is the same as that appearing between the broad faces of the waveguide when whisker and crystal are absent. This assumption will be examined in more detail later. For the TE_{01} mode (fig. 5.14) the peak electric field E_{max} occurs at the centre of the broad face, and is related to the incident power, P, by:

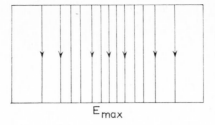

Fig. 5.14. Instantaneous distribution of the microwave electric field in the TE_{01} wave-guide mode. The field lines are bunched most closely in regions of maximum electric field.

$$P = \frac{E_{max}^2}{Z_0} \frac{ab}{4} \tag{5.4}$$

where Z_0 is the characteristic impedance of the waveguide and a and b are respectively its long and short dimensions. The peak microwave voltage V_1 may therefore be defined by:

$$V_1^2 = (bE_{max})^2 = \frac{2b}{a}(2Z_0P) = 2ZP \tag{5.5}$$

where we shall call Z the impedance of the fundamental frequency circuit. As the ratio $2b/a$ is unity, or nearly so, for conventional waveguides, the two impedances are usually the same, and equation (5.5) is the normal a.c. circuit relationship. Under typical conditions Z would be of the order of

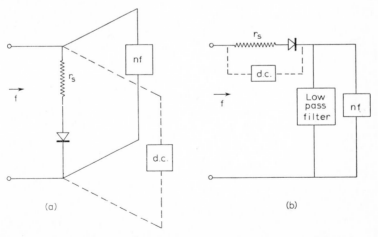

Fig. 5.15. Equivalent circuits for diode harmonic generators; (a) parallel configuration, (b) series configuration.

500 Ω, so that a power of 1 mW would correspond to a voltage V_1 of 1 V, whilst 100 mW would produce 10 V. The peak to peak microwave voltage would be twice these values. It should be noted that relation (5.5) holds only if the contact is perfectly matched to the microwaves; if power is reflected it must be modified accordingly.

The equivalent circuit and typical conduction cycles for a series harmonic generator are shown in figs. 5.15b and 5.16. This treatment neglects any nonlinearities in the diode characteristic and assumes equal forward spreading and backward avalanche resistances, approximations borne out in practice (fig. 5.5). OHL et al. [1959] have analysed the behaviour of a diode d.c. biased so that only forward conduction takes place during the microwave cycle (fig. 5.16a); a rather different approach is used here in order to illustrate the effect of varying fundamental and harmonic impedances. Normally one assumes that the non-linear resistance of the diode yields harmonic currents when a fundamental voltage ($V_1 \cos \theta$) is applied; instead one can say that the diode presents a time-dependent conductance $G(\theta)$ to this voltage. By comparing harmonic currents, it is possible to make these two representations equivalent:

$$I = (I_0 + I_1 \cos \theta + \ldots + I_n \cos n\theta + \ldots)$$
$$= (G_0 + G_1 \cos \theta + \ldots + G_n \cos n\theta + \ldots) \cdot V_1(\cos \theta - \cos \phi). \quad (5.6)$$

Current flow is restricted to the periods when $-\phi < \theta < \phi$ by the applied d.c. bias, $V_0 = V_1 \cos \phi$. The two representations become equivalent if:

$$G_0 = \phi/\pi r_s$$
$$G_n = 2 \sin n\phi/n\pi r_s. \quad (5.7)$$

Equation (5.6) holds only so long as all harmonic currents flowing through

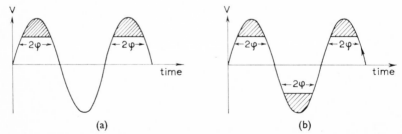

Fig. 5.16. Current flow (shaded) in a diode harmonic generator conducting (a) in a forward direction only, (b) symmetrically in the forward and reverse direction.

the diode are short-circuited. As soon as a harmonic load G_H (for example, a parallel resonant circuit) is inserted in order to withdraw nth harmonic power, a new voltage ($V_n \cos n\theta$) appears across the diode and must be subtracted from the V_1 term in (5.6). This gives rise to a new set of harmonic currents, denoted here by primes. The algebra to follow is greatly simplified by use of the relations (5.8), which parallel closely quantities defined by OHL et al. [1959]:

$$
\left.
\begin{aligned}
a &= \tfrac{1}{2}(G_{n-1} - 2G_n \cos \phi + G_{n+1}) = \frac{2}{\pi r_s} \frac{(\sin n\phi \cos \phi - n \cos n\phi \sin \phi)}{n(n^2 - 1)} \\[2mm]
b &= G_0 - G_1 + \tfrac{1}{2}G_{2n} = \frac{1}{\pi r_s}\left(\phi + \frac{\sin 2n\phi}{2n}\right) \\[2mm]
c &= G_0 - G_1 + \tfrac{1}{2}G_2 = \frac{1}{\pi r_s}\left(\phi - \frac{\sin 2\phi}{2}\right).
\end{aligned}
\right\} \quad (5.8)
$$

When the nth harmonic is terminated by a load of conductance G_H:

$$I'_n = I_n - bV_n = I_n - bI'_n/G_H$$

$$P_n = \frac{I'^2_n}{2\,G_H} = \tfrac{1}{2}I_n^2 \frac{G_H}{(G_H + b)^2} = \tfrac{1}{2}a^2 V_1^2 \frac{G_H}{(G_H + b)^2}, \quad (5.9)$$

where P_n is the available nth harmonic power. This is greatest when $G_H = b$,

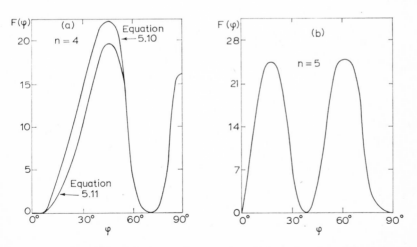

Fig. 5.17. The variation of the harmonic generation efficiency functions with conduction angle, ϕ. (a) $F(\phi)/b^2 = a^2/4\,bc$ (eq. (5.10)) and $4\,a^2/(b^{\frac{1}{2}} + c^{\frac{1}{2}})^4$ (eq. (5.11)). (b) $F(\phi)/B^2 = (A/\cos \phi)^2$ (eq. (5.14)).

i.e. when the harmonic generator is impedance matched to the harmonic waveguide. If we neglect the small effect on the current I_1 of terminating the nth harmonic, the power absorbed at the fundamental frequency is:

$$P_1 \text{ (abs.)} = \tfrac{1}{2}I_1 V_1 = \tfrac{1}{2}c V_1^2$$

and the impedance of the harmonic generator at this frequency is therefore $1/c$. Thus the harmonic generator cannot be simultaneously matched to two waveguides of the same impedance unless $b=c$, when $\phi = \tfrac{1}{2}\pi$. At smaller conduction angles we find that, if the waveguides are separately matched ($G_H = b$; $G_F = c$):

$$\frac{P_n}{P_1} = \frac{a^2}{4 bc} \tag{5.10}$$

whilst, if both waveguides have the same impedance ($G_H = G_F = (bc)^{\frac{1}{2}}$):

$$\frac{P_n}{P_1} = \frac{4a^2}{(b^{\frac{1}{2}}+c^{\frac{1}{2}})^4} \tag{5.11}$$

where P_1 is the *incident* fundamental power and G_H and G_F are respectively the harmonic and fundamental waveguide conductances.

In agreement with the work of OHL et al. [1959], expressions (5.10) and (5.11) are largest at small conduction angles. However the quantities b and c will then be small, and parasitic losses due to the contact capacitance, C, become serious. It is shown later in this section (eq. (5.18)) that the power output of practical millimetre wave generators varies as $(b/\omega C)^2$, and so a more realistic appraisal of the effect of varying the conduction angle will be obtained by multiplying both (5.10) and (5.11) by b^2. The angular variation of the resulting expressions is shown in fig. 5.17a for a representative even harmonic; they differ only slightly and the power at $\phi = \tfrac{1}{2}\pi$ is within 1.5 dB of the maximum power available. Odd harmonics behave similarly, but show a zero at $\tfrac{1}{2}\pi$ and a maximum at a somewhat smaller angle. Thus parasitic capacitance has the effect of raising the angle of near-optimum performance close to that of half wave rectification ($b = c$), for which the efficiency is:

$$\frac{P_n}{P_1} = \frac{4}{\pi^2(n^2-1)^2}. \tag{5.12}$$

The assumptions used to derive equation (5.12) apply when n is large, and tend to break down when second or third harmonic power is being withdrawn. A further assumption, that the diode conducts only in the forward direction, becomes incorrect at power levels of the order of 10-100 mW. If an alternative conduction cycle of fig. 5.16b is assumed, the coefficients G_n in equation (5.7) are each multiplied by a factor $1+(-1)^n$. This makes the odd coefficients vanish, and with them, the even harmonic currents, as is to be expected from the symmetry of the conduction cycle. The terms of (5.8) take on a rather different form, denoted here by capital letters:

$$
\left.
\begin{aligned}
A &= \frac{4}{\pi r_s} \frac{(n \sin n\phi \cos \phi - \cos n\phi \sin \phi)}{n(n^2-1)}, \\[2mm]
B &= \frac{2}{\pi r_s}\left(\phi + \frac{\sin 2 n\phi}{2n}\right), \\[2mm]
C &= \frac{2}{\pi r_s}\left(\phi + \frac{\sin 2 \phi}{2}\right).
\end{aligned}
\right\} \quad (5.13)
$$

The conduction angle ϕ is now set by the ratio between diode breakdown voltage, E_b, and microwave driving voltage, V_1

$$
\cos \phi = \frac{E_b}{2V_1}.
$$

The harmonic power produced is:

$$
P_n = \tfrac{1}{2} A^2 V_1^2 \frac{G_H}{(G_H+B)^2} = \tfrac{1}{8} E_b^2 G_H \left(\frac{A}{\cos \theta}\right)^2 \frac{1}{(G_H+B^2)}. \quad (5.14)
$$

Once more we allow for parasitic capacitance by multiplying (5.14) by B^2; it then becomes clear that for best results, $G_H \ll B$ and the bracketed expression $(A/\cos \phi)^2$ should be maximised. Fig. 5.17b shows that this expression has a set of equally large peaks; in other words, increasing the microwave drive beyond that needed to produce a conduction angle of $\pi/2n$ has been shown to yield no further increase in harmonic output. The "saturated" harmonic power available at this conduction angle is found by substituting back in equation (5.14), still assuming that $G_H \ll B$:

$$
P_n = \tfrac{1}{8} E_b^2 \, G_H \left(\frac{A}{B \cos \phi}\right)^2. \quad (5.15)
$$

This expression is correct for odd harmonics; it also applies for even harmonics if one uses the coefficients of (5.8) and assumes a conduction angle of $\tfrac{1}{2}\pi$. In both cases, $G_H = 1/Z$,

$$P_n \text{ (odd)} = \frac{2n^2}{\pi^2(n^2-1)^2} \frac{E_b^2}{Z}$$

$$P_n \text{ (even)} = \frac{2}{\pi^2(n^2-1)^2} \frac{E_b^2}{Z}.$$

(5.16)

The periodic variation of harmonic output with conduction angle implied by eqs. (5.11) and (5.14) has never been observed experimentally, but with this one exception the conclusions reached are in fair semiquantitative agreement with experimental measurements. OHL et al. [1959] have compared experimental and theoretical harmonic generation efficiency using a diode and a microwave drive for which the assumptions leading up to (5.12) are valid, with the results shown in fig. 5.18. There is a remarkably close agreement between the theoretical curve (c), corresponding to (5.12), and the experimental curve (d), especially when it is borne in mind that the latter curve has

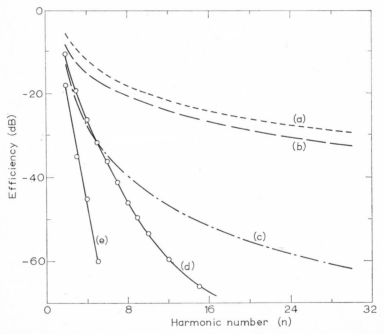

Fig. 5.18. Efficiency of diode harmonic generation as a function of harmonic number. Curve (a) is the $1/n^2$ ideal limit. Curves (b) and (c) are the calculated efficiencies in the respective cases of perfect matching and the more realistic fixed 90° conduction angle. Curve (d) represents the experimental results obtained with bombarded silicon diodes and curve (e) the results with conventional silicon diodes (from OHL, BUDENSTEIN and BURRUS [1959]).

not been corrected to allow for the frequency response of the crystal detector used. In section 3 it will be shown that the output of such a detector falls at a rate inversely proportional to the square of the frequency, or 6 dB per octave, and when this correction is made the two curves coincide much more closely. Curve (b) corresponds to a diode matched at both fundamental and harmonic frequencies, and for this optimum harmonic output occurs at small conduction angles. Although moves have been made in the direction of this double matching by using harmonic waveguide of lowered impedance (see the earlier practical section), the extreme impedance ratios required at small conduction angles have yet to be tried experimentally. It must be admitted that the efficiency possible with this double matching is quite high, closely approaching the theoretical limit of $1/n^2$ which has been shown by PAGE [1958] to represent the highest efficiency obtainable from any nonlinear positive resistance. This limit corresponds to curve (a).

The phenomenon of saturation of harmonic output at high drive powers is well known. It was first noticed for untreated silicon diodes (JOHNSON et al. [1954]) and probably accounts for the poor results of curve (e) in fig. 5.18. It has recently been observed in a gallium arsenide 70 Gc to 140 Gc doubler (BAUER et al. [1966]), a maximum output of slightly less than 1 mW being obtained with a saturating drive power of only 10 mW. Typical diodes of this material break down under a reverse voltage of 3 V (BURRUS [1966]), as compared with the 6–10 V of treated silicon diodes, which can therefore operate at much higher power levels. The results of fig. 5.18 were obtained with 200 mW of drive, for example. At still higher powers the writer has noted a marked loss of even harmonics, illustrated in the grating spectrum of fig. 5.19, which was produced by a diode with a characteristic as shown in fig. 5.5 and driven by $\frac{1}{2}$ W of power at 35 Gc.

It should be possible to predict the microwave power required for saturation from equation (5.5) by equating the peak to peak microwave voltage to the diode breakdown voltage, but in practice the agreement is very poor. Much better agreement is obtained by assuming that the microwave voltage at the diode is one half of the above value, despite the fact that the conclusions of equation (5.5) are supported by rigorous treatments based on the theory of waveguides (YAMASHITA and BAIRD [1966]). This modification does not invalidate the arguments of the preceding section, for the whisker structure can be considered to be an ideal transformer which reduces the voltage by a factor of two whilst reducing the impedance by a factor of four (so that the power relation (5.5) remains unaltered). It is merely necessary to note that this factor of four should be allowed for when matching diode

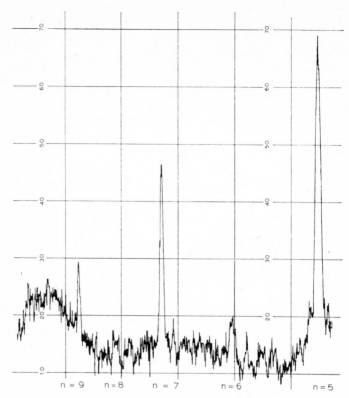

Fig. 5.19. Harmonics produced from a bombarded diode whose characteristic is shown in fig. 5.5, using a 35 Gc source of power approximately $\frac{1}{2}$W, and a reflection grating system with Golay detector. Even harmonics have almost completely disappeared (courtesy of K. D. Froome).

and waveguide impedances. In practice the size of the contact is adjusted by varying the contact pressure, and so matching takes place as part of the harmonic optimisation process.

It is easily shown from equation (5.16) that the maximum second harmonic power available from a diode of 3 V breakdown voltage matched to a waveguide of impedance 500 Ω is 1.6 mW, in quite good agreement with the experimental value of about 1 mW quoted earlier. The power available at higher harmonics is naturally much less, so that diode harmonic generators are inherently low power devices which can be expected to produce microwatts rather than milliwatts of short wavelength power. These diodes can be driven at powers up to twice those required for saturation before the damaging effects of thermal dissipation become noticeable (BAUER et al.

[1966]), but there is little point in doing so or in applying short pulses of even larger microwave powers, because in neither case is there more harmonic power available than predicted by equation (5.16).

A phenomenon that occurs in most harmonic generators is that of harmonic reinforcement, in which returning a low harmonic to the nonlinear element produces an increase in output at higher harmonics. Effectively this amounts to introducing terminations, or idler circuits, at more than one harmonic in the equivalent circuit of fig. 5.15b. The effect of this can be examined theoretically by evaluating the higher harmonic currents by means

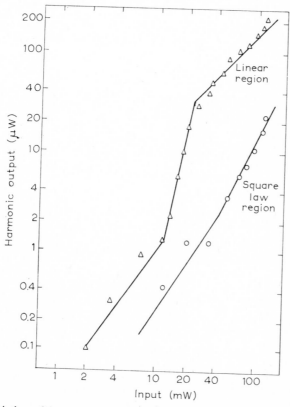

Fig. 5.20. Variation of harmonic power with fundamental power at fourth and fifth harmonics of 24 Gc. The straight lines drawn at the high power levels have slopes that correspond to exact linear and square law relationships between input and output powers. The fifth harmonic (o) was produced by inserting a filter section reflecting fourth harmonic (△) between harmonic generator and detector. (△ = no high pass filter, o = fourth harmonic reflected.)

of equation (5.6) when the nth harmonic current is not short circuited,

$$I'_{n+1} = I_{n+1} - \tfrac{1}{2}(G_1 + G_{2n+1})V_n. \tag{5.17}$$

As the expression in parentheses is positive for all values of the conduction angle ϕ, the best $(n+1)$th harmonic output is clearly obtained when the nth harmonic current is short circuited, by a lossless idler circuit, and not when power is being withdrawn at the nth harmonic. This explains the superiority of the series harmonic generator (fig. 5.15b) over the parallel configuration (fig. 5.15a), as in the former case all harmonics below cutoff are reactively short circuited by the harmonic waveguide, whereas in the latter such harmonic tuning as does occur must be carried out by means of filters beyond the diode itself, and it is rarely possible to short circuit several harmonics simultaneously. It is not necessarily true that the best harmonic output is obtained when *all* lower harmonics are short circuited; for example, the $(n+3)$th harmonic is optimised by open circuiting the nth harmonic when the conduction angle is close to $\tfrac{1}{2}\pi$. The best practical compromise is reached when the first few harmonics are short circuited by the structure of the harmonic generator and higher harmonics are terminated by means of microwave filters of the type described earlier in this section. The performance of such a filter used to improve the fifth harmonic output by suitably terminating the fourth is illustrated in figs. 5.20 and 5.21.

The results obtained can only be qualitatively explained by the preceding theory; for example the square law variation of fifth harmonic power is characteristic of a nonlinear process mixing the fourth harmonic and fundamental, and must be due to the near square law curvature of the diode characteristic, whilst the fall in impedance observed at the fundamental frequency is much greater than would be predicted from the preceding theory. However other workers have observed both harmonic reinforcement and a harmonic output proportional to some exponent of the fundamental power (OHL et al. [1959], COLEMAN and BECKER [1959], BAUER et al. [1966]) and it would appear generally true that high harmonics can be optimised by using filter sections to terminate lower ones, rather than absorbing them in the same detector. The use of a suitable idler termination can even produce harmonics that would otherwise be completely suppressed, as will be illustrated for varactor diodes in section 4.

2.2. Limitations of semiconductor harmonic generators

The ultimate limit to semiconductor harmonic generator performance is set by harmonic saturation, which depends on the back breakdown voltage.

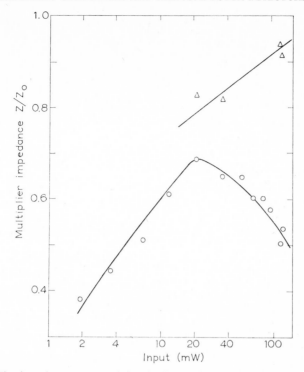

Fig. 5.21. The impedance presented by the harmonic generator to the fundamental waveguide (determined from the standing wave ratio within the latter) as harmonic terminations are varied, other parameters such as d.c. bias and harmonic waveguide tuning remaining unaltered. When the fourth harmonic ($\triangle$) is absorbed by a matched detector, the harmonic generator forms a good match; when the harmonic is reflected by means of a filter section (thus optimising the fifth harmonic) the impedance at the fundamental falls sharply, as would be expected if the fifth harmonic (o) were produced by beating fourth and fundamental.

Treated diodes with breakdown voltages up to 30 V have been produced (BURRUS [1964]), but their performance as submillimetre wavelength generators is inferior to those which break down at 5–6 V, at any rate when a fundamental power of 200 mW is used. It is possible that this is due to an increased curvature of the characteristic and that they would perform better with watts of drive, but the greater length of the junction and longer carrier transit times may also be responsible for this poorer performance. The prospect of even a tenfold increase in submillimetre wave power produced by these techniques seems quite remote.

An alternative method of reaching shorter wavelengths is to raise the fundamental frequency to 100 Gc or more. It was shown at the end of section

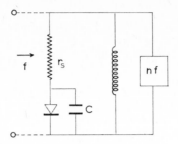

Fig. 5.22. The equivalent circuit of a harmonic generator, taking into account parasitic contact capacitance. The resonating inductance to tune this out is provided by a tuning stub in the mm waveguide, but perfect tuning is made impossible by the presence of the intervening diode spreading resistance.

1 that the diode capacitance does not appreciably affect its performance even at these high frequencies, but we must now consider the nature of the harmonic output circuit more carefully. When a harmonic is terminated by a load (i.e. a lossy idler circuit), the diode capacitance offers a shunt path to the harmonic current, with an equivalent circuit shown in fig. 5.22. Tuning the harmonic circuit is equivalent to inserting an inductive reactance across the load that resonates with the diode capacitance, but perfect tuning is not possible because of the intervening spreading resistance r_s. At the

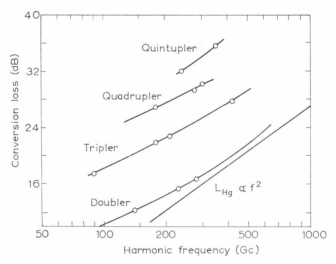

Fig. 5.23. Harmonic generation conversion loss at various frequencies for several harmonic orders (from BAUER et al. [1966]).

harmonic frequencies $\omega C r_s$ is already greater than unity, and circuit analysis shows that:

$$\frac{\text{Power dissipated in load}}{\text{Maximum power available}} = \frac{1}{1+(\omega C r_s)^2}. \qquad (5.18)$$

Because of the switching action of the fundamental power, the effective spreading resistance is really $1/b$ (e.g. (5.8)) rather than r_s. With this modification the parasitic losses of equation (5.18) have been earlier shown to play a significant part in the optimisation of harmonic generator performance. The experimental data of fig. 5.23 show a (frequency)^2 variation in good agreement with the equation, and lead to the conclusion that improved performance at submillimetre wavelengths calls for even smaller contact areas and diodes of higher cutoff frequency (table 5.2). Unfortunately such diodes can withstand only limited fundamental powers, and the shortest wavelengths to date have been obtained from strongly driven bombarded silicon diodes. Nevertheless fig. 5.23 shows that a 70 Gc fundamental can produce harmonics as efficiently as the 25 Gc source of fig. 5.18d.

Fundamental frequency	Highest harmonic observed	Highest harmonic calculated
32 Gc	18 GORDY [1960]	18 (assumed)
58 Gc	12 JONES and GORDY [1964]	14
140 Gc	4 BAUER et al. [1966]	10
280 Gc	2 BAUER et al. [1966]	8

By combining eqs. (5.12) and (5.18) it can be seen that the power available at any frequency f_n varies as f_1^4/f_n^6, where f_1 is the drive frequency, and so a doubling of the latter can only produce an increase of sixty per cent in the output frequency. As the table shows, the trend of the experimental results is far less favourable than this, possibly because of the difficulty of making loss free components at such short wavelengths. It should be emphasised that the tabulated results refer to frequencies that have been propagated from a harmonic generator to a detector and are therefore useful for spectroscopy. Much higher frequencies can appear within the harmonic generating diode itself, and experimental observations of harmonic mixing at 1800 Gc (0.17 mm wavelength) have recently been made (WOODS and STRAUCH [1966]), but devices of this kind fall more properly into the realm of submillimetre detectors rather than harmonic generators.

On the basis of the above results, it seems unlikely that semiconductor harmonic generators will ever produce 0.1 mm wavelength power, but their present usefulness as short millimetre wavelength sources should rapidly extend into the 0.25–1 mm range as suitable driving sources become more generally available.

2.3. SPECTROSCOPY WITH HARMONIC GENERATORS

Of the many fields in which spectroscopy at low millimetre and submillimetre wavelengths is and will be important (see ch. 1), crystal harmonic generators have up to now been used in studies of molecular rotation spectra, electron spin resonance, antiferromagnetic resonance, cyclotron resonance, plasma and atmospheric investigations. With the exception of the last two, which appear in section 3, this work will be reviewed here in order to illustrate the particular experimental methods employed.

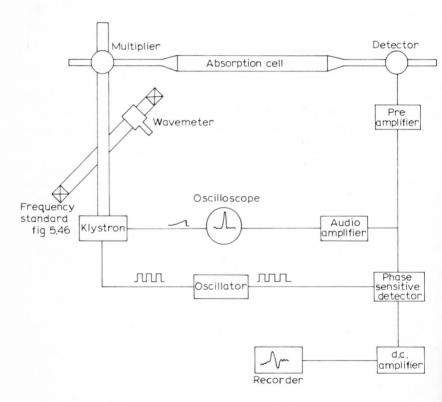

Fig. 5.24. Block diagram of a gaseous absorption spectrometer as used at millimetre wavelengths.

2.3.1. *Molecular rotation spectra*

Figure 5.24 is a block diagram of a typical millimetre wavelength gas spectrometer.

The absorption cell is a section of centimetre waveguide between 50 cm and 2 m long, linked to harmonic generator and detector by taper sections. Mica or Terylene windows seal it at each end so that working pressures in the 10–100 micron region may be used. A search for a spectral absorption is carried out by sweeping the frequency of the klystron fundamental source electronically, and feeding the detector output through an audio amplifier back to an oscilloscope which derives its time base from the klystron sweep, lines then appear as sharp "blips" on the oscilloscope trace. The audio amplifier generally has a passband of the order of 10 kc in order that it should be able to record narrow lines. The sensitivity of this system is limited by amplifier and detector noise, which varies inversely as the square root of the passband (cf. section 3). It could be reduced a hundred times, say, by using a 1 cps passband, but the penalty that must be paid is that lines would be distorted and reduced in height if they were crossed in a time of less than a few seconds, and it is no easy matter to maintain a stable output from the detector and amplifier over this period.

If noise is a problem, a better method of gaining the advantages of a narrow passband is to switch the klystron frequency rapidly back and forth between two values and to amplify the detector output at the switching frequency before passing it through a "phase-sensitive" detector (also known as a "lock-in", or "homodyne" detector). The latter is a circuit that compares the amplified signal from the crystal detector with the output of the switching oscillator and rejects it unless the two remain phase-coherent for an appropriately long period, e.g. about 1 second to give an effective passband of 1 cps. The klystron frequency is changed slowly by mechanical means and the phase-coherent output is fed to a recorder which traces out any spectral lines as their frequency is crossed by the klystron source (fig. 5.12). The lines appear as their first derivatives when this technique is used, and so tend to lie on a severely fluctuating baseline that corresponds to the first derivative of the power versus frequency output characteristic from the harmonic generator. Some improvement at the cost of sensitivity may be obtained by amplifying and "phase detecting" at twice the switching frequency, which displays lines as their second derivatives, a form that resembles the original line shape and makes measurement of line positions more reliable. The more sophisticated techniques of Stark modulation (TOWNES and SCHAWLOW [1955]) used at lower frequencies are rarely used at millimetre wavelengths because the spectra observed are generally rather insensitive to external electric fields and because the special absorption cells required have a high attenuation at these wavelengths (a cell design that may solve the latter difficulty has recently been described by LIDE [1964]).

Gases with absorption lines classified as medium to strong at centimetre wavelengths give very strong absorptions indeed in the low millimetre and submillimetre wavelengths. For example, the gas carbon oxysulphide (OCS), which is widely used as a microwave absorption standard, shows rotational absorption lines at every harmonic of 12163 Mc, or 24.6 mm wavelength. The following table shows how far microwave radiation of various wavelengths falling at the peaks of these absorption lines can travel through the gas at 10–100 micron pressure before its power is attenuated to 1/e, or 37%, of its initial value.

Wavelength	Path length for 37% attenuation
12.3 mm	200 m
3.075 mm	3 m
0.77 mm	5 cm

This feature assists greatly in the setting up of harmonic generators because an absorption line in this substance at any harmonic will be clearly revealed so long as the harmonic power is detectable; this use was discussed earlier in this section and illustrated in fig. 5.12. The reason why a spectral line falls close to every harmonic of the fundamental used is to be found in the quantum mechanics of rotating molecules. The allowed rotational energies of a linear molecule like OCS are:

$$E_J = \frac{h^2}{8\pi^2 I} J(J+1) \tag{5.19}$$

and transitions are governed by the selection rule $J \rightarrow J+1$, where J is an integral quantum number representing the rotational angular momentum and I is the moment of inertia of the molecule about its centre of gravity. It follows that a ladder of transitions exist at frequencies given by:

$$f = \frac{h}{4\pi^2 I}(J+1) = 2B(J+1) \tag{5.20}$$

where $J = 0, 1, 2\ldots$ and, in the particular case of OCS, $2B = 12162.96$ Mc. If the klystron fundamental is set at frequency $2B$, or any multiple of this, a transition will thus appear at every harmonic of this fundamental frequency.

Equations (5.19) and (5.20) neglect the effect of centrifugal stretching as the molecule rotates; when this is taken into account the transition frequencies become:

$$f = 2B(J+1) - 4D(J+1)^3, \tag{5.21}$$

where D is a constant very much smaller than the rotational constant B. When the total output from a harmonic generator is passed through OCS gas the transitions do not occur all at exactly the same frequency setting of the fundamental. They are displaced by an amount proportional to the square of the harmonic number, n, in terms of the fundamental frequency setting, as implied in (5.21). The appearance in fig. 5.12 of *six* clearly spaced spectral lines (fourth to ninth harmonic) as the fundamental frequency varies by 3.5 Mc is a vivid demonstration of the extremely high resolution possible in gas spectroscopy. A similar example is the tracing of fig. 5.25, in which

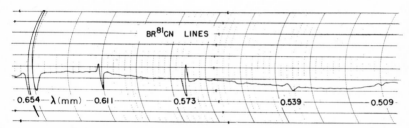

Fig. 5.25. Spectrum of five rotational transitions in gaseous BrCN, at the fourteenth to eighteenth harmonic of a 9 mm wavelength klystron. The separation between the extreme lines in this spectrum is only 2.2 Mc at the fundamental frequency, and is caused by centrifugal stretching of the molecule (from GORDY [1960]).

the spectrum of BrCN is displayed with a klystron fundamental near 9 mm wavelength (in this case, $8B$). The harmonics from the fourteenth to the eighteenth are responsible for the five lines.

Measurements of such spectra yield extremely accurate data for molecular rotational and distortion constants. In some cases even more information is available; fig. 5.26 shows the $J = 0 \rightarrow 1$ transition of gaseous HCl at 0.48 mm wavelength to consist not of one but of three lines (JONES and GORDY [1964]). The splittings between them are caused by interactions of the electric quadrupole moments of the Cl nuclei with the electrons within the molecule, and may be interpreted to yield information on the spatial distribution and densities of the latter.

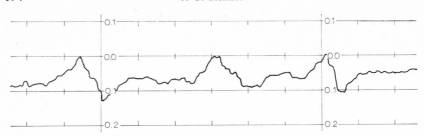

Fig. 5.26. Recorder tracing of the three hyperfine components of the $J = 0 \rightarrow 1$ rotational transition of HCl^{35} at 0.48 mm wavelength. The two outside components are separated by approximately 35 Mc (from JONES and GORDY [1964]).

Still further, the *frequency* of the above transition has been measured to an accuracy of 10^{-6}, and, when combined with precision determinations of the *wavelength* of transitions of higher J in the near infra-red, leads to a determination of the velocity of light. The result obtained, $c = 299792.8 \pm 0.4$ km/sec, is comparable in accuracy with the best previous determinations, and shows how submillimetre wave measurements can act as a bridge between precision radio frequency and near infra-red standards. The same publication lists an absorption line of CO at 0.43 mm, the shortest wavelength measurement made up to the present with a crystal harmonic generator.

For larger, nonlinear molecules, transition intensities do not rise so rapidly with frequency, and enough power for spectroscopy is generally available only out to 1 mm wavelength. Rotational assignments for most molecules with undetermined parameters can be made in the conventional 6 mm–3 cm band, but in a fair number of cases millimetre wavelength studies can give information not available at longer wavelengths. Some asymmetric molecules, notably bent linear chains, show spectra that are almost independent of one of the rotational constants until high J values are reached at millimetre wavelengths; hydrazoic acid, HN_3, is one example (KEWLEY et al. [1964]). Even the very much heavier molecule, chloroform, has been usefully studied at short millimetre wavelengths (FAVERO and MIRRI [1963]). At low frequencies, its spectrum is difficult to measure and analyse because the quadrupole structure due to the Cl nuclei is not well resolved, and the lines are extremely broad. At high J values the quadrupole structure disappears, leaving narrow lines which permit the precise measurement of rotational and distortion constants. A further example of a molecular spectrum that could be only partly identified at centimetre wavelengths is that of methyl alcohol. This gives a profuse spectrum at all wavelengths which is caused by a combination of molecular asymmetry, a relative twisting of methyl and

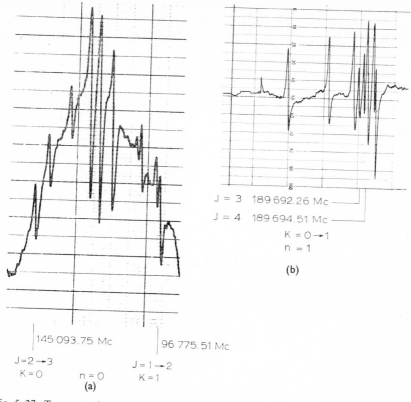

$J = 3$ 189 692.26 Mc

$J = 4$ 189 694.51 Mc

$K = 0 \rightarrow 1$

$n = 1$

(b)

145 093.75 Mc   96 775.51 Mc

$J = 2 \rightarrow 3$ $J = 1 \rightarrow 2$

$K = 0$ $n = 0$ $K = 1$

(a)

Fig. 5.27. Two recorder tracings of millimetre wavelength lines of methyl alcohol (a) superimposed groups of transitions at fourth harmonic ($J1 \rightarrow 2$) and sixth harmonic ($J2 \rightarrow 3$) of 24 Gc, (b) a group of Q branch transitions ($J \rightarrow J$), involving relative torsion of the methyl and hydroxyl groups, at the fifth harmonic of 38 Gc. The complex structure of the spectra is caused by the combined effects of molecular asymmetry and internal torsion.

hydroxyl groups during rotation, and centrifugal distortion, but only a few lines have so far been assigned and fitted (IVASH and DENNISON [1953]) to the molecular parameters. Measurements at millimetre wavelengths (BAKER and LEES [1966]) such as those shown in fig. 5.27 have resulted in the assignment of many more lines and a clarification of the complex effects of internal torsion and centrifugal stretching in this molecule.

A most promising line of research that is just commencing is the study of free radicals, molecules in excited states and molecular beams at short wavelengths (DEES and SHEPPARD [1963], STRAUCH et al. [1964]). The importance of such studies lies in the detailed information they can contribute

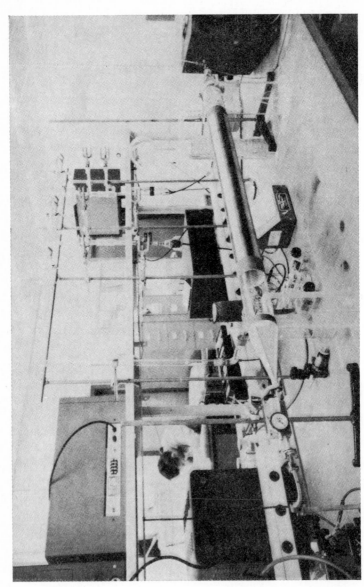

Fig. 5.28. Photograph of a millimetre-wave free-radical spectrometer (courtesy of J. J. Gallagher).

about the electronic structure of molecules. Millimetre wavelengths are especially suited and sometimes essential to this kind of work. The stronger absorptions allow shorter absorbing paths and more rapidly responding detection systems to be used; metal waveguide cells which quickly decompose unstable radicals may be replaced by glass systems through which the millimetre waves are focussed by horns and PTFE lenses (fig. 5.28). Alternatively a Fabry-Perot interferometer which confines the active substance in a small volume whilst having a very much longer effective travel path for the millimetre waves may be used (STRAUCH et al. [1964]).

Unstable radicals can be generated directly by a high power radio frequency discharge (KEWLEY et al. [1963]) or through the initial production of atoms which then undergo further chemical reaction (POWELL and LIDE [1964]). Figure 5.29a shows two lines at different harmonics in the spectrum

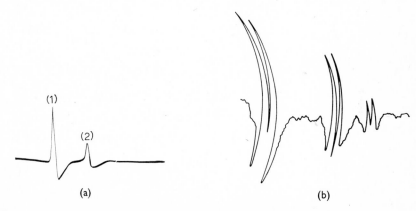

(a)   (b)

Fig. 5.29. Spectra of unstable molecules and free radicals: (a) Two transitions of the rather unstable molecular fragment CS (from KEWLEY et al. [1963]). (1) $J = 1 \rightarrow 2$ transition at 97981.007 Mc using the 3rd harmonic of klystron fundamental frequency; (2) $J = 3 \rightarrow 4$ transition at 195954.16 Mc using the 6th harmonic of klystron fundamental frequency. Spacing between the two lines is due to centrifugal distortion terms. (b) The $J = \frac{3}{2} \rightarrow \frac{5}{2}$ transition at 250 Gc of the stable radical NO in an electronically excited state. The doublets are caused by interaction between electronic and molecular rotation; the splitting into three groups by magnetic interactions involving the nitrogen nuclear spin (from FAVERO et al. [1959]).

of the radical CS, produced by the former method, whilst fig. 5.29b shows the 1.2 mm wavelength spectrum of the first excited electronic state of the stable radical NO. In the latter case the lines are all hyperfine components of the same transition, the large scale splittings being due to the nuclear spins of the nitrogen atoms and the doublet separations to the electron spin of

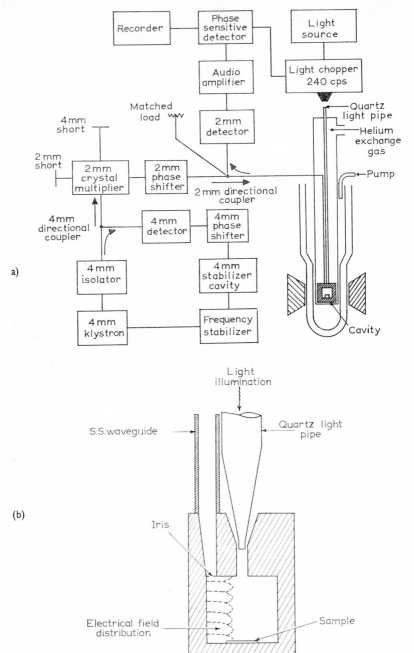

Fig. 5.30. Spectrometer used to observe cyclotron resonance in semiconductors at 2 mm wavelength and liquid helium temperature (from STICKLER et al. [1962]). (a) Block diagram of 2 mm cavity spectrometer, (b) Details of TM_{016} spectrometer sample cavity.

the radical. A feature of the NO spectrum common to many linear radicals is that it can be observed only at millimetre wavelengths, because the presence of electronic angular momentum sets a lower limit to the value that J, representing the total angular momentum, can take. As a result the ladder of transitions described by eq. (5.21) does not extend to a frequency as low as $2B$ as it would for a normal molecule.

The brief summary given here shows how far millimetre wavelengths have already been exploited by gas spectroscopists, even with the limited powers available. As these powers improve, the technique will be used increasingly to throw light on many of the features of molecular bonding that are at present still obscure.

2.3.2. Cyclotron, magnetic and antiferromagnetic resonance

The block diagram of fig. 5.30 shows a cavity spectrometer for the study of solids at 2 mm wavelength and low temperatures. This particular spectrometer was designed for the study of cyclotron resonance (STICKLER et al. [1962]).

The 4 mm source is locked in frequency to a reference cavity by standard techniques (INGRAM [1955]) and the harmonics at 2 mm are reflected from a cavity immersed in liquid helium and returned through a directional coupler to a 2 mm detector. Varying the magnetic field on a sample inside the latter cavity will result in successive resonant absorptions by the electrons and holes within it, with a consequent change in power reflected to the 2 mm detector. As in the previous section, high sensitivity is obtained by phase-sensitive detection of the reflected signal which, in this particular case, is modulated by varying the carrier concentration within the sample by shining light on it, and interrupting the light at 240 cps. The cavity itself is made oversize, because of fabrication difficulties, and the microwave electric field goes through zero six times along its length. This does result in a lower oscillating field at the sample for a given incident 2 mm power, but the absorptions are sufficiently intense to overcome this loss.

Cyclotron resonance is the excitation of the helical motion of an electron or other current carrier in a steady magnetic field about the field direction. The characteristic frequency of this motion is given by

$$f = \frac{qH}{2\pi m^* c} \tag{5.22}$$

where q and m^* are respectively the charge and effective mass of the carrier, H is the magnetic field and c the velocity of light. As $q/2\pi mc$ has the value

1.4 Mc per gauss for a free electron, it would seem that a field of 100 kG would be required to produce resonant absorption at 2 mm wavelength. But current carriers in semiconductors often behave as if they had very small effective masses m^*, related to the shapes of the energy bands, and the field for resonance may therefore be 5–50 times smaller, values easily obtained in any laboratory. The advantage of using such short wavelengths for cyclotron resonance is that, even at liquid helium temperature, the lifetime of a carrier between collisions is of the order of 10^{-10} seconds. Unless it travels round its cyclotron orbit in less time than this the oscillating dipole that it produces is interrupted randomly by collisions, and the resonance is excessively damped, and perhaps unobservable. The higher the cyclotron frequency the better, therefore, and measurements have been limited to 2 mm wavelength only because power of the order of a milliwatt is required. The detail which can be observed at 2 mm is shown in the cyclotron resonance spectra of silicon and germanium in fig. 5.31. Clear lines are seen for electrons in the conduction band and many weaker ones for holes in the valence band, and

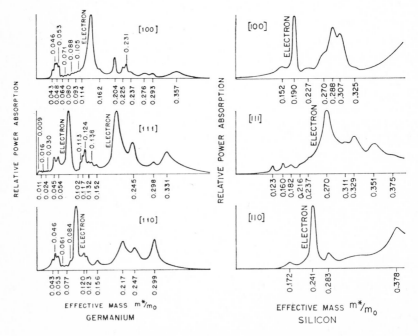

Fig. 5.31. Cyclotron resonance spectra in crystalline semiconductors, displayed by varying the d.c. magnetic field. This field is expressed in terms of an effective mass by eq. (5.22) from STICKLER et al. [1962].

the broadening and less of detail due to carrier collisions is evident in the silicon spectrum. There are many more lines present than can be accounted for on the simple classical picture leading to eq. (5.22), and the interpretation of the quantum effects producing them provides a great deal of information about the electronic structure of these materials. A convenient feature of studies of this kind is the presentation of spectra by varying the magnetic field rather than the frequency, a practice common in all types of magnetic resonance.

Very little conventional electron spin resonance has been carried out at millimetre wavelengths because of the high magnetic fields required. The condition for resonant absorption becomes:

$$f = g \frac{qH}{2\pi mc} \tag{5.23}$$

where g, the gyromagnetic ratio of the ion or radical involved, is normally close to the value 2. A field of the order of 50 kG is therefore required at 2 mm wavelength, and although this value is now attainable it is hardly convenient even with a superconducting magnet. Further, the transitions are induced by the microwave magnetic field, rather than by the electric field as in cyclotron resonance, and are some 10^4 to 10^5 times weaker, so that considerably more power is required to observe the spectra. On the whole millimetre wave work has up to now been limited to substances with "zero field splitting" such as ruby (MOCK [1960]), in which the applied magnetic field is used to supplement an internal crystal field effect, and to antiferromagnetic resonance in such substances as MnO and MnF_2, where the lining up of adjacent spins antiparallel to each other results from exchange interactions *equivalent* to a built-in magnetic field of the order of 100 kG (JOHNSON and NETHERCOT [1959]). The techniques used are essentially those described for cyclotron resonance, differing only in details of cavity structure and in detection methods, and the results obtained can be related to the nature of the crystalline field and exchange forces in such lattices.

3. Semiconductor detectors

The asymmetric conduction characteristic of a metal-to-semiconductor contact fits it not only for harmonic generation but also for the conversion of millimetre wave signals to direct current and for the mixing of two such signals of different frequencies. The first use is known as *video* detection;

the rectified current through the diode produced by the incident radiation is amplified by a video frequency system with a bandwith ranging from kc to Mc, depending on the speed of response required. A greater sensitivity is obtained with the second mode of use, known as *superheterodyne* detection, in which the diode mixes the low power signal with the output of a high power local oscillator working at a frequency close to that of the signal. The resulting diode current fluctuates at a frequency equal to the difference between signal and local oscillator frequencies, and this intermediate frequency current is amplified by a radio frequency amplifier. The two modes of use involve rather different principles and techniques, and will therefore be given separate treatment here.

3.1. VIDEO DETECTION

Millimetre wave detectors naturally bear a close resemblance to the harmonic generators of section 2, the principal difference lying in the absence of the fundamental frequency waveguide and a corresponding shortening of the metal whisker across the millimetre waveguide shown in figs. 5.8–5.10. The semiconductor materials used are however rather different; p-type silicon, n-type germanium and p-type gallium arsenide have all been used, but of these high conductivity aluminium or boron doped silicon has given the best results at submillimetre wavelengths, and the practical discussion to follow will be confined to this material.

The initial procedures of electropolishing and pointing a tungsten wire and setting up a contact for a detector are exactly the same as those for a harmonic generator. However in this case only very light contact pressures, corresponding to 0.1–0.5 g force, are used, because the contact area must be kept down to a minimum for good millimetre wave performance. After the first contact, the semiconductor crystal is rotated so that the pointed metal whisker scrapes over it and produces brief bursts of rectified output from the incident radiation. The magnitude of these bursts gives some indication of the best performance to be expected, and they should be followed up by a slight increase of pressure and more rotation until a stable output is obtained. Usually a slow withdrawal of the crystal after this process, without further rotation, will result in a series of near-optimum contacts that are reproducible but depend critically on the contact pressure. The whole process is very much more tedious and time consuming than setting up a harmonic generator, and experience is the only guide as to when the point of diminishing returns is reached. It must be admitted that the most serious hazard to a good contact is the experimenter who is trying to obtain a better one.

Good contacts are very susceptible to mechanical shock, unlike those of harmonic generators, and it is rare for them to survive overnight. However they can be remade by a slight alteration in contact pressure without further adjustment and in this sense are stable for weeks. Even when the whisker must be removed for further electrolytic pointing, it is usually possible to remake the contact as satisfactorily as ever. Best results for longer wavelengths are obtained when the crimp in the whisker almost enters the detector waveguide, but for wavelengths much shorter than cutoff the wire length should be optimised experimentally. One irritating feature of a good contact is that its output tends to drift down to about two thirds of the value when first made over the course of some minutes, and that during this period the

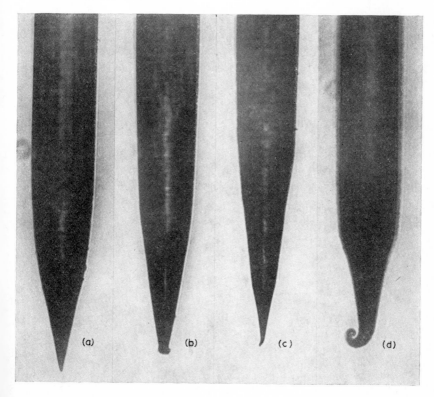

Fig. 5.32. Photomicrographs of a 0.05 mm diameter tungsten whisker used in millimetre wave detectors: (a) before contact; (b) after a successful contact has been made; (c) after excessive pressure has been applied to a delicate point; (d) when a contact has been completely lost.

amplitude flickers noticeably at the rate of a few cps. Contacts which show exceptional instability of this kind may be improved by "tapping", a sharp blow to the crystal mount parallel to the whisker. This invariably leads to a loss of output, but a change in contact pressure then results in a contact more stable than before. As a guide to sound operation, fig. 5.32 shows the appearance of a detector whisker at several stages during the life of a contact.

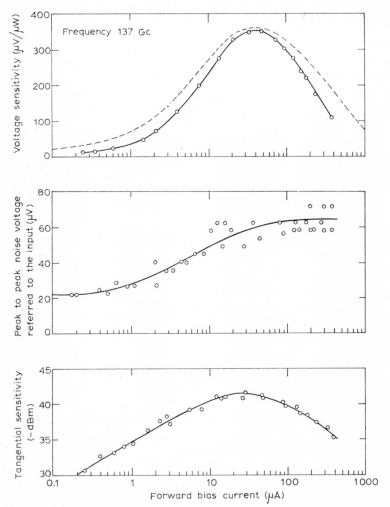

Fig. 5.33. Experimental curves for a commercial germanium detector at 2 mm wavelength. Tangential sensitivity is defined on page 216. The dotted curve represents the theoretical sensitivity assuming a zero bias capacitance of 0.023 pF (from MEREDITH and WARNER [1963]).

Diodes of n-type germanium (contacting a whisker of titanium) produce more stable contacts, but only because they are initially "formed" by the passage of a brief but heavy surge of current. Although they can be used as current sources without external bias, they must be forward biased to produce the best voltage output (fig. 5.33). These features are a considerable handicap in a search for a good millimetre wave contact, and use of such diodes has so far been confined to wavelengths at which ample power is available. N-type gallium arsenide should form an excellent detector material according to the reasoning of the theoretical discussion to follow, despite the fact that it suffers from the same practical disadvantages as germanium. In practice contacts made between phosphor bronze and gallium arsenide perform well

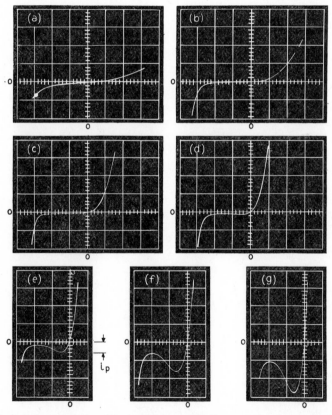

Fig. 5.34. $I-V$ characteristics of typical backward diodes made by electrically "forming" a gallium point contact on n-type germanium. (a) Initial contact, no intentional forming. (b)–(c) a.c. forming. (d)–(g) Pulse forming. Scale: 0.2 V/cm horizontal, 0.2 mA/cm vertical (from BURRUS [1963]).

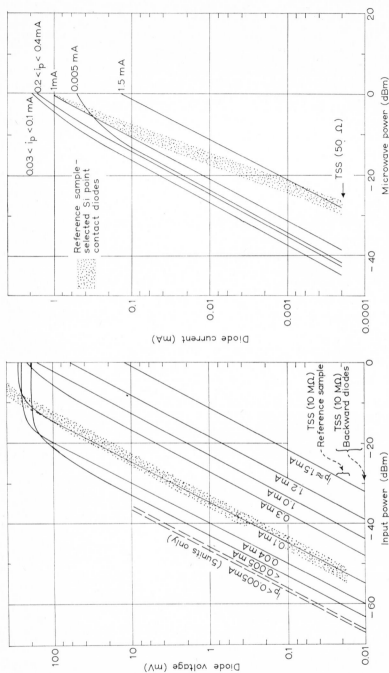

Fig. 5.35. The d.c. voltage and the d.c. current for backward diodes as functions of input microwave power at 55 Gc. (Diode loads 10 MΩ and 50 Ω respectively; bandwidth 40 kc.) From BURRUS [1963].

at first, but deteriorate very rapidly (BURRUS [1966]), presumably because of atmospheric attack, and success has been obtained up to the present with sealed units operating at wavelengths above 1 mm (BAUER et al. [1966]).

Considerable work on backward diodes of n-type germanium has been carried out by BURRUS [1963]. Some d.c. characteristics are shown in fig. 5.34, whilst the millimetre wave performance of representative diodes is illustrated in fig. 5.35. The best diodes have characteristics resembling those of tunnel diodes, but with rather small peak currents (i_p), corresponding to small contact areas. Some work has also been carried out with true tunnel diodes (CHASE and CHANG [1963]), but the results do not justify the extra complexity of the biasing circuits required. Backward diodes prove to be competitive with the best silicon diodes at wavelengths longer than 1.5 mm, and indeed are superior as current rather than voltage detectors, but no substitute has yet been found for silicon at submillimetre wavelengths.

3.2. THEORY OF VIDEO DETECTION

An equivalent circuit for a metal to semiconductor contact is reproduced in fig. 5.36. The asymmetrical diode characteristic is represented by a voltage dependent resistance R, shunted by a voltage independent contact capacitance C.

This capacitance and the spreading resistance r_s together form a potential dividing network that reduces the applied millimetre wavelength voltage V_1 to a smaller value V_b across the diode barrier layer itself. As the frequency increases a progressively larger voltage must be applied to the detector

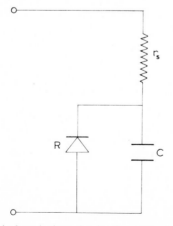

Fig. 5.36. Electrical equivalent circuit of a millimetre wave detector.

in order to maintain the same output because of this network. At any one angular frequency ω the whole equivalent circuit presents an impedance:

$$Z = r_s + 1/(1/R + j\omega C) = \frac{1 + r_s/R + j\omega C}{1/R + j\omega C}. \qquad (5.24)$$

The imaginary part of Z is tuned out by means of a short circuiting stub in the wave guide beyond the detector; the real part should be matched to the waveguide impedance Z_0 to ensure complete absorption of the incident millimetre wave power. The absorbed power is given by:

$$P = \tfrac{1}{2}V_1^2 \left(\text{real part of } \frac{1}{Z}\right) = \frac{V_1^2}{2r_s}\frac{(r_s/R)(1 + r_s/R) + (\omega C r_s)^2}{(1 + r_s/R)^2 + (\omega C r_s)^2}. \qquad (5.25)$$

The quantity $\omega C r_s$ plays an important role in detector performance, both in matching it to the incident power and in determining its sensitivity; it will be shown later to be purely a function of the detector material and contact area. However its value is not too critical, for over half of the incident power is absorbed so long as the real part of Z lies between one fifth and five times the waveguide impedance Z_0.

The barrier voltage produced by the microwave voltage V_1 is:

$$\frac{V_b^2}{V_1^2} = \frac{1}{(1 + r_s/R)^2 + (\omega C r_s)^2}. \qquad (5.26)$$

Combining relations (5.25) and (5.26) leads to:

$$\frac{V_b^2}{P} = \frac{2r_s}{(r_s/R)(1 + r_s/R) + (\omega C r_s)^2}. \qquad (5.27)$$

The performance of a detector depends on the relative magnitudes of the two terms in the denominator of (5.27) and will be considered after an expression for the low frequency sensitivity has been obtained. The current flowing into a short circuit that is produced by the rectification of the barrier voltage may be found by expanding the diode characteristic in a Taylor series about the origin,

$$i = i_0 + v\left(\frac{\mathrm{d}i}{\mathrm{d}v}\right)_0 + \tfrac{1}{2}v^2\left(\frac{\mathrm{d}^2 i}{\mathrm{d}v^2}\right)_0 + \dots.$$

When this is averaged over a microwave cycle, the first and all odd terms disappear, and even terms depend on the average value of the appropriate power of $\cos\theta$,

$$I_{\text{d.c.}} = \tfrac{1}{4}V_b^2\left(\frac{\mathrm{d}i^2}{\mathrm{d}v^2}\right)_0 + \tfrac{1}{64}V_b^4\left(\frac{\mathrm{d}^4 i}{\mathrm{d}v^4}\right)_0 + \dots. \qquad (5.28)$$

This expression may be put in closed form in terms of hyperbolic Bessel functions (Handbook of Chemistry and Physics) if the diode characteristic is assumed to follow the form (5.2) as derived in section 1,

$$I = I_0 (e^{\alpha V} - 1). \tag{5.2}$$

Then, as $(d^n I/dV^n)_0 = \alpha^n I_0$, expression (5.28) becomes:

$$I_{d.c.}/I_0 = H_0(\alpha V_b) - 1$$

$$I_{d.c.}/I_0 = \tfrac{1}{4}(\alpha V_b)^2 + \tfrac{1}{64}(\alpha V_b)^4 + \ldots \tag{5.29}$$

where H_0 is the hyperbolic Bessel function of zero order. Two kinds of resistance can be defined for the diode; the first, R, is the average barrier resistance presented to the microwaves, and the second, $R_{d.c.}$, that presented at the output terminals. These are given by:

$$\frac{1}{R} = \alpha I_0 [1 + \tfrac{1}{8}(\alpha V_b)^2 + \ldots] = 2\alpha I_0 \frac{H_1(\alpha V_b)}{\alpha V_b}, \tag{5.30}$$

$$\frac{1}{R_{d.c.}} = \alpha I_0 [1 + \tfrac{1}{4}(\alpha V_b)^2 + \ldots] = \alpha(I_{d.c.} + I_0). \tag{5.31}$$

These zero-bias parameters can readily be converted to the corresponding ones at an external bias current I by replacing the quantity I_0 by $(I+I_0)$ wherever it appears – thus the current sensitivity of a diode rises and its resistance falls with increasing forward bias.

An alternative measure of detector sensitivity is the open circuit voltage V_0 appearing across the diode when direct current is not permitted to flow; it is given by an equation analagous to (5.2),

$$I_{d.c.} = I_0(e^{\alpha V_0} - 1).$$

Thus

$$V_0 = \frac{1}{\alpha} \ln (1 + I_{d.c.}/I_0) = \frac{1}{\alpha} \ln H_0(\alpha V_b) = \tfrac{1}{4}\alpha V_b{}^2 - \tfrac{1}{64}\alpha^3 V_b^4 + \ldots. \tag{5.32}$$

As V_b^2 is proportional to the incident power (eq. (5.27)) it is clear that the sensitivities given by (5.29) and (5.32) are proportional to the power only at low levels, when αV_b is less than unity. This corresponds to a few microwatts, from the discussion of section 2. The exact behaviour of the functions derived above is shown graphically in fig. 5.37, from which it appears that proportionality of the open circuit voltage is maintained at quite large values of αV_b, but that the short circuit current deviates very markedly from this approximation once αV_b exceeds unity. The experimental curves for silicon diodes in fig. 5.35 confirm the conclusions reached here,

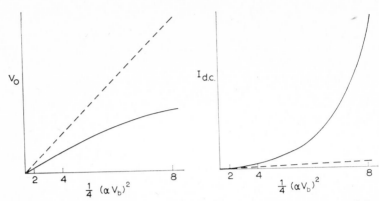

Fig. 5.37. The rectified voltage (V_0) and current ($I_{d.c.}$) produced by an ideal detector, plotted as a function of the microwave voltage (αV_b). The dotted lines represent extrapolations of the sensitivity at very low power levels.

and demonstrate the unsoundness of the common misconception that the short circuit current in microwave diodes varies linearly with power up to milliwatt power levels.

The effect of contact capacitance on the open circuit voltage sensitivity V_0/P may be introduced by using eq. (5.27):

$$\frac{V_0}{P} = \frac{\frac{1}{4}\alpha V_b^2}{P} = \frac{1}{2}\alpha \frac{r_s}{(r_s/R)(1+r_s/R)+(\omega C r_s)^2}. \tag{5.33}$$

In this configuration R will take on a value of the order of a megohm, whilst r_s is a few ohms. Thus the condition $r_s/R < (\omega C r_s)^2$ will hold, and (5.33) may be approximated as:

$$\frac{V_0}{P} = \frac{1}{2}\alpha \frac{r_s}{(\omega C r_s)^2}. \tag{5.34}$$

The condition for microwave matching (eq. (5.25)) may be approximated in the same way as

$$Z_0 = r_s(1+1/(\omega C r_s)^2). \tag{5.35}$$

Thus

$$\frac{V_0}{P} = \frac{1}{2}\alpha(Z_0 - r_s) \sim \frac{1}{2}\alpha Z_0. \tag{5.36}$$

Although we have reason to believe from the behaviour of harmonic generators (sec. 2) that the relation $V_b^2 = 2ZP$ does not hold, this does not affect the preceding argument. As in that case, an ideal matching transformer may be inserted to alter V_b and Z in such a way that the above relation is maintained, whilst a variation of this kind leaves (5.36) unaltered. It follows that for a detector matched to 500 Ω waveguide and for which $\alpha = 20 \text{ V}^{-1}$, the sensitivity will be 2.5 V/mW. An extra factor of one half has been inserted here to take account of the discrepancy between the initial and the mean slope of the voltage sensitivity curve of fig. 5.37. This result is in good agreement with the experimental figures for silicon diodes shown in fig. 5.35. It also follows from (5.34) and (5.35) that a diode made from any given semiconductor material can be matched by a suitable choice of contact-dimension, and that unless this dimension is reduced as the frequency increases the response will fall off as the square of the frequency. The smaller the quantity $\omega C r_s$ can be made, the better the performance at high frequencies; this quantity is tabulated for various semiconductors in table 5.1. Although silicon appears the least suitable detector material on this criterion, it turns out in practice to produce extremely small contacts that function well at submillimetre wavelengths, even though the lack of "forming" leads to very poor mechanical stability.

The use of diodes as voltage generators is not practicable when a rapid response to microwave pulses is called for, because the effect of a high output resistance and stray capacitance is to limit the response time to tens of microseconds or longer. Instead the output resistance is deliberately lowered by the application of forward bias, and a current amplifier is used to amplify the output pulses. Germanium (MEREDITH and WARNER [1963]) and gallium arsenide (BAUER et al. [1966]) have proved to be the best detectors under these conditions, probably because they show a smaller increase of storage capacitance with forward bias than silicon, with its long minority carrier lifetime. However aluminium-doped silicon is also satisfactory (SHURMER [1964a]), and only boron-doped silicon shows so little improvement in sensitivity with forward bias that it has been used mainly as a voltage detector.

Assuming a linear relation between detector current and incident power, the current sensitivity with forward bias is given by combining equations (5.27), (5.28) and (5.29):

$$\frac{I_{\text{d.c.}}}{P} = \tfrac{1}{2}\alpha \frac{r_s/R_{\text{d.c.}}}{(r_s/R)(1 + r_s/R) + (\omega C r_s)^2}. \tag{5.37}$$

The quantity r_s/R is no longer so small as when the same diode is used as a voltage detector, but it is still of the order of 0.01–0.1, and may usually be neglected. The current sensitivity then becomes:

TABLE 5.1
Properties of semiconductor materials

	p-type silicon	n-type germanium	n-type gallium arsenide	n-type germanium backward diode
Carrier density, N	2×10^{19} per cm³	2×10^{18} per cm³	7×10^{17} per cm³	7×10^{19} per cm³
Carrier mobility, b	70 cm²/V sec	800 cm²/V sec	3750 cm²/V sec	160 cm²/V sec
Resistivity, $\varrho = 1/Nqb$	0.005 Ω cm	0.004 Ω cm	0.0024 Ω cm	0.00056 Ω cm
Dielectric constant, ε	12	16	11	16
Barrier height, ϕ	0.3 V	0.45 V	0.8 V	0.45 V
Barrier capacitance, $C = \dfrac{\frac{1}{4}\pi d^2 (\varepsilon \varepsilon_0 Nq)^{\frac{1}{2}}}{2\phi}$	0.187 pF	0.056 pF	0.020 pF	0.329 pF
Spreading resistance, $r_s = \varrho/2d$	25 Ω	20 Ω	12 Ω	2.8 Ω
Cutoff frequency, $f_c = 1/2\pi C r_s$	34 Gc	142 Gc	663 Gc	173 Gc

$q\ $ = electronic charge, 1.6×10^{-19} coulomb
ε_0 = $(1/36\pi) \times 10^9$
$d\ $ = contact diameter, 10^{-4} cm

$$\frac{I_{\text{d.c.}}}{P} = \tfrac{1}{2}\alpha\, \frac{r_s/R_{\text{d.c.}}}{(\omega C r_s)^2}. \tag{5.38}$$

The use of $R_{\text{d.c.}}$ in eqs. (5.37) and (5.38) considerably extends their range of validity, as the product $I_{\text{d.c.}}R_{\text{d.c.}}$ remains proportional to the incident power over a much wider range than either term alone. This is of course equivalent to saying that the output voltage varies linearly with power over a wider range than does the current, as has already been shown. MEREDITH and WARNER [1963] have analysed the 2 mm wavelength performance of a germanium diode over a wide range of forward bias and obtain excellent agreement between theory and experiment with very reasonable diode para-meters. However it is not possible to estimate the sensitivity of any diode as easily as was done for voltage detectors because of the unknown parameter $R_{\text{d.c.}}$; it is typically a few kilohms at the milliwatt power level, and so a well matched diode will have a current sensitivity of the order of 1 mA/mW at centimetre wavelengths. The small contacts necessary at millimetre wave-lengths lead to a larger value of $R_{\text{d.c.}}$ and a fall in current sensitivity, and

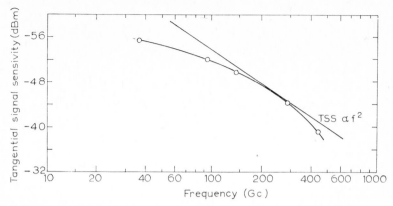

Fig. 5.38. Curve based upon measured sensitivities of semiconductor diode detectors at frequencies in the millimetre wave spectrum. The straight line is drawn for comparison and has the decrease in sensitivity to be expected as diode parasitics become dominant. In calculating the slope of this straight line, it was assumed that there was no decrease in mount efficiency (from BAUER et al. [1966]). (Video bandwith = 1 Mc, o = measured points.)

at submillimetre wavelengths in particular diodes have found use only as voltage detectors. The (frequency)^2 variation of sensitivity of current detectors is illustrated in fig. 5.38, in which the tangential signal sensitivity represents the minimum detectable power (cf. page 216).

The increased sensitivity of backward and tunnel diode detectors arises from the new principles on which they operate. These devices do not follow the relation (5.2) which formed the basis of the previous theoretical treatment; instead their behaviour is dominated by tunnelling currents with quite a different voltage dependence. This may be approximated as a cubic polynomial function of the voltage (SHURMER [1964b]) so that all the higher order terms of (5.29) and subsequent equations vanish. Thus backward and tunnel diodes give voltage and current outputs proportional to the incident power over a much wider range than normal diodes (fig. 5.35). The exact sensitivity depends on the degree of overlap of n-type conduction band and p-type valence band; calculations confirm the three to five fold increase observed (SHURMER [1964b]). The deterioration at high frequencies is no worse than that of conventional diodes (table 5.1) but the necessity for "forming" sets a low limit on contact area and hence on $\omega C r_s$. Even so backward diodes reach half the voltage sensitivity of a good silicon diode at 1 mm wavelength and show a superior current sensitivity at 1.5 mm wavelength (BURRUS [1963]) and are therefore to be preferred to silicon diodes at all but submillimetre wavelengths.

3.3. PROPERTIES OF SEMICONDUCTOR MATERIALS

Table 5.1 lists the properties that determine the spreading resistance and contact capacitance of four semiconductors that have been used as detectors (OHL et al. [1959], MEREDITH and WARNER [1963], BURRUS [1963] and DELOACH [1964]), with an estimate of the cutoff frequency of a 1 micron diameter contact in each case. The dimensions of practical contacts vary so markedly that these cutoff frequencies are no guide to the relative performances of diodes of the various materials; instead the experimental measurements on high frequency detector parameters have been used to estimate the contact dimensions and the practical cutoff frequencies, as given in table 5.2. It is

TABLE 5.2

Experimental detector parameters

	p-type silicon	n-type germanium	n-type gallium arsenide	n-type germanium backward diode
Contact diameter	10^{-5} cm	7×10^{-5} cm	10^{-4} cm	3.5×10^{-5} cm
Parameters (calculated)	$r_s = 250\ \Omega$ $C = 0.0019$ pF	$r_s = 28\ \Omega$ $C = 0.028$ pF	$r_s = 12\ \Omega$ $C = 0.020$ pF	$r_s = 8\ \Omega$ $C = 0.040$ pF
Parameters (experimental)		$r_s = 24\ \Omega$ $C = 0.023$ pF (a)	$r_s = 12\ \Omega$ $C = 0.017$ pF (b)	$r_s = 7.3\ \Omega$ $C = 0.038$ pF (c)
Cutoff frequency (experimental)	335 Gc (estimated)	288 Gc	780 Gc	574 Gc

(a) MEREDITH and WARNER [1963].
(b) DELOACH [1964].
(c) BURRUS [1963].

interesting to note that although, size for size, silicon forms the poorest and gallium arsenide the best, the practical results do not match the trend. The reason appears to be that it is very difficult to "form" gallium arsenide contacts of less than a micron diameter, whilst silicon pressure contacts may well be ten times smaller. These dimensions are much smaller than the apparent whisker point dimensions of fig. 5.32, and evidently contact takes place at only a few isolated spots on the whisker point itself. This explains the extreme mechanical instability of such contacts, which are only to be preferred at submillimetre wavelengths for which the "formed" contacts of other materials become too large.

3.4. Noise in video detectors

The ultimate sensitivity of any detector is set by noise generated within it and subsequent amplifier circuits. As the quantity hf/kT is only 0.05 for 1 mm wavelength radiation at room temperature, it is a good approximation to neglect quantum effects and to treat this noise in the purely classical manner that has been developed for electrical noise at lower frequencies (BELL [1960]). This treatment has been applied to nonlinear detectors by several authors (TORREY and WHITMER [1948], SMITH et al. [1957]); the results to be quoted here have been presented in a systematic manner by SMITH [1951].

There are three significant sources of detector noise:

(a) Johnson noise, an equilibrium thermodynamic property of all electrical circuits.

(b) Shot noise, a nonequilibrium fluctuation in the rate of transit of carriers across the barrier layer.

(c) Inverse frequency, or flicker, noise, a nonequilibrium effect in current carrying semiconductors whose basic causes are still obscure.

Taking account of Johnson noise alone, we may say that a detector exchanges an incoherent noise power of kTB_{in} with its surroundings even in the absence of any incident radiation. B_{in} represents the available frequency bandwith, extending from the waveguide cutoff up to a frequency at which the detector response given by equations (5.33) or (5.37) has fallen off to one half of its low frequency value. The effect of rectifying this noise power is to produce a similar band of noise extending from zero frequency to an upper limit of B_{in}. A coherent millimetre wave signal will give a d.c. output that can be distinguished from these random noise fluctuations by integration over a suitably long time. This is equivalent to passing the detector output through a circuit of small bandwidth, B_{out}, as would normally be present within the following amplifier. For brevity it is assumed here that the detector is a square law device and that the output circuit is a resonant circuit; other forms of detector and of output circuits lead to results of similar form that differ only in a numerical constant (SMITH [1951]). When coherent millimetre wave radiation falls on the detector the ratios between signal and noise powers, S, before and after rectification are related by:

$$S_{out}^2 = S_{in}^2 \, B_{in}/B_{out}. \tag{5.39}$$

This equation only applies for small values of S_{in} because the noise power is assumed independent of whether or not a signal is present. However the coherent radiation itself produces excess noise due to the mixing properties of the detector, and when S_{in} is large the correct equation is:

$$S_{out} = \tfrac{1}{2}S_{in}. \tag{5.40}$$

To find an expression for the minimum detectable power we must make some assumption as to the minimum detectable value of S_{out}. A widely used definition is that of *tangential signal sensitivity* (TSS), which is the power required to give an output equal to the peak to peak noise amplitude. It is measured in dBm – decibels relative to 1 mW – so that, for example, a TSS of -60 dBm corresponds to a minimum detectable power of 10^{-9} W. As the peak to peak noise amplitude is some four to six times greater than its r.m.s. value, depending on how the former is defined, a suitable minimum value for S_{out} would be 25, corresponding to a ratio of 5 between d.c. and r.m.s. noise voltage output.

When a detector is used to observe radiation against an incoherent background, as in astronomical or plasma investigations, eq. (5.39) may be used to give the minimum detectable power,

$$P_{min} = 5kT(B_{in}B_{out})^{\tfrac{1}{2}}. \tag{5.41}$$

If on the other hand small variations in a radiation power P are to be observed, as is the case in absorption spectroscopy, eq. (5.40) leads to a minimum detectable relative absorption of:

$$\left(\frac{\Delta P}{P}\right)_{min} = 5\left(\frac{2kTB_{out}}{P}\right)^{\tfrac{1}{2}}. \tag{5.42}$$

Thus a tenfold increase in sensitivity is attainable only at the cost of increasing either the incident power or the observation time a hundredfold.

Before comparing the conclusions of this section with experiment it is necessary to allow for the fact that this generalised treatment assumes that all the incident power is absorbed by the nonlinear resistance of the detector. We already know that this is very far from the case; indeed combining eqs. (5.25) and (5.35) shows that:

$$\frac{P_{barrier}}{P_{input}} = \frac{V_b^2/2R}{V_1^2/2Z_0} = \frac{Z_0}{R}. \tag{5.43}$$

The zero bias barrier resistance of a typical germanium diode would be about 250 kΩ (MEREDITH and WARNER [1963]) whilst Z_0 is of the order of

500 Ω; thus the apparent sensitivity is five hundred times less than eq. (5.41) would predict. If we make this correction, and assume an input bandwidth of 100 Gc and an output bandwidth of 1 Mc, the tangential sensitivity works out as 3×10^{-9} W, or -55 dBm, in good agreement with the experimental data for the low frequency diodes of fig. 5.38. The effect of parasitic capacitance across the barrier is to lower the sensitivity as the frequency rises (eq. (5.38)), and so video diodes are not altogether satisfactory, although still useful, at submillimetre wavelengths.

TABLE 5.3

Comparison of detectors at a wavelength of 2 mm (from MEREDITH and WARNER [1963])

Type of detector	Minimum detectable power when $B_{out} = 1$ cps	Input bandwidth	Minimum detectable temperature change when $B_{out} = 1$ cps
Golay cell	2×10^{-10} W	15 Gc*	960 °C
Evacuated barretter	4×10^{-11} W	15 Gc*	190 °C
Crystal video radiometer with a forward biased germanium diode	2.5×10^{-11} W	15 Gc*	120 °C
1.5 °K carbon bolometer	10^{-11} W	15 Gc*	48 °C
Harmonic mixer radiometer	1.3×10^{-14} W	2×10 Mc	46 °C
Superheterodyne radiometer with fundamental mixing	7×10^{-15} W	2×30 Mc	8.3 °C
1.5 °K InSb photoconductive detector	10^{-12} W	15 Gc*	4.8 °C

* Restricted to 10 per cent to obtain adequate frequency resolution for radiometry.

The comparisons between different detectors at 2 mm wavelength in table 5.3 show that video diodes are inferior to 1.5 °K thermal detectors (ch. 4), and should normally only be used when their fast response time of microseconds or less is necessary. This has always presented problems in submillimetre wave absorption spectroscopy, in which power levels available rarely exceed a microwatt. Only rather strong absorptions are observable, restricting work to the study of rather simple gas molecules and intense absorption bands in solids. At the higher power levels available at longer millimetre wavelengths, by contrast, the limit is set by carrier noise (eq. (5.42)), and it may be advantageous to use a microwave bridge system to cancel out power not absorbed by the substance of interest.

The conclusions reached up to the present are not greatly affected by the inclusion of other sources of detector noise; their main effect is to set the way in which the detector should be used. *Shot noise* takes the form of a fluctuating current with r.m.s. value:

$$\delta i^2 = 2qI_{\text{d.c.}}B_{\text{out}}. \tag{5.44}$$

This produces a noise voltage that increases gradually with forward bias and much more rapidly with reverse bias (TORREY and WHITMER [1948]). *Inverse frequency* noise has a power distribution given by:

$$P_{\text{N}} = \frac{CI^2_{\text{d.c.}}}{f} B_{\text{out}}. \tag{5.45}$$

This inverse frequency dependence has been observed in various semiconductors (BELL [1960]) over a range of nine octaves – from 10^{-4} cps to 10^5 cps – and appears to be a very fundamental property of such substances. There is still doubt as to whether it is caused by surface effects or by fluctuations in the equilibrium carrier populations, but whatever the case it is especially noticeable in small point contacts which have a high current density and surface to volume ratio; the constant C may well be as large as 10^{-5}. Thus when the rectified current is of the order of 1 mA inverse frequency noise is more important than Johnson noise, kTB_{out}, at all frequencies up to the microwave range, but when the rectified current is only 1 μA inverse frequency noise is no longer important at frequencies above a few kc. It is therefore advantageous to use voltage detection without any forward bias when this source of noise is to be minimised. Under conditions of backward bias both shot and inverse frequency noise increase very rapidly with applied voltage (TORREY and WHITMER [1948]), and it is now believed that this increase is associated with the onset of avalanche breakdown. In the case of backward and tunnel diodes, on the other hand, the mechanism of conduction is such that inverse frequency noise should be much less than that in a normal diode (ENG [1961]); the experimental evidence on this point has so far been rather conflicting (BURRUS [1963], SHURMER [1964b]).

The practice of integrating a detector output over long periods to obtain a narrow output bandwidth is now seen to be undesirable when inverse frequency noise is present, as is normally the case in absorption spectrometers working at high power levels. A much better technique is the use of phase sensitive detection as described in the account of gas spectroscopy in section 2. The desired signal is somehow modulated at a frequency high enough to make inverse frequency noise relatively small – 100 kc is a typical value

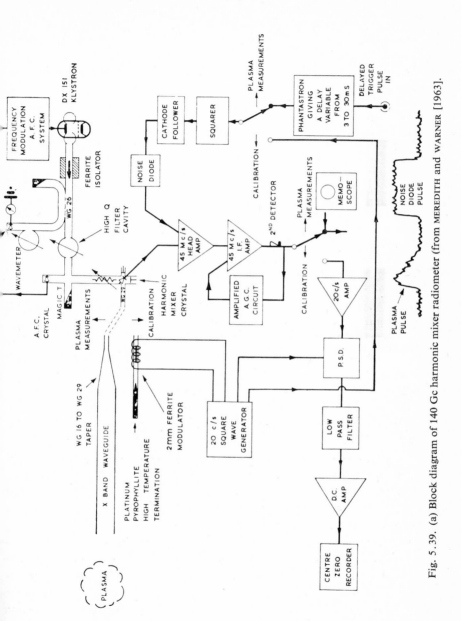

Fig. 5.39. (a) Block diagram of 140 Gc harmonic mixer radiometer (from MEREDITH and WARNER [1963].

for a gas spectrometer – and the detector output is amplified by a narrow-band amplifier tuned to this frequency before being integrated within a phase sensitive rectifying system. The narrow output bandwidth is then centred about the high modulation frequency rather than about zero frequency as would otherwise be the case. Only the desired absorption signal itself should be modulated; modulation of the unabsorbed power that is incident on the detector will result in low frequency noise being converted to modulation frequency noise by means of the mixing properties of the detector, as already discussed in connection with eq. (5.40).

3.5. SUPERHETERODYNE DETECTION

Millimetre wave spectroscopy as such has up to the present been limited to video detection, for reasons connected with the inconvenience of supplying an additional tuneable local oscillator rather than with any inherent difficulty in the superheterodyning process itself. Small amounts of power have been detected at frequencies as high as 600 Gc (BAUER et al. [1966]), and MEREDITH and WARNER [1963] have developed a superheterodyne *radiometer* operating at 140 Gc which will be described here.

The purpose of this radiometer, whose block diagram appears in fig. 5.39a, was to measure the 140 Gc emission from the high energy plasmas produced by ZETA at Harwell. It used a 70 Gc klystron as a local oscillator; this frequency was simultaneously doubled and mixed with the desired plasma emission signal in a germanium detector. The intermediate frequency (45 Mc) current produced was then amplified and rectified by a second detector, the output of which was observed directly by oscilloscope and compared with the known output from a noise diode (acting as a source of random microwave noise). The remainder of the rather complicated circuitry served the purpose of calibrating the radiometer with a standard heat source at a temperature of 870 °C.

As the primary limitation on the sensitivity of any superheterodyne system is set by fluctuations in local oscillator amplitude, which produce proportionate intermediate frequency fluctuations, it is necessary to take special precautions to prevent these fluctuations from appearing at the output. One method used was to insert the local oscillator power through a filter cavity, whose long ringing time would suppress rapid power fluctuations, whilst at the same time preventing drift of the local oscillator frequency by an automatic frequency control system (INGRAM [1955]). A more broadband method, which does however require a local oscillator close in frequency to

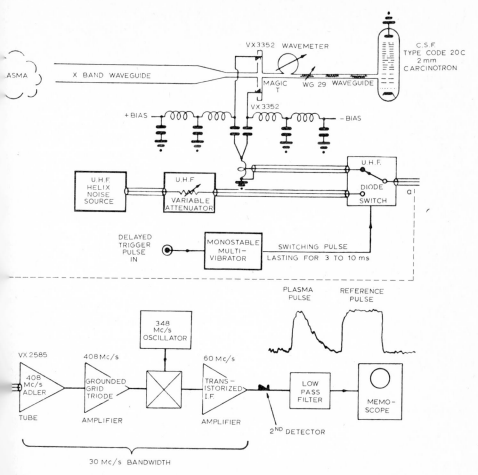

Fig. 5.39. (b) Block diagram of 140 Gc superheterodyne radiometer with fundamental mixing. (From MEREDITH and WARNER [1963].)

the signal, was subsequently used by the same authors. This involves the use of a balanced mixer, consisting of two crystal diodes fed simultaneously with signal power in phase and local oscillator power in antiphase. The *difference* between the two diode currents is amplified, resulting in a cancellation of local oscillator noise before amplification. The whole process closely resembles that of phase sensitive detection at lower frequencies.

The first form of the radiometer described is particularly interesting because it employed the principle of harmonic mixing, using a local oscillator at a frequency approximately one half that of the signal. Recently other workers have shown that harmonic mixing is feasible at signal frequencies as high as 600 Gc (BAUER et al. [1966]), using local oscillators at 140 Gc and 280 Gc, and given detailed descriptions of the operation of a superheterodyne radiometer using these techniques. WOODS and STRAUCH [1966] have even been able to detect 1800 Gc harmonics of a 300 Gc source in this way, and in so doing have proved the feasibility of coherent detection at 0.17 mm wavelength. It would appear that harmonic mixer detection is likely to assume importance in the submillimetre range. (See also ch. 4, section 8.)

3.6. THEORY OF SUPERHETERODYNE DETECTION

The significant difference between video and superheterodyne detection is that the latter restricts the detector response to a very narrow range of wavelengths. A video detector is exposed to the whole spectrum of millimetre wave noise within its input bandwidth, B_{in}, and the maximum sensitivity attainable corresponds to an effective noise bandwidth of $(B_{in}B_{out})^{\frac{1}{2}}$. In a superheterodyne detector, the local oscillator produces excess noise at the intermediate frequency, given by an equation analagous to (5.40). This excess noise arises from two sidebands separated from the local oscillator frequency by the intermediate frequency, each with a bandwidth equal to that of the intermediate frequency amplifier, B_{IF} (fig. 5.40).

If a signal is present at a frequency within either of these two sidebands it too is converted to the intermediate frequency and should in principle be observable if the signal power exceeds the total noise power, kTB_{IF}, within the appropriate sideband. However allowance must be made for

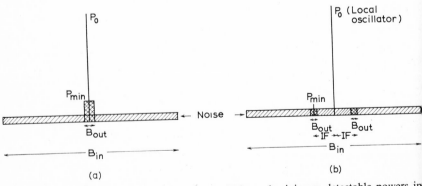

Fig. 5.40. Schematic diagram of noise bandwidths and minimum detectable powers in video (a) and superheterodyne (b) systems.

noise generated by the other sideband, or *image*, frequency; this is normally done by assuming that the signal power suffers a conversion loss of 3 dB between millimetre wave input and intermediate frequency output, half being converted to the intermediate frequency and the other half to the image frequency. The minimum detectable signal thus becomes $2kTB_{IF}$. Normally, after amplification, the intermediate frequency voltage is rectified by a second detector, and use of eq. (5.39) leads to a tangential sensitivity of:

$$P_{min} = 10kT(B_{IF}B_{out})^{\frac{1}{2}}. \qquad (5.46)$$

Typical intermediate frequency bandwidths range from 1 to 100 Mc, and such a superheterodyne system is two to three orders of magnitude more sensitive than the best video detector. Moreover some sensitivity is lost by the use of a second detector; use of phase sensitive detection at the intermediate frequency would equalise the effective values of the two bandwidths B_{IF} and B_{out}, and so lead to a limiting tangential sensitivity of $10\,kTB_{out}$. This is some six orders of magnitude more sensitive than video detection, and closely approaches the ultimate limit set by the thermodynamic nature of noise itself. It should however be borne in mind that this increase in sensitivity is obtained at the cost of a much reduced range of observation at millimetre wavelengths, and finds application mostly in high resolution spectroscopy and communications work. If signals entering over a wide range of frequencies are to be observed, as in some forms of radiometry or grating spectroscopy, then the wideband response of a video detector is essential despite its lesser sensitivity.

It was shown in the previous discussion of practical detectors that a diode makes a very poor low level video detector because only a small part of the incident power is available for rectification. Superheterodyne detectors suffer much less severely from this failing, and indeed at centimetre wavelengths practical detectors regularly approach a sensitivity within a factor of ten of the optimum quoted above. The discrepancy in performance between an ideal and a practical detector is expressed by a noise factor, F, given by:

$$F = L(F_{IF}+t+t'-1), \qquad (5.47)$$

where L = conversion loss of detector,
F_{IF} = noise factor of intermediate frequency amplifier,
t = noise temperature ratio of detector,
t' = noise temperature ratio due to local oscillator.

The first term represents a practical conversion loss and is normally only 1 or 2 dB greater than the ideal value of 3 dB. The second term is a noise temperature ratio that takes into account the non-ideal behaviour of amplifier and detector and the noise produced by fluctuations in local oscillator power. It represents the factor by which the noise due to each one of these exceeds Johnson noise at 290 °K.

The theory of frequency conversion has been worked out by TORREY and WHITMER [1948] by assuming that the local oscillator produces a time varying conductance within the mixer itself. The treatment is essentially similar to that used to account for the reinforcement of harmonics in section 2, but with a somewhat greater algebraic complexity in order to take account of the terminations of the currents flowing through the mixer at the various linear combinations of signal and local oscillator frequencies. If the local oscillator voltage is represented by $V_L \cos \omega_L t$, the time varying conductance may be written:

$$g = \frac{\mathrm{d}I}{\mathrm{d}V} = g_0 + 2g_1 \cos \omega_L t + 2g_2 \cos 2\omega_L t + \dots . \qquad (5.48)$$

The minimum conversion loss, L, proves to be:

$$L = 2 \frac{1 + (1-\eta)^{\frac{1}{2}}}{1 - (1-\eta)^{\frac{1}{2}}} \qquad (5.49)$$

where

$$\eta = \frac{2g_1^2}{g_0(g_0 + g_2)}.$$

The detector diode characteristic of (5.2) is the most appropriate at the local oscillator power levels used, and for this the conductance components become associated Bessel functions (Handbook of Chemistry and Physics),

$$g_n = \alpha I_0 H_n(\alpha V_b). \qquad (5.50)$$

MEREDITH and WARNER [1963] have computed the conversion losses for a diode whose parameters were measured at 2 mm wavelength, using both fundamental mixing, described above, and second harmonic mixing, in which the local oscillator frequency is approximately half the signal frequency. Their results are shown in fig. 5.41.

The conversion loss is high at small local oscillator voltages, but falls toward a minimum value little greater than the theoretical optimum of 3 dB as this voltage rises above 0.2 V. At these relatively high voltages the variation in the second term of eq. (5.47), the noise temperature ratio, becomes important because the crystal noise ratio t increases in direct

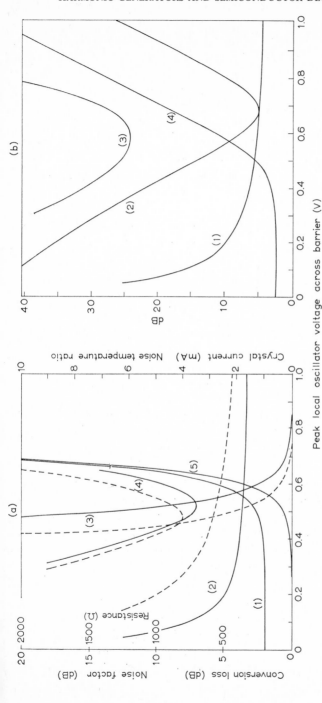

Fig. 5.41. (a) Theoretical curves for fundamental and second harmonic mixing when both spreading resistance and barrier capacitance are neglected. $I = I_0 (\exp (\alpha V) - 1)$, $I_0 = 0.1 \ \mu A$, $\alpha = 20 \ V^{-1}$, $r_s' = 0$, $C = 0$, $F_{IF} = 1.5$, $t = 1.5$ at $\frac{1}{2}$mA, $t' = 0$. (1) Noise temperature ratio; (2) conversion loss when perfectly matched; (3) input resistance at signal frequency; (4) overall noise factor; (5) crystal current; —— fundamental mixing; – – – second harmonic mixing. (b) Performance curves for 140 Gc radiometer with harmonic mixing. $r_s = 20 \ \Omega$, $C = 0.06 \ pF$, $\alpha = 20 \ V^{-1}$, $I_0 = 0.1 \ \mu A$, $F_{IF} = 1.8$, $t = 1.8$ at $\frac{1}{2}$mA, $t' = 2.8$ at $\frac{1}{2}$mA. (1) low frequency conversion loss for second harmonic mixing; (2) loss due to barrier capacitance and spreading resistance at 140 Gc; (3) overall noise factor at 140 Gc; (4) loss due to intermediate frequency amplifier, crystal and local oscillator noise. (From MEREDITH and WARNER [1963].)

proportion to the rectified diode current. The overall noise factor, F, goes through a minimum at a local oscillator voltage in the neighbourhood of 0.5 V, corresponding to a microwave power of 0.25 mW. Surprisingly, this optimum local oscillator voltage is less for second harmonic mixing than for fundamental mixing, and the noise factor is only some 2 dB worse. These conclusions have been borne out by experiment (MEREDITH and WARNER [1963]).

The effects of spreading resistance and barrier capacitance on the performance of such a mixer are twofold. Firstly it will be necessary to increase the applied local oscillator power as the frequency increases in order to maintain the applied voltage V_L, and the conversion loss L constant. Indeed it is more meaningful to specify mixer performance at a given rectified current than a given local oscillator power. Secondly the signal power available at the junction, P_R, will also decrease as the frequency increases, as shown in eq. (5.43),

$$\frac{P_R}{P} = \frac{1}{1 + r_s/R + (\omega C)^2 r_s R}. \tag{5.43}$$

Thus the conversion loss at frequency ω, L_ω, is related to the hypothetical low-frequency conversion loss, L_0, by:

$$L_\omega = L_0[1 + r_s/R + (\omega C)^2 r_s R]. \tag{5.51}$$

The diode barrier resistance R is no longer set by the signal power but by the local oscillator drive (see fig. 5.41), and is only a few hundred ohms rather than the hundreds of kilohms of a low level video detector. It is however rarely possible to make a contact that is able to withstand the local oscillator power and yet so small that the frequency dependent term of (5.51) is negligible. In the diode of fig. 5.41 the conversion loss at 140 Gc is degraded by almost 10 dB, but nonetheless its performance is greatly superior to that of a video detector, in which the microwave signal suffers a loss of nearly 30 dB even before it is rectified. The overall experimental noise figure of the above diode system was 25 dB, in excellent agreement with calculations.

Figure 5.42 shows the conversion loss of various fundamental and harmonic mixers (using gallium arsenide diodes) at signal frequencies up to 560 Gc (BAUER et al. [1966]). Even at this frequency the second harmonic conversion loss is only 10 dB worse than at 140 Gc, and so systems of this kind will maintain their superior over other kinds of detectors (table 5.3)

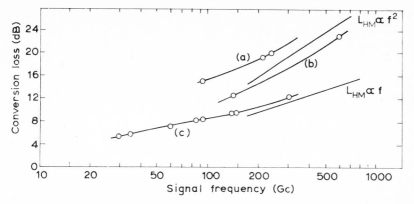

Fig. 5.42. Conversion loss of fundamental (c) and harmonic (third (a) and second (b)) mixers as a function of frequency. Straight lines have been drawn with slopes in accordance with selected laws and are shown for comparison (from BAUER et al. [1966]). o = measured points.

through most of the submillimetre range. It might be more realistic to ask how well a given local oscillator would detect successive harmonics of its own frequency; a projection of fig. 5.41 suggests a conversion loss comparable with the harmonic generation losses of fig. 5.18, or roughly 6 dB a harmonic at high harmonics. This would seem quite promising for harmonics up to the fifth or sixth, and indeed Strauch et al. have shown that it is possible to carry out harmonic mixer detection at 0.17 mm wavelength, using a 1 mm source (WOODS and STRAUCH [1966]).

The considerations governing the choice of detector materials for video detectors apply even more forcefully to superheterodyne mixers, whose contact dimensions are necessarily larger in order to withstand the local oscillator power. In practice there seems little to choose between the materials of table 5.1, though germanium is mostly restricted to longer wavelengths, whilst silicon and gallium arsenide are used almost equally in the submillimetre region. The latter material gives a fundamental mixing conversion loss at 125 Gc of only 6.8 dB when mounted so that it can be moved at right angles to the microwave electric field (SHARPLESS [1963]), as compared with 8.5 dB for the best silicon diode available.

Backward diodes are not expected to perform any better than those of normal materials, as their cutoff frequencies are much the same (table 5.2). They do possess the important advantage that their conversion loss is almost as low at microwatt local oscillator powers as it is in the more usual milliwatt power region (OXLEY [1964]). The reason for this is the same as that behind the exceptionally linear rectifying characteristic of a backward diode used as a video detector; the diode current is approximately a cubic function of the voltage, with the exponential character of (5.2) largely suppressed, and the conversion loss for such a characteristic may be shown to rise much less rapidly with decreasing local oscillator voltage than that for an exponential characteristic. BURRUS [1963] has shown that the conversion loss of a good backward diode at 60 Gc rises by only 6 dB as the local oscillator power is lowered from 1 mW to 10 μW, as compared with a rise of 22 dB for a silicon diode. Forward biasing the silicon diode does reduce this discrepancy considerably, owing to the lowering of the barrier resistance, R, with a corresponding reduction in the frequency losses given by (5.43). However the superiority of the backward diode at local oscillator power levels of a few tens of microwatts makes it exceptionally suitable for superheterodyne mixing at short millimetre wavelengths, where the available power is limited and frequency losses are exceptionally severe for the high resistance diodes that would otherwise be employed.

Superheterodyne mixers suffer from the same sources of noise as do video detectors, and the effects of Johnson noise have already been considered in the preceding theoretical discussion. The linear rise of noise temperature t with forward current (MEREDITH and WARNER [1963]) is due to *shot noise*, and this normally limits the amount of forward bias that can be applied. *Inverse frequency noise* is generally made negligible by choosing an intermediate frequency of 10 Mc or more, although even so it will appear if the diode is reverse biased, as may happen when no d.c. return path is supplied for the diode rectified current. There is some evidence that this inverse frequency noise is less for backward diodes than for normal diodes (BURRUS [1963] and OXLEY [1964]) and that they can be operated at distinctly lower intermediate frequencies. An additional source of noise in millimetre wave systems is *local oscillator noise*; whether the local oscillator power is generated electronically or by a harmonic generation process its spectrum is that of a single frequency surrounded by noise sidebands which spread out to several hundred Mc on each side at millimetre wavelengths. Unless these noise sidebands are supressed by a balanced mixer or in some other way they are the predominant source of detector noise (fig. 5.41). For this reason there is considerable advantage to be gained by the use of a travelling wave microwave amplifier as a first intermediate frequency stage, followed by a second mixer (MEREDITH and WARNER [1963], BAUER et al. [1966]). Furthermore this enables the bandwidth of the detection system to be perhaps a thousand times higher than that of a conventional superheterodyne receiver.

The performance of two superheterodyne systems at 2 mm wavelength is compared with that of other detectors in table 5.3. It should be noted that these systems excel in detecting small amounts of coherent power, but are less effective in radiometric work where radiation over a wide frequency band is to be sampled. At submillimetre wavelengths such detectors can be expected to supplement the more convenient thermal and photoconductive detectors as narrow-band sources come into use.

4. Charge storage diodes and ferrites

In sections 2 and 3 we considered the use of nonlinear *resistors* for frequency conversion. This is necessarily a very inefficient process; the efficiency of generating the nth harmonic cannot exceed $1/n^2$, for example (PAGE [1958]), and in a superheterodyne system the local oscillator power goes entirely to waste. By contrast the use of a nonlinear *reactance* makes it feasible in principle to convert all the power available at a fundamental frequency to any harmonic, and to carry out a heterodyning process in which both local oscillator and signal powers become available at the intermediate frequency. The reason for this difference lies in the ability of the reactance to store energy and to release it at the appropriate points of an electrical cycle, whilst itself not dissipating any power. As long ago as 1831, FARADAY [1831] recognised this principle as applicable to elastic materials, and in 1883 Lord Rayleigh made some detailed studies of it in connection with the properties of sound (STRUTT, LORD RAYLEIGH [1894–'96]). Interest in electrical devices based on it died away with the advent of the thermionic valve, however, and was not rekindled until van der Ziel, in 1948, pointed out the potentialities of such devices for microwave amplification. In 1957 Suhl proposed the use of a ferrite as a microwave amplifier (SUHL [1957]), a proposal soon verified experimentally by WEISS [1957], and this triggered off a wave of investigation that has continued to the present day. Improved solid state technology has led to a continuing development in ferrites and the appearance of many new diode sources of millimetre wave power. Of these the varactor and tunnel diode are well established as centimetre wavelength amplifiers and oscillators, and more recently the step recovery diode and the avalanche diode oscillator have outclassed the former respectively as harmonic generators and milli-metre wave sources. In this section we consider harmonic generators only, leaving tunnel and avalanche diode oscillators to the next. Experimental data on the use of these at millimetre wavelengths is as yet very meagre, and so a brief account of the theory of operation of each device together with such experimental information as is available will be given here.

4.1. VARACTORS

Any semiconductor diode shows a reverse bias capacitance that varies with voltage in a manner described by eq. (5.3). However, to ensure that carriers can cross the depletion layer sufficiently rapidly to give a good millimetre wavelength performance, the junction must normally be of the abrupt kind, with a depletion capacitance given by eq. (5.52):

$$C = \frac{dQ}{dV} = C_0(1+V/\phi)^{-\frac{1}{2}}. \tag{5.52}$$

Integration yields the variation of stored charge, Q, with reverse voltage, V:

$$Q = 2\phi C_0(1+V/\phi)^{\frac{1}{2}}. \tag{5.53}$$

The assumption made in (5.53) is that when the voltage reaches a forward value equal to the semiconductor energy step ($V = -\phi$) the depletion layer disappears, and, with it, the stored charge. It is convenient to eliminate the square root operation by writing:

$$V = Q^2/4\phi C_0^2 - \phi. \tag{5.54}$$

If the static charge, Q_0 (produced by a voltage V_0), is now varied sinusoidally by an amount $Q_1 \sin \omega t$, we find:

$$
\begin{aligned}
V &= \frac{(Q_0+Q_1 \sin \omega t)^2}{4\phi C_0^2} - \phi \\
&= V_0 + \frac{Q_0 Q_1}{2\phi C_0^2} \sin \omega t + \frac{Q_1^2}{4\phi C_0^2} \sin^2 \omega t \\
&= V_0 + (S_0 \sin \omega t + S_1 Q_1 \sin^2 \omega t)Q_1.
\end{aligned}
\tag{5.55}
$$

The quantities S_0 and S_1 form part of a nonlinear elastance, S, which we shall use to describe the voltage response of the varactor just as, in section 2, we used a nonlinear conductance to describe the current characteristic of a rectifying diode. However in this case expression (5.55) is sufficiently simple to make the use of time-dependent parameters unnecessary, for it may be rewritten as:

$$V = V_0 + \tfrac{1}{2}S_1 Q_1^2 + S_0 Q_1 \sin \omega t - \tfrac{1}{2}S_1 Q_1^2 \cos 2\omega t. \tag{5.56}$$

Thus voltage fluctuations at a frequency 2ω appear across the depletion layer when the charge is modulated at a frequency ω. This charge modulation may be produced by driving the varactor from a current source $I_1 \cos \omega t$, for which:

$$I_1 \cos \omega t = \frac{d}{dt}(Q_1 \sin \omega t); \quad I_1 = \omega Q_1. \tag{5.57}$$

The varactor now behaves as an ideal reactance, for the voltage across it at frequency ω is in quadrature with the current and no power is absorbed. If however an "idler" circuit is provided to allow the flow of second harmonic current a very different situation arises. Figure 5.43 shows such an idealised idler configuration, with a resistance R_2, passing only the second harmonic frequency, 2ω.

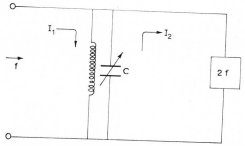

Fig. 5.43. Idealised varactor diode in frequency doubling circuit.

The idler current flows through the varactor as well as through R_2, and so gives rise to an additional charge modulation at frequency 2ω. Using eqs. (5.56) and (5.57), we may write:

$$I_2 = -V_2/R_2; \quad I_2 \cos 2\omega t = \frac{d}{dt}(Q_2 \sin 2\omega t); \quad I_2 = 2\omega Q_2. \tag{5.58}$$

Equation (5.55) must now be modified to:

$$V = V_0 + S_0(Q_1 \sin \omega t + Q_2 \sin 2\omega t) + S_1(Q_1 \sin \omega t + Q_2 \sin 2\omega t)^2$$

$$= \text{terms of eq. (5.55)} + \tfrac{1}{2}S_1 Q_2^2 + S_0 Q_2 \sin 2\omega t +$$

$$+ S_1 Q_1 Q_2 \cos \omega t + \text{terms in } 3\omega, 4\omega \ldots. \tag{5.59}$$

The new second harmonic term is once more purely reactive, but the new fundamental frequency term is in phase with the driving current I_1, producing an effective series resistance, R_1, that does dissipate power. The following power relations are easily derived:

$$\left.\begin{array}{l} P_1 = \tfrac{1}{2}V_1I_1 = \tfrac{1}{2}(S_1Q_1Q_2)\,(\omega Q_1) = \tfrac{1}{2}\omega S_1Q_1^2Q_2, \\[2mm] P_2 = \tfrac{1}{2}V_2I_2 = \tfrac{1}{2}(\tfrac{1}{2}S_1Q_1^2)\,(2\omega Q_2) = \tfrac{1}{2}\omega S_1Q_1^2Q_2, \\[2mm] R_1R_2 = V_1V_2/I_1I_2 = S_1^2I_1^2/4\omega^4. \end{array}\right\} \qquad (5.60)$$

Hence all the power absorbed at the fundamental frequency is converted to second harmonic, and by a proper choice of load resistance R_2 it is possible to match R_1 to the internal resistance of the current source and so to obtain maximum power transfer. However an upper limit is set on the allowable value of I_1 by the reactive voltages produced in the varactor; these are the terms preceded by S_0 in eq. (5.59), and the voltage swing to which they correspond must not be so large as to drive the varactor into forward conduction or avalanche breakdown. This limitation corresponds to the *maximum reactive power*, or *normalised power*, that the varactor can handle.

A further feature of varactor harmonic generator that follows from eq. (5.56) is that higher harmonics cannot be generated at all unless second harmonic current is allowed to flow. In general one or more idler circuits tuned to intermediate harmonics must be supplied in order to generate a specific high harmonic, and it may be shown that the efficiency of harmonic generation will remain 100% if these idlers are all short circuits – a situation analagous to that already found for rectifying harmonic generators in section 2.

Real varactors show a series resistance in addition to a voltage variable capacitance (fig. 5.44). This gives rise to a cutoff frequency, f_c, defined in terms of the resistance and capacitance at zero bias:

$$f_c = 1/2\,\pi C_0 r_s. \qquad (5.61)$$

Varactors with cutoff frequencies in the range 250–500 Gc are now commercially available and a 800 Gc gallium arsenide diode has been described in the literature (DELOACH [1964] and table 5.2). When such varactors are used as harmonic generators in the 1–10 Gc region doubling efficiencies of 90% and tripling efficiencies of 75% are readily obtainable in practice, but the presence of series resistance so degrades the varactor performance at high frequencies that these efficiencies soon become comparable with the much poorer figures for rectifying harmonic generators. A detailed theoretical

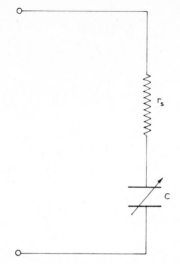

Fig. 5.44. Electrical equivalent circuit of a real varactor diode.

study by PENFELD and RAFUSE [1962] has led to the general conclusions summarised in table 5.4 for varactors driven at a frequency within a factor of ten of cutoff. Not only does the efficiency for the higher harmonics fall off very steeply as the fundamental frequency increases, but the input power

TABLE 5.4

The varactor harmonic generator at frequencies near cutoff
(from PENFELD and RAFUSE [1962])

Harmonic number	Short circuited idlers at	Efficiency
2	–	3.9×10^{-3} $(f_c/f)^2$
3	$2f$	6.08×10^{-5} $(f_c/f)^4$
4	$2f$	5.96×10^{-8} $(f_c/f)^6$
5	$2f, 3f$	16.6×10^{-10} $(f_c/f)^8$
5	$2f, 4f$	2.33×10^{-10} $(f_c/f)^8$
6	$2f, 3f$	2.87×10^{-12} $(f_c/f)^{10}$
6	$2f, 4f$	0.91×10^{-12} $(f_c/f)^{10}$
8	$2f, 4f$	8.67×10^{-19} $(f_c/f)^{14}$

f = fundamental frequency; f_c = cutoff frequency.
Optimum source resistance: r_s
Optimum load resistance: r_s
Maximum power input: $\dfrac{(E_B + \phi)^2}{2r_s} \left(\dfrac{f}{f_c}\right)^2$
Breakdown voltage: E_B.

required for this efficiency to be attained also rises; indeed the maximum second harmonic output turns out to be independent of frequency and takes on a value of approximately 6 mW for a varactor of 6 V breakdown voltage and 12 Ω resistance (cf. table 5.2), whilst higher harmonic powers will be still lower. Because the efficiency is so low this maximum power may not be attained, as the input power will tend to be limited by thermal dissipation within the varactor spreading resistance rather than by considerations of reactive capacity alone. A further practical point is that the optimum source and load resistance are so low that matching must be carried out by reducing the waveguide height; a ratio as extreme as 18 : 1 has been used (DELOACH [1964]) in place of the normal 2 : 1. In addition, careful attention must be given to the provision of idler circuits; some frequencies must be short circuited and others left open. The net result is that efficient varactor harmonic generators tend to be very narrow band and difficult to tune.

In the case of frequency doubling the situation is much easier, and conversion from 4 mm to 2 mm wavelength with only 5.4 dB loss has been reported (BAUER et al. [1966]). Similar experiments by the author, using a 250 Gc varactor mounted centrally across both fundamental and harmonic waveguides (fig. 5.45), have not been very encouraging; the doubled power output at 4 mm was less than from a commercial rectifier diode, possibly due to the inadequate matching techniques used. Other workers have reported a 10 dB loss with a better matched 8 mm–4 mm system (COLEMAN [1963]). Table 5.5 compares the optimum efficiencies for a realistic varactor doubler, with the observed performance of a bombarded silicon harmonic generator (OHL et al. [1959]). The varactor can produce more power at low harmonics

TABLE 5.5

Comparison of varactor and bombarded silicon diode
harmonic generators at 35 Gc

Harmonic number	Computed conversion loss (350 Gc varactor)	Experimental conversion loss (silicon diode, fig. 5.18)
2	4 dB	11 dB
3	2.5 dB	19 dB
4	12 dB	27 dB
5	8 dB	32 dB
6	16 dB	36 dB
8	41 dB	46 dB

Optimum drive power for varactor: 150 mW.

Fig. 5.45. Photograph of an integrated 35 to 70 Gc varactor doubler. The encapsulated diode (bottom centre) is mounted in a freely rotatable mount across the fundamental waveguide. A pressure contact is made with a spring loaded brass wire passing across the millimetre waveguide and through a PTFE bush separating the two waveguides (scale in centimetres).

(if it can withstand the drive power) but at high harmonics it shows little improvement over the rectifier diode, and is unlikely to be competitive at submillimetre wavelengths unless the cutoff frequency is very markedly increased. The data of table 5.2 offer little hope of such a further increase, for although silicon pressure contacts can be made even smaller, their poor backward breakdown characteristic does not lend itself to varactor operation, whilst the limit of size for "formed" germanium and gallium arsenide contacts seems already to have been reached.

Although varactors have proved rather disappointing as millimetre wave power sources, they are finding considerable application in precision spectroscopy. The high resolving power of gaseous spectrometers (section 2) requires a comparable precision in frequency measurement, which is accomplished by comparing the frequency of the microwave klystron source with a "ladder" of hamonics generated from a very stable standard in the 100 kc–10 Mc region. Figure 5.46 shows a typical harmonic generating chain, in which the output from a 5 Mc standard quartz crystal oscillator is multiplied to 60 Mc in sharply tuned stages, and then further multiplied to 540 Mc in a broadband system. The resulting mixture of frequencies is used to drive a varactor mounted across a waveguide and so to generate all harmonics of 60 Mc above the waveguide cutoff frequency.

Nowadays it is practical to generate milliwatts of power at 10 Gc by direct multiplication from 60 Mc, using chains of varactors without any external power source. However such chains must be sharply tuned for high efficiency, and are not really suitable for broadband spectroscopy. The system described above uses a single varactor of 100 Gc cutoff frequency and generates power of the order of a microwatt at 10 Gc and less than a picowatt at 40 Gc. The low efficiency is a concomitant of the fact that power is available at *every* microwave harmonic of 60 Mc. Formerly microwave spectroscopists used detector diodes as the harmonic generating element of this system, but in the writer's experience varactors have proved distinctly superior, giving 10–100 times more power at any one harmonic, and reaching harmonics as high as the eightieth where detector diodes find difficulty in reaching the fiftieth.

Frequency measurement is carried out by comparing the klystron frequency with an adjacent varactor harmonic in a superheterodyne detection system. A fraction of the klystron power is bled off to act as local oscillator, and the resulting intermediate frequency, which must lie between 0 and 30 Mc, is detected by a high sensitivity tunable communications receiver. In practice the klystron frequency, f, is swept electronically so that the condition:

$$f = 60N \pm R \text{ Mc},$$

where R is the receiver setting and N any integer, is fulfilled at more than one point on the frequency sweep. At each such point a sharp "blip", or frequency marker, appears on the oscilloscope presentation of the detected microwave power (fig 5.46), and frequencies are readily measured by ad-

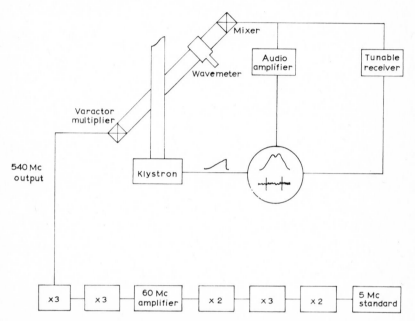

Fig. 5.46. Block diagram of a frequency standard used for the precise measurement of microwave frequencies and the phase locking of the frequency of a microwave source.

justing the very narrow markers to coincide with a spectral line of interest.

A slight modification of this technique makes it possible to "phase lock" a microwave klystron to the low frequency standard source. The intermediate frequency obtained as above is amplified by a wideband radio frequency amplifier until its amplitude is great enough to "saturate" a phase sensitive detector, in which it is compared with a stable radio frequency reference source of, for example, 30 Mc. The d.c. output from this detector is fed into the frequency regulating section of the klystron power supply in such a way as to oppose any shift in the intermediate frequency from the value corresponding to the reference. In a properly designed system, it is impossible for this frequency to shift in phase with respect to the reference by more than a quarter cycle (PETER and STRANDBERG [1955], POYNTER and STEFFENSEN [1963]), and so the stability of the low frequency standard is automatically conferred on the klystron itself. Considerably more varactor harmonic power is required for phase locking than for frequency measurement, but by the use of intermediate oscillators this has been done at frequencies of up to 70 Gc (STRAUCH et al. [1964], [1966]). Such a phase locked klystron can of course be used as a secondary frequency standard to generate varactor or rectifier diode harmonics up to 70–100 Gc, frequencies unattainable by multiplier chains of the type already described.

Phase locked klystrons also find use as spectroscopic sources in their own right, and have been used to reveal hyperfine structure not otherwise resolvable in gaseous spectra. Structure of this kind is due to nuclei of rather small electric quadrupole moment, such as D, ^{14}N and ^{17}O, and also to magnetic coupling between nuclei of the type normally observed only in radio frequency nuclear magnetic resonance spectra. The latter effects are shown in the millimetre wave electric resonance spectrum of H_2S, reproduced in fig. 5.47.

Not only does phase locking improve the resolving power of a spectrometer, but also its sensitivity. Even with very careful stabilisation of power supplies and temperature, a klystron tends to drift in frequency by perhaps 1 Mc per hour and to jitter randomly by some 10 kc every second. These effects normally make it impossible to improve the sensitivity by increasing the post-detector integration time beyond a few seconds, but with phase locking it has proved possible to reduce drift to a few kc per hour and to take several hours to scan a few lines (FLYGARE and LOWE [1965]).

Varactors are also used as mixers, but not in the same way as rectifying diodes. It may be shown from the Manley-Rowe relations (MANLEY and ROWE [1959], BLACKWELL and KOTZEBUE [1961]) obeyed by all ideal non-linear energy storage devices, that power can be transferred from a high pumping frequency to two lower frequencies whose sum makes up the pump frequency, but the efficiency for conversion to a low intermediate frequency is very poor. This mode of use, known as parametric amplification, is not at all suitable for conversion of a microwave to a radio frequency, but rather for the amplification of a microwave signal by a higher frequency pumping source. Another mode of use, the up-converter, is just the reverse of that described above; the varactor mixes radiofrequency and microwave power to give an output at the sum of the two frequencies. This latter mode offers the possibility of producing a tunable superheterodyne system with only one microwave source (fig. 5.48).

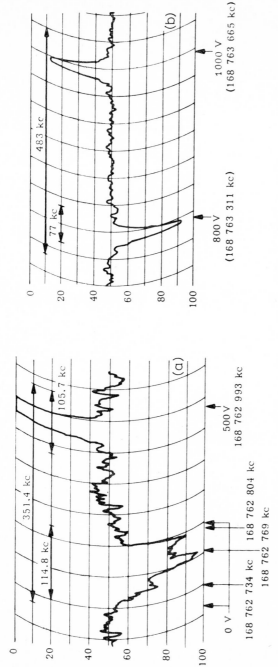

Fig. 5.47. Molecular beam electric resonance spectrum of the $1_{01} \rightarrow 1_{11}$ rotational transition of H_2S at 168.7 Gc. These spectra of extremely high resolution are produced at the seventh harmonic of a klystron phase locked to a crystal oscillator and presented by modulation of an applied electric field. (a) Square wave modulation 0 to 500 V, (b) square wave modulation 800 to 1000 V. The structure of the zero field line is due to magnetic coupling between the nuclear spins and molecular rotation (from STRAUCH et al. [1966]).

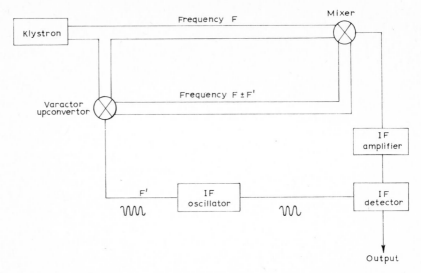

Fig. 5.48. Block diagram of idealised superheterodyne spectrometer using a varactor to generate the power for spectroscopy from the local oscillator source.

The upper sideband (sum frequency) produced by mixing the radio frequency and a phase locked microwave signal is used as a spectroscopic source, and tuned by adjustment of the radio frequency oscillator. The intermediate frequency produced after superheterodyne detection is the same as that of the above oscillator, which may therefore be used as a reference source in a very narrow band phase sensitive detector, thus minimising noise at the output. Such a system has been used at a fixed wavelength near 8 mm with a rectifier (not varactor) mixer generating both upper and lower side-bands of the microwave frequency (BROWN et al. [1965]), but to the author's knowledge, no tunable varactor system of this kind has been attempted. In practice the author has found a real varactor to give both upper and lower side-bands almost equally, with conversion losses at 10 Gc of the order of 6–8 dB, increasing rapidly with frequency, but the sensitivity of such a system would make it well worth while.

4.2. STEP RECOVERY DIODES

When varactors came into widespread use as high efficiency harmonic generators, it was soon found that the best results were obtained when forward current was allowed to flow during part of the conduction cycle. This cannot be explained on the basis of a simple variation of capacitance with bias voltage, and it was eventually realised that quite a different mechanism must be responsible for these unexpected results. This charge storage mechanism (PENFELD and RAFUSE [1962]) has been described in section 1, and it should be made clear that although it depends on the occurrence of forward current flow it is still a reactive property, with a nonlinearity very much more pronounced than that of a varactor. The varactor capacitance variation under reverse bias is still present, but does not contribute significantly to the diode performance because the charge stored during the forward cycle is usually much greater than that stored under reverse bias. As the Manley-Rowe relations (MANLEY and ROWE [1959], BLACKWELL and KOTZEBUE [1961]) still apply, a step recovery diode is capable of generating high harmonics with an efficiency that may approach 100%; it is superior to a varactor in that no idler circuits are required and problems such as the simultaneous tuning of several circuits, the interaction between output and input circuits, and the possibility of parametric oscillations are largely eliminated.

In practice a step recovery diode is used in the parallel configuration of fig. 5.49. It is reverse biased (usually by a suitably chosen d.c. load resistor)

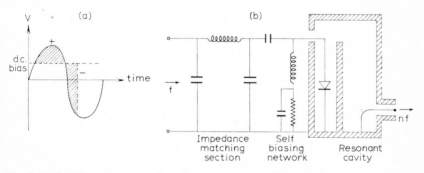

Fig. 5.49. (a) The current waveform in a step recovery diode, backward biased for optimum efficiency. The charge injected during forward bias (shaded) has all been recovered when the diode reaches maximum reverse bias, and at this point the diode switches off sharply. (b) A practical parallel configuration for the step recovery diode harmonic generator.

so that it does not conduct until the fundamental voltage reaches about 20° conduction angle; the stored charge (shaded) is then exhausted when the fundamental cycle reaches its peak reverse voltage and maximum current is flowing. At this point the diode switches sharply to its normally low reverse current operation, suddenly diverting the fundamental current into the tuned harmonic circuit and thereby setting it "ringing" in synchronism with the fundamental frequency. The whole process is reminiscent of the operation of an electronic class C amplifier. High efficiency is obtained only if the harmonic circuit is sufficiently selective to reject all but one harmonic, and if the fundamental source is suitably matched to the low impedance of the heavily conducting diode, but under these circumstances the commercial literature quotes efficiencies up to 30% for the production of several hundred milliwatts of power at 2 Gc from a 100 Mc source. This is far beyond the capabilities of either a single varactor or a rectifier diode, but the process cannot as yet be extended to higher frequencies because the fastest diode switching time now available is 10^{-10} seconds; the prospect of useful millimetre wave generation by this technique does therefore seem very remote.

The future of the step recovery diode as part of a frequency standard chain is however assured. When mounted in a nonresonant waveguide such a diode can generate all frequencies above cutoff; in practice brief pulses of 8–11 Gc frequency have been observed each time a GaAs diode is switched by a short pulse (DIETRICH and SHARPLESS [1964]). These pulses are synchronised to the frequency of the fundamental driving waveform, and it has proved possible to amplify them by means of a travelling wave tube and by further harmonic generation with a gallium arsenide rectifier diode to produce synchronous pulses of 90 Gc frequency (DIETRICH [1961]). If particular harmonics are selected by means of a cavity wavemeter (DIETRICH [1962]), these synchronous pulses may be used either as a millimetre wave frequency standard or to phase lock a millimetre wave klystron. In this way the stability of a low frequency standard can ultimately be conferred on harmonics at submillimetre wavelengths which might then be used to test the stability of other submillimetre sources.

4.3. FERRITES

It is well known that ferromagnetism, as shown by iron and certain other metals and alloys, is due to the presence of unbalanced electron spins, which tend to couple together and give rise to magnetised domains within a material. When an increasing magnetic field is applied these domains gradually line up so that their magnetisation is parallel to the applied field, until at a sufficiently high field all the domains are lined up and the material is said to be saturated. This process gives rise to a nonlinear variation of magnetisation with applied field and is in principle suitable for parametric amplification and harmonic generation, but the high conductivity of metals prevents the penetration of microwave radiation into the bulk material.

Ferrites consist of sintered mixtures of metal oxides, such as Fe_2O_3 and Al_2O_3, which are still ferromagnetic but very poor conductors, and are therefore usable at microwave frequencies.

The physical effect of a d.c. magnetic field is to cause electron spin magnetisation to precess about the field direction at a frequency given by $f = gqH/2\pi mc$, where g is the gyromagnetic ratio of an electron (approximately 2), q and m its charge and mass, H the d.c. field in gauss, and c the velocity of light. If an oscillating magnetic field of this frequency is also present it will interact with the precessing spin and increase the amplitude of precession if it is circularly polarised in the appropriate phase; energy can thus be fed from the microwave magnetic field into the electron spin system. This mechanism is utilised in the ferrite waveguide *isolator*, in which microwaves travelling in one direction have the wrong polarisation and do not interact with the ferrite spins, but any returning microwaves have the opposite polarisation and are strongly absorbed by the resonant process described above, thus ensuring that no system of standing waves can be built up.

If the microwave field is sufficiently large to partly saturate the ferrite spins, harmonic generation will take place, the spins precessing at a rate that has components not only of frequency f, but also $2f$, $3f$, etc. The practical problems of harmonic generation therefore consist of supplying a sufficiently large microwave field and of extracting the harmonics from the spin system. Driving powers of the order of kilowatts are required, and must be supplied from pulsed magnetrons, and the ferrite must be carefully shaped and placed at the optimum waveguide position. In general the behaviour of a ferrite spin system is very much more complex than described here (AULD [1962]) and this shaping and positioning has been largely a matter of trial and error. Two geometries that have been used successfully by AYRES [1959] for 4 mm to 2 mm doubling are shown in fig. 5.50.

In the previous discussion, dissipative energy losses within the ferrite were ignored; in practice these are quite important and produce a broadening ΔH of the relation between frequency and d.c. field that may amount to several kilogauss. The higher the saturation magnetisation of the material, M_s, the better, and Ayres found that the second harmonic output at 2 mm varied in proportion to $M_s/\Delta H$. The material for which this is largest is single crystal yttrium iron garnet (YIG), but it appears difficult to couple into and out of this as well as for simpler ferrites. The maximum power obtained was 50 W pulsed, at an efficiency of a few percent, and no higher harmonics than the second were observed.

Subsequent work has confirmed this general behaviour, in obtaining

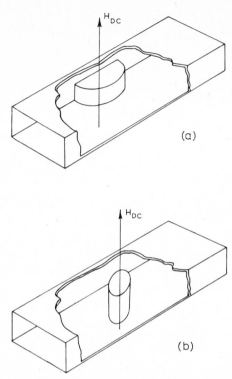

Fig. 5.50. Typical waveguide configurations of ferrite harmonic generators. (a) Half-disk geometry. The disk height is about 60 per cent of the waveguide height, and the disk diameter is about two-thirds the waveguide width. (b) Centered post geometry. The post diameter is about one-third the waveguide width, and the post height is about 90 per cent of the wave guide height (from AYRES [1959]).

doubling efficiencies of a few percent with higher harmonics present in only very small amount, and it may be concluded that ferrites show the same limited nonlinearities as do varactors, but that the problems of providing appropriate idler circuits to generate high harmonics have yet to be solved in the former case. Nonetheless ferrites are the only harmonic generators capable of giving millimetre wave power outputs of watts, or even kilowatts, when pulsed; they thrive on high power inputs and are virtually indestructible, and could find a regular use in specialised applications such as the low-temperature spectroscopy of phonons in solids and liquids.

5. Semiconductor diode oscillators

The devices discussed in the preceding sections have all been passive generators of millimetre waves, requiring some form of microwave or radio-frequency input power. In this section we consider three types of semiconductor that can convert d.c. power directly to millimetre wavelengths without any intervening microwave stage; the tunnel diode, the Gunn effect "diode" and the avalanche diode. Each operates by a different mechanism, but the net effect of this mechanism is always to produce a negative resistance that is sufficient to cancel out the positive resistance of a millimetre waveguide system, and thereby to generate sustained oscillations.

5.1. TUNNEL DIODES

The tunnel diode was introduced in 1958 by ESAKI [1958], and was rapidly taken up as a radio frequency oscillator and computer element. Its development as a millimetre wave generator has been carried out largely by Trambarulo and Burrus, and a detailed report on the techniques used and results obtained was made by BURRUS [1961]. Very little fundamental change has since taken place, and the following account summarises the above report.

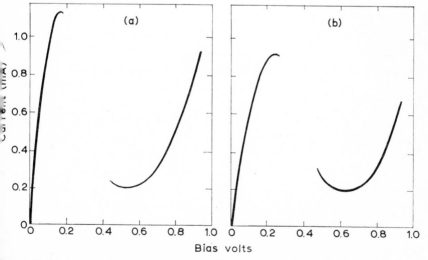

Fig. 5.51. Forward $V-I$ characteristics of representative Esaki diodes with point contact geometry. (a) Diode of p-type GaAs with formed tin point contact. (b) Diode of n-type GaAs with formed zinc point contact (from BURRUS [1961]).

The most successful millimetre wave source by far is heavily doped n-type gallium arsenide. Both p- and n-type tunnel diodes have been made (fig. 5.51) with very similar d.c. characteristics, the origin of which is explained in section 1, but the n-type diode has oscillated at a frequency three times higher. No doubt the high carrier mobility (cf. table 5.1) is responsible, for the limiting frequency seems set by a combination of spreading resistance and barrier capacitance just as in the case of detector diodes.

Both in principle and in practice, a tunnel diode oscillator is very simple to set up. The equivalent circuit of fig. 5.52 shows that the device must merely

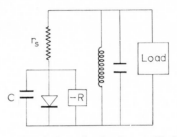

Fig. 5.52. Electrical equivalent circuit of an oscillating tunnel diode.

be put in parallel with a tuned circuit and forward biased until its negative resistance $(-R)$ is less than the positive resistance of the load. The exact oscillation frequency depends somewhat on the bias used (possibly because of variation of the diode capacitance with bias) and a range of 1–2% can be obtained by varying the bias. The mount used is shown in fig. 5.53; it consists of a short circuited waveguide of dimensions 3.1 mm × 0.25 mm (to give a match to the low impedance of the tunnel diode), tapered up to a more conventional size for measurements. The d.c. biasing network includes a shunt resistor less than $(-R)$ in magnitude, so that low frequency parasitic oscillations or switching to a region of positive resistance cannot take place.

The power output at 4 mm wavelength, together with the d.c. characteristic, as the forward bias is varied, appears in fig. 5.54 in the case of a weakly oscillating diode. Strongly oscillating diodes tend to jump between several different frequencies as the bias varies.

The maximum output obtainable from a tunnel diode corresponds approximately to a swing over all of the negative resistance characteristic – roughly 0.35 V and 0.8 mA peak to peak for the diode of fig. 5.51. This represents a power of 35 μW, showing that tunnel diodes are intrinsically

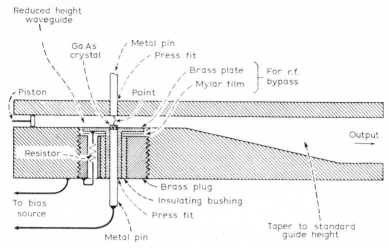

Fig. 5.53. Cross section of a representative tunnel diode oscillator in simple waveguide circuit (from BURRUS [1961]).

low power devices. In practice the whole negative resistance characteristic is not covered (fig. 5.54) and typical power outputs are even less. Typical power outputs at various frequencies are shown in table 5.6.

An upper limit for the frequency of oscillation of a tunnel diode has been derived by YAMASHITA and BAIRD [1966]. This depends on the relative values of spreading resistance r_s and negative resistance, $-R$, but in general works

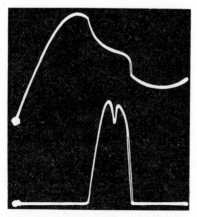

Fig. 5.54. D.c. characteristic of a weakly oscillating tunnel diode (upper) and the detected millimetre wave output (lower) as the applied voltage is swept at 60 cps. The absorption pip in the lower trace is from a cavity wavemeter tuned to 81 Gc (from BURRUS [1961]).

TABLE 5.6

Tunnel diode power outputs

Frequency	Power
50 Gc	50 μW
80 Gc	25 μW
103 Gc	0.3 μW

out as comparable to or less than the resistive cutoff frequency $f_c = 1/2\pi C_0 r_s$. This does not depend markedly on the degree of doping, but gallium arsenide diodes, which would be expected to give the best results from table 5.1, have the unfortunate property of deteriorating in performance very rapidly in the course of time, despite all the efforts that have been put into their fabrication technology (BURRUS [1966]).

Thus tunnel diodes are not seriously competitive with harmonic generators as millimetre wave power sources, although they remain useful as switches and detecting devices. Interest has tended to shift to diodes of the type to be described in the following section.

5.2. GUNN EFFECT AND AVALANCHE DIODE OSCILLATORS

Following the success of the tunnel diode as a compact solid state oscillator, further work on new semiconductor types has led in 1965 to the production of solid state oscillators operating by quite different mechanisms.

In 1964 GUNN [1964] reported that small slabs of bulk n-type gallium arsenide and indium phosphide showed current instabilies in electric fields of the order of 3000 V/cm. He discovered that strong microwave oscillations of frequency 1–6 Gc were taking place in the material, and that the oscillations were remarkably coherent and had a period equal to the transit time of the electrons across the semiconducting slab. Subsequent work has yielded continuous power outputs of over 10 mW (HAKKI and IRWIN [1965]) and pulsed outputs as high as 2.5 W (QUIST and FOYT [1965]) in the above frequency region. It has also proved possible to phase lock the oscillations to a radio frequency source, and so the Gunn effect "diode" (so called because of its two terminals, for no semiconductor junction is present) proves to be a microwave source with a performance comparable to that of a klystron. The extension of such a device to millimetre wavelength operation requires a factor of ten decrease in the slab thickness (at present 20–50 μ) and work on the growth of epitaxial layers is now in progress. Already harmonics of the rather nonsinusoidal oscillations have been observed in the 20–30 Gc range, and there seems no reason to regard these figures as an upper limit, though it must be admitted that the basic cause of the oscillations is as yet only qualitatively understood (HAKKI and KNIGHT [1965]).

Another development of 1965 has been the avalanche diode, a mechanism for which was first proposed by READ [1958]. The process of carrier multiplication during avalanche breakdown results in a (magnified) output current that is delayed in time behind a sinusoidal input voltage because multiplication only takes place when the electric field is greater than breakdown; the delay is in fact a quarter cycle. By arranging that these carriers are driven across an intrinsic undoped region before reaching the other side of the junction the delay can be increased to a half cycle, thus making the current rise as the voltage falls and producing a negative junction resistance at a frequency set by the size of the junction barrier layer. It now appears that almost any p-n junction diode can be made to oscillate by driving it into avalanche breakdown with large voltage pulses; continuous operation is normally precluded by thermal dissipation effects. The highest frequencies have been obtained by BURRUS [1965], who reports pulsed outputs as high as 350 mW at 50 Gc and 1 mW at 85 Gc from p-n silicon diodes in waveguide mountings similar to those previously described for tunnel diodes. Like Gunn diodes, the frequency was found to be coherent by cavity wavemeter standards, and also like Gunn diodes, harmonics were present and 300 Gc output was just barely observable from strongly oscillating 50 Gc diodes.

These devices are already seriously competitive with conventional sources of longer millimetre wavelengths, and it does seem possible that, with the steady present day improvement in small junction manufacturing techniques, they will eventually form useful millimetre wavelength spectroscopic sources, for their simplicity and convenience count greatly in their favour.

6. The plasma arc harmonic generator

Electrical discharges in low pressure gases are characterised by a long glowing plasma and marked striations near the cathode. Immediately adjacent to the cathode is the Crooke's dark space, in which electrons are accelerated by the positive space charge of the plasma until they are energetic enough to excite the gas molecules with which they collide, with resulting emission of light, and even to ionise neutral molecules with the formation of positive ions and more electrons. The plasma itself is a highly conducting mixture of positive ions and electrons moving in opposite directions. The effect of increasing the gas pressure is to make the plasma contract in diameter, because collisions with gas molecules slow down the rate of radial diffusion of individual plasma ions and electrons. The Crooke's dark space also becomes shorter because of the reduced distance travelled by electrons between collisions. At pressures of the order of one hundred atmospheres the plasma is only 0.05 mm in diameter and the cathode dark space a little over 10^{-7} cm wide (fig. 5.55). The resulting electric field across this dark

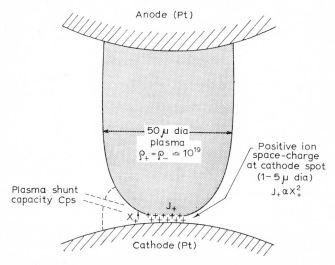

Fig. 5.55. The plasma-metal junction (from FROOME [1963]).

space is nearly 10^8 V/cm, a value so high that electrons are dragged out of the cathode by the field itself (FROOME [1963]) rather than released by positive ion bombardment, as occurs at lower pressures. This bombardment is however sufficiently intense to melt the very small cathode spot, so that some thermionic emission of electrons reinforces the field emission that takes place anyway. The plasma is largely composed of vaporised electrode material rather than of the surrounding gas, and so it is properly an arc rather than a gas discharge.

Many metals have been found suitable as electrodes for such a discharge, but platinum has the best chemical and electrical stability. Originally pure argon at several hundred atmospheres was used as the discharge gas, but it has since been found that the addition of 8% of hydrogen reduces the size of plasma and cathode spot so effectively that good operation is possible at one hundred atmospheres pressure.

Figure 5.55 shows that the plasma arc is closely analogous to a semiconductor to metal point contact, with the plasma taking the role of the bulk semiconductor and the cathode space the role of the barrier layer. The carrier density within the plasma is 10^{19} carriers/cm^3, comparable with typical semiconductor densities (table 5.1), but the lower carrier mobility leads to a somewhat higher plasma resistivity of 0.04 Ω cm. The "barrier" capacity has been calculated by FROOME [1963] to be 0.03 pF, and to this must be added the shunting capacity of the plasma itself and the interelectrode capacity, making a total of 0.05 pF. As the total resistance of the plasma under working conditions is 14–20 Ω, the whole device falls in the range between the germanium diodes of table 5.2.

The rectifying action of the arc is however very different, and merits detailed description. The electric field at the cathode (X^+) varies as the square root of the positive ion current density (J^+), but the electron current density (J^-) is a rapidly increasing exponential function of the field X^+, as described by FROOME [1963]. For all practical purposes there is no conduction until this field reaches a value of well over 10^7 V/cm, and then the electron current rises so rapidly that any further applied voltage is dropped across the plasma resistance rather than across the cathode space. This is the same situation as in a semiconductor diode biased to backward breakdown, and one would expect similar efficiencies of harmonic generation. Two features favour the plasma arc generator; first there is no conduction analagous to "forward" conduction in a semiconductor diode, for the electrodes cannot interchange roles in the time of a microwave cycle, and second the cathode spot is self renewing and virtually indestructible. Even low harmonic generation efficiencies can be tolerated, because there is no limit to the fundamental power that the arc can dissipate. The only practical limit so far has been the availability of high power millimetre wavelength sources; an unfortunate property of the plasma arc is that if the microwave drive ceases for as long as a microsecond the plasma diffuses radially outwards, and the arc will not re-strike when power is once more applied. Pulsed magnetron power sources are therefore useless, and the highest continuous power so far available has been 20 W at 8.7 mm wavelength. There is also a low limit to the useful drive set by the requirement that a voltage variation of the order of 10^7 V/cm must appear across the cathode space to produce any significant change in field emission; this low limit is in the region of a few watts. In practice, then, the plasma arc generator utilises a power range between that of the low level semiconductor harmonic generator and the pulsed ferrite multiplier, even though it is in principle superior to both of them.

The details of such a generator are shown in figs. 5.56 and 5.57. The anode wire acts as pickup aerial for the fundamental radiation, and the 0.05 mm long arc is struck across the harmonic waveguide. This guide is of circular cross-section, for ease of fabrication rather than on grounds of low millimetre wave attenuation, because the mode excited is the TE_{11} mode and radiation transmitted out to free space by means of a conical horn is polarised in the plane of the arc. In operation the arc is struck from

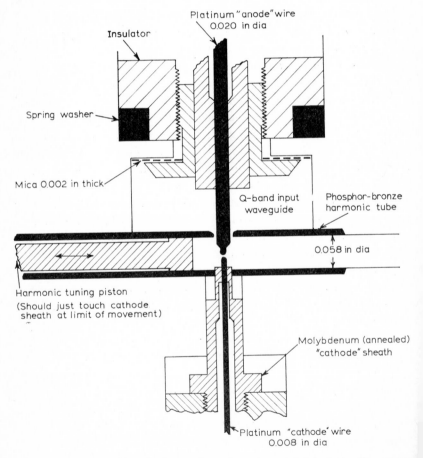

Fig. 5.56. Plasma-metal junction harmonic generator-harmonic tube design (from FROOMI [1963]).

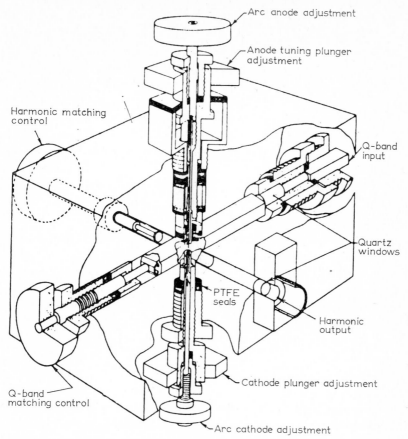

Fig. 5.57. Plasma-metal junction harmonic generator (from FROOME [1963]).

Calculated and measured harmonic output power

Harmonic no.	Frequency (Gc)	Calculated maximum power output (microwatt)	"Best-ever" measured output (microwatt)
6	210	200	100
12	420	3	1
20	700	0.1	0.01
29	1015	0.007 ($n = 30$)	0.001

a d.c. supply, taking about $\frac{1}{2}$ A at 25 V, and the microwave drive then switched on. This drops the voltage across the generator to 3–5 V without any change in the rectified current; evidently the latter is maintained by short pulses of microwave current, so that a conduction angle of less than 180° occurs. The exact value of this conduction angle is determined by the ratio of microwave driving voltage to the voltage necessary for the onset of field emission; Froome has estimated these to be respectively 60 V (peak to peak) and 16 V (d.c.), leading to a conduction angle of about 70°. The exact value depends on how much microwave power is reflected by the arc, the assumption here being that 10 W is absorbed and 10 W reflected. This conduction angle cannot be varied by adjustment of the d.c. bias, as in the case of semiconductor multipliers, because a value of bias less than the 16 V quoted above will cause the arc to go out, and at greater values the micro-wave drive takes control. It has proved possible to run (but not to strike) the arc in the absence of d.c. bias, but the output has never been as good as when bias is present.

Once the arc is running the millimetre wave output is optimised by adjustment of its position and that of the electrodes with respect to the harmonic waveguide, and by short circuiting plungers in both fundamental and harmonic waveguides. To avoid transfer of platinum between the electrodes, with a resulting slow movement of the arc, the d.c. bias is reversed at 5000 cps frequency, with a switching time so fast (BRADSELL [1963]) that the arc cannot go out during reversals. All the adjustments described must take place within high pressure argon gas, and the controls are designed as differential screw plungers passing through PTFE (Teflon) seals. The fundamental and harmonic radiation pass through quarter inch thick quartz seals inside their respective waveguides. The whole harmonic generator is mounted within a thickwalled metal box that has been made as small as a three inch cube; the gas leak rate is sufficiently low to permit operation for weeks or months between refillings.

The theory of the plasma arc harmonic generator is basically the same as that for multipliers discussed in section 2; Froome has made a calculation that allows for the losses due to plasma resistance at both fundamental and harmonic frequency, on the lines of the detector calculations of section 3, and obtains the figures shown in fig. 5.57. The agreement between experiment and his calculations is quite good, despite a tailing off of the observed power in the submillimetre region. The experimental conversion efficiencies, assuming a 10 W drive, are distinctly worse than those quoted in fig. 5.18, even when allowance is made for the fifty per cent increase in fundamental frequency used by Froome, but the actual available powers at submillimetre wavelengths are of course nearly two orders of magnitude greater.

A typical run through the harmonics of the plasma arc generator, using

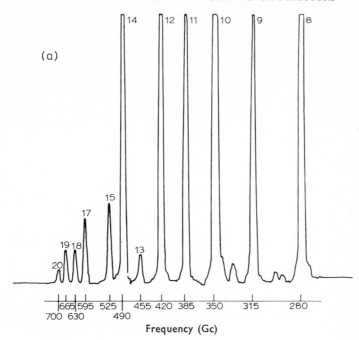

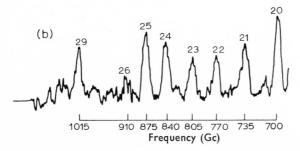

Fig. 5.58. The output of a plasma-metal junction microwave harmonic generator. The harmonics are numbered by multiples of the fundamental frequency, namely 35 Gc. Atmospheric water vapour absorbs the 16th harmonic at 0.54 mm. The output in the 13th appears low because of poor output coupling at this frequency. The deflexions between the 8th and 9th; 9th and 10th harmonics are grating 2nd order effects (from FRCOME [1963]).

a grating spectrometer and high sensitivity Golay detector is shown in fig. 5.58.

Still further output could be obtained from this generator by raising the drive level, for there is no sign of harmonic saturation at 20 W input (KNAPP [1965]). Alternatively the arc might be mounted in a cavity to increase the effective microwave electric field. Although such a device might well produce still more submillimetre wavelength harmonics, it would be less attractive as a spectroscopic source because of lack of tunability.

6.1. SPECTROSCOPY WITH THE PLASMA ARC GENERATOR

The generator giving the harmonic output shown in fig. 5.58 is in practice very critically adjusted with respect to its driving frequency, and a change of as little as 5–10 Mc will result in considerable loss of harmonics. Considerable changes in frequency cause complete loss of harmonics, despite readjustment of all the variable tuning devices described earlier, for the arc itself appears to act as some form of resonant cavity. Martin and Knapp have modified the generator so that it acts as a broadband submillimetre source, with a range of 10 W tunable klystrons as fundamental sources (KNAPP [1965], MARTIN and KNAPP [1966]). Although the submillimetre output obtained so far has fallen below that quoted by Froome by at least an order of magnitude, useful spectroscopy has been possible down to 0.6 mm wavelength (fig. 5.59). Harmonics are separated from each other by a small grating spectrometer and, with mechanical tuning of the klystrons giving a $\pm 5\%$ scan in fundamental frequency, successive harmonics provide a continuous submillimetre spectral coverage.

Long path transmission spectra for several gases in the 0.5–1 mm range have been obtained, and detailed studies of line broadening in nitrous oxide made. This spectrometer already shows considerable promise in investigation of broad spectra in gases and solids, and work at higher resolution will soon become possible with the advent of electronic stabilisation techniques for the exceptionally powerful and rather noisy microwave sources that must be used.

Conclusion

The field of semiconductor and related millimetre wave devices has undergone a most encouraging change in the last few years, for it can now be said that the operation of nearly all the generators and detectors that have been described in the preceding pages is quantitatively understood, and the problems they present are largely the technical ones of matching and mounting them in suitable holders. Work at wavelengths below 1 mm is now

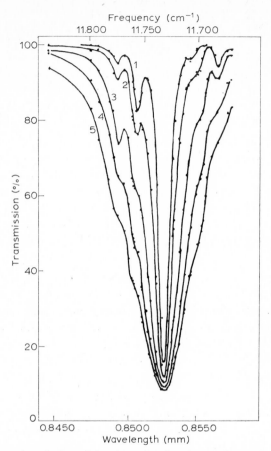

Fig. 5.59. Pressure broadening of the absorption line due to the J 13 → 14 rotational transition of gaseous N_2O at 0.85 mm wavelength. Curves 1 to 5 correspond respectively to pressures of 20, 40, 80, 120 and 160 mm Hg (from MARTIN and KNAPP [1966]).

becoming more common, and beachheads have been established at still shorter wavelengths below 0.5 mm, by direct harmonic generation (FROOME [1960]) and by harmonic mixer detection (BAUER et al. [1966]). Although there is a tendency to regard harmonic generation as a stopgap technique until something better comes along, it should be emphasised that this technique is an essential part of high resolution spectroscopy and very probably will always be superior to other methods of submillimetre wave detection. The various harmonic generators – semiconductor, plasma arc, and ferrite – occupy an ascending scale in drive power with roughly comparable milli-metre wavelength efficiencies, and the choice of which to use must depend on whether power output or ease of tunability is the most important consideration. Only the plasma arc generator can be said in itself to have extended the range of harmonic generation; the others have succeeded through a successful scaling down to accept shorter drive wavelengths, and in this respect are a tribute to modern millimetre wave tube design. Already the gulf between millimetre waves and far infrared radiation has been crossed, offering the possibility of comparing the stability of a far infrared laser with a radio frequency standard, and of introducing coherent radio techniques in regions where high resolution has been notoriously difficult to obtain.

The great strides made in semiconductor technology in recent years have revolutionised millimetre wave detection (BURRUS [1966]) and now appear on the verge of producing new millimetre wave sources. In this field progress is so rapid that any prediction becomes obsolete almost as soon as it is made, and new devices seem to appear almost daily. For example, in the recent literature there are reports of a new detector operating by the thermoelectric effect of carriers heated by the incident radiation (HARRISON and ZUCKER [1966]), which will operate at room temperature or, with greater sensitivity, when cooled, and is expected to respond uniformly to all wavelengths, and of a possible new generator of millimetre waves that operates by Josephson tunnelling of carriers between two superconductors separated by a thin insulating layer (LANGENBERG et al. [1966]), an effect that was predicted for the first time only in 1963. There can be no doubt that spectroscopists will soon be able to make measurements in the 0.2 mm–2 mm range with the same ease that now characterises work at centimetre and near infra-red wavelengths, thanks to the happy synthesis of microwave and optical techniques that is taking place.

Acknowledgements

The author would like to express his appreciation to the many millimetre wave workers who appear in these pages for patiently clarifying the details of their working techniques, and in particular to thank Dr. K. D. Froome and Mr. J. J. Gallagher for extensive information and helpful discussions.

References

B. A. AULD, J. Appl. Phys. **33** (1962) 112.

W. P. AYRES, IRE Trans. MTT. **7** (1959) 62.

J. G. BAKER and R. M. LEES, to be published; also R. M. LEES, Ph. D. Thesis, Univ. of Bristol (1966).

R. J. BAUER, M. COHN, J. M. COTTON and R. F. PACKARD, Proc. IEEE **54** (1966) 595.

D. A. BELL, Electrical Noise (Van Nostrand, 1960).

L. A. BLACKWELL and K. L. KOTZEBUE, Semiconductor Diode Parametric Amplifiers (Prentice-Hall, New York, 1961).

J. A. BRADSELL, J. Sci. Inst. **40** (1963) 225.

G. BROWN, D. R. MASON and J. S. THORP, J. Sci. Inst. **42** (1965) 648.

C. A. BURRUS, J. Appl. Phys. **32** (1961) 1031.

C. A. BURRUS, IEEE Trans. MTT. **11** (1963) 357.

C. A. BURRUS, Solid State Electronics **7** (1964) 219.

C. A. BURRUS, Proc. IEEE **53** (1965) 1256.

C. A. BURRUS, Proc. IEEE **54** (1966) 575.

P. E. CHASE and K. K. N. CHANG, IEEE Trans. MTT. **11** (1963) 560.

P. L. CLOUSER and W. GORDY, Phys. Rev. **134** (1964) A863.

P. D. COLEMAN and R. C. BECKER, IRE Trans. MTT. **7** (1959) 54.

P. D. COLEMAN, IEEE Trans. MTT. **11** (1963) 277.

J. W. DEES and A. P. SHEPPARD, Electronics (1963) p. 10.

B. C. DELOACH, IEEE Trans. MTT. **12** (1964) 15.

A. F. DIETRICH, Proc. IRE **49** (1961) 972.

A. F. DIETRICH, Rev. Sci. Inst. **33** (1962) 486.

A. F. DIETRICH and W. M. SHARPLESS, IEEE Trans. MTT. **12** (1964) 316.

S. T. ENG, IRE Trans. MTT. **9** (1961) 419.

L. ESAKI, Phys. Rev. **109** (1958) 603.

M. FARADAY, Phil. Trans. Roy. Soc. London **121** (1831) 299.

P. G. FAVERO, A. M. MIRRI and W. GORDY, Phys. Rev. **114** (1959) 1534.

P. G. FAVERO and A. M. MIRRI, Nuovo Cimento **30** (1963) 502.

W. H. FLYGARE and J. T. LOWE, J. Chem. Phys. **43** (1965) 3645.

K. D. FROOME, Nature **186** (1960) 959.

K. D. FROOME, Quantum Electronic Conference, Paris (1963), eds. D. Grivet and N. Bloembergen, Vol. 2, p. 1527.

W. GORDY, Proc. Symp. on Millimeter Waves (Polytechnic Press, Brooklyn, New York, 1960).

J. B. GUNN, IBM J. Res. Develop. **8** (1964) 141.

B. W. HAKKI and J. C. IRWIN, Proc. IEEE **53** (1965) 80.

B. W. HAKKI and S. KNIGHT, Solid State Communications **3** (1965) 89.

Handbook of Chemistry and Physics, A143 (Chemical Rubber Co., Cleveland, Ohio).

R. I. HARRISON and J. ZUCKER, Proc. IEEE **54** (1966) 588.

D. J. E. INGRAM, Spectroscopy at Radio and Microwave frequencies (Butterworths, London, 1955).

E. V. IVASH and D. M. DENNISON, J. Chem. Phys. **21** (1953) 1804.

C. M. JOHNSON, D. H. SLAGER and D. A. KING, Rev. Sci. Inst. **25** (1954) 213.

F. M. JOHNSON and A. H. NETHERCOT Jr., Phys. Rev. **114** (1959) 705.

G. JONES and W. GORDY, Phys. Rev. **135** (1964) A295.

R. KEWLEY, K. V. L. N. SASTRY, M. WINNEWEISER and W. GORDY, J. Chem. Phys. **39** (1963) 2856.

R. KEWLEY, K. V. L. N. SASTRY and M. WINNEWEISER, J. Mol. Spect. **12** (1964) 387.

W. C. KING and W. GORDY, Phys. Rev. **93** (1954) 407.

P. F. KNAPP, Ph. D. Thesis, Univ. of London (1965).

D. N. LANGENBERG, D. J. SCALAPINO and B. N. TAYLOR, Proc. IEEE **54** (1966) 560.

D. R. LIDE Jr., Rev. Sci. Inst. **35** (1964) 1226.

J. H. MANLEY and H. E. ROWE, Proc. IRE **47** (1959) 2115.

D. H. MARTIN and P. F. KNAPP, Proc. IEEE **54** (1966) 528.

R. MEREDITH and F. L. WARNER, IEEE Trans. MTT. **11** (1963) 397.

R. MEREDITH, F. L. WARNER, Q. V. DAVIS and J. L. CLARKE, Proc. IEEE. **III** (1964) 241.

J. B. MOCK, Rev. Sci. Inst. **31** (1960) 551.

J. L. MOLL, S. KRAKAUER and R. SHEN, Proc. IRE **50** (1962) 43.

J. L. MOLL, Physics of Semiconductors (McGraw-Hill, New York, 1964).

R. S. OHL, B. P. BUDENSTEIN and C. A. BURRUS, Rev. Sci. Inst. **30** (1959) 765.

T. H. OXLEY, J. Elec. Control **17** (1964) 1.

C. H. PAGE, Proc. IRE **46** (1958) 1738.

P. J. PENFELD and R. A. RAFUSE, Varactor Applications (MIT Press Cambridge, Mass., 1962).

M. PETER and M. W. P. STRANDBERG, Proc. IRE **43** (1955) 869.

F. X. POWELL and D. R. LIDE Jr., J. Chem. Phys. **41** (1964) 1413.

R. L. POYNTER and G. R. STEFFENSEN, Rev. Sci. Inst. **34** (1963) 77.

T. M. QUIST and A. G. FOYT, Proc. IEEE **53** (1965) 303.

W. T. READ Jr., Bell Syst. Tech. J. **37** (1958) 401.

W. M. SHARPLESS, Bell Syst. Tech. J. **42** (1963) 2496.

H. V. SHURMER, Proc. IEEE. **III** (1964a) 257.

H. V. SHURMER, Proc. IEEE. **III** (1964b) 1511.

J. H. SIMPSON and R. S. RICHARDS, Physical Principles and Applications of Junction Transistors (Oxford University Press, 1962).

R. A. SMITH, F. E. JONES and R. P. CHASMAR, Detection and Measurement of Infrared Radiation (Oxford, University Press, 1957).

R. A. SMITH, IEE Monographs **98** (1951) 43.

J. J. STICKLER, H. J. ZEIGER and G. S. HELLER, Phys. Rev. **127** (1962) 1077.

R. G. STRAUCH, R. E. CUPP, M. LICHTENSTEIN and J. J. GALLAGHER, Symp. on Quasi-Optics (Brooklyn Polytech. Inst., 1964).

R. G. STRAUCH, R. E. CUPP, V. E. DERR and J. J. GALLAGHER, Proc. IEEE **54** (1966) 506.

J. W. STRUTT, LORD RAYLEIGH, Theory of Sound (Second ed., MacMillan, London, 1894–1896).

H. SUHL, J. Appl. Phys. **28** (1957) 1225.

H. C. TORREY and C. A. WHITMER, Crystal Rectifiers (McGraw-Hill, New York, 1948).

C. H. TOWNES and A. L. SCHAWLOW, Microwave Spectroscopy (McGraw-Hill, New York 1955) ch. 10.

C. W. VAN ES, M. GEVERS and F. C. DE RONDE, Philips Tech. Rev. **22** (1960) 115.

M. T. WEISS, Phys. Rev. **107** (1957) 317.

E. G. WESSEL and R. J. STRAIN, IEEE Trans. MTT. **12** (1964) 139.

D. R. WOODS and R. G. STRAUCH, Proc. IEEE **54** (1966) 673.

E. YAMASHITA and J. R. BAIRD, Proc. IEEE **54** (1966) 606.

CHAPTER 6

COHERENT SOURCES USING ELECTRON BEAMS

BY

P. N. ROBSON

University of Sheffield, Sheffield, England

1. Introduction

The purpose of this chapter is to review the characteristics of both commercial and experimental free electron sources of radiation below 2 mm wavelength, and also to provide some insight into the problems involved in scaling such sources to oscillate at even higher frequencies. At the time of writing (early 1966), the experimental spectroscopist, intending to work at wavelengths of 2 mm and below, and contemplating the use of commercially available electron tubes as fundamental sources, would find no more than six tubes available. One of these is a reflex klystron generating 2 mm wavelength radiation (VAN IPEREN et al. [1963]), and the remainder are backward wave oscillators* (YEOU [1965]) covering the range 2 mm to 0.4 mm. There are, however, several approaches in development in the laboratory and these, too, will be discussed in this chapter.**

Many of the problems involved in constructing submillimetre tubes can be appreciated most easily by considering the klystron oscillator and section 3 is therefore devoted to this type of valve, with particular reference to the minimum current required to start oscillation and to efficiency. The single commercially available klystron for this wavelength range is described in this section and is used as a basis for predicting what is likely to be the minimum wavelength obtainable from klystron oscillators. Klystron frequency multipliers appear to have a higher ultimate output frequency than the self-excited klystron and recent progress in this approach is outlined.

In section 4 it is shown that travelling wave interactions, where electrons move in synchronism with a slow electromagnetic wave, are capable of achieving shorter wavelengths than the essentially lumped klystron interaction. Section 5 is devoted to the backward wave oscillator which is based on

---

* The French refer to these tubes as 'O-type carcinotrons' and this term has found fairly universal acceptance as an alternative to backward-wave oscillator or B.W.O.
** *Footnote added in press.* Varian Associates now manufacture a range of reflex klystrons covering 140–170 GHz. Hughes Aircraft supply a B.W.O. generating 2 watt over the range 135–150 GHz.

this conclusion; particular consideration is given to the starting current for oscillation in order to assess how much further B.W.O.'s are likely to advance into the infra-red spectrum. The rather stringent power supply requirements for these valves are also touched on.

The limitations of the magnetron as a source of short millimetre waves are considered in section 6.

The short wavelength limit for coherent free electron sources can, in principle, be extended to beyond 100 μ by using a longer wavelength source to bunch spatially the electrons in a relativistic beam. The harmonic radiation from this beam is then coupled out in one of several possible ways discussed in section 7.

Recently an oscillator capable of producing coherent cyclotron radiation at millimetre and submillimetre wavelengths has been reported and this is described in section 8. This tube, which has been demonstrated to have a tuning range greater than one octave, appears to have potential in the short submillimetre region if the necessary high magnetic fields can be produced conveniently.

2. Progress in the coherent generation of millimetre and submillimetre waves

The first truly coherent millimetre wave source was the smooth anode magnetron of CLEETON and WILLIAMS [1936] with which they succeeded in generating a wavelength of 6 mm. Further development of the magnetron and the use of multi-cavity anodes was done predominantly at centimetric wavelengths for radar purposes. After 1945 several groups, notable amongst these being the Columbia Radiation Laboratory, attempted to scale the multi-cavity magnetron to higher frequencies. The present day short wavelength limit for the magnetron is 2.5 mm (see section 6) and it seems unlikely that this will be reduced since other types of tube, notably the backward wave oscillator, have greater potentialities.

In 1946 the first millimetre-wave reflex klystron was reported by LAFFERTY [1946]. His tube, generating 4.15 mm wavelength radiation represented a considerable technical achievement, particularly when it is realised that nearly twenty years later, no reflex klystron has been made to oscillate at less than 2.0 mm wavelength. This is considered to be very near the ultimate capability of the reflex klystron (VAN IPEREN [1959]).

The first travelling wave tube amplifier to operate in the millimetric band was described by MILLMAN [1951]. This valve could have been made into a self excited, tunable oscillator, by coupling output back to input in suitable phase. However about this time it was realised that the feedback required to sustain oscillation could automatically be provided by utilising a travelling wave structure in which the phase and group velocities were oppositely directed (KOMPFNER et al. [1953]). This was the backward wave oscillator or B.W.O. In 1957, KARP [1957] reported a B.W.O. oscillating at around 1.5 mm wavelength, electronically tunable over a 13% bandwidth and having an output power of several milliwatts. Since this time, the short wavelength limit of the B.W.O. has been pushed steadily downwards by Convert and his colleagues; to 0.9 mm in 1960, 0.7 mm in 1961, 0.6 mm in 1962, 0.5 mm in 1963, and recently to just less than 0.4 mm (YEOU et al. [1965]). Fig. 6.1 shows the performance of some of these tubes. However a fundamental limit is believed to lie near 0.1 mm unless radically new cathode forms can be devised (see section 5.3).

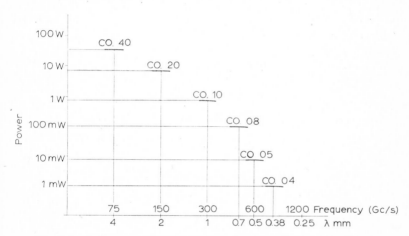

Fig. 6.1. Performance of C.S.F. backward wave oscillators (after Yeou).

With the advent of linear electron accelerators, tightly bunched relativistic electron beams were made available and these provided a current source containing high harmonics of the bunching frequency. MOTZ [1951] suggested a means whereby these travelling current waves could be made to radiate efficiently into an overmoded waveguide surrounding the beam. Radiation was observed down to 100 μ using the beam from a 3.5 MeV accelerator, and with a 100 MeV beam, optical frequencies were seen. Other suggestions have been advanced and tested for obtaining harmonic energy from the beams of linear accelerators (WILLSHAW [1960]), but no significant improvements on the results of Motz et al. have been reported in the submillimetre range

(MOTZ et al. [1953]). The equipment required for high energy beams is complex and this approach may be of limited interest to spectroscopists.

An alternative method for producing a stream of electrons containing a fundamental component of current in the submillimetre region exists in principle by irradiating a photo-electric surface with two laser beams whose frequencies differ by the required amount. Heterodyning is achieved since the emitted photo-current is proportional to the total intensity of the incident optical flux. Possible tube configurations, suitable for short wavelength generation, have been discussed by Cullen (CULLEN [1963]; CULLEN et al. [1963]) and mixing has been observed at 31Gc/s (WITTWER [1963]) between two axial modes of a ruby laser, but submillimetre radiation has not yet been generated in this way.

The most recent development is in the generation of coherent cyclotron radiation by a beam of electrons gyrating in an intense uniform magnetic field. This possibility was considered by PANTELL [1959], HIRSHFIELD and WACHTEL [1964] and SCHNEIDER [1959], and was recently very clearly demonstrated by BOTT [1964, 1965] using superconducting magnets to generate magnetic fields of sufficient intensity to give radiation in the short millimetre and submillimetre region.

Reference must also be made to the recent development of gas lasers for the submillimetre region but these are described in ch. 1 rather than in this chapter because they are not based on an electron beam interaction.

3. Klystron oscillators

3.1. STARTING CURRENT FOR THE TWO CAVITY KLYSTRON OSCILLATOR

We begin by reviewing the operation of the two cavity klystron (fig. 6.3a). A focussed cylindrical electron beam is accelerated from a suitable electron gun towards the input cavity resonator, or buncher cavity. After crossing the cavity gap where the beam becomes velocity modulated, it drifts along in a field free region and finally traverses the gap of a second cavity, or catcher, before striking the collector electrode. A signal injected into the first cavity results in an electric field appearing across the cavity gap and, since the gap is normally sufficiently narrow that the transit time of electrons across it is a small fraction of an r.f. cycle, the kinetic energy of an electron crossing the gap is changed by an amount directly proportional to the r.f. voltage across the gap at the instant of transit. The electrons in the beam will therefore be speeded up or slowed down depending on the instantaneous phase of the gap voltage. In the drift region following this cavity fast electrons approach those which crossed the gap at an earlier portion of the cycle, when the phase of the gap voltage was such as to decelerate them. Electrons therefore tend to form into clusters or bunches in the drift space with the result that an a.c. convection current is set up on the beam.

The amplitude of the fundamental component of current in the beam is a slowly varying function of drift distance z from the buncher, being zero when z is zero. The form this function takes depends on the degree of mutual interaction between electrons in the beam due to their own space charge. In low density beams the space charge debunching is small but in many practical klystron amplifiers it is necessary to take it into account. This is most conveniently done by treating the electron stream initially as a monoenergetic, drifting, compressible, charged fluid. The velocity modulation induced by the buncher is considered to be a small time-varying perturbation on the steady flow and this modulation creates a small amplitude time-varying component of convection current at the bunching frequency. This linearised hydrodynamic approach is referred to as space-charge wave theory whereas the purely ballistic treatment, which ignores space charge, is called kinematic theory (BECK [1958]).

These theories provide different expressions for the fundamental component of convection current i_z; these are given in eqs. (6.1) and (6.2).

Kinematic theory

$$i_z = -2I_0 J_1\left(\frac{\omega z V_1}{2u_0 V_0}\right) \cos \omega \left(t - \frac{z}{u_0}\right); \qquad (6.1)$$

Space charge wave theory

$$i_z = -\frac{I_0 V_1}{2V_0}\left(\frac{\omega}{\omega_p}\right) \sin \left(\frac{\omega_p z}{u_0}\right) \cos \omega \left(t - \frac{z}{u_0}\right), \qquad (6.2)$$

where $V_1 \sin \omega t$ is the voltage developed across the buncher gap, u_0 is the unperturbed beam velocity and V_0 the corresponding potential ($\frac{1}{2} mu_0^2 = eV_0$), z is distance measured from the buncher, I_0 is the d.c. beam current. The plasma frequency, ω_p, is a measure of the space charge density in the beam and is equal to $(J_0 e/u_0 \varepsilon_0 m)^{\frac{1}{2}}$ where J_0 is the d.c. current density, e/m is the electronic charge to mass ratio and ε_0 the permittivity of free space. The fundamental component of current density has its first maximum when $\omega z V_1/2u_0 V_0 = 1.84$ corresponding to the first maximum of the Bessel function, $J_1(X)$ if kinematic theory is appropriate, or when $\omega_p z/u_0 = \frac{1}{2}\pi$ if space charge wave theory more correctly describes the conditions of operation.

In the klystron amplifier the output or catcher cavity is normally placed at the position of maximum current modulation. The convection current induces a voltage across the gap of the output cavity, which is tuned to the same frequency as the input cavity, in time antiphase with the current, thereby extracting maximum power from the modulated beam.

The power gain in the two cavity klystron can be described and analysed in the following way. Fig. 6.2 shows a simplified lumped equivalent circuit for

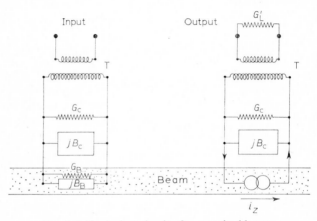

Fig. 6.2. Equivalent circuit of two cavity klystron.

the two cavity klystron where input and output cavities are considered to be identical. Near resonance each cavity can be represented by a perfect transformer T, a shunt susceptance jB_c and the conductance G_c. At resonance B_c is zero and the conductance G_c represents the cavity losses caused by the finite conductivity of the cavity walls. The turns ratio of the transformer T is determined by the degree of coupling between the cavity and the waveguide to which it is connected. If the transit time of the electrons across the buncher gap is not a small fraction of a cycle, then net power is transferred to the beam. This can be represented in fig. 6.2 by loading the buncher cavity with a further shunt admittance $G_B + jB_B$. Normally however, both these quantities are small and in the present approximation will be neglected.

The catcher cavity is terminated by the load admittance G_L' (assumed purely resistive for the moment), which transformed by T appears as G_L in parallel with the cavity conductance G_c. The modulated beam, passing between the gaps of the catcher cavity, can be shown to induce a current i_z into the cavity, equal to the convection current on the beam at the position of the catcher and given by either eq. (6.1) or (6.2). Thus referring to fig. 6.2 we have

$$\text{Input power} = \tfrac{1}{2} V_1^2 G_c, \tag{6.3}$$

$$\text{Output power} = \frac{A^2 I_0^2}{2(G_c + G_L)}, \tag{6.4}$$

where $A = 2J_1\left(\dfrac{\omega z V_1}{2u_0 V_0}\right)$ if kinetic theory is appropriate

or $A = \dfrac{V_1}{2V_0}\left(\dfrac{\omega}{\omega_p}\right) \sin\left(\dfrac{\omega_p z}{u_0}\right)$ if space charge wave theory is appropriate.

The power gain, found by dividing (6.4) by (6.3) can be made greater than unity if the d.c. beam current I_0 is sufficiently large. With a power gain greater than unity, the two cavity klystron can obviously be made into an oscillator by coupling a fraction of the output power back to the input cavity. However a total loop phase shift equal to $2\pi n$ radians where n is any positive integer, must be maintained and this requires a suitable form of adjustable phase shifter in the feedback loop.

The starting current for oscillation can readily be found, assuming the phase shift condition is satisfied, by noting that if the output resonator is connected directly to the input resonator, then $G_L = G_c$. Setting the power gain equal to unity for the starting current, gives from (6.3) and (6.4)

$$\frac{A^2 I_0^2}{2G_c} = 2V_1^2 G_c. \tag{6.5}$$

We have the choice of two relations for A. If we are only concerned with predicting the starting current for oscillation, then at the threshold of oscillation, V_1 must be vanishingly small and the Bessel function may be written

$$J_1\left(\frac{\omega z V_1}{2u_0 V_0}\right) \approx \frac{\omega z V_1}{4u_0 V_0}.$$

Thus the starting current is given by

$$(I_0)_{\text{start}} = \frac{4G_c V_0 u_0}{\omega z} \quad \text{if space charge is neglected}, \tag{6.6}$$

$$\text{or } (I_0)_{\text{start}} = \frac{4G_c V_0 u_0}{\omega z}\left[\frac{\omega_p z/u_0}{\sin(\omega_p z/u_0)}\right] \quad \text{when space charge is considered.} \tag{6.7}$$

For the case $\omega_p z/u_0 \ll 1$, eqs. (6.6) and (6.7) give the same value for the starting current. In general however since the term in square brackets in (6.7) is always greater than unity, the start-oscillation current is greater the larger the space charge density in the beam. This result is to be expected intuitively since the effect of space charge is to inhibit electron bunching.

The two cavity self-excited oscillator just described has been little used in practice, its chief drawbacks being:

(a) two cavities have to be tuned simultaneously to resonance,

(b) the total loop phase shift is frequency sensitive and therefore some variable phase control must be included in the feedback path.

These disadvantages are overcome in the reflex klystron, considered in the next section.

3.2. STARTING CURRENT AND EFFICIENCY OF THE REFLEX KLYSTRON

A schematic diagram of the reflex klystron is shown in fig. 6.3b. A single cavity C is used to perform the dual role of buncher and catcher. After passing through the cavity, the electron beam enters a region of retarding electric field rather than a field free drift region as previously. The retarding field is produced by a suitably shaped repeller or reflector electrode R held at a potential $-V_R$ negative with respect to the cathode. Thus electrons are caused to reverse their direction of motion some distance in front of the reflector electrode and return through the cavity gap. Electrons that are accelera-

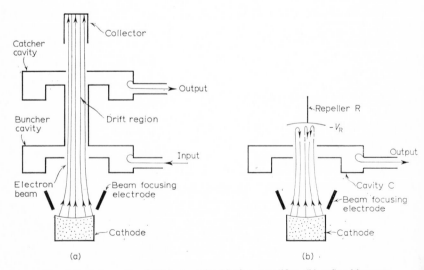

Fig. 6.3. Schematic of (a) two cavity klyston amplifier, (b) reflex klystron.

ted by the r.f. field on first crossing the cavity gap penetrate deeper into the retarding field and thus take longer to return to the cavity than do electrons decelerated on crossing the gap. The deceleration of electrons in the reflector region is uniform if the electric field in this region is constant, which closely approximates the situation in many reflex klystrons.

Thus, as with the two cavity klystron, the initial velocity modulation set up by the cavity, causes current modulation to appear on the beam. The equation, corresponding to eq. (6.1) for the fundamental component of current modulation on the returning beam at the cavity gap is

$$i_z = 2I_0 J_1 \left(\frac{\omega z V_1}{2 u_0 V_0} \right) \sin \left(\omega t - \frac{\omega z}{u_0} - \tfrac{1}{2}\pi \right), \qquad (6.8)$$

where the symbols have the same meaning as previously except that z is now the total distance travelled by an unperturbed electron, into the reflector region and back to the cavity. Thus z is a function of the potential on the reflector electrode. Two differences are noted when comparing eqs. (6.1) and (6.8); a change of sign due to the reversal of the direction of current flow and an extra phase lag of $\tfrac{1}{2}\pi$ radians. The latter occurs because in the two cavity klystron an electron bunch forms around the electron that passed through the buncher one quarter cycle before the peak accelerating r.f. voltage, whereas in the reflex klystron, a bunch forms about an electron that passed through one quarter cycle after the peak.

From eq. (6.8) and remembering that the modulating voltage is $V_1 \sin \omega t$, the electronic admittance of the returning beam $Y_e = G_e + j B_e$ is defined by:

$$G_e = \frac{- \text{In phase component of } i_z}{V_1} = \frac{-2I_0}{V_1} J_1 \left(\frac{\omega z V_1}{2 u_0 V_0} \right) \cos \left(\frac{\omega z}{u_0} + \tfrac{1}{2}\pi \right),$$

$$(6.9)$$

$$B_e = \frac{- \text{Leading quadrature component of } i_z}{V_1} =$$

$$= \frac{+2I_0}{V_1} J_1 \left(\frac{\omega z V_1}{2 u_0 V_0} \right) \sin \left(\frac{\omega z}{u_0} + \tfrac{1}{2}\pi \right). \qquad (6.10)$$

The effect of the returning beam is to load the equivalent circuit of the cavity with a shunt conductance G_e and shunt susceptance B_e, both of which are functions of the transit angle $\omega z / u_0$ in the reflector region. This is shown in fig. 6.4. We note from this figure that the resonant frequency is determined by the condition

$$B_e + B_c + B_L = 0 \qquad (6.11)$$

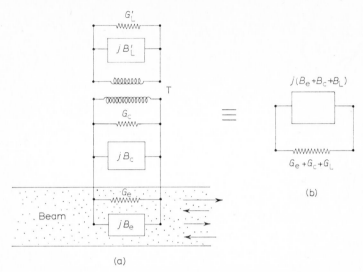

Fig. 6.4. Equivalent circuit of reflex klystron; (a) complete circuit, (b) reduced version of (a).

where B_L is the susceptance associated with the load. Oscillation can occur because the total shunt conductance $G_e + G_c + G_L$ can be negative since G_e can be negative. For the start-oscillation condition:

$$G_e + G_c + G_L = 0 \qquad (6.12)$$

i.e. oscillations are undamped. At the start-oscillation condition V_1 will be small and using therefore the small argument approximation for the Bessel function, from (6.9) and (6.12)

$$(I_0)_{\text{start}} = \frac{(G_c + G_L)2V_0}{\theta \cos (\theta + \tfrac{1}{2}\pi)} \qquad (6.13)$$

where $\theta = \omega z/u_0$.

Minimum start-oscillation current occurs when $\cos (\theta + \tfrac{1}{2}\pi) = 1$, i.e.

$$\theta = (n + \tfrac{3}{4})2\pi, \qquad n = 0, 1, 2, \text{etc.} \qquad (6.14)$$

where n is known as the mode number.

With this condition

$$(I_0)_{\text{start}} = \frac{(G_c + G_L)V_0}{(n + \tfrac{3}{4})\pi}. \qquad (6.15)$$

Had the space charge wave expression for convection current been used to obtain the d.c. starting current rather than the kinematic equation then the right-hand side of (6.11) would have been multiplied by a factor $\omega_p \theta / \omega \times \sin(\omega_p \theta / \omega)$, as was the case for the two cavity klystron examined in the preceeding section. Since from eq. (6.10) $\theta \approx \pi$ and in most practical klystrons, $\omega_p / \omega \ll 1$, this correction factor is close to unity and will be neglected in what follows. If the d.c. beam current exceeds $(I_0)_{start}$ the peak voltage V_1 across the resonator gap will build up, and the steady state value is determined by (6.12). From (6.9) and (6.12),

$$\frac{2I_0}{V_1} J_1\left(\frac{\theta V_1}{2V_0}\right) \cos\left(\theta + \tfrac{1}{2}\pi\right) = G_c + G_L \tag{6.16}$$

and the output power of the device is $\tfrac{1}{2}V_1{}^2 G_L$.

We are now in a position to understand the observed behaviour of the reflex klystron both as regards its frequency of oscillation and its output power, as the reflector voltage is varied and all other parameters are kept constant. In fig. (6.5) typical curves of output power and frequency are

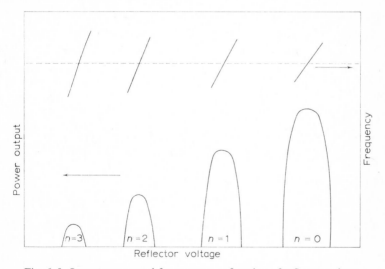

Fig. 6.5. Output power and frequency as a function of reflector voltage.

shown as a function of the reflector voltage which in turn determines the transit angle θ in the reflector region. As θ departs from the value $(n + \tfrac{3}{4})2\pi$, the electronic conductance G_e becomes less negative and eventually oscillations cannot be sustained. This is the explanation of the discrete modes of oscillation seen in fig. 6.5. More detailed solution of equation (6.16) shows that the maximum power in any one mode occurs when $\theta = (n+\frac{3}{4})2\pi$ and generally decreases monotonically as n increases, i.e. as the reflector voltage becomes less negative. This can be understood qualitatively since, as n increases, an electron spends longer between leaving and returning to the cavity and therefore optimum bunching will be obtained with a lower r.f. gap voltage. The reduction in gap voltage implies a reduction in output power. Thus although eq. (6.15) predicts a starting current which decreases as the mode number n increases, the efficiency also decreases.

The output frequency is observed from fig. 6.5 to vary with reflector voltage and thus to provide some degree of electronic tuning. This is to be understood by noting, from eq. (6.10), that the electronic conductance B_e depends on θ and hence on the reflector voltage. Since the frequency of oscillation is determined by eq. (6.11), it will alter as B_e varies in order to maintain the equality. Changes in load susceptance will also cause the frequency to change, by a similar argument, even though the reflector voltage remains constant.

The efficiency of a reflex klystron depends on the load conductance G_L and this can readily be altered by changing the degree of coupling between the cavity and the output waveguide. Remembering that the ouput power is equal to $\frac{1}{2}V_1^2 G_L$, substituting for G_L from (6.16), and differentiating the resulting expression to find the maximum power, the following relationships are obtained

$$J_0(X) = \frac{2G_c}{G_0\theta} \tag{6.17}$$

and for the efficiency η,

$$\eta = \frac{X^2 J_2(X)}{\theta} \tag{6.18}$$

where $J_0(X)$ and $J_2(X)$ are Bessel functions of the 1st kind of zero order and second order respectively; $X = \theta V_1/2V_0$, and $G_0 = I_0/V_0$.

3.3. REFLEX KLYSTRON SCALING

We are now in a position to appreciate the problems involved in scaling klystrons to operate at shorter wavelengths. A wavelength of about 2 mm is the limit for a commercially available klystron at the present time, e.g. the Philips type DX 247. Fig. 6.6 shows a sectional view of a similar valve designed for 2.5 mm operation. A key to the component parts and some important dimensions are provided in the caption to this figure.

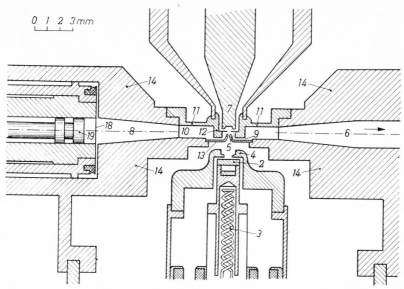

0 1 2 3mm

Fig. 6.6. Central portion of reflex klystron for 2.5 mm waves. 2. L cathode; 3. heater; 4. focusing electrode; 5. resonant cavity; 6. output waveguide; 7. repeller; 8. waveguide with shorting plunger (not shown); 9. quarter-wave transformer; 10. annular space (9, 10 and 8 together form the matching transformer between the resonant cavity 5 and the output waveguide 6); 11. thin wall allowing copper section, 12, to be moved axially in relation to the copper section, 13, by means of an external tuning mechanism (mechanical tuning); 14. copper block in which central portion is mounted; 18. mica window; 19. shorting plunger.

Diameter of opening in electrode 4 0.6 mm   Diameter of holes in 12 and 13   0.15 mm
Diameter of resonant cavity 5 . . .1.0 mm   Diameter of waveguides 6 and 8 2.0   mm
Height of resonant cavity 5   . . . 0.4 mm   (after Van Iperen).

The accelerating voltage for this tube, between cathode and resonator is 2400 to 2500 V, and the total d.c. beam current is in the region of 16 mA. In order to pass this current through the resonator without significant interception, the beam is focussed from an active area of cathode some 600 μ diameter, down to about 80 μ diameter at its narrowest point. The current density at this point is slightly greater than 300 A/cm², and the power density in the beam is therefore 0.75 MW/cm². A bandwidth of some 15% is obtainable by mechanical tuning; in order to do this the top half of the cavity (12) and the reflector (7) are moved axially by means of an external tuning mechanism. The thin flexible diaphragm (11) permits this motion. Alignment of the electrodes must be accurate to better than several microns and facilities are provided for adjustments to be made when the tube is in operation. The average output power is approximately 20 mW and the efficiency is therefore less than 1 %. Both maximum output power and maximum tuning range is found to occur for the $\theta = (10\frac{3}{4})2\pi$ and $\theta = (11\frac{3}{4})2\pi$ modes. The output is along the waveguide (6); the plunger (19) is optimised for maximum output power at a given frequency.

Two problems are immediately obvious from studying fig. 6.6 and the preceding paragraph. Mechanical tolerances are extremely small on tubes operating at this wavelength and the problems of heat dissipation, since eventually most of the beam current alights on the resonator, are considerable. Less obviously, the electric field, particularly in the reflector region, is sufficiently high to cause vacuum breakdown unless care is taken.

Suppose now we wish to scale the above tube down to a wavelength $1/S$ times its design wavelength where S is greater than unity. This is to be done by scaling all linear dimensions $1/S$ times, including the cathode dimensions but keeping all d.c. voltages constant. The problems of breakdown, heat dissipation and tolerances will not be taken into account, it being assumed in some way that they can be overcome. Assuming for the moment that the cathode emission remains space charge limited, the total beam current I_0 does not change. The following quantities remain invariant under this form of scaling: I_0, V_0, G_0, θ. The cavity shunt conductance however increases $\sqrt{S}$ times if a normal skin effect law is assumed to account for resonator losses. Reference to eq. (6.13) suggests that the minimum starting current $(G_L = 0)$ will increase as $\sqrt{S}$, and $J_0(X)$ from eq. (6.17) will also increase as $\sqrt{S}$. When the numerator and denominator in (6.17) are equal, $J_0(X) = 1$, $X = 0$, and from (6.18) the efficiency is zero. VAN IPEREN [1959] has shown there are good reasons for believing that the 2.5 mm klystron could only be scaled by a factor $S = 2$ before the efficiency falls to zero.

One initially obvious way to maintain $J_0(X) < 1$ is either to increase G_0 or θ to compensate for the increase in G_c as wavelength decreases. It is found in practice that for values of θ greater than about $(10+\frac{3}{4})2\pi$ the starting current starts to increase as θ increases rather than decrease as eq. (6.13) suggests. This is attributed to the failure of simple kinematic theory to predict the fundamental component of convection current for long transit angles in the reflector region since space charge effects and aberrations in the reflector field are not taken into account. Thus one is left with the only alternative of increasing G_0, either by increasing the current I_0, or decreasing the voltage V_0. Decreasing the voltage is not practicable since the transit time of an electron across the gap of the resonator becomes an increasing fraction of an r.f. cycle, which has the effect of further increasing G_c.

The cathode current density for the 2.5 mm valve is seen to be some 5

A/cm^2 which comes near to the limit attainable from the best thermionic emitters under conditions of continuous operation. In a valve scaled $1/S$ times, the cathode current density must increase S^2 in order to maintain the total beam current constant. Since this is obviously impossible, the cathode area must be made larger and the degree of beam convergence increased. As the area convergence is increased however it becomes increasingly difficult to maintain the same minimum beam diameter at the focus. The defocussing effect is caused because electrons are emitted from the cathode, not necessarily normal to the cathode surface, with a range of thermal velocities (PIERCE [1949]). More detailed calculations (VAN IPEREN [1959]) suggest that because emission velocities limit the maximum current that can be focussed through a given klystron gap, and since this maximum decreases with wavelength because the gap diameter decreases, it is impossible to provide the starting current required for wavelengths below 1 mm by using electrostatic focussing. The work of Ash however (ASH [1963]), who has considered the use of a highly convergent magnetic field to compress the electron beam, suggests that a current density in excess of 2500 A/cm^2 can be produced in a 2 kV beam in this manner. This method of focussing would, of course, add to the complexity of the reflex klystron. If new cathode materials, having emission densities significantly greater than say 10 A/cm^2, were available, or if magnetic compression proved feasible, then the lower wavelength limit of the klystron could possibly be reduced to below 1 mm wavelength. The remaining problems of heat dissipation, electric field breakdown in the reflector region and reflector alignment would still be formidable however.

3.4. KLYSTRON FREQUENCY MULTIPLIERS

The convection current produced by velocity modulating an electron beam contains not only a fundamental component at the bunching frequency but also harmonic components. In this connection it is interesting to note that if the modulating voltage could be made to have a triangular, rather than sinusiodal waveform as a function of time, and if space charge were neglected, then perfect delta function bunching could be obtained. In this ideal state, all harmonics of the fundamental would be present in equal amplitude.

A klystron frequency multiplier resembles a two cavity klystron with the buncher cavity driven by an external "fundamental" source and with the catcher cavity tuned to a harmonic of this drive frequency. The frequency stability and fractional tuning range can be made no greater than those of the source. There are however no starting current requirements.

Accurate theoretical prediction of the harmonic current density in the beam of a multiplier is difficult since, with input drives as large as are feasible, small signal conditions cannot be invoked. The problem has been studied actively by two groups in recent years (KING et al. [1963], VAN IPEREN et al. [1965]) and considerable progress has been made. No commercial valves exist at the time of writing but recently an experimental multiplier, starting from a fundamental wavelength of 8 mm and producing an output power of 30 mW at the tenth harmonic has been reported (KUIJPERS [1965]). The tuning range is some 5%. These devices would appear to be highly promising.

3.5. REFLEX KLYSTRON POWER SUPPLIES

Both the output power and frequency of a reflex klystron depend markedly on the voltages applied to its resonator grid and reflector and these voltages must be carefully regulated. The heater current also requires careful stabilisation since it determines, in part, the temperature of the tube which, through dimensional changes, causes the frequency to alter. For example, in the case of the 2 mm klystron described in section 3.3, 1 mA change in heater current (normal value 1.83 A) will alter the frequency by 18 Mc/s.

For a general discussion of stablised voltage supplies suitable for reflex klystrons the reader is referred to the book by BENSON [1957]. A power supply that would be suitable for the above klystron is described by WARNER [1950]. The E.H.T. voltage required (2.6 kV max) for this klystron is greater than that provided by many commercial power supplies designed for tubes giving longer wavelengths.

4. Travelling wave interactions

4.1. EXTENDED INTERACTION KLYSTRONS

We have seen in preceeding sections that in order to modulate and demodulate the electron beam in a klystron effectively, the transit time for electrons to traverse both the buncher and catcher gaps must be a small fraction of a r.f. period. If the electron beam velocity remains fixed, then the gap length must scale as wavelength in order to keep the transit angle constant. If instead of using a resonant cavity, a travelling wave structure is used to modulate and demodulate the beam, then the transit time along the structure may be many cycles long. In this case it is necessary that the phase velocity of the wave supported by the travelling wave structure be very closely matched to the electron beam drift velocity. Thus individual electrons remain in essentially a constant field during the period of time they spend in traversing the coupler. The requirements for a suitable modulating structure then are that it can support a wave having a phase velocity much less than the velocity of light (e.g. $0.1c$ for a 2.5 kV beam) in order to synchronise with the electron beam, and also that the wave shall have an axial component of electric field to accelerate or decelerate electrons. Such structures are commonly referred to as slow wave structures.

Suppose that the two resonant cavities of a klystron are replaced by two resonant slow wave structures. The first structure modulates the beam in the same manner as the bunching cavity, and the second structure acts as a catcher. In order to determine the start oscillation condition, the equivalent conductance of one of these resonant systems has to be calculated and compared with that of a klystron cavity. The calculation can be conveniently done as follows. A resonant standing wave field on the slow wave structure may be decomposed into two oppositely travelling waves of equal amplitude.

Each component has a maximum axial component of electric field E at the position of the beam and an associated total power flux P. The quantity $E^2/2 \, \beta^2 P$, where β is the propagation constant of the wave, is called the coupling impedance Z_c and has the dimensions of resistance. If the attenuation constant for each travelling wave component is α then the power in each wave decays, as $P \exp -2\alpha z$. Assuming $\alpha z \ll 1$, the power dissipated in losses per component of the travelling wave is $2\alpha L P$, where L is the structure length. Thus the total power loss in the standing wave is $4\alpha L P$ while the peak energy attained by an electron traversing the structure in synchronism with one component of the standing wave is EL, expressed as a voltage. The oppositely directed travelling wave appears, to electrons in the stream, to move past them at twice the electron drift velocity, and this produces no cumulative effect. An equivalent conductance G_c' can then be defined such that

$$G_c' = \frac{2 \text{ Power dissipated}}{(\text{Peak voltage})^2} = \frac{8\alpha P L}{E^2 L^2} = \frac{4\alpha}{\beta^2 L Z_c}. \qquad (6.19)$$

If attenuation is due to ohmic losses and scales with frequency according to the normal skin effect law, then $\alpha/\beta \sim \lambda^{-\frac{1}{2}}$. Since Z_c remains invariant on scaling and $\beta \sim \lambda^{-1}$ we have from (6.19):

$$G_c' \sim \frac{\lambda^{\frac{1}{2}}}{L}. \qquad (6.20)$$

If the whole travelling wave coupler were to be scaled in direct proportion to wavelength, so that $L \sim \lambda$, from eq. (6.19) $G_c \sim \lambda^{-\frac{1}{2}}$ which is just the same rate as for the klystron cavity. However with the travelling wave coupler, although it is natural to scale the transverse dimensions proportionally to wavelength, to maintain the coupling impedance and phase velocity constant the interaction length L need not be scaled since electrons and wave always move in synchronism.

A system of the sort just described could be made into an oscillator by providing some coupling between the two resonant slow wave structures. Referring to eq. (6.13), the starting current is directly proportional to cavity loss conductance. Thus with travelling wave input and output couplers the starting current required, according to (6.20) is inversely proportional to coupler length. Travelling wave couplers would therefore seem to offer considerable advantages at short wavelengths, where it becomes increasingly difficult to provide sufficient current in cavity klystrons to give much power or even to start oscillations. It is not possible in practice however to increase the coupler length without limit. Equation (6.19) was derived with the assumption that $\alpha L \ll 1$ which is not the case for arbitrarily large values of L.

This principle has recently been used directly to provide a high-power source for wavelengths of several millimetres (DAY and NOLAND [1965]). For short wavelengths, sources based on an extension of the idea are more successful. It turns out to be unnecessary to separate the bunching and catching slow wave structures in order to provide signal gain or oscillation. This was first realised by KOMPFNER [1946] and resulted in the travelling wave amplifier and later in the voltage tunable backward wave oscillator described in the following sections.

4.2. TRAVELLING WAVE AMPLIFIER

The travelling wave amplifier will be described initially since an understanding of the gain mechanism is helpful later in considering the corresponding oscillators. A schematic view of a typical amplifier is shown in fig. 6.7. The electron beam traverses a single slow wave structure which is not made resonant. The input signal is coupled into the slow wave structure at the electron gun end and the output is taken from the collector end.

Consider initially a signal injected at the gun end. The wave associated with this signal will travel along the structure with a phase velocity directed from gun to collector, which is assumed equal, in the first instance, to the electron beam drift velocity. At any point in time the axial electric field distribution due to this wave varies with distance sinusoidally as shown in fig. 6.8. Electrons entering the slow wave structure when the field is zero

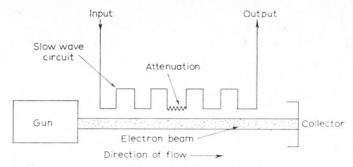

Fig. 6.7. Schematic of travelling wave amplifier.

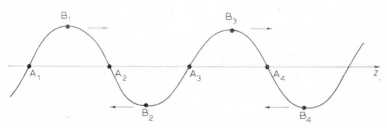

Fig. 6.8. Bunching of electrons in an almost synchronous travelling wave field.

(A_1, A_2, A_3, A_4 etc.) drift with the wave and their phase relative to the wave remains unchanged. Electrons at points such as B_1, B_3, are accelerated and drift towards the phase stable electrons at A_2 and A_4 respectively. Electrons at points B_2, B_4, are decelerated towards the phase stable electrons at A_2 and A_4 respectively. Thus electron bunches tend to form around the phase stable electrons at A_2, A_4 etc. In order for energy to be extracted from the beam and fed into the travelling wave, more electrons must be positioned in decelerating phases than in accelerating ones and this is not the case when there is exact synchronism between wave and electron stream. If however the wave moves slightly slower than the electron drift velocity, then the centres of gravity of the bunches move from the point A_2, A_4 etc. into the decelerating regions of field between A_2B_2, A_4B_4 etc. In this manner energy is given up to the wave which eventually grows exponentially in amplitude with distance travelled from the gun end. Since the electric field is continuously modulating the electron stream, the convection current on the beam also grows exponentially.

The behaviour of the travelling wave tube has been analysed in considerable detail (PIERCE [1950], BECK [1958]), both with and without space charge being taken into account. No attempt will be made here to reproduce any of these analyses in detail but the following points may be noted:

(1) Gain is achieved only if the electron beam and travelling wave have almost the same phase velocities. If the slow wave structure is dispersive there is in general only one frequency at which synchronism is obtained for a given beam voltage. However most travelling wave tubes are designed to be broad band amplifiers and this requires that the phase velocity of the travelling wave remains constant over a wide frequency range. A wire-wound helix is an almost ideal structure in this respect since it can be designed to be almost completely non-dispersive over several octaves (PIERCE [1950]).

(2) The travelling wave tube can be made to oscillate by feeding back a portion of the output power to the input. Feedback can in fact readily occur along the slow wave structure itself, particularly as a result of multiple reflections at the input and output transitions. These spurious oscillations can be removed either by severing the slow wave structure at some point along its length so that there is no direct feedback path, or, more commonly by introducing considerable distributed loss at some point along the slow wave structure in order to attenuate any backward travelling signal. In either case the amplifier operates somewhat similarly to the extended interaction klystron with separate input and output travelling wave couplers, described in section 4.1 except that the couplers are not made resonant but are both terminated in matched load impedances. The gain along each section is only approximately half the total gain before severing, and thus the chance of self oscillation in either section is considerably reduced. The introduction of the sever, or the attenuation, is to cause the overall gain to be reduced by several decibels, a small price however for the improved stability (PIERCE [1950]).

(3) The calculated gain depends on whether space charge debunching is taken into account. Kinematic analysis which neglects space charge debunching (PIERCE [1950]) shows that the travelling wave amplitude eventually increases as $\exp{(\pi \sqrt{3} CN)}$ where $C = (Z_c I_0 / 4V_0)^{\frac{1}{3}}$ and $N = \beta L / 2\pi$. Here Z_c is the coupling impedance, I_0 and V_0 the d.c. beam current and voltage respectively, β the propagation constant of the wave along the structure, and L the structure length (see section 4.1). The effect of both space charge and ohmic losses along the slow wave structure is to decrease the gain coefficient below the value given above. The gain of a typical low power travelling wave amplifier might be around 30 dB.

5. The backward wave oscillator

The backward wave oscillator (B.W.O.) resembles closely the traveling wave tube except that no intentional circuit attenuation is introduced along the slow wave structure to suppress feedback from output to input. However, the output port is now at the gun end of the structure while the collector end

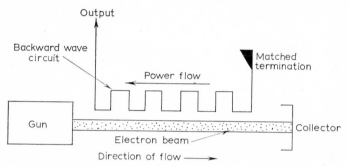

Fig. 6.9. Schematic of backward wave oscillator.

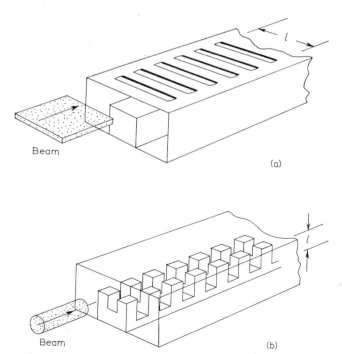

Fig. 6.10. (a) The Karp slow wave structure; (b) the Vane slow wave structure.

is normally terminated in a matched load, or in some cases, left untermi-nated. A schematic layout of a B.W.O. is shown in fig. 6.9.

Although the helix slow wave structure has been used in some longer wavelength B.W.O.'s (the mode used is however not that used for forward wave amplification in the T.W.A.), two other types have been more common-ly used for tubes operating at 2 mm wavelengths and below. These are shown in fig. 6.10. Both are modified forms of ridged rectangular wave-guide with periodic discontinuities. In the case of the Karp structure, fig. 6.10a, the periodic loading is produced by cutting transverse slots in the top face of the waveguide, whereas in the Vane structure, fig. 6.10b, these slots are cut in the ridge. In the case of the Karp structure, the electron beam, normally a strip beam, is arranged to graze either the upper or lower surface of the slotted wall. For the Vane structure, a cylindrical beam traverses the region between the top of the ridge and the opposite waveguide wall; alterna-tively an axial groove is cut in the ridge and the beam is fired along this.

5.1. BACKWARD WAVE SPACE HARMONICS

Before going on to discuss the mechanism of oscillation in the B.W.O., it is appropriate at this stage to consider the dispersion characteristics for perio-dically loaded structures of the type shown in fig. 6.10. It is customary to present the dispersion characteristics of waveguides in terms of the depend-ence of angular frequency ω on propagation constant β. In the absence of the periodic loading, i.e. for homogeneously filled waveguides, it is well known that the dispersion law is given by

$$\beta^2 = \frac{\omega^2}{c^2} - k_c^2$$

where c is the velocity of light and k_c the cut-off wave number. The dispersion curve is a hyperbola, with the asymptotes $\beta = \pm \omega/c$ and shown by the solid lines in fig. 6.11. Positive values of β we will understand to apply to waves propagating from left to right, and negative values to waves from right to left. The effect of the periodic loading is to produce strong Bragg reflec-tion when $\beta D = \pm n\pi$ where n is an integer and D is the periodic length. This results in a series of stop and pass bands, shown dotted in fig. 6.11, the band edges occurring at values of β given by $\beta D = \pm n\pi$. In general we are only interested in propagation in the lowest pass band.

The dispersion curve for any pass band is not restricted to the first Bril-louin zone, $-\pi \le \beta D \le \pi$, but exists for all values of β from $-\infty$ to $+\infty$ and is an even function of β, having a periodicity $2\pi/D$ (SLATER [1950]). This

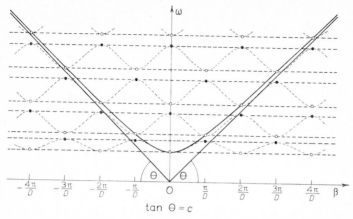

Fig. 6.11. Dispersion curve for homogeneously filled non-periodic waveguide (solid), and pass band structure when periodically loaded (dotted).

follows from a theorem due to Floquet which states essentially that in any lossless periodic structure, the wave function at any point on the structure can only differ from the wave function one period away by a phase factor $\exp - j\theta = \exp - j\beta_0 D$, where $\theta = \beta_0 D$ is the phase shift per periodic cell. The most general expression for the wave function in the direction of propagation z, satisfying these conditions at a given frequency, is of the form

$$\sum_{n=-\infty}^{\infty} A_n \exp j\{\omega t - (\beta_0 + 2\pi n/D)z\}$$

where A_n is an amplitude coefficient and ω is the angular frequency of the wave. It is thus apparent that at any frequency within a pass band, an infinite number of partial or component waves propagate, each having a different propagation constant: such partial waves are commonly called *space harmonics* since they are harmonically related in β rather than ω. Reference to fig. 6.11 and the relationship given above shows that the propagation constant of the nth space harmonic of this wave is given by $\beta_n = \beta_0 + 2\pi n/D$ where β_0 is the propagation constant in the first Brillouin zone for the frequency concerned.

For a wave of given frequency carrying energy from left to right along the guide, and thus by our convention having positive group velocity, only the space harmonics with positive gradient $d\omega/d\beta$ are present. The relative amplitudes A_n of the set of space harmonics which constitute this complete

travelling wave are determined by the shape of the periodic structure only
and not by the manner in which the wave is excited.

Suppose now we consider a signal at a specific frequency ω', conveying
energy from right to left along such a periodic structure, i.e. from collector
to gun end. Since energy is travelling in the negative z direction, only the
space harmonics with negative $d\omega/d\beta$ as shown solid in fig. 6.12 are involved.

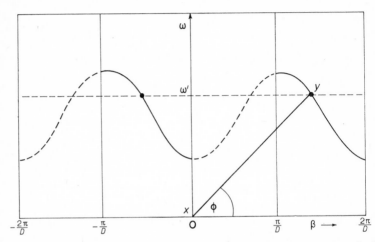

Fig. 6.12. Space harmonics excited in B.W.O. operation (solid) $\tan \varphi = u_0$, the beam
velocity.

The space harmonic present in the first Brillouin zone, normally called the
fundamental, is seen to have a negative phase velocity. However, the space
harmonics in the range π/D to $2\pi/D$, $3\pi/D$ to $4\pi/D$ etc., all have positive
phase velocities and one of these, with suitable choice of frequency and
periodicity D, can be made synchronous with an electron beam drifting from
left to right. In general the amplitude of successive space harmonics involved
in a particular wave decreases with increasing $|n|$ and for this reason only
the space harmonic in the range π/D to $2\pi/D$ is normally used in this way.
Since the phase and group velocities of this space harmonic are oppositely
directed it is called the first backward wave space harmonic. In a B.W.O. it
is usually the only one which couples strongly to the beam; all other space
harmonics are sufficiently far away from synchronism to produce negligible
coupling. Although only the one space harmonic directly interacts with the
drifting electron stream, the energy it may extract is divided between itself
and all the other space harmonics with which it is coupled to make up the
complete travelling wave.

Consider now how oscillations might build up from noise fluctuations in such a system. Suppose a small noise signal develops on the slow wave structure near the collector end. Some of this energy will propagate along the circuit towards the gun and in doing so a first backward space harmonic component will be set up having its phase velocity in the same direction as the electron beam. If the noise frequency is such that the phase velocity of this space harmonic is very slightly less than the beam velocity, then, as with the travelling wave tube (see section 6.1), d.c. energy can be extracted from the electron beam and converted into wave energy, thus causing the amplitude of the circuit wave to grow. The noise signal, at least that component in a narrow frequency range, will be greater on arrival at the gun end of the tube than it would have been if no beam were present. We have an amplifier that is inherently regenerative, even if the slow wave structure is perfectly matched at both ends, since the wave building up towards the gun end, is continuously modulating the electron stream, which is flowing towards the collector and in turn giving up energy to the circuit on its way. If the beam current is sufficiently large the tube will break into oscillation at almost that frequency for which the phase velocity of the first backward wave is equal to the electron beam drift velocity. If the beam current is less than required for start oscillation then narrow band regenerative amplification is possible.

The first backward wave space harmonic is highly dispersive as reference to fig. 6.12 shows; thus the oscillation frequency will be tunable over a wide range by varying the beam velocity. The tangent of the radius vector XY in fig. 6.12 is equal to the phase velocity ω/β. For any given velocity u_0, the point of intersection of a radius vector subtending an angle arc tan u_0 with the first backward space harmonic dispersion curve gives very closely the frequency of oscillation. We shall see later that it is not possible to obtain oscillation throughout the complete pass band, from high frequency to low frequency cut-off, by varying the beam velocity, but only over a restricted range of perhaps 30% of the total pass band width.

The width of the pass band can be estimated from the following considerations. The low frequency cut-off is almost that of the unloaded ridge waveguide propagating its dominant transverse electric mode. The low frequency cut-off is hardly affected by the loading since, at cut-off, the current flow in the waveguide walls and ridge is purely transverse to the axis. Thus the slots in the top wall, or in the ridge, do not seriously perturb this transverse current flow. In order to determine the high frequency cut-off consider the slots in the Karp structure. In isolation, without any mutual coupling, or the proximity of the ridge, they would be resonant at a free space wavelength λ

such that $\lambda = 2l$ where l is the slot length. It can be shown that a periodic array of such slot resonators do not in fact exhibit any mutual coupling since, rather remarkably, electric and magnetic coupling between adjacent slots cancel out exactly. It is the purpose of the ridge, placed in close proximity to the slots, to destroy this balance. The high frequency cut-off is marked by the fact that the group velocity is zero and no energy can propagate; thus the slots once more behave as if uncoupled and we can conclude therefore that the high frequency cut-off wavelength is given by $\lambda \approx 2l$. For the Vane structure the same sort of argument applies, but the slots in the ridge, at the high frequency cut-off, since they are open circuited at one end, resonate at $\lambda = 4l$ where l is the depth of the slot. This relationship then gives the high frequency cut-off wavelength approximately.

5.2. STARTING CURRENT FOR THE B.W.O.

The starting current required for the B.W.O. has been analysed by several authors (HEFFNER [1954], JOHNSON [1955]). An elementary analysis would take no account of space charge or ohmic losses; each of which have the effect of increasing the starting current. In the case of the travelling wave amplifier we have seen that an analysis of this kind predicts that the amplified wave builds up as $\exp(\pi\sqrt{3}\,CN)$ in the absence of space charge and losses, where C and N have been defined in section 4.2(3). Since the gain coefficient is proportional to the product CN, it would appear reasonable to expect, in order for there to be sufficient regeneration in the B.W.O. for oscillation to start, that this product be greater than a given value. Calculation (HEFFNER [1954]) shows that oscillation is, in fact, possible when $CN > 0.314$. Recasting this inequality, the start oscillation current is given by

$$(I_0)_{\text{start}} = \frac{32\pi^3(0.314)V_0}{Z_c(\beta L)^3}$$

$$\approx \frac{300\,V_0}{Z_c(\beta L)^3}. \qquad (6.21)$$

In particular the starting current is seen to be proportional to L^{-3} where L is the structure length. It would therefore appear that the starting current could be reduced without limit by increasing L. This result is, however, only valid when no circuit attenuation is present which is far from the case in submillimetre wave tubes. Karp, for example, estimates some 60 dB ohmic loss along the slow wave structure used in his experiments at 1.5 millimetres (KARP [1957]).

It is necessary, in order to be able to predict starting currents with any accuracy, to include both losses and space charge. Here we follow the treatment of CONVERT et al. [1959] since these workers have been particularly concerned with the ultimate frequency limit attainable with the B.W.O.

These authors show that the amplitudes of the axial electric field distribution E_z and convection current I_z vary with distance z measured from the gun end, as

$$E_z = A \exp(\tfrac{1}{2}\alpha z) \cos(\beta Dz - \phi) \tag{6.22}$$

$$I_z = B \exp(\tfrac{1}{2}\alpha z) \sin(\beta Dz) \tag{6.23}$$

where A and B are constants that need not concern us here, and

$$\beta D = \tfrac{1}{2}\left[\frac{Z_c}{Z_B}\beta^2 - \alpha^2\right]^{\tfrac{1}{2}}, \tag{6.24}$$

$$\sin\phi = \frac{\alpha}{\sqrt{(Z_c\beta^2/Z_B)}}, \qquad Z_B = \frac{2\omega_p}{\omega}\frac{V_0}{I_0}. \tag{6.25}$$

α is the voltage attenuation coefficient, Z_c the coupling impedance for the first backward wave and ω_p the plasma frequency, defined as in section 3.1. When there is no attenuation, $\alpha = 0$ and hence $\phi = 0$ from (6.25). The electric field then has a cosine distribution and the convection current a sine distribution with distance. Since the electric field must be zero at the collector end if we assume perfectly matched terminations, $\beta DL = \tfrac{1}{2}\pi$, where L is the structure length. Referring to (6.22) and (6.23), the current modulation is seen to increase sinusoidally towards the collector end whereas the electric field increases towards the gun end, in accordance with the considerations of section 5.1. The efficiency of the B.W.O. is consequently always low because the power extracted from the beam is proportional to the integral, along the circuit, of the product (in phase component of a.c. modulation on beam) × (a.c. field on structure) and at every point one or other of these quantities is small. This is in contrast to the T.W.A. where both electric field and current modulation increase towards the collector end.

The start oscillation condition is $\beta DL = \tfrac{1}{2}\pi$. Putting $\alpha = 0$, we have

$$(I_0)_{\text{start}} = \frac{2\pi^2 V_0}{Z_c(\beta L)^2}\frac{\omega_p}{\omega}. \tag{6.26}$$

This expression goes over to equation (6.21) for zero space charge in the manner described by HEFFNER [1954]. The start oscillation current is now proportional to L^{-2} which is a slower rate of variation with L than the L^{-3} dependence predicted when space charge is neglected. It would appear once again, however, that by increasing L, the starting current could be made indefinitely small.

It is not until losses are considered that a lower limit on the wavelength of oscillation emerges. In this case, from eq. (6.22), the start oscillation condition becomes

$$\beta DL - \phi = \tfrac{1}{2}\pi$$

or

$$\beta DL = \tfrac{1}{2}\pi + \text{arc sin} \frac{\alpha}{\beta \sqrt{(Z_c/Z_B)}}. \tag{6.27}$$

Using this equation and equation (6.24) the starting current can be determined. As expected, it is found to increase above the value given by (6.26) as α increases. An upper limit on the allowable attenuation is obtained by noting from equation (6.24) that if $\alpha = \beta\sqrt{(Z_c/Z_B)}$, then $\beta D = 0$ and oscillations are not possible for any length of line. Thus only if $\alpha < \beta\sqrt{(Z_c/Z_B)}$, is it possible for the tube to oscillate. The above inequality can be written:

$$(I_0)_{\text{start}} > \frac{2(\omega_p/\omega)V_0}{Z_c} \left(\frac{\alpha L}{\beta L}\right)^2. \tag{6.28}$$

The minimum starting current is thus proportional to the square of the total circuit loss αL and this suggests that every effort should be made to keep this small. Once this inequality is satisfied, the circuit length has to be long enough to satisfy eq. (6.27). Equation (6.28) determines, as we shall see later, the minimum wavelength likely to be generated by a B.W.O. and it will be used in section 5.4 to scale existing submillimetre wave tubes to their limit. Before doing this, however, some of the existing B.W.O.'s operating at wavelengths below 2 mm will be described in the following section.

5.3. SOME MILLIMETRE AND SUBMILLIMETRE B.W.O.'S

The first tube to operate below 2 mm wavelength was constructed by Karp using the slow wave structure which bears his name (KARP [1957]). The mechanical realisation of this structure and the dimensions used for his lowest wavelength tube are shown in fig. 6.13. This tube was voltage tunable over the range 1.5 → 1.7 mm and the output power at midband was estimated to be some 0.2 mW. The slotted waveguide wall was fabricated from a grid of molybdenum tapes, cross sectional dimensions 0.003″ × 0.005″, wound 200 turns per inch and then gold brazed onto the support frame. Thin,

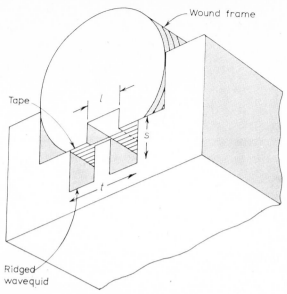

Fig. 6.13. Mechanical realisation and dimensions of Karp's 1.6 mm oscillator; $l = 0.024''$, $t = 0.122''$, $s = 0.061''$ (after Karp).

photo-etched molybdenum foil has also been used to form such a slotted wall (ALLISON [1960]). Fig. 6.14 shows schematically the complete tube layout. The cathode was a tungsten hairpin and the beam was focussed by immersing the whole tube in an axial magnetic field of approximately 3000 oersted. At midband, 1.6 mm wavelength, the beam voltage was 2.5 kV and the cathode current density J_0 at start oscillation was approximately 5 A/cm². The total starting current can be obtained if the effective useful cross sectional area of the beam is known. The periodic components of the fields can be shown to decay with distance away from a slow wave structure of this type as $\exp - \beta y$ where y is distance from the tapes, and β is the axial propagation constant. The effective area of the beam is therefore of order l/β where l is the length of a slot. We have previously seen that $l \approx \frac{1}{2}\lambda$, thus the effective area of the beam is approximately $(\lambda^2/4\pi)(u_0/c)$ where u_0 is the electron beam velocity and c the velocity of light. With $V_0 = 2.5$ kV, $u_0/c = 1/10$, $J_0 = 5$ A/cm², $\lambda = 1.5$ mm, the effective starting current is found to be just less than 1 mA. It is interesting to note that only a skin of electrons near to the structure interact usefully; in this particular example the skin thickness $1/\beta$ is only 25 microns.

The plasma frequency ω_p can be calculated ($\omega_p = \sqrt{(J_0 e/u_0 \varepsilon_0 m)}$) from the

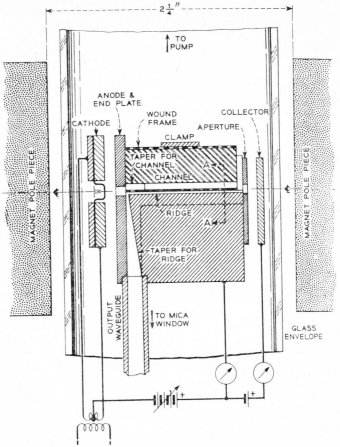

Fig. 6.14. Demountable backward-wave oscillator tube, 100–200 Gc (schematic)
(after Karp).

cathode current density J_0 and the beam velocity u_0, giving a value of $\omega_p/\omega \approx 1/500$. The attenuation αL can be estimated from Karp's results to be almost 8 nepers, and the coupling impedance for the first backward wave space harmonic is usually considered to lie in the range $1 \rightarrow 10\ \Omega$. This quantity is difficult to measure experimentally and also to calculate theoretically with any accuracy. Putting the above values into eq. (6.28) and assuming $Z_c = 2\ \Omega$ gives $(I_0)_{start} > 1$ mA, in reasonable agreement with the observed value.

Suppose that this tube is now scaled to shorter wavelengths still by changing all transverse dimensions in proportion to wavelength. The beam voltage is assumed to remain constant, thus synchronism is still maintained in the scaled tube. Assuming once again a normal skin effect variation of α with frequency, we find from eq. (6.28)

$$(J_0)_{\text{start}} \propto \lambda^{-4}$$

where $(J_0)_{\text{start}}$ is the starting current density. This represents a very rapid increase in $(J_0)_{\text{start}}$ as frequency increases. In order to generate 0.8 mm, for example, the cathode current density must increase 16 times, to some 80 A/cm^2. This is much greater than can be obtained directly from either oxide coated or dispenser type cathodes or even tungsten cathodes under continuous operation. Thus some form of electron gun design is required which would cause the electron beam to converge from the cathode, thus increasing the current density. In this particular example, an area convergence ratio of about 16 would be needed.

The Karp structure in the form described could no doubt be built to operate below 1 mm wavelength but it has poor thermal properties. The thin tapes are ill designed to conduct away heat produced by electron bombardment and it is only too easy, when aligning the magnetic focussing field, to cause the whole beam to strike the tapes. If this is not sufficient to melt them it can still cause serious distortion. Pulsed operation, with a duty cycle much less than unity is always one way of overcoming this problem.

So far, only dimensional scaling has been considered. It is possible also to increase the beam voltage V_0. The periodicity of the slow wave structure must then increase (see fig. 6.12) in order that the phase velocity matches the increased beam velocity. This changes both the coupling impedance Z_c and the attenuation constant α. There are, however, good reasons for believing that $Z_c \propto V_0$ and $\alpha \propto V_0^{-\frac{1}{2}}$, giving from eq. (6.28), $(I_0)_{\text{start}} \propto V_0^{-\frac{1}{2}}$. This represents a very slow reduction in starting current with increase in beam voltage. However, since the d.c. beam power has been increased by increasing V_0, the output power of the tube, once the oscillation threshold has been reached, is likely to be greater than before. It may be that with the Karp structure any advantage in using a more energetic beam is offset by the inability of the structure to withstand the increased power density in the beam.

The low wavelength limit of the Karp structure is considered to be around 1 mm and no one has improved upon Karp's results. The C.S.F. group (YEOU [1965]) have been able to extend the limit to 0.38 mm by using the Vane structure. This type of structure is more robust and better suited to conducting away the heat produced by electrons striking the vanes. Great care however has also been taken in the design of suitable high convergence guns in order to produce the high current densities needed for these tubes.

The form of the C.S.F. submillimetre tubes is shown schematically in fig. 6.15. The Vane slow wave structure is milled from high purity oxygen-free

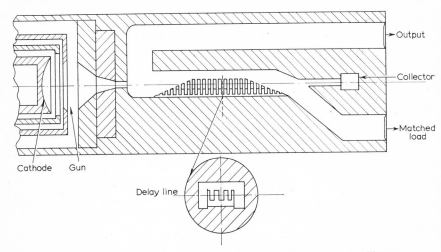

Fig. 6.15. Sectional view (schematic) of C.S.F. backward wave oscillators.

copper and is tapered at its ends in order to facilitate matching to the plain waveguide. In some of the shorter wavelength tubes no external termination is used at the collector end of the slow wave structure. The pitch D between consecutive vanes is of order $\lambda/10$ and in particular for the 0.4 mm tube is 55 microns. The height of the ridge is of order $\frac{1}{4}\lambda$. Some 200 vanes are used in the submillimetre tubes. Tolerances of approximately 1 micron are maintained, and the slots in the ridge are cut by using a single tooth tungsten carbide milling cutter, 9 mm diameter, 10 microns thick. Slow wave structures considered suitable for operating down to 0.1 mm wavelength have been manufactured.

The electron guns have an area convergence of several hundred. In most tubes the cathode loading is 5 A/cm² although it is considered that higher values could be used without cathode deterioration. The beam is focussed down to a diameter of order $\lambda/10$ and maintained parallel with an axial magnetic field of around 8000 oersted, produced either by a solenoid or permanent magnet. The power density in the beam reaches several megawatt/cm² and a water cooled collector is normally used.

All submillimetre tubes have a rectangular output waveguide designed for

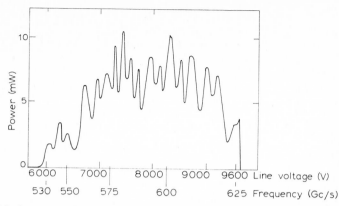

Fig. 6.16. Output power as a function of line voltage for C.S.F. 0.5 mm B.W.O. (after Yeou).

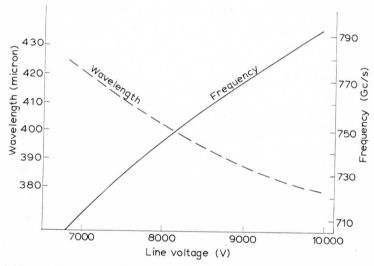

Fig. 6.17. Frequency versus line voltage for C.S.F. 0.4 mm oscillator (after Yeou).

dominant mode operation at 2 mm wavelength. Although this waveguide would support many high order modes in the case of all the tubes operating below 1 mm wavelength, the output is found to be almost completely TE_{01}. Fig. 6.16 shows the output power as a function of line voltage for a 0.5 mm tube. The structure on this curve is caused by multiple reflections from small discontinuities within the tube, possibly between the output window and the transition from slow wave structure to waveguide. In fig. 6.17, the frequency versus line voltage for the C.S.F. 0.4 mm backward wave oscillator is plotted.

The frequency stability is obviously very dependent on the regulation of the power supply; for example, fig. 6.17 suggests a 1% change in line voltage would produce a 0.25% change in frequency. In this respect the backward wave oscillator is more difficult to maintain stable than the reflex klystron. The resonant frequency of the reflex klystron is determined essentially by the cavity, but can be changed slightly by altering the reflector voltage. In the case of the Philips 2 mm klystron, for example, a 1% change in reflector voltage will cause a 0.01% frequency change approximately.

No quantitative information is available on the line widths of these sources. WARNER et al. [1965] however have mixed the outputs of two similar 2 mm C.S.F. backward wave oscillators and observed audio frequency beats.

5.4. THE SCALING OF SUBMILLIMETRE B.W.O.'S TO SHORTER WAVELENGTHS

Let us now consider the ultimate frequency of operation of a backward wave oscillator of the type just described where the current density in the electron beam is increased by the use of a convergent electron gun. Convert has listed three contributions to the effective losses (CONVERT et al. [1963]). These are:
(a) The ohmic circuit losses α_1. If a normal skin effect frequency law is assumed then $\alpha_1/\beta \propto 1/\sqrt{\lambda}$.
(b) Imperfections in the periodicity of the slow wave circuit. These have the effect of attenuating a wave propagating along the structure by back-scattering of energy and conversion to other modes. If the deviations from exact periodicity, ΔD, in successive cells, spaced on average D apart, are uncorrelated, then the effective attenuation constant α_2 is given by:

$$\alpha_2 = \frac{\overline{\Delta D^2}}{D^3} \left[\frac{v}{v_g} - 1 \right]^2$$

where $\overline{\Delta D^2}$ is the mean square deviation, v is the phase velocity and v_g the group velocity. (This explains incidentally why oscillations are not observed close to the high frequency cut-off despite the fact that the coupling impedance Z_c tends to ∞ there. Since v_g tends to zero at cut-off, the quotient α_2^2/Z_c can be shown to tend to infinity at this frequency since α_2^2 goes to infinity faster than Z_c. Thus the inequality, eq. (6.28), can never be satisfied near cut-off.) As tubes are scaled to shorter wavelengths $\overline{\Delta D^2}/D^2$ increases due to the difficulties in maintaining the same fractional tolerances.
(c) Electrons are emitted from the cathode with a range of thermal energies and this spread is magnified in the focussed beam by an amount proportional to the area convergence ratio S of the gun. This random velocity spread on the uniform drift velocity has the effect of increasing the starting current

and can be allowed for by introducing a third attenuation constant α_3 where α_3/β is proportional to S. The maximum current density that can be drawn from the cathode is fixed. Thus as the convergence S is increased in order to produce the required starting current needed for shorter wavelengths, the α_3 term becomes comparable with the ohmic loss term α_1 and eventually increase in S no longer helps in satisfying equation (6.28). The total effective attenuation constant α, in equation (6.28), is the sum of $\alpha_1 + \alpha_2 + \alpha_3$.

Taking account of all these terms and assuming that the maximum current density available from a thermionic cathode cannot be much greater than 10–20 A/cm^2, Convert has shown that the minimum wavelength likely to be generated by the Vane type B.W.O. oscillator in its present form is probably around 0.1 mm. If however new forms of high density emitters become available the situation may be different. Towards this end, interest has arisen in the possible use of field emission cathodes. The technology of such cathodes is not sufficiently advanced at present to hazard a guess as to their eventual usefulness, but certainly the current densities attainable from them are much higher than can be obtained from more conventional thermionic emitters.

5.4. Power supplies for b.w.o.'s

As we have seen in section 5.1, the frequency of a B.W.O. is determined by the velocity of the beam traversing the slow wave structure. The oscillation frequency of a C.S.F. 2 mm B.W.O., for example, changes from 120 to 140 Gc/s as the line voltage changes from -3.5 kV to -6 kV, thus giving a frequency sensitivity of about 8 Mc/s per volt. For the 0.4 mm tube the sensitivity is some 30 Mc/s per volt. Thus a very high degree of voltage stability and absence of ripple is needed to ensure a constant monochromatic signal. This can only be achieved by careful circuit design in which high stability components, particularly resistors and reference elements are used, together with error feedback amplifiers having very high loop gains.

As an example of what can be achieved, some characteristics of a power supply due to WARNER et al. [1965] will be described. This unit, originally designed for the C.S.F. 2 mm B.W.O. is suitable also for some of the shorter wavelength tubes. The voltages and currents provided are given in the following table:

Electrode	Voltage range	Maximum current
Cathode	-2 kV to -6 kV w.r.t. earth	150 mA
Anode	0 to $+2$ kV w.r.t. cathode	5 mA
Grid	10 to -60 V w.r.t. cathode	
Heater	0 to $+8$ V w.r.t. cathode	2.5 A

The grid voltage is used to control the focusing of the beam.

The ripple on each output voltage is less than 1 mV peak to peak and when the mains voltage is changed by 10%, cathode and anode voltages change by less than 0.002%, and grid and heater voltages by less than 0.01%. By mixing the output of two similar 2.0 mm B.W.O.'s together, each connected to an individual power supply, in a crystal diode, the beat note was observed to remain within the range $\pm$ 1 Mc/s for about 10 min and during this period it drifted through the audio range 7 times.

6. The cavity magnetron as a source of short millimetre waves

The multi-cavity magnetron, used so successfully in radar at centimetric wavelengths has been scaled down, with minor modifications in form, to 2.5 mm wavelength (PLANTINGA [1964]). This wavelength is considered to be very close to the ultimate that can be achieved. The chief modifications found in millimetre wave magnetrons are the absence of cavity strapping, which is normally used to prevent mode jumping, and a small increase in the total number of cavities. Mode jumping is overcome by interlacing two sizes of cavity around the circumference of the magnetron block (the so-called rising-sun magnetron). This has the effect of increasing the mode separation between the required mode and all other possible modes. Some characteristics of this 2.5 mm magnetron are given in the table below:

Peak output power	2.5 kW
Mean power	0.5 W
Magnetic field	25000 oersted
Anode voltage	9 kV
Peak current	14 A
Current density at cathode	400 A/cm^2
Pulse length	0.1 μs
Cathode diam.	0.60 mm
Anode diam.	0.95 mm
No. of cavities	22

The scaling laws for magnetrons suggest that if the dimensions are scaled proportionally to the wavelength required, the magnetic field inversely proportional to wavelength, and the voltage kept constant, then the current and output power remain unchanged. The magnetic field and the starting voltage can both be reduced by increasing the number of resonant cavities around the magnetron anode block. This results not only in increased manufacturing difficulties at short wavelengths but, more seriously, in decreased heat conduction from the block due to the removal of extra metal. The whole of the

cathode current is of course intercepted on the surface of the precision formed anode block, rather than being dissipated, as in the B.W.O., on a comparatively massive collector. This together with the inability of cathodes to
sustain the large current densities required, are the principle reasons for the
short pulse operation used. It is also particularly difficult to tune magnetrons
of this type since the cavity cannot conveniently be distorted, and tuning is
only possible by perturbing the fringing fields at the ends of the cavity block.

Harmonic output can be obtained from a magnetron and as far back as
1947 workers at Columbia Radiation Laboratory induced a 3.3 mm pulsed
magnetron to generate several hundred microwatts of third harmonic (1.1
mm) (LOUBSER et al. [1949]). Once again, however, the tuning range is very
limited.

Since the demands of radar in this frequency range are as yet more or less
non existent and since the magnetron's fixed frequency and pulsed operation
characteristics make it unsuitable for spectroscopic and diagnostic measurements, there is little possibility that there will be any significant further
development to higher frequencies.

7. Harmonic generators using relativistic electron beams

Klystron and backward wave oscillators have been described in preceding
sections. These are limited by two important factors when attempting to
produce higher frequencies.

(a) The difficulty of providing the starting current required. This limitation
is not brought about because the total current is large but because this current has to be focused, and then contained, in a beam whose transverse area
is typically $\lambda^2/100$.

(b) The transverse dimensions of the slow wave structure are of order $\frac{1}{2}\lambda$.
This poses problems in making the structure at very short wavelengths, and
also in ensuring that it is sufficiently robust to withstand accidental bombardment by the electron beam. Ruggedness and constructability thus become
almost the sole criteria for choosing a particular slow wave structure for submillimetre wavelengths.

As we have already seen (section 3.4), the klystron harmonic generator
has no minimum starting current, but the fabrication of the harmonic
cavity is still difficult and the electron beam has still to be focused down to an
area of order $\lambda_h^2/100$, where λ_h is the harmonic wavelength, in order to pass
through the holes in the resonator gap. Very tight bunching is also required
if high harmonics are to be generated. It has also been noted that in general

travelling wave interactions are advantageous at short wavelengths rather than lumped interactions using resonant cavities.

A number of harmonic generators have been described in which the above difficulties are circumvented. These utilise travelling wave interactions in extracting energy from tightly bunched beams. (COLEMAN et al. [1959] provides a review of these methods.) The travelling wave structures are normally smooth walled, overmoded cylindrical waveguides whose transverse dimensions are sometimes several wavelengths long, and thus prevent fewer problems of manufacture.

In these devices the bunched beam is normally produced by a travelling wave linear accelerator operating at a frequency corresponding to a wavelength of around 10 cm. Coleman and his colleagues have described other methods, which use a number of resonant cavities in cascade (COLEMAN et al. [1959]). Since the electron beam is usually relativistic (greater than 1 MeV) with all electrons moving very nearly at the velocity of light, there is little debunching of the beam after exit from the accelerator.

Such a bunched beam comprises a line current which can contain high harmonics of the bunching frequency. We can write its time and z dependence as:

$$I_z = \sum_{n=-\infty}^{\infty} I_n \exp jn \left(\omega t - \frac{\omega}{u_0} z \right), \qquad (6.29)$$

where I_n is the amplitude of the nth harmonic and u_0 is the electron beam velocity, normally close to c. Since all the component current waves have phase velocities less than the velocity of light, they do not radiate directly into free space; some coupling device is required to allow them to do this.

One approach is to direct the beam through a small diameter tunnel made in a block of dielectric material of relative permittivity $\varepsilon_r(\varepsilon_r > 1)$. The current waves are able to excite Čerenkov radiation in the dielectric material which propagates at a characteristic angle arc cos $(c/u_0\sqrt{\varepsilon_r})$ to the z axis where u_0 is the electron velocity. A suitable coupler, designed to facilitate the extraction of the emitted radiation from the dielectric block is shown in fig. 6.18 (COLEMANN [1961]). The radiation is totally reflected at the first dielectric-air interface (surface 1) and falls on the second interface (surface 2) at the Brewster angle and thus suffers no reflection. The shortest coherent wavelength observed using the Čerenkov principle appears to be 8.3 mm where approximately 1 watt peak power was generated using a 50 mA, 1 megavolt beam, bunched at $\lambda \approx 10$ cm (COLEMAN [1961]).

Another approach to the problem of coupling is to induce a transverse

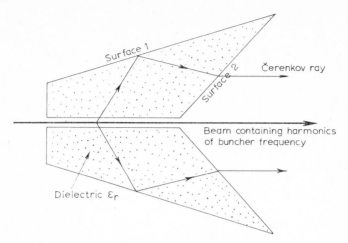

Fig. 6.18. Čerenkov coupler, after Coleman.

(or axial) oscillatory motion on the electron trajectories. Returning to eq. (6.29), the line charge density ρ in the beam is given by I/eu_0, where e is the electronic charge, since all electrons have the same velocity. Thus:

$$\rho = \frac{1}{eu_0} \sum_{n=-\infty}^{\infty} I_n \exp jn \left(\omega t - \frac{\omega z}{u_0} \right). \tag{6.30}$$

Suppose now these electrons are caused to oscillate transversely to their direction of motion by some spatially periodic electric or magnetic field acting as a small perturbation. Alternatively a similar perturbation might be produced by another travelling wave. As a result of this perturbation the electrons acquire a transverse velocity dependence of the form $\exp j(\omega_p t + \beta_p z)$. The agency producing the perturbation is sometimes referred to as the pump and the corresponding frequency and propagation constant are therefore given the subscript p. Since current density is the product of charge density and the velocity vector, it follows that, as a result of the perturbation, a transverse current wave I_t of the following form is induced on the beam,

$$I_t = \sum_{n=-\infty}^{\infty} A_n \exp j \left[(n\omega + \omega_p)t - \left(\frac{n\omega}{u_0} - \beta_p \right) z \right]. \tag{6.31}$$

The phase velocity of the nth component of this transverse current is thus $(n\omega + \omega_p)/(n\omega/u_0 - \beta_p)$ and by suitable choice of ω_p and β_p can be made greater than the velocity of light in vacuo. Thus those components whose phase velocities are greater than, or equal to the velocity of light will radiate directly into free space. It is normal however to surround the beam by a smooth walled waveguide which acts in the manner of a light pipe, thus containing the emitted radiation. Radiation is strongest into those waveguide modes which at frequency $n\omega + \omega_p$ have a propagation constant $|n\omega/u_0 - \beta_p|$ and thus have a phase velocity to match that of the current wave.

In 1951, Motz et al., using a bunched beam from a 2 MeV linear accelerator, operating at a wavelength of 10 cm, generated harmonic peak powers of several watt in the wavelength region 100μ to 1 mm (MOTZ et al. [1953]). In order to produce the transverse velocity perturbation, the beam was shot between the poles of a linear array of magnets whose polarities were alternately reversed (fig. 6.19). In this case $\omega_p = 0$ since the perturbation is not

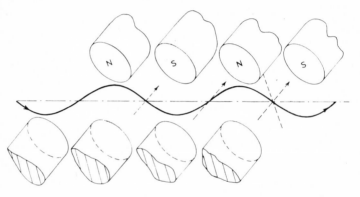

Fig. 6.19. Magnetic undulator, after Motz.

time varying. MALLORY et al. [1963] at Stanford University have reported observing 40 μW of peak power at 400 μ and 8 mW at 1.0 mm using a scheme similar to Motz's and a 3.5 MeV beam from an accelerator operating at $\lambda = 3$ cm.

Experiments in which the transverse velocity perturbation is produced by a travelling electromagnetic field have also been described (SIRKIS et al. [1964], ROBSON [1965]) but the shortest wavelength generated by this technique so far reported appears to be 4 mm. In these experiments the radiated signal is at $|n\omega + \omega_p|$ and is thus not limited to harmonics of the bunching frequency.

In interactions of the type described, the waveguide is generally highly overmoded. However, since the field pattern for the dominant mode at least is large over most of the waveguide cross section, the greater part of the injected electron beam is effective, although this may be several wavelengths in diameter. This is in contrast to the Karp and Vane slow wave structures where the useful transverse beam dimensions are only of order $\lambda/10$.

Against devices employing relativistic beams may be cited the very low efficiency, normally $\ll 1\%$; the complexity of the ancilliary equipment needed to produce the prebunched beam; the fact that output is pulsed (typically some 1 000 p.p.s., each pulse lasting several microseconds); the X-ray hazard from the beam, and also the fact that, since the frequency of the linear accelerator is normally fixed, the harmonic spectrum cannot readily be tuned.

The problems involved in making very small slow wave circuits and carefully focused electron beams are considerably reduced with the fast wave generators just described: fast wave, since the radiation is into a mode whose phase velocity is greater than the velocity of light. This simplicity is only obtained, however, at the expense of having to use a very sophisticated bunching system. It is natural to enquire if travelling wave interactions, where the excited wave produces its own bunching, as in the B.W.O., can be made to occur in smooth-walled highly overmoded waveguide. Recently this has been shown to be possible at millimetre and submillimetre wavelengths by BOTT [1964, 1965] and his tube is described in the next section.

8. A coherent source of millimetre and submillimetre cyclotron radiation

Fig. 6.20 is a schematic diagram of one of the tubes constructed by Bott. A convergent electron gun is used to accelerate electrons up to 20 kV potential

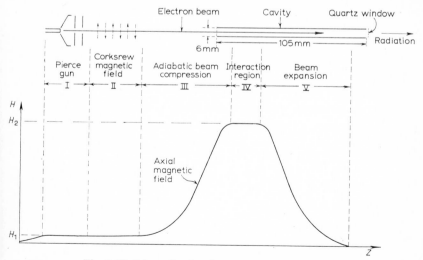

Fig. 6.20. Schematic of cyclotron generator after Bott.

in region I. In region II a uniform low magnetic field H_1 is perturbed by a transverse corkscrew magnetic field which imparts a controlled amount of the electron beam's transitional energy to rotational. In region III the beam is adiabatically compressed by the magnetic field so that in region IV its diameter is reduced in the ratio $(H_1/H_2)^{\frac{1}{2}}$ and its transverse component of kinetic energy increased in the ratio $(H_1/H_2)^{-1}$. In region V the beam expands and is collected on the walls of the cavity.

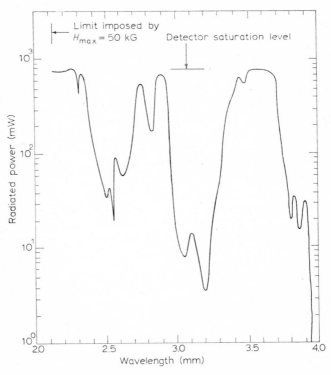

Fig. 6.21. Output power versus wavelength for cyclotron generator (after Bott).

The high magnetic field for this particular experiment was derived from a superconducting solenoid and had a maximum value of 50 kG. In region IV the gyrating electrons radiate into the low Q overmoded cavity, formed by the short circuited cylindrical waveguide and the quartz output window, at the cyclotron frequency $\omega_c = e\mu_0 H_2/m$. If there were no cooperative effects between the radiation field and the electrons, then the radiation would be in the nature of fairly narrow band noise centred around the cyclotron frequency. If this were the case for the conditions pertaining in Bott's experiment, it can be shown that the noise would be distributed over approximately a 10% bandwidth and the output power would be some 100 μW per ampere injected beam current. As reference to fig. 6.21 shows, where output power as a function of wavelength is plotted, it is considerably in excess of the incoherent value since beam currents much less than 1 A were used. The fractional line width has been measured to be less than 5×10^{-5} for a fixed magnetic field H_2, and the radiated power is observed to be at the cyclotron frequency $e\mu_0 H_2/m$. Thus the output must possess a high degree of coherence.

The sorting mechanism which ensures coherence is not fully understood. There are at least two possible mechanisms, which together or separately, might be responsible. The first, suggested by PANTELL [1959] is that the transverse rotational velocity compounded with the transverse magnetic field of the excited wave produces an axial Lorentz force which causes bunching in a similar manner to that in the travelling wave tube or backward wave oscillator. The second mechanism relies on purely rotational sorting, and requires that the relativistic change in mass, as the electrons either gain or lose energy, be taken into account (HSU et al. [1965]). This mechanism can also be understood quantum mechanically, since the dependence of electron mass on energy leads to a non-uniform spacing of the allowed Landau levels, a necessary requirement for obtaining net stimulated emission (SCHNEIDER [1959], HIRSHFIELD et al. [1964]).

This tube seems particularly rich in second harmonic; Bott has noted some 10 mW at 1.3 mm. In an earlier tube using a pulsed magnetic field of up to 100 kG, cyclotron radiation of approximately 1 mm wavelength was observed and second harmonic also (BOTT [1964]). It is not possible to predict the short wavelength limit of this tube at the present stage but it appears to be limited by the availability of high magnetic fields rather than any difficulty in obtaining sufficient starting current.

References

J. ALLISON, Proc. I.E.E. **107B** (1960) 295.

E. A. ASH, Millimeter wave generation research at the Standard Telecommunication Laboratories. In: Proc. 2nd Colloquium on Microwave Communication, Budapest (Publishing House of the Hungarian Academy of Sciences, Budapest, 1963) p. 47.

A. H. W. BECK, Space charge waves (Pergamon Press, London, 1958).

F. A. BENSON, Voltage stabilised supplies (Macdonald, London, 1957).

I. BOTT, Proc. I.R.E. **53** (1964) 330.

I. BOTT, Physics Letters **14** (1965) 293.

E. E. CLEETON and N. H. WILLIAMS, Phys. Rev. **50** (1936) 1091.

P. D. COLEMAN and R. C. BECKER, Trans. I.R.E. MTT-7 (1959) 42.

P. D. COLEMAN, Čerenkov radiation approach to the submillimeter problem. In: Advances in Quantum Electronics (Columbia University Press, New York and London, 1961) p. 581.

G. CONVERT, T. YEOU and B. PASTY, Millimetre wave O-carcinotrons. In: Proc. Symp. Millimetre Waves, New York 1959 (Polytechnic Press, Brooklyn N.Y.) p. 313.

G. CONVERT, T. YEOU and P. C. MOUTON, The generation of submillimetre waves. In: Proc. 4th Intern. Congr. on Microwave Tubes, Scheveningen 1962 (Centrex Publishing Company, Eindhoven, 1963) p. 739.

A. L. CULLEN, Proc. I.E.E. 110 (1963) 475.

A. L. CULLEN and J. A. JONES, Proposals for millimetric photo-mixing using surface waves. In: Proc. Symp. on Optical Masers (Polytechnic Press Brooklyn, N.Y., 1963) p. 585.

W. R. DAY and J. A. NOLAND, Reported at the Boulder Millimetre Wave and Far Infrated Conference, August 1965.

H. HEFFNER, Proc. I.R.E. 42 (9954) 930.

J. L. HIRSHFIELD and J. M. WACHTEL, Phys. Rev. Letters 12 (1964) 533.

T. W. HSU and P. N. ROBSON, Electronics Letters 1 (1965) 84.

H. R. JOHNSON, Proc. I.R.E. 43 (1955) 684.

G. KING, L. SOLIMAR and E. A. ASH, Experimental investigation of non-linear phenomena in electron beams at fundamental and harmonic frequencies. In: Proc. 4th intern. Congr. on Microwave Tubes (Centrex Publishing Company, Eindhoven, 1963) p. 668.

A. KARP, Proc. I.R.E. 45 (1957) 496.

R. KOMPFNER, Wireless World 52 (1946) 369.

R. KOMPFNER and N. T. WILLIAMS, Proc. I.R.E. 41 (1953) 1602.

W. KUIJPERS, Reported at British Radio Spectroscopy Group Conf., Malvern, 1965.

J. M. LAFFERTY, J. Appl. Phys. 17 (1946) 1061.

J. H. N. LOUBSER and C. H. TOWNES, Phys. Rev. 76 (1949) 178.

K. B. MALLORY, R. H. MILLER and P. A. SZENTE, 1963, Paper presented at I.R.E. Millimetre and Submillimetre Conf. Orlanda, U.S.A.

S. MILLMAN, Proc. I.R.E. 39 (1951) 1035.

H. MOTZ, J. Appl. Phys. 22 (1951) 527.

H. MOTZ, W. THON and R. N. WHITEHURST, J. Appl. Phys. 24 (1953) 826.

R. H. PANTELL, Electron beam interaction with fast waves. In: Proc. Symp. on Millimetre Waves, New York 1959 (Polytechnic Press, Brooklyn N.Y.) p. 301.

J. R. PIERCE, Travelling wave tubes (D. Van Nostrand Co., Princeton, N. J., 1950).

J. R. PIERCE, Theory and design of electron beams (D. Van Nostrand Co., Princeton, N. J., 1949) Ch. 8.

G. H. PLANTINGA, Philips Tech. Rev. 25 (1964) 217.

P. N. ROBSON, A parametric electron beam doubler from 35 Gc/s to 70 Gc/s. In: Proc. 5th Intern. Congr. on Microwave Tubes, Paris 1964 (Academic Press, New York and London, 1965) p. 138.

J. SCHNEIDER, Phys. Rev. Letters 2 (1959) 504.

J. C. SLATER, Microwave electronics (D. van Nostrand Co., Princeton, N. J., 1950) Ch. 8.

B. B. VAN IPEREN, Reflex klystrons for millimetre waves. In: Proc. Symp. on Millimetre Waves, New York 1959 (Polytechnic Press of the Polytechnic Institute of Brooklyn, Brooklyn, N.Y.) p. 149.

B. B. VAN IPEREN, G. H. PLANTINGA and TH. I. SPRENGER, 1963, Paper presented at I.R.E. Millimetre and Submillimetre Conf. Orlando, USA.

B. B. VAN IPEREN and H. J. C. A. NUNNINK, The velocity modulated electron beam as a harmonics generator for millimetre and submillimetre waves. In: Proc. 5th Intern. Congr. on Microwave Tubes, Paris 1964 (Academic Press, New York and London, 1965) p. 124.

C. C. T. WANG and M. D. SIRKIS, Trans. I.R.E., E.D. 11 (1964) 266.

F. L. WARNER, A stabilised power unit for klystrons and travelling wave tubes, T.R.E. Technical Note No. 82 (1950).

F. L. WARNER and P. HERMAN, A highly stabilised power unit for C.S.F. millimetre wave carcinotrons, Royal Radar Establishment Memorandum No. 1962 (1965).

W. E. WILLSHAW, A survey of the present day position on the generation and amplification of millimetre waves. In: Proc. 3rd intern. Congr. on Microwave Tubes, Munich 1960 (Academic Press, New York, 1961).

N. C. WITTWER, Appl. Phys. Letters 10 (1963) 194.

T. YEOU, Generation des ondes millimétriques et submillimétriques. In: Proc. 5th Intern. Congr. on Microwave Tubes, Paris 1964 (Academic Press, New York and London, 1965) p. 151.

CHAPTER 7

TECHNIQUES OF PROPAGATION AT MILLIMETRE AND SUBMILLIMETRE WAVELENGTHS

BY

D. J. KROON and J. M. VAN NIEUWLAND

Philips Research Laboratories, N.V. Philips' Gloeilampenfabrieken, Eindhoven, The Netherlands

PAGE

1. Introduction

There are two possible directions from which to approach the experimental problem of guiding millimetre and submillimetre waves, namely from the optical and microwave sides.

The first way, which has its origin in geometrical optics, uses lenses, prisms and mirrors with dimensions many times the wavelength. This method would imply that in the construction of suitable instrumentation for 1 mm wavelength, elements about 2000 times as large as the corresponding elements in optical instrumentation would have to be used. This would lead to structures several metres in size if high quality is required. The other approach, starting with microwave techniques involving instruments like waveguides, directional couplers, plungers, etc., would require a scaling down to match with the desired wavelength. Since these instruments are of the order of the wavelength in dimensions a submillimetre microwave spectrometer would be very small and extremely difficult to construct. Moreover, small waveguides tend to be highly attenuating.

It is clear that both methods, though having outstanding properties in their own wavelength ranges, tend to fail in the short millimetre region. Therefore we should investigate combinations of pure optical and pure waveguide methods, involving instruments whose dimensions are a few times the wavelength. This necessitates a full consideration of the influences of boundary effects and the electromagnetic description of the wave propagation has to be used, rather than its ray-optical approximation. Starting from Maxwell's equations we shall derive in section 2 some general considerations about wave propagation and attenuation in various wave-guiding structures.

A survey is then given of practical wave-guiding structures. Sections 3 and 4 deal with the propagation of waves through metallic tubular waveguides. Another way of concentrating electromagnetic energy within a certain region is through the use of dielectrics. This leads to structures like the H-guide and trough-line to be discussed in section 5, and to the dielectric rod, image-line and V-line discussed in section 6. Finally we will say something about the multi-mode quasi-optical transmission lines, using lenses, in section 7. Particular attention will be paid to the attenuation in all these guiding structures. Section 8 gives a description of some ancillary components for use with the different structures, such as methods for exciting waves, bends and couplers, attenuators, etc.

2. Summary of relevant electromagnetic theory

2.1. GENERAL CONSIDERATIONS

The calculation of the electromagnetic field within the guiding structures to be described in this chapter, is based upon the solution of the Maxwell field equations. Since there are many textbooks in which the general foundations, solutions and applications of the Maxwell field equations can be found, we shall confine ourselves to a short summary of what will be necessary for our purposes. The practical transmission lines which we shall consider, are all of regular cross-section (rectangular, circular etc.) and furthermore they are all uniform, i.e. the geometrical and physical properties of the cross-section do not vary along the direction of propagation. Different media (dielectric, metal or air) may be used in the construction of these transmission lines. The physical properties of these linear, homogeneous and isotropic media are described by a scalar dielectric constant $\varepsilon\varepsilon_0$ and a scalar permeability $\mu\mu_0$; ε_0 and μ_0 are the dielectric constant and permeability of free space while ε and μ are respectively the relative dielectric constant and relative permeability of the medium. The Maxwell field equations, for time harmonic fields with time variation exp $j\omega t$, can then be written as follows

$$\text{curl } E = -j\omega\mu_0\mu H$$
$$\text{curl } H = \sigma E + j\omega\varepsilon_0\varepsilon E \qquad (7.1)$$

with σ the conductivity of the medium.

A new complex relative dielectric constant, which includes all the contributions from conduction currents, can be defined as

$$\varepsilon = \varepsilon' - j\varepsilon'', \text{ with } \varepsilon'' = \sigma/\omega\varepsilon_0$$

resulting in the following expression for the second equation in (7.1.)

$$\text{curl } H = j\omega\varepsilon_0\varepsilon E.$$

For a typical dielectric medium ε'' is much smaller than ε', whereas for a metal ε'' is very large compared to ε'. Using this formalism for the dielectric constant we may derive general expressions for wave propagation which can be applied to the various special cases by substituting appropriate values for ε' and ε''.

Consider a structure of two media, having a geometry in the x, y plane as in fig. 7.1, the inner having a relative permittivity ε_1 and permeability μ_1, the outer ε_2 and μ_2. The inner as well as the outer medium may be a metal, a dielectric or vacuum, provided it is uniform.

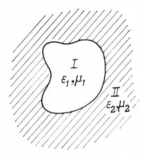

Fig. 7.1. Cross-section of a general wave-guiding structure made up of two media, I and II. ε and μ are the relative permittivity and relative permeability respectively.

The field variation along the direction of propagation (the z-direction) of the electromagnetic waves propagating along this structure will be denoted by $\exp-\mathrm{j}\delta z$, where the propagation constant $\delta = \beta-\mathrm{j}\alpha$ (α and β real) is a complex quantity, its real part representing the phase constant or wave-vector and its imaginary part the attenuation constant. The time dependence is as $\exp \mathrm{j}\omega t$, and so the phase velocity is ω/β. The z-components of the electric field vector E and the magnetic field vector H may be given as solutions of the wave equation in both media:

$$(E_z)_{1,2} = f_{1,2}(q_1, q_2) \exp(-\mathrm{j}\delta z) \exp(\mathrm{j}\omega t)$$
$$(H_z)_{1,2} = g_{1,2}(q_1, q_2) \exp(-\mathrm{j}\delta z) \exp(\mathrm{j}\omega t) \qquad (7.2)$$

where q_1, q_2 and z refer to the three space coordinates in a coordinate system appropriate to the geometry of the guiding structure; the subscripts 1 and 2 refer to medium I and medium II respectively.

In structures where the geometrical configuration of the cross-section is such that separable coordinate systems can be used, such as rectangular and cylindrical coordinate systems, the functions $f_{1,2}(q_1,q_2)$ and $g_{1,2}(q_1,q_2)$ are separable in two parts, each part depending on one space coordinate.

The longitudinal components (z-components) can than be written:

$$(E_z)_{1,2} = P_{1,2}(q_1)R_{1,2}(q_2) \exp(-j\delta z) \exp(j\omega t) \quad \Big\}$$
$$(H_z)_{1,2} = S_{1,2}(q_1)T_{1,2}(q_2) \exp(-j\delta z) \exp(j\omega t) \quad \Big\} \quad (7.2a)$$

and the other field components $E_{q_1}, E_{q_2}, H_{q_1}$ and H_{q_2} may be derived from these by application of the Maxwell field equations (7.1). Since both E_z and H_z are solutions of a second order differential equation, the solutions (7.2a) contain 4 integration constants for each of the two media, so 8 integration constants have to be determined. Each set of constants determines a certain pattern for the field distribution in the cross-section of the transmission line which does not vary along the propagation direction of the guide and is called a *mode*.

The integration constants can be determined by application of the special conditions set by the physical properties of the structure. A first condition is that the fields are finite and single valued. Furthermore all waves are "outgoing" waves towards infinity ("radiation condition"); which means that in physical media, being more or less lossy, the fields vanish at infinity, decaying even faster than $1/r^2$ to avoid sidewards radiation.

These conditions select the classes of function of P, R, S and T and leaves us with 4 constants, which can be determined by the application of the boundary conditions at the interface between medium I and II. At the interface between two media, where no electric currents can flow on the surface (e.g. two dielectrics), the boundary condition is that the tangential components of the electric field vector E and the magnetic field vector H are continuous across the interface. When one of the media is a perfect electric conductor the boundary conditions require that the tangential component of the electric field vector E vanishes at the interface. Application of the appropriate boundary conditions results in 4 homogeneous linear equations in the 4 unknown constants. A non-vanishing solution of these equations is obtained only when the determinant of the coefficients of the unknown constants is zero. This leads to the so-called *characteristic equation*, containing ε_1, ε_2, μ_1, μ_2, δ and the geometry of medium I, represented here by r_0,

$$F(\varepsilon_1, \varepsilon_2, \mu_1, \mu_2, \delta, r_0) = 0. \quad (7.3)$$

The solutions of this equation for specified values of ε, μ and r_0 give the values of the propagation constant δ, belonging to each mode and as a function of frequency. This characteristic equation will be very useful in the calculation of attenuation.

2.2. MODAL DESCRIPTION

The mathematical representation of an electromagnetic field within a uniform wave-guiding structure is in the form of a superposition of an infinite number of wave types or *modes* (MARCUVITZ [1951]), a given mode corresponds to a specific solution of the characteristic equation (7.3). Each mode is characterized by a specific field distribution in a cross-section of the guide; this field distribution is determined by the cross-sectional shape of the given guide and, save for the amplitude factor, is identical at every cross-section along the guide.

The transmission modes may be assigned to different classes. The most general type of transmission modes is the set of modes in which both electric and magnetic field vector have longitudinal and transverse components; these modes are called *hybrid modes*.

Other types are the *transverse magnetic modes* (TM or E modes) where the *magnetic* field vector is perpendicular to the direction of propagation, while the *electric* field vector has a longitudinal component and the *transverse electric modes* (TE or H modes) where the *electric* field vector is everywhere perpendicular to the direction of propagation, while the *magnetic* field vector has a longitudinal component. If both vectors are perpendicular to the direction of propagation the modes are called *transverse electromagnetic modes* (TEM modes).

The distinction between different modes of one type is indicated by adding two subscripts m and n, which relate to the number of nodal lines of the electromagnetic field components appearing in the cross-sectional plane. For instance the well known dominant mode in rectangular metallic waveguides is denoted by TE_{10}; the H_z-component of this mode has *one* nodal line parallel to the y-axis and no nodal line parallel to the x-axis. For other modes the correlation between the subscripts and nodal lines may be slightly different; we refer to MARCUVITZ [1951] for further discussion. No modes exist in which either the electric field or the magnetic field is totally longitudinal.

As noted above, the variation along the direction of propagation of the amplitudes of the fields is denoted by $\exp(-j\delta z)$; $\delta = \beta - j\alpha$ being the propagation constant. Its real part, the phase constant β, represents the periodicity of the electromagnetic field along the z-axis and $\lambda_g = 2\pi/\beta$ is called the *guide wavelength*. The propagation constant δ, and therefore the guide wavelength

λ_g, depend upon the operating frequency and the particular transmission mode.

In structures surrounded by perfect conductors the guide wavelength may become infinite at a frequency which is called the *cut-off frequency*. In structures surrounded by non-metallic media the frequency at which the guide wavelength becomes equal to the wavelength in the surrounding medium is called the cut-off frequency. In both cases waves cannot propagate in the particular mode at frequencies lower than cut-off; for metallic waveguides there is reflection of the incident wave rather than transmission and in the other wave-guiding structures (such as the dielectric rod) the wave is not constrained to the structure and is therefore not guided by it.

Each mode has its own cut-off frequency, the cut-off frequencies of the various transmission modes of a guide may be arranged in ascending order of magnitude. The lowest of these frequencies is the absolute cut-off frequency for the structure and the corresponding mode is the *principal* or *dominant* mode.

For frequencies below this absolute cut-off frequency no wave can propagate through the structure. If the guide is excited by a signal with a frequency above the absolute cut-off but below the next higher, then a wave will travel along the guide only in the dominant mode.

Increasing the frequency above several other cut-offs means a possible propagation in an increasing number of modes. As a first classification of guiding structures we therefore distinguish between single-mode and multi-mode propagation.

In the conventional use of standard waveguides (section 3) at microwave frequencies the dimensions of the guide and the method of exciting the fields are such that only one mode can carry the electromagnetic energy. In other transmission lines, e.g. the oversized waveguide (section 4) the geometry of the guide allows the existence of several modes together at the particular frequency, but the excitation system is designed so that the energy is transferred only into one mode. In these cases it is important to prevent disturbances in any way of the propagation in this mode (e.g. by defects or discontinuities in the guide) otherwise the transmission of energy will be transferred partially or completely to one or more of the other possible modes, the so-called *spurious* modes.

The energy transmission involves losses, depending on the media, the propagating mode and the wavelength. In determining the most suitable guide and mode for a particular experiment these losses play a very important role. Particularly at short wavelengths it may be desirable to use single-mode propagation in structures capable of guiding many modes, as we shall see. This is done at the risk of mode-conversion to spurious, and perhaps more lossy, modes.

2.3. ATTENUATION CONSTANT

In order to determine the most suitable mode for the propagation of the electromagnetic energy, the knowledge of the attenuation constant is of vital importance. The solution of the characteristic equation (7.3) gives for every mode its specific propagation constant $\delta = \beta - j\alpha$, α being the attenuation constant.

In general the solution of the characteristic equation cannot be obtained in explicit form. Even for regular cross-sectional shapes of the waveguide structures, such as rectangular or cylindrical, the unknown δ may appear in the argument of transcendental functions, for instance trigonometric or cylinder functions, and solutions can be obtained only with the aid of numerical methods. If, however, the properties of the media are assumed to be ideal (infinite conductivity for metals, lossless dielectrics), δ becomes real and the characteristic equation simplifies. The transmission constant for a real case might then be calculated as a perturbation using the solution for this idealized case, i.e. the assumption is made that the modes are unchanged in form by the introduction of losses. In general this assumption is valid although in the idealized case some modes may be forbidden which can occur in the non-ideal case (e.g. TM_{m0} modes in circular metallic waveguides), but since the attenuation constants of such modes are in any case rather high we need not consider them. Based on this assumption are two methods of calculating the attenuation of a propagating wave. The most commonly used method starts with the computation of the dissipated power per unit length dP/dz where P is the power flux through the guide, given by

$$P = \tfrac{1}{2} \int_{\substack{\text{cross-}\\ \text{section}}} [E \times H^*]_z \, dS.$$

The attenuation constant is then directly given (MARCUVITZ [1951]) by

$$\alpha = -(2P)^{-1} \frac{dP}{dz}.$$

A second method, particularly useful for circular cross-sections, starts immediately from the characteristic equation, and involves differentiation rather than integration.

We introduce a new quantity $v = (\lambda_0/2\pi)\,\delta = v' + jv''$ where $v' = \lambda_0/\lambda_g$ and $v'' = -(\lambda_0/2\pi)\alpha$, λ_0 being the free space wavelength. The characteristic equation now reads

$$F(\varepsilon_1, \varepsilon_2, \mu_1, \mu_2, v, r_0) = 0\,.$$

This is expanded in a Taylor series as follows, putting $v = v_0 + \Delta v$ where v_0 is real, and Δv complex

$$0 = F(\varepsilon_1, \varepsilon_2, \mu_1, \mu_2, v_0 + \Delta v, r_0)$$
$$= F(\varepsilon_1, \varepsilon_2, \mu_1, \mu_2, v_0, r_0) + \left(\frac{\partial F}{\partial v}\right)_{v=v_0} \Delta v + \ldots \, . \qquad (7.4)$$

If $|\,\Delta v\,|$ is small we neglect higher order terms and find

$$\Delta v = -\frac{F(\varepsilon_1, \varepsilon_2, \mu_1, \mu_2, v_0, r_0)}{(\partial F/\partial v)_{v=v_0}}\,. \qquad (7.5)$$

Hence

$$\alpha = -\frac{2\pi}{\lambda_0}\,\mathrm{Im}\,[\Delta v] = \frac{2\pi}{\lambda_0}\,\mathrm{Im}\left[\frac{F(\varepsilon_1, \varepsilon_2, \mu_1, \mu_2, v_0, r_0)}{(\partial F/\partial v)_{v=v_0}}\right]\,. \qquad (7.6)$$

If, for instance, medium II is a metal, with ε_2'' very large compared to ε_2', then $\varepsilon_2 \approx -j\varepsilon_2''$. In that case we may neglect all powers of ε_2'' except the few highest, thus finding an approximate expression for F and a first order value for the attenuation constant. We shall illustrate this in section 3.2 for a circular waveguide.

For dielectric media we can obtain another simplified expression for Δv. In that case we make use of the fact that $\varepsilon = \varepsilon' - j\varepsilon''$, with ε'' very small and write the Taylor expansion (7.4) thus:

$$0 = F(\varepsilon_1' - j\varepsilon_1'', \varepsilon_2' - j\varepsilon_2'', \ldots, v_0 + \Delta v, r_0)$$
$$= F(\varepsilon_1', \varepsilon_2', \ldots, v_0, r_0) - j\varepsilon_1''\left(\frac{\partial F}{\partial \varepsilon_1}\right)_{\substack{\varepsilon_1 = \varepsilon_1' \\ v = v_0}} +$$
$$- j\varepsilon_2''\left(\frac{\partial F}{\partial \varepsilon_2}\right)_{\substack{\varepsilon_2 = \varepsilon_2' \\ v = v_0}} + \Delta v\left(\frac{\partial F}{\partial v}\right)_{\substack{\varepsilon_1 = \varepsilon_1' \\ \varepsilon_2 = \varepsilon_2' \\ v = v_0}} + \ldots \qquad (7.7)$$

Taking for v_0 the value which follows from the idealized lossless case, we have $F(\varepsilon_1', \varepsilon_2', \ldots, v_0, r_0) = 0$ and thus

$$\Delta v = \frac{[j\varepsilon_1''(\partial F/\partial \varepsilon_1)_{\varepsilon_1 = \varepsilon_1'} + j\varepsilon_2(\partial F/\partial \varepsilon_2)_{\varepsilon_2 = \varepsilon_2'}]}{[(\partial F/\partial v)_{v = v_0}]} \tag{7.8}$$

from which again, since $\alpha = -(2\pi/\lambda_0)\mathrm{Im}[\Delta v]$, we can determine α.

It should be noted that, using the MKS system the attenuation constants given by the expressions above are in nepers/metre. This is related to the more commonly used unit, dB/metre, by 1 Np = 8.686 dB.

2.4. CIRCULAR WAVE-GUIDING STRUCTURES

The foregoing discussion can be particularly easily applied to the calculation of the properties of wave-guiding structures with circular cross-sections.

Suppose that medium I has the shape of an infinitely long cylinder with circular cross-section, of radius a and dielectric constant $\varepsilon_1 = \varepsilon_1' - j\varepsilon_1''$, and is surrounded by medium II, characterized by $\varepsilon_2 = \varepsilon_2' - j\varepsilon_2''$; $\mu_1 = \mu_2 = 1$.

The time-independent parts of the longitudinal components of the electric and magnetic fields in media I and II are given by (SCHELKUNOFF [1943]):

$$
\left.
\begin{aligned}
(E_z)_{\mathrm{I}} &= A\, J_m\left(\frac{pr}{a}\right) \exp(-jm\varphi) \exp(-j\delta z) \\[2mm]
(H_z)_{\mathrm{I}} &= B\, J_m\left(\frac{pr}{a}\right) \exp(-jm\varphi) \exp(-j\delta z) \\[2mm]
(E_z)_{\mathrm{II}} &= C\, K_m\left(\frac{qr}{a}\right) \exp(-jm\varphi) \exp(-j\delta z) \\[2mm]
(H_z)_{\mathrm{II}} &= D\, K_m\left(\frac{qr}{a}\right) \exp(-jm\varphi) \exp(-j\delta z)
\end{aligned}
\right\} \tag{7.9}
$$

where

$$(p/a)^2 = \omega^2 \varepsilon_0 \mu_0 \varepsilon_1 - \delta^2,$$

$$(q/a)^2 = \delta^2 - \omega^2 \varepsilon_0 \mu_0 \varepsilon_2,$$

m an integer and r, φ and z being the cylindrical coordinates. In the expressions (7.9) the conditions that the fields should be finite, single valued and vanishing at $r \to \infty$ are already applied. J_m and K_m are the mth order Bessel function and modified Hankel function respectively and these contain the radial dependences of the fields.

From Maxwell's equations the angular field components can be derived from the longitudinal components:

$$E_\varphi = (-\omega^2\varepsilon_0\varepsilon\mu_0+\delta^2)^{-1}\left[\frac{m\delta}{r}E_z - j\omega\mu_0\left(\frac{\partial H_z}{\partial r}\right)\right],$$

$$H_\varphi = (-\omega^2\varepsilon_0\varepsilon\mu_0+\delta^2)^{-1}\left[\frac{m\delta}{r}H_z + j\omega\varepsilon_0\varepsilon\left(\frac{\partial E_z}{\partial r}\right)\right]. \quad (7.10)$$

The boundary condition at $r = a$ requires

$$\left.\begin{array}{ll}(E_\varphi)_{\mathrm{I}} = (E_\varphi)_{\mathrm{II}} & (H_\varphi)_{\mathrm{I}} = (H_\varphi)_{\mathrm{II}} \\ (E_z)_{\mathrm{I}} = (E_z)_{\mathrm{II}} & (H_z)_{\mathrm{I}} = (H_z)_{\mathrm{II}}\end{array}\right\} \text{ at } r = a. \quad (7.11)$$

Substitution of (7.9) and (7.10) in (7.11) results in four homogeneous linear equations. The vanishing determinant of the coefficients of the amplitudes A, B, C and D gives the characteristic equation for the circular wave-guiding structure, whose solutions determine the propagation constants for the various modes as a function of frequency

$$F(\varepsilon_1, \varepsilon_2, v, a) =$$
$$[\varepsilon_1 U + \varepsilon_2 V]\,[U+V] + \frac{m^2 v^2}{(2\pi a/\lambda_0)^2}(\varepsilon_2-\varepsilon_1)^2 J_m^2(p)K_m^2(q) = 0$$

where

$$\left.\begin{array}{l}U = j(\varepsilon_2-v^2)(\varepsilon_1-v^2)^{\frac{1}{2}}J_m'(p)K_m(q) \\ V = (\varepsilon_1-v^2)(\varepsilon_2-v^2)^{\frac{1}{2}}J_m(p)K_m'(q)\end{array}\right\} \quad (7.12)$$

with

$$J_m'(p) = \left[\frac{\mathrm{d}J_m(pr/a)}{\mathrm{d}(pr/a)}\right]_{r=a}; \quad K_m'(q) = \left[\frac{\mathrm{d}K_m(qr/a)}{\mathrm{d}(qr/a)}\right]_{r=a}.$$

The modes for an empty circular metallic pipe waveguide can be found by putting $\varepsilon_1 = 1$ and $\varepsilon_2 \to \infty$ in eq. (7.12). The attenuation is found by application of eq. (7.5). This will be demonstrated in section 3.2. For the dielectric rod we should put $\varepsilon_2 = 1$ and $\varepsilon_1 = \varepsilon' - j\varepsilon''$, with ε'' small. The attenuation is found by using eq. (7.8). This is described in section 6.

3. Standard waveguides

3.1 Modes

The conventional method of short distance transmission of electromagnetic energy in the dm, cm and mm wavelength regions is by standard metallic waveguides of circular or rectangular cross-section. The dimensions and geometry of these guides are such that usually only one mode can exist, the already mentioned dominant mode. For the rectangular waveguide this is the TE_{10} mode and for the circular waveguide the TE_{11} mode. Their electric field lines in the cross-sectional plane of the guides are shown in fig. 7.2.

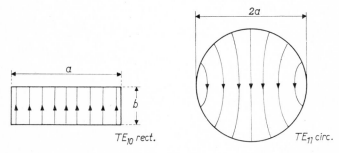

Fig. 7.2. Dominant mode electric field-patterns in rectangular and circular waveguides.

The cut-off wavelength λ_c of the TE_{10} rectangular guide mode is equal to $2a$, and for the TE_{11} circular guide mode 3.412 times the radius of the cross-section. For the standard rectangular waveguide the ratio b/a is usually 0.5, giving for the next higher modes (TE_{20} and TE_{01}) a cut-off wavelength of $\lambda_c = a$, half that of the dominant mode. For a circular guide the next higher mode (TM_{01}) has a cut-off wavelength of $\lambda_c = 2.613$ times the radius. For both rectangular and circular guides the guide wavelength is related to the free-space wavelength λ_0, by

$$\lambda_g = \lambda_0[1 - (\lambda_0/\lambda_c)^2]^{-\frac{1}{2}}.$$

From the above quoted figures we see that the dimensions of standard waveguides are of the order of the wavelength. This means from the view-point of manufacture that standard guides can be machined or electroformed with sufficient accuracy down to about 1 mm wavelength. At wavelengths shorter than this, however, the manufacture of guides will be very difficult.

3.2. ATTENUATION

A second important limitation to the range of suitability of the standard waveguides is set by the attenuation due to losses, especially the dissipation in the metallic walls. As an example we shall calculate the attenuation of a circular guide, using the general procedure described in section 2.4. Substituting in eq. (7.12) the value $\varepsilon_1 = 1$, and taking only the highest and second highest powers of the large ε_2, the characteristic equation reduces to

$$F(\varepsilon_2, v) = U^2 + \varepsilon_2 V^2 + \varepsilon_2 UV + \frac{m^2 v^2}{(2\pi a/\lambda_0)^2} \varepsilon_2^2 J_m^2(p) K_m^2(q) = 0. \qquad (7.13)$$

In order to simplify eq. (7.13) we make now the distinction between TM and TE modes. These modes are easily found by putting $\varepsilon_2 = \infty$ (idealized perfectly conducting wall). For this extreme value of ε_2, eq. (7.13) reduces to $J_m(p) J_m'(p) = 0$ and is therefore satisfied by two solutions, either $J_m(p_0) = 0$, or $J_m'(p_0) = 0$, the first characterizing the TM modes, the second the TE modes, with

$$p_0 = (2\pi a/\lambda_0)(1-v_0^2)^{\frac{1}{2}}.$$

With $\varepsilon_2 = -j\varepsilon_2''$, eq. (7.13) for TM modes simplifies to

$$F_{TM}(-j\varepsilon_2'', v_0) = (1-v_0^2)(-j\varepsilon_2''-v_0^2)^2 J_m'^2(p_0) K_m^2(q_0).$$

Application of eq. (7.5) gives then

$$\Delta v_{TM} \approx \frac{(1-j)\lambda_0}{2\pi a v_0 (2\varepsilon_2'')^{\frac{1}{2}}}.$$

According to eq. (7.6) the attenuation becomes

$$\alpha_{TM} = 1/[v_0 a (2\varepsilon_2'')^{\frac{1}{2}}].$$

It is common practice to introduce the surface resistance, $R_s = (\omega\mu/2\sigma)^{\frac{1}{2}}$ and the free-space impedance $\zeta = (\mu_0/\varepsilon_0)^{\frac{1}{2}}$ and with $\varepsilon_2'' = \sigma/(\varepsilon_0\omega)$ (section 2.1) and $v_0 = [1-(\lambda_0/\lambda_c)^2]^{\frac{1}{2}}$, α_{TM} can be written as

$$\alpha_{TM} = \frac{R_s}{\zeta a}[1-(\lambda_0/\lambda_c)^2]^{-\frac{1}{2}}.$$

In a similar way the attenuation constant for TE modes is

$$\alpha_{TE} = \frac{R_s}{\zeta a}[1-(\lambda_0/\lambda_c)^2]^{-\frac{1}{2}}\left[\frac{m^2}{p_{0_{mn}}^2-m^2} + (\lambda_0/\lambda_c)^2\right]$$

where $p_{0_{mn}}$ is the nth non-vanishing root of $J_m'(p_0) = 0$.

The same method may be used for calculating the wall losses in a rectangular guide, albeit in a slightly more complicated way. Here the boundary conditions at the wall-intersections cause some difficulties in deriving the characteristic equation. The problem has to be split into two parts, each part giving the calculation of the loss in two opposite parallel walls, not perfectly conducting, while the other two walls are assumed to be perfect conductors. The sum of the separate attenuation constants is the attenuation constant of the complete guide.

The other method using the Poynting theorem as indicated in section 2.3, is somewhat simpler in this case. Without calculation we give the attenuation constants for TM modes and TE modes in rectangular guides (MARCUVITZ [1951])

$$\alpha_{TM} = \frac{2R_s}{\zeta a} \left[\frac{m^2 + n^2 a^3 / b^3}{m^2 + n^2 a^2 / b^2} \right] \left[1 - \left(\frac{\lambda_0}{\lambda_c} \right)^2 \right]^{-\frac{1}{2}} \quad \text{for TM modes} \quad (7.14)$$

where $m,n = 1, 2, 3, 4, \ldots$
and

$$\alpha_{TE} = \frac{R_s}{\zeta a} \left[\frac{\delta_n m^2 b/a + \delta_m n^2}{m^2 b/a + n^2 a/b} \left[1 - \left(\frac{\lambda_0}{\lambda_c} \right)^2 \right]^{\frac{1}{2}} + \right.$$

$$\left. + \frac{(\delta_n + \delta_m b/a)(\lambda_0/\lambda_c)^2}{[1 - (\lambda_0/\lambda_c)^2]^{\frac{1}{2}}} \right] \quad \text{for TE modes} \quad (7.15)$$

where $m,n = 0, 1, 2, 3, \ldots$ with $m = n = 0$ excluded and

$$\delta_m = 1 \quad \text{if} \quad m = 0$$
$$\delta_m = 2 \quad \text{if} \quad m \neq 0.$$

In order to decide, from the viewpoint of attenuation, on the suitability of the standard waveguide in the different wavelength regions, it is of course important to consider the wavelength dependence of the attenuation. We know that in order to ensure the single-mode operation the frequency of the signal wave has to be in between the lowest and the second lowest cut-off frequency. This means that the guide has to be designed in a form which is appropriate to the operating wavelength, and thus that the ratio between the wavelength and the dimensions of the guide must be practically constant. Taking the ratio λ_0/λ_c constant in the expressions above for the attenuation constants for the dominant modes of rectangular and circular waveguides, we see that the attenuation constant increases with decreasing wavelength, according to $\lambda_0^{-\frac{3}{2}}$ (R_s varies with $\lambda_0^{-\frac{1}{2}}$).

The attenuation per metre, however, is frequently not the best criterion for most laboratory equipments, because the necessary lengths of waveguides and those of components also normally diminish at shorter wavelengths. The attenuation per wavelength, $\alpha\lambda_0$, is much more significant. But even $\alpha\lambda_0$ increases with decreasing wavelength for both modes in proportion to $\lambda_0^{-\frac{1}{2}}$. For the TE_{10} mode in rectangular waveguides eq. (7.15) leads to

$$\frac{\alpha\lambda_0}{R_s} = \frac{2}{\zeta}\frac{\lambda_0}{2a}\frac{a}{b}\frac{1+2(b/a)(\lambda_0/2a)^2}{[1-(\lambda_0/2a)^2]^{\frac{1}{2}}}$$

and with $\zeta = 376.62\ \Omega$ (free space impedance)

$$\frac{\alpha\lambda_0}{R_s} = 0.53 \times 10^{-2}\frac{\lambda_0}{2a}\frac{a}{b}\frac{1+2(b/a)(\lambda_0/2a)^2}{[1-(\lambda_0/2a)^2]^{\frac{1}{2}}} \tag{7.15a}$$

For standard waveguide, having $a/b = 2$ and $a = \frac{3}{4}\lambda_0$ this reduces to

$$\frac{\alpha\lambda_0}{R_s} = 119 \times 10^{-3} \quad dB/\Omega. \tag{7.15b}$$

For rectangular waveguides with a conductivity of 5.8×10^7 Siemens/metre, we thus calculate an attenuation of 0.85×10^{-2} dB per wavelength or 2.1 dB per metre for 4 mm guides, 1.1×10^{-2} dB per wavelength or 5.5 dB/metre for 2 mm waveguides, 1.7×10^{-2} dB per wavelength or 17 dB/metre at 1 mm, and 2.4×10^{-2} dB per wavelength or 48 dB per metre for 0.5 mm guides. In practice, however, owing to imperfections in the surfaces of the guide, the measured values of the attenuation constant are about twice as high as these computed values.

Some significant measured figures for standard rectangular copper waveguides are

$\alpha = 3.5$–5.3 dB/m (WG 26) at 4.3 mm wavelength and

$\alpha = 11.4$ dB/m (WG 29) at 2.1 mm wavelength

(BENSON and STEVEN [1963]).

Circular waveguides are not often used in the short millimetre wavelength region. The losses of the circular guide in the dominant mode are comparable to those of rectangular guide, but the single-mode bandwidth of the circular guide mode is much smaller. For rectangular guide the ratio of the two longest cut-off wavelengths is 2, but for circular guides it is only 1.31.

We conclude that the standard rectangular guide is suitable for wavelengths above 2 mm, but for the propagation of waves shorter than 2 mm other techniques may have to be used both from the constructional point of view and due to the excessively high attenuation.

4. Oversized waveguides

One of the possible techniques entailing lower losses and easier construction for shorter wavelengths is the oversized waveguide. At a given wavelength an oversized guide is one which is large enough to propagate many higher order modes in addition to the dominant mode.

Mostly the rectangular oversized guide is at least ten times larger than the conventional guide in each cross-sectional dimension; the ratio a/b usually remains close to 2. Oversizing can also be applied to circular guides and to one dimension of a rectangular guide, the latter resulting in the so-called "tall guide", which has lower attenuation than the normal oversized guide, as we shall see. For oversized guides (large λ_c) the guide wavelength λ_g, given by $1/\lambda_g^2 = 1/\lambda_o^2 - 1/\lambda_c^2$, becomes very close to the free space wavelength λ_0.

4.1. MODES

If the oversized guide is fed by careful tapering from standard-size waveguide, the same mode as is propagated in the feeding guide is transferred to the oversized system. As far as the rectangular guide is concerned this means that here too the TE_{10} mode is the dominant one. The field distribution in the cross-sectional plane though on larger scale, is the same as in the standard guide. In oversized guides higher, "spurious", modes can exist, however. Fig. 7.3 is a useful mode chart for determining these spurious modes. The cut-off conditions for various modes are plotted, as determined by the expression for the cut-off wavelength of TM_{mn} and of TE_{mn} modes in rectangular guides

$$\lambda_c = \frac{2\,(ab)^{\frac{1}{2}}}{[m^2 b/a + n^2 a/b]^{\frac{1}{2}}}. \tag{7.16}$$

The horizontal lines in this chart are the cut-off curves for the TE_{01}, TE_{02} etc. modes, while the vertical lines are cut-off curves for the TE_{10}, TE_{20} etc. The other curves represent the cut-offs of the modes indicated in the figure (from TM_{11} and TE_{11} up to TM_{55} and TE_{55}). The modes which may exist in an oversized guide are found by drawing a line at an angle of $45°$ to the vertical through any point appropriate to the ratio a/b. Such a line represents any oversized waveguide with that aspect ratio a/b. Each intersection of this $45°$-line with the cut-off curves, below the operating point a/λ_0 where λ_0 is the operating wavelength, represents the possible existence of a spurious mode pertaining to the intersected curve. Consider, for example, the standard

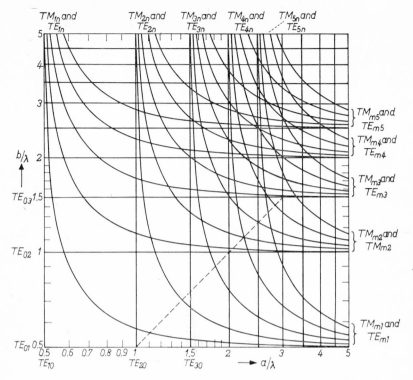

Fig. 7.3. Mode chart for rectangular waveguides. Each line represents the cut-off wavelength of the indicated mode.

rectangular waveguide with a/b equal to 2, operated at a wavelength λ_0 a little shorter than $3a$ or a little more than two times oversized. The dashed $45°$ line in the figure represents this guide. We see that in this case 24 modes other than the fundamental TE_{10} mode can exist starting with TE_{01}, TE_{20}, TE_{11}, TM_{11} etc. All kinds of rectangular guides with different aspect ratios can be considered in this way. From this mode chart we may draw the conclusion that careful launching of the fundamental mode is very important if single-mode propagation is desired, because even in only slightly oversized structures many modes can exist.

For circular oversized waveguides the cut-off wavelengths are simply given by

$$\lambda_c = \frac{2a}{p_{mn}} \qquad \text{for TM modes}$$

and

$$\lambda_c = \frac{2a}{p'_{mn}} \quad \text{for TE modes,}$$

where p_{mn} and p'_{mn} are respectively the nth non-vanishing roots of $J_m(p) = 0$ and $J'_m(p) = 0$, and a the radius of the tube. The first few longest cut-off wavelengths are given in table 7.1.

TABLE 7.1

Cut-off wavelengths for modes in circular waveguides

	mode	λ_c/a
dominant mode	TE_{11}	3.412
	TM_{01}	2.613
	TE_{21}	2.057
low-loss mode	TE_{01}	1.640
	TM_{11}	1.640
	TE_{31}	1.495
	TM_{21}	1.224

4.2. ATTENUATION

The expressions (7.14) and (7.15) for the theoretical attenuation constants are also valid for the oversized guide. It can easily be seen from these expressions that for constant frequency, enlarging the dimensions gives a reduction of the attenuation, provided that the dominant mode is maintained. From eq. (7.15a) and for the "standard" ratio $a/b = 2$

$$\frac{\alpha\lambda_0}{R_s} = 1.06 \times 10^{-2} \frac{\lambda_0}{2a} \frac{1+(\lambda_0/2a)^2}{[1-(\lambda_0/2a)^2]^{\frac{1}{2}}}.$$

For small values of $\lambda_0/2a$, i.e. for use as an oversized guide this reduces to

$$\left(\frac{\alpha\lambda_0}{R_s}\right)_{\text{oversized}} \approx 1.06 \times 10^{-2}(\lambda_0/2a) \quad \text{Np}/\Omega$$
$$= 9.2 \times 10^{-2}(\lambda_0/2a) \quad \text{dB}/\Omega.$$

For example a 3 cm rectangular guide (X-band) used for 2 mm wave propagation has a theoretical attenuation of 0.23 dB/m while the theoretical attenuation in the standard 2 mm guide would have been about 4.6 dB/m; the use of the oversized guide thus reduces the attenuation by a factor of 20. The theoretical attenuation of four standard rectangular guides (designed for normal use at 2, 4, 8 and 30 mm) when used as oversized guides for the wavelength region 0.3 mm − 9.0 mm, is illustrated in fig. 7.4. It can be seen

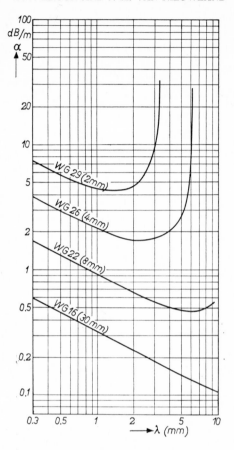

Fig. 7.4. Theoretical attenuation of the dominant mode as a function of wavelength for four standard guides, used as standard oversized waveguides.

that an increasing degree of oversizing results in a decreasing attenuation. Further, using a standard guide, one can very easily reduce the attenuation by an additional factor of 2 for oversized propagation by turning the guide 90 degrees, so that the electric field is parallel to the largest inner dimension of the guide so that $a'/b' = 0.5$ (tall guide). The attenuation of the same standard guides but now in this turned position follows from eq. (7.15a)

$$\left(\frac{\alpha\lambda_0}{R_s}\right)_{\text{tall}} = 0.27 \frac{\lambda_0}{2a'} \frac{1+4(\lambda_0/2a')^2}{[1-(\lambda_0/2a')^2]^{\frac{1}{2}}}$$

which for small $\lambda_0/2a'$ reduces to

$$\left(\frac{\alpha\lambda_0}{R_s}\right)_{\text{tall}} \approx 0.27 \times 10^{-2}(\lambda_0\ 2a') \qquad \text{Np}/\Omega$$

$$= 2.3 \times 10^{-2}(\lambda_0/2a') \qquad \text{dB}/\Omega.$$

The theoretical attenuation of a 2 mm wave in an X-band guide is thus reduced to about 0.12 dB/m. The attenuation of the TE_{10} mode in different standard guides, used as tall guides, is shown in fig. 7.5.

In order to compare the attenuation of a TE_{10} dominant mode in rectangular oversized waveguides, having different ratios a/b, with the attenuation of normal (not oversized) waveguides at the same wavelength, normalized plots of α/α_{st} are presented in fig. 7.6. These curves show that the ratio α/α_{st} decreases rapidly with increasing degree of oversizing. Up to about four

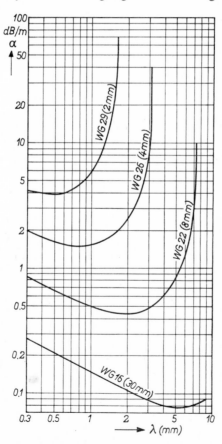

Fig. 7.5. Theoretical attenuation of the dominant mode as a function of wavelength of four standard guides, used as tall guides.

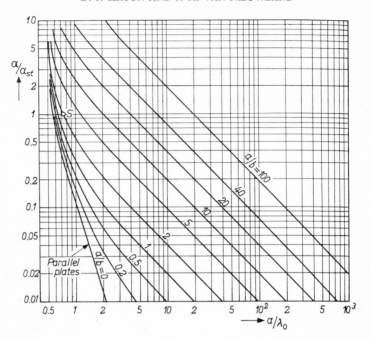

Fig. 7.6. Theoretical attenuation of the dominant mode of rectangular oversized guides, normalized to the attenuation of standard guides for the same wavelength, as a function of degree of oversizing (a/λ_0) for different ratios a/b. The point S represents a standard guide, used in the conventional way.

times oversize the relative attenuation factor of the normal guide ($a/b = 2$) decreases faster than inversely to the degree of oversizing. For further over-sizing the decrease becomes inversely proportional. The dependence on the ratio a/b is clearly shown by the various curves; diminishing a/b for constant a/λ_0, that is making the guide "taller", results in a decreased relative attenuation.

It should be noted that the attenuation of TM modes has a more compli-cated wavelength dependence for large degree of oversizing (KARBOWIAK [1958]; MARTIN [1960]).

Experimental values for the attenuation constant have been given by BLED et al. [1964] .The attenuation constant of a 3 cm standard waveguide, used as an oversized waveguide is given in table 7.2. As in the case of standard waveguides, the measured values differ from the calculated values by a factor of 2 to 4. Again the discrepancy between calculated and measured values of the attenuation may be attributed to imperfections in the surfaces of the

TABLE 7.2

Attenuation constant of a standard 3 cm waveguide used as an oversized guide

wavelength	calculated value	experimental value
4 mm	0.16 dB/m	0.25 dB/m
2 mm	0.23 dB/m	0.5 dB/m
1 mm	0.32 dB/m	1 dB/m
0.65 mm	0.4 dB/m	~ 1.6 dB/m

guide; the increase of this discrepancy towards shorter wavelength suggests that the ratio of the defect size to the wavelength determines the influence which defects have on attenuation.

4.3. PARALLEL-PLATE AND TALL GUIDES

The decrease of the attenuation for smaller ratios a/b noted in the preceding section might suggest extending the width b to infinity, while the other dimension, a, is kept the same. In this structure, called the parallel-plate guide, the modes may be regarded as limiting forms of the modes in a rectangular waveguide. This set of modes, bounded only in one direction by a conducting wall, has both a discrete (in the finite direction) and a continuous character. One of these modes is the parallel-plate "low-loss" mode, the limiting form of dominant TE_{10} rectangular waveguide mode, with the electric field parallel to the plates. The attenuation constant for this mode, which can be derived from eq. (7.15a), is

$$\alpha = \frac{R_s}{\frac{1}{2}\zeta a} \frac{(\lambda_0/2a)^2}{[1-(\lambda_0/2a)^2]^{\frac{1}{2}}} \qquad (7.17)$$

with a cut-off wavelength $\lambda_c = 2a$. This mode, with no longitudinal currents (which cause high losses) thus has a very small attenuation which decreases with increasing frequency for fixed a; for sufficiently short wavelengths ($\lambda_0 \ll \lambda_c$) as $\lambda_0^{\frac{3}{2}}$. (Note the $\lambda_0^{-\frac{1}{2}}$ dependence of R_s.) However, the appropriate guide for a certain wavelength would correspond to a constant ratio of (λ_0/a) and then there is an increasing attenuation with decreasing wavelength, according to $\lambda_0^{-\frac{3}{2}}$, although the losses are still very small. Here too, oversizing of the dimension a entails lower losses, approaching in the limit $\lambda_0 \ll \lambda_c$, an a^{-3} dependence for constant frequency (see fig. 7.6).

In practice the parallel-plate guide cannot be realized because it requires infinitely wide plates. Its low losses, however, justify the search for approaches with roughly the same properties. As indicated by GRIEMSMANN

[1963] three guides do approach this operation: the tall guide, the groove guide and the dielectric H-guide, the last two being discussed in the next sections, and the first having been introduced in the preceding section.

The tall guide, being essentially an oversized rectangular waveguide with $a/b \leq \frac{1}{2}$, has a field configuration approaching that of the parallel plate guide. The attenuation of the TE_{10} mode, normalized as a ratio to the attenuation of the conventional guide, is included in fig. 7.6 for values $a/b = \frac{1}{2}, \frac{1}{5}$. From eq. (7.15a) it can be derived that for every ratio a/b there is an optimum wavelength λ_m for which the attenuation is a minimum. The relation between a/b and λ_m is given by

$$a/b = \frac{6(\lambda_c/\lambda_m)^2 - 2}{(\lambda_c/\lambda_m)^2[(\lambda_c/\lambda_m)^2 - 3]} \, . \qquad (7.18)$$

From this equation it is easily seen that shorter wavelengths require a smaller value for a/b, for minimum attenuation; i.e. the optimum guide becomes "taller" at shorter wavelengths. This minimum attenuation, however, is still four times the attenuation of the parallel-plate guide, as can be seen from

$$\frac{(\alpha_{\text{tall}})_{\min}}{\alpha_{\text{par. pl}}} = \frac{a}{2b}(\lambda_c/\lambda_0)^2 + 1$$

where for very small a/b we can say

$$(\lambda_c/\lambda_0)^2 \approx 6 \, b/a$$

so that $(\alpha_{\text{tall}})_{\min}/\alpha_{\text{par. pl}} = 4$.

4.4. GROOVE-GUIDE

The difficulty with the parallel-plate guide (discussed in the preceding section) using finite parallel plates is loss by sidewards radiation of the electromagnetic energy. In the groove-guide radiation is prevented by shaping the plates in such a way that the field distribution decreases exponentially from the centre. There are grooves in the two parallel walls located in the central region of the guide cross-section, running along the guide as indicated in fig. 7.7.

These grooves support a low-loss TE mode with the main electric field component parallel to the plates, as in the ideal case. However, the electric field lines are slightly curved in the cross-sectional plane in order to end perpendicular at the plates. TISCHER [1963] gives a general theory of the groove-guide using conformal mapping and estimates the values of cut-off and guide wavelengths. GRIEMSMANN [1963] gives theoretical information about attenuation in groove-guides.

According to his calculation attenuation for a guide with a separation of 7.3 mm at the centre groove and 7.1 mm elsewhere is about 0.015 dB/m for 300 Gc/s (1 mm), and about 0.0066 dB/m for 1000 Gc/s (0.3 mm).

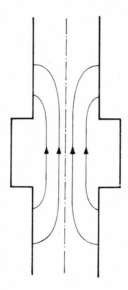

Fig. 7.7. Cross-section of groove-guide with electric field pattern of TE mode.

4.5. LIGHT-PIPES

Light-pipes are metallic pipes (brass or cupro-nickel) about 1 cm or more in diameter and frequently used for wavelengths less than 1 mm in conjunction with spectrometers and interferometers using broad-band (hot-body) sources and relatively low resolutions. They are essentially greatly oversized guides, used without mode discrimination, so that most of the energy is transmitted in many very high order modes. The propagation is then most easily described in geometrical optical terms by a nearly plane wave passing through the pipe by multifold reflection against the wall. Since infrared reflectivities are high they are very convenient and effective over distances of a metre or so.

5. H-guides

The H-guide represents an attempt to make use of the low loss properties of a parallel-plate guide (section 4.3) avoiding the loss of power by sideways radiation from plates of finite width by field containment. An exponential decay of the fields in the sidewards direction is obtained by placing a dielectric slab between the conducting strips, as is indicated in fig. 7.8.

Some properties of the H-guide have been analyzed by TISCHER [1959], GRIEMSMANN et al. [1959], and an extensive derivation of all possible field distributions has been published by MORSE and BEAM [1956]. An experimental study of the H-guide in the millimetre wave region has been published by TAKIYAMA et al. [1962].

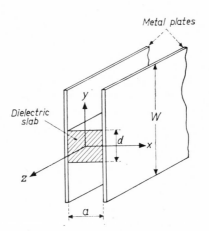

Fig. 7.8. The H-guide.

5.1. MODES

Morse and Beam conclude that both transverse electric and hybrid modes (i.e. modes with both an electric and a magnetic field component in the direction of propagation) can propagate through this structure. However, a transverse magnetic mode cannot exist. The lowest transverse electric mode has zero cut-off frequency and is therefore the dominant mode. The properties of this mode have been calculated and experimentally verified by Morse and Beam and by COHN [1959]. However, this mode has a non-vanishing H_y component which means that in the parallel strips there are longitudinal currents that cause high losses at short wavelengths. The attenuation of this mode is comparable with that of the conventional rectangular guide mode.

The hybrid modes can be divided into two types, one characterized by the electric field component in the y-direction being zero (transverse electric sidewards; TE_s) and the other by the magnetic field component in the y-direction being zero (transverse magnetic sidewards; TM_s).

The latter type has no longitudinal currents and hence the attenuation due to metal loss decreases as the frequency increases, as in the case of the parallel-plate guide (cf. section 4.3). A description of the field pattern of the low-loss TM_s mode is given by GRIEMSMANN [1959]. The main component of the electric field is, as in the parallel plate guide and the groove guide, parallel to the plates. Due to the rapid exponential decay of the fields in the sidewards direction, no radiation occurs when finite plates of convenient width are used.

Since the TE_s modes, having an H_y component, produce longitudinal currents, the attenuation is higher than for the TM_s modes.

Both TM_s and TE_s modes can be subdivided in terms of the symmetry of the E_y and the H_y distributions about the geometrical plane of symmetry ($y = 0$) into symmetrical and anti-symmetrical mode-types. Four different mode-types of the hybrid modes thus exist, satisfying the following characteristic equations (GRIEMSMANN [1959]). These equations represent the relation between the guide wavelength ($v' = \lambda_0/\lambda_g$) and the geometrical and physical properties of the guide for the different mode-types.

$$\tan \varphi = \varepsilon[(\tau-1)/(\varepsilon-\tau)]^{\frac{1}{2}} \qquad TM_s \text{ sym} \qquad (7.19a)$$

$$\tan \varphi = -\frac{1}{\varepsilon}[(\varepsilon-\tau)/(\tau-1)]^{\frac{1}{2}} \quad TM_s \text{ asym} \qquad (7.19b)$$

$$\tan \varphi = [(\tau-1)/(\varepsilon-\tau)]^{\frac{1}{2}} \qquad TE_s \text{ sym} \qquad (7.19c)$$

$$\tan \varphi = -[(\varepsilon-\tau)/(\tau-1)]^{\frac{1}{2}} \qquad TE_s \text{ asym} \qquad (7.19d)$$

where $\tau = (n\lambda_0/2a)^2 + v^2$, n being an integer, ε the relative dielectric constant of the slab and $\varphi = (\pi d/\lambda_0)(\varepsilon-\tau)^{\frac{1}{2}}$. The tangent functions of the symmetric modes have their arguments in the odd quadrants, whereas the asymmetric modes are located in the even quadrants. Inspection of these equations shows that $1 \le \tau \le \varepsilon$, so that if ε is small $\tau \approx 1$. Eq. (7.19) can easily be solved numerically.

As has been remarked above the TM_s sym is a low-loss mode and is therefore recommended for use. To avoid the excitation of other modes a mode-filter is required. The TM_s sym mode has a vanishing sidewards impedance at the central plane, $y = 0$, which means that a conducting sheet may be

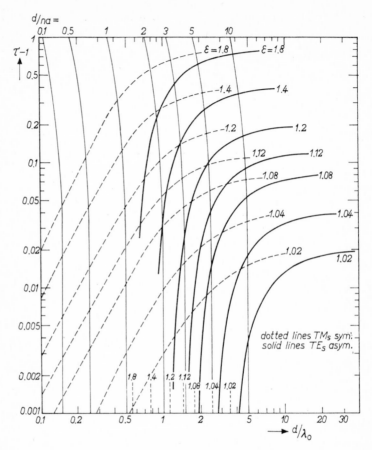

Fig. 7.9. The parameter $\tau = (n\lambda_0/2a)^2 + v^2$ as a function of d/λ_0 for different values of ε for the TM_s sym and TE_s asym modes in the H-guide. Dotted lines represent the TM_s sym modes and solid lines the TE_s asym modes. Lines of constant d/na are drawn to facilitate calculation of the cut-off wavelength for a given guide.

inserted at this plane without disturbing the field pattern. The TM_s asym mode and the TE_s sym mode are eliminated in this way, but the TE_s asym mode may still exist, since for this mode too the sidewards impedance vanishes at the symmetry plane. We therefore examine the TE_s asym and the TM_s sym modes more closely. The solutions of the characteristic equations (7.19a and d) are presented in fig. 7.9. Here the value of $\tau - 1 = (n\lambda_0/2a)^2 + v^2 - 1$ is plotted against d/λ_0 for different values of ε, where a is the separation of the metallic plates and d is the width of the dielectric strip. For large values of d/λ_0, for both modes $\tau - 1 \rightarrow \varepsilon - 1$, or, in other words, the guide wavelength becomes equal to that of a dielectric-filled parallel plate guide and all energy propagates in the dielectric.

For small values of d/λ_0 the two modes behave differently. Decreasing d/λ_0 causes τ to approach 1 and, considering first the behaviour of the TE_s asym mode for $\tau \to 1$, we see from eq. (7.19d) that $\varphi \to \frac{1}{2}\pi$ and therefore $d/\lambda_0 \to \frac{1}{2}(\varepsilon-1)^{\frac{1}{2}}$. This corresponds to the asymptote to which the TE_s asym curves in fig. 7.9 approach. For given d and ε the wavelength $\lambda_{cr} = 2d(\varepsilon-1)^{-\frac{1}{2}}$ is called the critical wavelength. If $\lambda_0 > \lambda_{cr}$ there exist no real value for τ, as a solution of the characteristic equation. This means that the sidewards decay of the fields is no longer exponential and hence loss due to radiation occurs.

For the TM_s sym mode $\varphi \to 0$ for $\tau \to 1$, and therefore the critical wavelength of this mode is infinite. At all wavelengths below the cut-off wavelength this mode can exist without sidewards radiation. Fig. 7.9 may also be used in the calculation of the cut-off wavelengths.

At cut-off $v \to 0$, and therefore $\tau \to (n\lambda_c/2a)^2$; where λ_c is the cut-off wavelength. In that case for each given value of $n\lambda_c/2a$ the corresponding value of d/λ_c can be found, at the different values of ε.

In order to facilitate the calculation of the cut-off wavelength of an H-guide of given dimensions a third set of curves has been drawn in fig. 7.9, namely lines of constant d/na. The cut-off wavelength of a guide with given values of d and a can be found from the value of d/λ_c at which the corresponding d/na curve intersects the curve of the appropriate ε.

Since the curves of constant d/na are nearly vertical lines the values of d/λ_c, and therefore the cut-off wavelengths, of the TE_s asym and TM_s sym modes are very close.

5.2. ATTENUATION

The losses in the H-guide consist of two parts: the losses in the dielectric and the losses due to dissipation in the metal plates. Because both are small they may be calculated separately.

The dielectric losses can be determined using the perturbation method discussed in section 2.3. Application of eqs. (7.7) and (7.8) to the characteristic equations (7.19) results in the following expression for the attenuation in the dielectric for any mode.

$$\alpha_\varepsilon = \frac{\pi}{\lambda_0}\frac{\tau}{v}\frac{1+(\sin 2\varphi)/2\varphi+(\varepsilon-\tau)[1-(\sin 2\varphi)/2\varphi]/\tau}{1+(\sin 2\varphi)/2\varphi+2\varepsilon[(\varepsilon-\tau)/(\tau-1)]^{\frac{1}{2}}(\cos^2 \varphi)/2\varphi}\tan\delta \quad \text{Np/m}$$

$$(7.20)$$

where $\tan\delta = \varepsilon''/\varepsilon'$ denotes the loss tangent of the dielectric and φ is the argument of the tangent function in the characteristic equation, $\varphi = (\pi d/\lambda_0)\,(\varepsilon-\tau)^{\frac{1}{2}}$. At very high frequencies $\tau \to \varepsilon$ and

$$\alpha_\varepsilon \approx \frac{\pi \varepsilon^{\frac{1}{2}}}{\lambda_0} \tan \delta \qquad \text{Np/m}. \qquad (7.21)$$

This is the expression for the attenuation of a uniform plane wave in the dielectric, in accordance with the fact, already mentioned, that in this limit

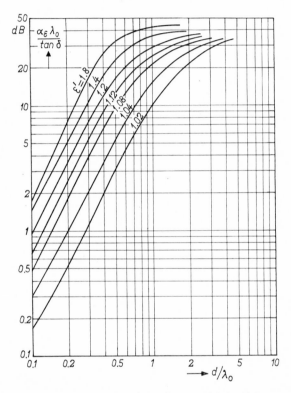

Fig. 7.10. Dielectric attenuation factor, $\alpha_\varepsilon \lambda_0/\tan \delta$ of H-guide for TM_s sym mode as a function of d/λ_0 for different values of ε. Plate separation of the H-guide $a = \frac{3}{4}\lambda_0$.

the wave propagates only in the dielectric strip. Of course these dielectric losses are a disadvantage of using dielectric media in waveguides, but nevertheless it is a very satisfactory method of confining electromagnetic energy, especially if the attenuation can be kept low by using dielectrics having small loss tangents. In fig. 7.10 the attenuation of the TM_s sym mode due to dielectric loss is plotted for a number of values of ε as a function of d/λ_0. In order to make this plot more universal $\alpha_\varepsilon \lambda_0/\tan \delta$ is plotted rather than α_ε. For the value of a, the separation of the metallic plates, a somewhat arbitrary choice has been made; the H-guide can be excited directly from standard waveguide if the separation of the plates has been chosen to be equal to the width, a, of the standard waveguide, used at a wavelength $\lambda_0 = \frac{2}{3}\lambda_c = \frac{2}{3}2a$ and therefore we have chosen $a = \frac{3}{4}\lambda_0$. Fig. 7.10 can also be used at other plate separations, provided the ordinate is multiplied by

$$[(\tau - 0.445)/[\tau - (\lambda_0/2a)^2]]^{\frac{1}{2}}$$

where the appropriate value of τ can be found from the TM_s sym curves in fig. 7.9.

For the attenuation due to dissipation in the metal we find for the TM_s sym mode

$$\alpha_m = \tag{7.22}$$

$$= 2\frac{R_s}{\zeta a}\left(\frac{n\lambda_0}{2a}\right)^2 \frac{\varepsilon}{\tau v} \frac{1+(\sin 2\varphi)/2\varphi + [(\cos^2 \varphi)/\varphi]\ [(\varepsilon - \tau)/(\tau - 1)]^{\frac{1}{2}}}{1+(\sin 2\varphi)/2\varphi + 2\varepsilon[(\varepsilon - \tau)/(\tau - 1)]\ (\cos^2 \varphi)/\varphi} \ \text{Np/m}$$

where R_s is the surface resistance of the metal and ζ the free space impedance. At high frequencies the expression for the metallic attenuation becomes

$$\alpha_m \approx 2\frac{R_s}{\zeta a}\left(\frac{n\lambda_0}{2a}\right)^2 \varepsilon^{-\frac{1}{2}} \quad \text{Np/m}. \tag{7.23}$$

Since R_s varies as $\lambda_0^{-\frac{1}{2}}$ the variation of α_m with wavelength is, for fixed a,

$$\alpha_m \sim \lambda_0^{\frac{3}{2}}. \tag{7.24}$$

This means a decrease of the attenuation due to calculated metallic losses with decreasing wavelength. In a similar way as for the dielectric attenuation, we consider $\alpha_m \lambda_0/R_s$ instead of α_m. It turns out that in the range $0.1 \le d/\lambda_0 \le 10$ and $1.02 \le \varepsilon \le 1.8$ the magnitude $\alpha_m \lambda_0/R_s$ is nearly independent of d/λ_0 and ε, having an average value

$$\alpha_m \lambda_0/R_s = 0.117(\lambda_0/2a)^3[(\tau - 0.445)/\{\tau - (\lambda_0/2a)^2\}]^{\frac{1}{2}} \ \text{dB}/\Omega, \tag{7.25}$$

which on the assumption of $a/\lambda_0 = \frac{3}{4}$, as above, becomes

$$\alpha_m \lambda_0/R_s = 34.7 \times 10^{-3} \quad \text{dB}/\Omega,$$

where

$$R_s = 10.88 \times 10^{-3}\ (10^7/\sigma\lambda_0)^{\frac{1}{2}} \quad \Omega,$$

with λ_0 in metres, and σ in Siemens/metre.

The total attenuation constant is the sum of α_ε and α_m the former increasing and the latter decreasing with decreasing wavelength (cf. eqs. (7.21) and (7.24)). This means that there is somewhere a minimum value of the attenuation constant, but this theoretical minimum will not coincide with the practical minimum because the imperfect smoothness and impurities of the metallic surfaces increase α_m especially at higher frequencies. But still the calculated attenuation is, due to the lack of longitudinal currents, three times smaller than the attenuation of conventional guides, as can be seen by comparing the attenuation per wavelength of the standard waveguide for the TE_{10} mode, as was given by eq. (7.15b),

$$(\alpha\lambda_0/R_s)_{st.w.} \approx 119 \times 10^{-3} \quad dB/\Omega$$

with the metal-attenuation of the H-guide given above

$$(\alpha\lambda_0/R_s)_{H-guide} \approx 34.7 \times 10^{-3} \quad dB/\Omega.$$

At 1 mm wavelength the attenuation due to metallic loss would be about 5 dB/metre.

For the rectangular waveguide we have seen in section 4 that a decrease in attenuation could be obtained by oversizing the guide, and the same possibility will hold for the H-guide. If the spacing between the metallic plates, a, is enlarged the metal losses decrease, according to eq. (7.25) about as fast as a^{-3} because the third factor in eq. (7.25)

$$[(\tau-0.445)/[\tau-(\lambda_0/2a)^2]]^{\frac{1}{2}}$$

will not change very much (e.g. for $\tau < 1.3$ a 15-times oversizing results in a 20% decrease of this factor). The dielectric losses in the H-guide are insensitive to oversizing, because this same factor governs the variation in the expression for $\alpha_\varepsilon \lambda_0/\tan\delta$ above. The attenuation of the oversized H-guide is thus limited by the dielectric losses. Taking a representative value for $\alpha_\varepsilon \lambda_0/\tan\delta \approx 5$ dB (cf. fig. 7.10), the ultimate attenuation of the H-guide for a loss tangent of about 10^{-4} is found to be

$$\alpha\lambda_0 \approx 5 \times 10^{-4} \quad dB.$$

The usual disadvantage of oversizing, i.e. the possibility of exciting spurious or higher order modes, applies in this case. In an n-times oversized H-guide the n-th order modes may occur, as implied by the cut-off condition:

$$\tau = (n\lambda_c/2a)^2.$$

The attenuation for an n-th order mode is at least n^2 times that of the lowest order mode, but since the metal attenuation of the lowest order mode in an oversized guide is reduced by a factor of about n^{-3} by the oversizing (see above), it can be concluded that the metal-loss attenuation of the highest order mode in an oversized waveguide is still of the order of $1/n$ times that of the lowest order mode in a standard H-guide. This order of magnitude consideration shows that oversizing will always have some advantage as far as attenuation is concerned. If precautions are taken in launching the lowest order mode in an oversized waveguide so that the excitation of higher order modes is avoided, and the mode purity of the TM_s sym mode is assured by use of mode filters, the losses should approach the dielectric loss limit quoted above.

5.3. CONSTRUCTION AND MEASUREMENTS

H-guides have been constructed and measurements made by GRIEMSMANN [1959] and TAKIYAMA et al. [1962]. Both used metallic plates of about 10 cm width separated by spacers, a few cm apart, at the edges of the plates. According to Takiyama's measurements the spacers did not seriously influence the attenuation when the width of the metallic plates was between 10 and 20 times the wavelength, depending on the width, d, of the dielectric strip. In order to prevent high dielectric loss, Griemsmann suggested the use of dielectric foam, which has a low dielectric constant and a small loss tangent, rather than a thin solid dielectric strip as was originally proposed by TISCHER [1959]. A problem that may arise at shorter wavelengths from the use of foam is a possible additional attenuation caused by scattering when the wavelength becomes comparable to the size of the cells in the dielectric foam. No connectors and flanges between H-guide sections are needed, because no currents are intersected by transverse slots and gaps in the walls. The large cross-sectional dimensions and the simplicity of fabrication are such that manufacturing is no problem for short wavelengths.

At 5.5 mm wavelength Takiyama et al. found an attenuation constant of 0.65 dB/m for an H-guide having $a = 4.78$ mm and $d = 14$ mm. The dielectric constant was $\varepsilon = 1.01$ and tan δ about 10^{-4}. If d was increased to 20 mm, the attenuation constant became 0.87 dB/m. In a slightly oversized guide, having $a = 9.56$ mm, the attenuation constant for the TM_s sym mode became 0.42 dB/m. These values are about 1.3 times the theoretical values for their guide. The discrepancy is attributed to imperfect smoothness of the copper surfaces. In order to isolate the attenuation caused by the metal, GRIEMSMANN [1959] used Nichrome plates instead of copper for the construction of an experimental H-guide. Due to the increased resistivity of the metal, the dielectric loss was neglibigle compared with the metal loss. In the wavelength range 6 to 11 mm the attenuation ranged from 1.05 dB/m to 4 dB/m, in accordance with the predicted $\lambda_0^{-\frac{3}{2}}$ behaviour. The magnitudes were nearly 1.5 times the calculated values.

5.4. Dielectric loaded trough-line

As discussed in section 5.1, for some modes it is possible to introduce a metallic sheet at the symmetry plane, $y = 0$, of the H-guide structure without disturbing the field distribution. This is possible for the TM_s modes with a symmetrical distribution of E_y, for the TE_s modes with an anti-symmetrical distribution of H_y, and for the pure TE modes with an anti-symmetrical distribution of H_y. For these modes the parts of the H-guide, on both sides of the metallic sheet, act independently and could be constructed separately to give what is called a dielectric loaded trough-line (fig. 7.11). The trough-line can be constructed more rigidly than the H-guide, without supports be-

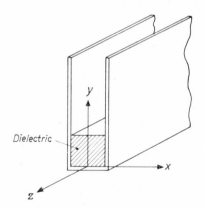

Fig. 7.11. Dielectric loaded trough-line.

tween the plates. Single-mode operation can be achieved as in the H-guide with a conducting wall inserted. The structure is smaller than the corresponding H-guide having a comparable attenuation and power-handling capacity. The attenuation due to losses in the parallel plates and in the dielectric is calculated in the same way as for the H-guide, but there is an additional component of the attenuation due to losses in the bottom plate.

Measurements and verification of the theoretical predictions of the guide wavelength, rate of field decay and attenuation for the pure TE mode have been performed by COHN [1960]. However, since the pure TE mode is not a low-loss mode, the attenuation is comparable with that of conventional standard rectangular waveguides. For hybrid modes better results can be predicted.

6. Dielectric rod guides

The problem of guiding electromagnetic waves along a dielectric rod was first treated by HONDROS and DEBEYE [1910]. Later the problem was re-investigated by CARSON et al. [1936] and formal solutions of the field equation in terms of cylinder functions were given by SCHELKUNOFF [1943]. Experimental investigations were performed by CHANDLER [1949] and were theoretically interpreted by ELSASSER [1949]. CULLEN et al. [1959] have applied the dielectric rod propagation for measurements of dielectric properties at millimetre wavelengths. Further investigations have been made by SCHULTEN [1960], and general plots of mode patterns have been published by BIERNSON and KINSLEY [1965].

It is known that certain electromagnetic modes can propagate along a dielectric without attenuation due to radiation, provided the rod is perfectly straight and no disturbances, such as supports are present. The propagation of electromagnetic waves within a dielectric is usually very lossy compared to the propagation through air or vacuum. However, in the case of the dielectric rod guide it can be arranged that the wave be guided by the dielectric but most of the electromagnetic energy travels outside the material in the surrounding air. The fraction which travels outside is determined by the dimensions of the rod and the dielectric constant. The more energy propagating outside the rod, the smaller the losses but also the looser the binding of the wave to the rod and the larger the radial extent of the field, so that the propagating mode is more easily disturbed with resultant losses due to radiation, etc.

6.1. MODES

In section 2.4 the general expressions for the z-components of the fields for any circular wave-guiding structure are given. Also given is the characteristic equation (7.12), whose solutions determine the propagation constants of the various modes as a function of frequency. Referring to section 2.4 this equation is

$$F(\varepsilon_1, \varepsilon_2, \mu_1, \mu_2, v, r_0) =$$
$$= (\varepsilon_1 U + \varepsilon_2 V)(U + V) + \frac{m^2 v^2}{(2\pi a/\lambda_0)^2}(\varepsilon_2 - \varepsilon_1)^2 J_m^2(p) K_m^2(q) = 0 \quad (7.12)$$

where
$$U = j(\varepsilon_2 - v^2)(\varepsilon_1 - v^2)^{\frac{1}{2}}J'_m(p)K_m(q)$$
$$V = (\varepsilon_1 - v^2)(\varepsilon_2 - v^2)^{\frac{1}{2}}J_m(p)K'_m(q)$$

with $v = (\lambda_0/2\pi)\delta$, J_m and K_m are the mth order Bessel function and modified Hankel function and

$$J'_m(p) = \left[\frac{\partial J_m(pr/a)}{\partial(pr/a)}\right]_{r=a} ; \quad K'_m(q) = \left[\frac{\partial K_m(qr/a)}{\partial(qr/a)}\right]_{r=a} ;$$

m being $0,1,2,\ldots$ and ε_1 and ε_2 are the relative dielectric constants of media I and II (fig. 7.1).
Recalling

$$(p/a)^2 = \omega^2\varepsilon_0\mu_0\varepsilon_1 - \delta^2 = (2\pi/\lambda_0)^2(\varepsilon_1 - v^2)$$
$$(q/a)^2 = \delta^2 - \omega^2\varepsilon_0\mu_0\varepsilon_2 = (2\pi/\lambda_0)^2(v^2 - \varepsilon_2)$$

we see that

$$p^2 + q^2 = (2\pi a/\lambda_0)^2(\varepsilon_1 - \varepsilon_2). \tag{7.26}$$

In practice medium II is air and therefore $\varepsilon_2 = 1$. Due to the oscillatory character of $J_m(p)$ the characteristic equation (7.12) gives, for a fixed value of m, an infinite number of discrete values for p, for each value of q. This means that in a p-q diagram we have an infinite number of curves that correspond to solutions of the characteristic equation. The actual values of p and q for a dielectric rod of given ε and radius a and a given wavelength can be found by superimposing the simultaneous relation between p and q in eq. (7.26), which forms a circle in the p-q plane. The intersections of this circle with the original p-q curves give the pairs p,q that are the solutions of equations (7.12) and (7.26). These pairs p,q define the modes which propagate along the rod.

We shall restrict ourselves to the modes with $m = 0$ and $m = 1$. For the value $m = 0$, which implies no angular variation of the fields (see eq. (7.9)) the characteristic equation reduces to

$$(\varepsilon_1 U + \varepsilon_2 V)(U + V) = 0$$

which can be separated into

$$\varepsilon_1 U + \varepsilon_2 V = 0 \tag{7.27}$$

or
$$U + V = 0. \tag{7.28}$$

Eq. (7.27) defines a mode with a vanishing longitudinal H-component (the TM circular-rod mode) and eq. (7.28) defines a mode with vanishing longitudinal E-component (the TE circular-rod mode), as can be shown by substitution in eq. (7.9).

If $m = 1$ there exists an angular dependence of the fields and the modes prove to be hybrid with both an E_z and an H_z component. Each hybrid mode can be denoted by HE_{1n}, where n is an ordinal number indicating the particular p-q pair. This ordinal number is related to the cut-off wavelength of that particular mode for a given rod as shall be shown in the next section. Of these hybrid modes the one of lowest order, i.e. the HE_{11} mode, has a field configuration similar to that of the TE mode in circular waveguides except that it has both E and H components in the direction of propagation.

6.2. CUT-OFF

All preceding wave-guiding structures were bounded by metallic surfaces and the cut-off wavelength was found by letting $v \to 0$ (or $\lambda_g \to \infty$). In the case of the dielectric rod, however, the longest wavelength for which the wave is really *guided* by the rod is given by $v \to 1$ (or $\lambda_g \to \lambda_0$) when the wave propagates with the phase velocity belonging to the surrounding medium and for longer wavelength the wire has no guiding influence. This cut-off wavelength can be found by letting q approach zero.

For the TE and TM circular-rod modes the cut-off wavelengths are found by letting $q \to 0$ in equations (7.27) and (7.28) and from this a value is obtained for p from $J_0(p) = 0$. The smallest value for p ($p = 2.405$) is then substituted in eq. (7.26) to give

$$\lambda_c = (2\pi a/2.405)\,(\varepsilon_1 - 1)^{\frac{1}{2}}.$$

For the hybrid modes HE_{1n}, p approaches a value given by $J_1(p) = 0$ as $q \to 0$. The already mentioned ordinal number n then corresponds to the ordinal number of the roots of $J_1(p) = 0$. The smallest value of p for which $J_1(p) = 0$ is zero, and therefore the cut-off wavelength of the HE_{11}, or "dipole" mode, is infinite. This means that this mode can exist for all wavelengths and it is the dominant mode of the circular rod. The next higher of all possible modes are the TE and TM circular rod modes considered above, so that if λ_0 is less than λ_c, i.e. if the radius, a, of the rod and the wavelength, λ_0, are such that

$$(2\pi a/\lambda_0)\,(\varepsilon_1 - 1)^{\frac{1}{2}} < 2.405,$$

only the dipole mode can propagate along the rod. This property in combination with the fact that its field configuration is similar to that of the TE_{11} mode in circular metallic waveguides so that this mode can be launched easily from a metallic guide, making it the most suitable for transmission purposes.

6.3. ATTENUATION

If no disturbances and bends are present and the wave is travelling in the proper mode no radiation occurs and the attenuation can be determined by considering the dielectric loss only. This attenuation may be calculated using the perturbation method discussed in section 2.3. ELSASSER [1949] used the Poynting theorem approach, but the same results can be obtained in a much simpler way by the alternative method of differentiating the characteristic equation. For the dielectric rod we assume the relative dielectric constant to be $\varepsilon_1 = \varepsilon' - j\varepsilon''$ with $\varepsilon'' \ll \varepsilon'$, while the relative dielectric constant of the surrounding air is equal to 1.

The *TE circular-rod modes* are characterized, according to eq. (7.28), by $U + V = 0$.

After substitution of U and V this is

$$F_{TE} = j(1-v^2)^{\frac{1}{2}}J_0'(p)K_0(q) + (\varepsilon_1 - v^2)^{\frac{1}{2}}J_0(p)K_0'(q) = 0. \qquad (7.29)$$

Differentiating with respect to ε_1 results in

$$\left[\frac{\partial F_{TE}}{\partial \varepsilon_1}\right]_{\substack{\varepsilon_1 = \varepsilon' \\ v = v_0}} = -\frac{1}{2}\left(\frac{2\pi a}{\lambda_0}\right)^2\left[f_0^2 + \frac{1}{p_0^2}(1+2f_0)\right], \qquad (7.30)$$

whilst differentiating with respect to v gives

$$\left[\frac{\partial F_{TE}}{\partial v}\right]_{\substack{\varepsilon_1 = \varepsilon' \\ v = v_0}} = v_0\left(\frac{2\pi a}{\lambda_0}\right)^2\left[f_0^2 + \frac{1}{p_0^2}(1+2f_0) - g_0^2 - \frac{1}{q_0^2}(2g_0-1)\right] \qquad (7.31)$$

where

$$f_0 = \frac{J_0'(p_0)}{p_0 J_0(p_0)}$$

and

$$g_0 = \frac{K_0'(q_0)}{q_0 K_0(q_0)}$$

with

$$p_0 = (2\pi a/\lambda_0)\,(\varepsilon' - v_0^2)^{\frac{1}{2}}$$

$$q_0 = j(2\pi a/\lambda_0)\,(1 - v_0^2)^{\frac{1}{2}}.$$

Using eqs. (7.7) and (7.8) we find

$$\alpha_{TE} = (\pi/\lambda_0)\varepsilon'\,R_{TE}\tan\delta \qquad Np/m,$$

where

$$R_{TE} = \left| \frac{1}{v_0} \frac{f_0^2 + (2f_0 + 1)/p_0^2}{f_0^2 + (2f_0 + 1)/p_0^2 - g_0^2 - (2g_0 - 1)/q_0^2} \right| \qquad (7.32)$$

(see fig. 7.12). The attenuation factor of the *TM circular rod modes* can be derived in a similar way, starting from their characteristic eq. (7.27) with $\varepsilon_2 = 1$. The attenuation is found to be

$$\alpha_{TM} = (\pi/\lambda_0)\varepsilon' \ R_{TM} \tan \delta \quad \text{Np/m}, \qquad (7.33)$$

where in this case

$$R_{TM} = \left| \frac{1}{v_0} \frac{[(\varepsilon' - 1)/q_0^2] \, (f_0^2 + 1/p_0^2)/(1/p_0^2 + 1/q_0^2) \, + \, v_0^2[f_0^2 + (2f_0 + 1)/p_0^2]}{\varepsilon'[f_0^2 + (2f_0 + 1)/p_0^2] - [g_0^2 + (2g_0 - 1)/q_0^2]} \right|$$

$$(7.34)$$

(see fig. 7.12).

For increasing $2a/\lambda_0$ both R_{TE} and R_{TM} go through a maximum and converge asymptotically to the value $(\varepsilon')^{-\frac{1}{2}}$. For this value of R the attenuation for both TE and TM-circular rod modes becomes

$$\alpha = (\pi/\lambda_0) \, (\varepsilon')^{\frac{1}{2}} \tan \delta \quad \text{Np/m},$$

which is equal to the attenuation of a plane wave within the dielectric medium. This is to be expected because for large cross-sections of the rod, or for very short wavelengths, all energy of the wave is travelling inside the dielectric. The *dipole mode* HE_{11} with $m = 1$, is characterized by the equation

$$F_{HE} = (\varepsilon_1 U + V) \, (U + V) - \left[\frac{v}{2\pi a/\lambda_0} \right]^2 (1 - \varepsilon_1) J_1^2(p) K_1^2(q) = 0.$$

The attenuation constant, derived in the same way as above becomes

$$\alpha_{HE} = (\pi/\lambda_0)\varepsilon' \ R_{HE_{11}} \tan \delta \quad \text{Np/m},$$

with

$$R_{HE_{11}} =$$
$$= \left| \frac{1}{v_0} \frac{[(\varepsilon' - 1)/q_0^2] \, (f_0^2 + 1/p_0^2 - 1/p_0^4)/(1/p_0^2 + 1/q_0^2) + (v_0^2 + \eta_0^2) X_0 + 4\eta_0 v_0/p_0^4}{X_0(\varepsilon' + \eta_0^2) + Y_0(1 + \eta_0^2) + (2\eta_0/v_0) \, [(\varepsilon' + v_0^2)/p_0^4 - (1 + v_0^2)/q_0^4]} \right|$$

$$(7.35)$$

where

$$\eta_0 = [(\varepsilon' f_0 + g_0)/(f_0 + g_0)]^{\frac{1}{2}}$$
$$X_0 = f_0^2 + (2f_0 + 1)/p_0^2 - 1/p_0^4$$
$$Y_0 = -g_0^2 - (2g_0 - 1)/q_0^2 + 1/q_0^4$$

with f_0, g_0, p_0 and q_0 as defined in eq. (7.31).

For large values of $2a/\lambda_0$ the attenuation constant for plane waves in the dielectric is again obtained.

From the values of R_{TE}, R_{TM} and R_{HE11} given respectively by equations (7.32), (7.34) and (7.35) the graphical illustration in fig. 7.12 for a relative permittivity $\varepsilon' = 2.56$ (polystyrene) is obtained, as calculated by Elsasser. In

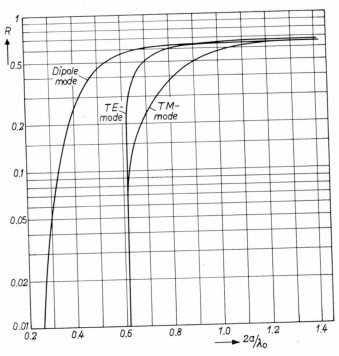

Fig. 7.12. Values of the attenuation factors, R_{TE}, R_{TM} and R_{HE11} as a function of $2a/\lambda_0$ for a rod with $\varepsilon' = 2.56$.

all cases the attenuation becomes small for small $2a/\lambda_0$. This is due to the fact that most of the energy is then transported outside the dielectric. The more $2a/\lambda_0$ approaches the cut-off value $2a/\lambda_c$ (being zero for the dipole mode and 0.613 for the TM and TE modes), the more energy is travelling outside the rod. At cut-off, where the rod no longer guides the wave in the appropriate mode the attenuation due to the rod becomes zero; this is in contrast to the results for other wave-guiding structures discussed earlier which are bounded by metal surfaces. The steep slopes of the R_{TE} and R_{TM} curves in fig. 7.12 show that the practical realization of a low-loss rod is very difficult; for the dipole-mode the construction is less critical. For smaller values of ε', more slowly increasing curves are obtained. This may suggest the use of dielectric foam (as in the case of the H-guide, section 5).

For the dipole mode the factor $\alpha_{HE11}\lambda_0/\tan\delta$ is plotted in fig. 7.13 as a function of $2a/\lambda_0$ for different values of the relative permittivity ε'. Some representative values, from this figure, assuming $2a/\lambda_0 = 0.3$, $\varepsilon' = 2.5$ and

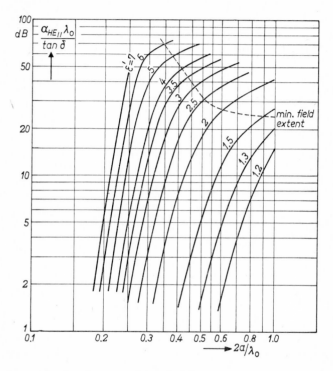

Fig. 7.13. Attenuation function $\alpha_{HE11}\lambda_0/\tan\delta$ of the circular dielectric rod for the dipole mode as a function of $2a/\lambda_0$ for different values of ε'. The dotted line represents the attenuation for minimum field extent.

$\tan\delta = 4 \times 10^{-4}$ are 0.34 dB/m, 0.68 dB/m, 1.36 dB/m and 2.72 dB/m for 4; 2; 1; and 0.5 mm respectively. These extremely low attenuation constants make the dielectric rod particularly suitable for use in applications where low-loss transmission is required, such as resonators. For application in other instrumentation the dielectric rod may cause some difficulties due to the loose binding of the wave to the rod, as we see below. A tighter binding of the wave is obtained if the diameter of the rod is increased. For minimum field extent (see next section) we require $2a/\lambda_0 = 0.5$ if $\varepsilon' = 2.5$. In this case the attenuation is ten times as high as in the example above, i.e. for 4;2;1 and 0.5 mm wavelength α is 3.4 dB/m; 6.8 dB/m, 13.6 dB/m and 27.2 dB/m respectively.

6.4. FIELD EXTENT

The intensity of the field in the transverse direction, outside the rod is characterized by a modified Hankel function that approaches zero with increasing distance nearly as exp $(-| q | r/a)$. The distance, d, from the surface of the rod to the point where the fields are decayed by a factor $1/e$ with respect to the field intensity at the surface is therefore

$$d = a/| q | = (\lambda_0/2\pi) (1-v^2)^{-\frac{1}{2}}.$$

This distance, d, decreases asymptotically to zero for increasing a/λ_0 and also decreases for increasing ε'.

The radius $r_b = (a+d)$ has therefore a minimum for some particular value of a. This "smallest field extent" is different for different values of ε'. This behaviour is illustrated in fig. 7.14, where the normalized $1/e$-diameter, $2r_b/\lambda_0$, is given as a function of $2a/\lambda_0$. It should be noted that at minimum field extent the attenuation is rather high, as indicated by the dotted line in fig. 7.13. For practical use a larger field extent with corresponding smaller attenuation may therefore be preferred. In fig. 7.14 we can see that for the values of $\varepsilon' < 5$ the minimum field extent is reached at a value $2a/\lambda_0$ smaller than the cut-off value of the next higher modes (TE and TM circular-rod modes). The corresponding cut-off value for the next-higher hybrid mode is 1.59 times higher than that of the TE and TM modes.

6.5. CONSTRUCTION AND MEASUREMENTS

Since the proper mode propagation is only obtained if the rod is perfectly straight and since supports disturb the field pattern and therefore cause radiation, the dielectric rod is most suitably applied as a stressed wire. It is therefore very useful in a resonator, where the wire can be mounted between two plane mirrors. At very short wavelengths the wire becomes very thin if the ratio $2a/\lambda_0$ is made small enough for low attenuation. This problem could be overcome by using dielectric tubes for which the dielectric constant is artificially lowered by the space-factor of the tube. For thin-walled dielectric tubes the field concentrates in the air inside the tube (MALLACH [1955]).

The influence of the ellipticity of the dielectric wire was investigated by CULLEN et al. [1959]. If a rod of elliptical cross-section is used, two distinct dipole modes will exist; having the transverse electric fields parallel to the

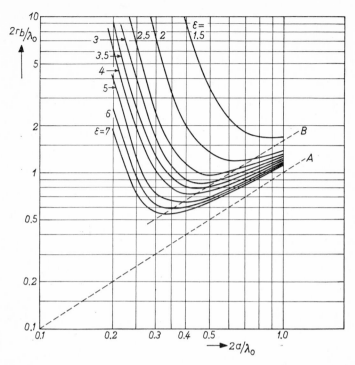

Fig. 7.14. Normalized $1/e$-diameter of the dielectric rod waveguides, $2r_b/\lambda_0$, as a function of the normalized rod diameter $2a/\lambda_0$, for different values of ε. The dotted line A represents the asymptote of all curves for large values of $2a/\lambda_0$. The line B gives the cut-off value $2a/\lambda_c$ for each ε of the TE and TM circular rod modes.

two axes of the ellipse. These two modes propagate with different guide wavelengths, λ_{g1} and λ_{g2}. If both modes are excited this may lead to an interference phenomenon, which can be characterized by a beat wavelength, $\lambda_B = \lambda_{g1}\lambda_{g2}/(\lambda_{g1}-\lambda_{g2})$. To avoid this a high accuracy in the rod circularity has to be achieved as is illustrated by Cullen's numerical example: at $\varepsilon' = 6.56$, $\lambda_0 = 8.50$ mm and for a nominal diameter 2.46 mm and an ellipticity of 10^{-3} the beat wavelength λ_B is already 1 metre.

6.6. DIELECTRIC IMAGE LINES

In the preceding paragraph it was shown that propagation with a low attenuation could be obtained if the main part of the electromagnetic energy guided by a dielectric rod travels outside the dielectric medium. The HE_{11}, or dipole mode, especially was shown to have low losses when the wave is bound loosely to the rod. A disadvantage of this loose binding is that obstacles, such as supports, very easily disturb the fields and excite radiating modes. Moreover the large field extent (the field is significant at least out to a radius about five times the $1/e$-radius r_b) in many cases makes a reduction of the effective guide cross-section desirable. The "dielectric image line" is one of the possible structures which may combine low-loss wave propagation with more easy handling. Since the field configuration of the dipole mode exhibits a plane of symmetry through the axis of the rod with the electric

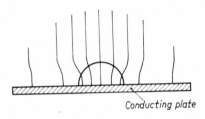

Conducting plate

Fig. 7.15. Dielectric image line with semi-circular dielectric rod. The electric lines of force are projected to a plane perpendicular to the direction of propagation and close in the z-direction.

field perpendicular to it, a conducting image plane can be used to replace half of the guiding structure, without disturbing the propagation of the dipole mode and, moreover, the boundary conditions at this conducting plane exclude the occurrence of the undesired higher loss modes of the TM type. Furthermore this conducting plane reduces the required cross-section and eliminates the problem of disturbing supports. The dielectric image line has been extensively studied by KING and SCHLESINGER [1952], [1955], [1957] and by SCHLESINGER and KING [1958].

A cross-section of the image line with semi-circular rod is shown in fig. 7.15. Here only the electric field projected onto the transverse plane is indicated; the complete field pattern is complicated, all three components of the electric and magnetic field being present.

6.7. ATTENUATION IN AN IMAGE LINE

The losses of the image line consist of two parts: the dielectric loss and the loss due to dissipation in the metal image surface. The attenuation due to dielectric loss is the same as the attenuation of the circular dielectric rod for the HE_{11} mode and therefore the attenuation curves in fig. 7.13 are also applicable for the image line. Radiation loss is avoided since reflecting supports are absent. The conduction loss, calculated by KING et al [1957], is in general less than the dielectric loss, except when the wave is very loosely bound and the dielectric loss becomes extremely small. For small values of $2a/\lambda_0$ the metal attenuation constant decreases with $2a/\lambda_0$ in the same rapid manner as the dielectric attenuation constant. In fig. 7.16 the metal attenuation function $\alpha_m \lambda_0/R_s$ is plotted as a function of $2a/\lambda_0$ for different values of the dielectric consant ε' of the semi-circular dielectric rod.

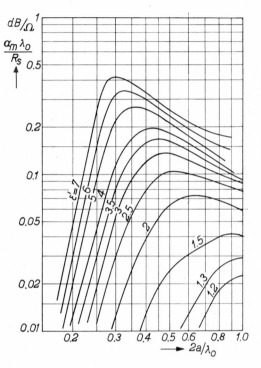

Fig. 7.16. Calculated metal attenuation function $\alpha_m \lambda_0/R_s$ of dielectric image line as a function of $2a/\lambda_0$ for different values of ε'.

This figure is based upon the expression for the metal attenuation derived by KING et al. [1957]. From this figure we may determine the attenuation due to metal loss in the image line, using the expression for the surface resistance

$$R_s = 10.88 \times 10^{-3} \, (10^7/\sigma\lambda_0)^{\frac{1}{2}} \quad \Omega \, ,$$

where σ is the conductivity in Siemens per metre. Since R_s depends on the wavelength, this attenuation will increase with decreasing wavelength.

As an example we may calculate the metallic attenuation constant, α_m, for $2a/\lambda_0 = 0.5$ and $\varepsilon' = 2.5$. We find for a copper image plane ($\sigma = 5.8 \times 10^7$ Siemens/metre) and for wavelengths of 4; 2; 1 and 0.5 mm respectively $\alpha_m = 1.86$; 5.27; 14.9 and 42 dB/m. The total attenuation of the image line is a superposition of this metal attenuation and the dielectric attenuation, α_ε. For the present example α_ε is as calculated in section 6.3, namely 3.4; 6.8; 13.6 and 27.2 dB/m for the respective wavelengths. The total attenuation then amounts to 5.26 dB/m for 4 mm, 12.07 dB/m for 2 mm, 28.5 dB/m for 1 mm and 69.2 dB/m for 0.5 mm.

In this example the wave is rather tightly bound to the dielectric, the values for ε' and $2a/\lambda_0$ being those for minimum field extent, and therefore the dielectric attenuation dominates at longer wavelengths. If the wave is more loosely bound to the rod, metal losses may be larger than the dielectric losses (e.g. for $2a/\lambda_0 = 0.3$, $\alpha_m = 0.55$; 1.57; 4.33 and 12.5 dB/m and $\alpha_z = 0.34$; 0.68; 1.36 and 2.72 dB/m at 4; 2; 1 and 0.5 mm respectively). It may be observed that the total attenuation is in any case lower if the wave is more loosely bound.

6.8. CONSTRUCTION AND MEASUREMENTS FOR IMAGE LINES

As the losses of the image line are mainly determined by the dielectric losses, it is desirable to construct the line such that most of the energy travels through air. In the case of an image line a half round dielectric tube or rod has to be mounted on a conducting plate, and this is difficult to construct at shorter wavelengths. Schlesinger and King therefore investigated the possibility of using other cross-sections for the dielectric, such as rectangular rods more or less imbedded in the image surface. In this case an axial slot or trench-cut has to be made into the conducting surface, into which the dielectric is mounted. The theory of Elsasser permits the exact calculation of the field distribution and losses for the circular rod, but a treatment of other cross-sections is very complicated and not yet performed. However, it turns out experimentally that some sizes of rectangular rods, which are easier to construct, give comparable results for the attenuation. Because the concentration of the field around the rod depends upon the volume of dielectric in regions of higher electric field, the shape of the dielectric cross-section will not influence very much the transmission system. The results of Schlesinger and King show that the guide wavelength is nearly independent of the cross-sectional shape of the rectangular rod. Comparing results of rods of miscellaneous shapes they find that rods having equal cross-sectional areas give comparable guide wavelengths. It is therefore reasonable to define an effective rod radius, a_e, such that $a_e = (O/\pi)^{\frac{1}{2}}$, where O is the cross-sectional surface area of the rod. Experiments have been reported by KING [1957] at 3 cm wavelength. An attenuation constant of 0.1 dB/metre was found in accordance with the theoretically predicted value. Experiments at 2.1 mm by M. J. KING et al. [1960] on image lines constructed of "Teflon" tape on a copper surface give values between 1.4 dB/metre and 3.2 dB/metre depending upon the thickness of the tape. A very simple construction, employing transparant adhesive tape containing some zinc-oxide, is shown in fig. 7.29. This gave, according to our measurements, better results than a "Teflon" wire partly imbedded in the aluminium image plane. The low attenuation of the image line would make it suitable for many experiments, although ancillary components have some disadvantages, as will be indicated in section 8, and deviations from the straight line, such as bends, even when carefully made, cause serious radiation loss.

6.9. THE V-LINE

A conducting plate which does not disturb the modal pattern in a dielectric rod guide (section 6.1) can also be inserted for hybrid modes with $m > 1$. The integer m determines the angular dependence of the field components and $m > 1$ means that there exist several planes, containing the axis of the rod, over which the angular field impedance is zero.

For instance, two perpendicular conducting plates, intersecting each other in the rod axis, will not disturb the field patterns of the hybrid mode with $m = 2$. Only one of the four sections need be constructed and this then forms a "V"-line.

V-lines can be constructed for many other values of m. The properties of these higher order hybrid modes are discussed by SCHELKUNOFF [1943] and SCHLESINGER et al. [1960], and the V-line itself is discussed by DIAMENT et al. [1961].

As in the case of the image line, the TM mode with axial electric field is eliminated by the conducting plates and so is the HE_{11} mode, so that the TE_0 mode would be the principal mode for the V-line. However, when the two conducting plates are insulated from each other in the apex of the V no radial currents can flow and even the TE_0 mode is eliminated. The dominant mode for this V-line with separated plates is the HE_{m1} mode. Experimental verification for these expectations of a V-line was obtained for the HE_{21} mode by Diament.

7. Beam guides

The wave-guiding structures described in the preceding sections have had a constant cross-section in every plane perpendicular to direction of the wave. Propagation then occurs in the form of "modes" in each of which the field pattern does not vary along the guide apart from the periodic variation associated with the wavelength and the attenuation due to losses. An alternative approach to the attainment of low-loss propagation is provided by "beam-guides". Here a beam is propagated essentially in free-space except that the divergence arising from the fact that the wavelength is comparable with the beam diameter is periodically corrected by equally spaced phase-transformers (e.g. lenses) along the path of the beam, as is illustrated in fig. 7.17.

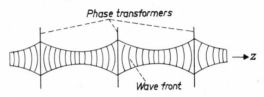

Fig. 7.17. Wave front correction by means of phase transformers in the beam guide.

As phase transformers GOUBAU et al. [1961] use lenses in a quasi-optical manner; *quasi*-optical because the ratio of lens diameter to wavelength is much smaller than in a geometrical optical application, so that diffraction effects are all-important. Goubau and VAN NIE [1964] reported extensive calculations of the electromagnetic fields guided in this manner, which are called "re-iterative beam-waves".

7.1. BEAM MODES

There are sets of re-iterative beams, called "beam modes", which satisfy the same orthogonality relations as the modes in an ordinary waveguide, that is to say they are transmitted independently. The field distribution over a plane perpendicular to the direction of propagation (the z-direction) depends on the z-coordinate in a way which varies from one beam mode to another but it turns out that the distortions of the phase planes with varying z are identical for all beam modes, so that each beam mode is correctly iterated by the same series of phase transformers and a composite beam can be propagated.

According to Goubau the lowest order beam mode has the smallest attenuation and is therefore the most important for transmission purposes. Quoting Van Nie, who considers the x- and y-components of the electromagnetic fields as a function of cylindrical position coordinates (for propagation in the z-direction) the electric field of the lowest order beam mode in the plane $z = 0$, where it is presumed to have a plane phase front, is (omitting the time harmonic part because we are considering a beam of a given single frequency)

$$E_x = E_{x0} \exp\left(-r^2/2r_0^2\right) \qquad (7.36)$$

where r is the radial coordinate, measured from the axis. This is a Gaussian distribution with width 2 r_0. After a propagation over a distance z the field distribution is in first approximation given by

$$E_x(z) = E_{x0}[1-\mathrm{j}z/kr_0^2]^{-1} \exp\left[-r^2/(2r_0^2-\mathrm{j}2z/k)\right] \exp\left(-\mathrm{j}kz\right) \qquad (7.37)$$

with $k = 2\pi/\lambda_0$, where $\lambda_0 < r_0$ is the wavelength of a plane wave of the same frequency. The real part of the exponent of the first exponential factor

$$\frac{-r^2k^2r_0^2}{2(k^2r_0^4+z^2)} \qquad (7.38)$$

describes the new breadth of the Gaussian distribution, i.e. the spread of the bundle of rays. The imaginary part of the same factor

$$-\mathrm{j}\frac{zr^2k}{2(k^2r_0^4+z^2)} \qquad (7.39)$$

describes the phase changes i.e. the curvature of the wave fronts.

Using a lens as a phase transformer this divergence may be corrected and the bundle of rays concentrated again. Expressions for focal distance and minimum diameter of the required lens are derived as follows. When a plane phase-front is present at the plane $z = -a$, a lens, situated at $z = 0$, if intended to recover a plane phase-front, has to compensate the phase distortion given by (7.39), and so it should produce the phase correction

$$\Phi = \frac{r^2ka}{2(r_0^4k^2+a^2)}. \qquad (7.40)$$

This can be achieved by a lens with a thickness, d, which varies parabolically with r, $d = \alpha r^2$. The phase correction produced by such a parabolic lens, at a distance r from the axis is

$$\Phi = \alpha r^2(\sqrt{\varepsilon_r\mu_r}-1)k, \qquad (7.41)$$

where ε_r and μ_r are the relative dielectric constant and permeability of the lens material. Now the optical focal distance of a lens, according to paraxial approximations, is

$$F = [2\alpha\{(\varepsilon_r\mu_r)^{\frac{1}{2}}-1\}]^{-1} \qquad (7.42)$$

and expressions (7.41) and (7.42) thus give the following expression for the phase correction produced by a parabolic lens of focal distance F

$$\Phi = kr^2/2F. \qquad (7.43)$$

The combination of (7.40) and (7.43) gives for the required focal distance,

$$F = a(1+r_0^4k^2/a^2). \qquad (7.44)$$

In order to define a beam diameter, tubes of constant energy flux have to be considered. These tubes have a z-dependent diameter, as the beam diverges and converges along the guide, which can be found by integrating the power over a cross-section with radius r. From this we find that the radius of a tube with constant energy flux is determined by

$$r^2r_0^2k^2(r_0^4k^2+z^2)^{-1} = \text{constant}.$$

The tube just covering the R.M.S. width of the Gaussian field distribution at $z = 0$ (eq.(7.36)) is found by putting the constant equal to unity. The local radius r_b of this tube is then given by

$$r_b^2 = (z^2/r_0^2k^2)+r_0^2. \qquad (7.45)$$

Consider now the more general situation as illustrated in fig. 7.18. The lens is situated at $z = 0$ and a Gaussian field distribution with plane phase front is present at $z = -a$ and is transformed by the lens into a plane phase front again in the plane $z = +b$.

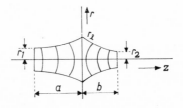

Fig. 7.18. Phase-correcting lens at $z = 0$. A plane wave front at $z = -a$ is transformed into a plane wave front at $z = +b$.

According to eqs. (7.40) and (7.43) the total phase correction of the lens required to compensate the phase distortions occurring along $-a < z < 0$ and $0 < z < b$ has to be

$$\Phi = \frac{kr^2}{2F} = \frac{akr^2}{2(r_1^4 k^2 + a^2)} + \frac{bkr^2}{2(r_2^4 k^2 + b^2)}$$

and therefore

$$F^{-1} = (a + r_1^4 k^2/a)^{-1} + (b + r_2^4 k^2/b)^{-1}. \qquad (7.46)$$

This is therefore the quasi-optical equivalent of the optical lens formula (instead transforming a point focus this transforms a plane phase front from a to b). In accordance with eq. (7.45) the beam radius or Gaussian width at the lens is given by

$$r_l^2 = a^2/r_1^2 k^2 + r_1^2 = b^2/r_2^2 k^2 + r_2^2 \qquad (7.47)$$

where r_1 and r_2 are respectively the Gaussian widths at a and b.

It should be noted that the lens diameter has to exceed the Gaussian beam diameter $2r_l$.

Eqs. (7.46) and (7.47) give us the necessary information for designing lenses that guide the lowest order mode. Due to the diffraction, the effective microwave focal distance, F_M, i.e. the distance from the lens to the plane of highest field intensity, i.e. smallest Gaussian width, for parallel incident beams $(a \to 0)$ is shorter than the optical focal distance. From eqs. (7.46) and (7.47) it follows that in this case

$$F_M = F[1 + F^2/k^2 r_l^4]^{-1}.$$

We will not describe here the properties of higher order beam modes; VAN NIE [1964a] gives a discussion of these.

7.2. ATTENUATION

The propagation losses in a lens system are caused by three phenomena (VAN NIE [1964]):

i) diffraction losses due to the finite diameters of the lenses,

ii) absorption losses in the media of the lenses,

iii) reflection losses at the surfaces of the lenses.

The diffraction losses can be minimized by making the beam diameter at the lens as small as possible and the other two sources of attenuation can be diminished by reduction of the number of lenses per metre. Therefore we have to look for smallest beam diameter, r_l, together with the longest path length $(a+b)$.

From eq. (7.47) it follows immediately that, for a given distance a, the minimum beam radius r_l is that corresponding to a beam radius in the object plane $r_l^2 = a/k$, i.e. the minimum value for r_l^2 is $2a/k$. In this case the path length $a+b$, derived from eq. (7.46), is

$$a+b = 2a^3(F^2+2a^2-2aF)^{-1}$$

which assumes a maximum value $2a$ for $F = a$. This means that in a lens system of identical lenses, the spacing between the lenses should be $2F$.

In such a system the diffraction loss bears direct relation to the maximum phase correction of each lens, given by $\Phi_{max} = kR^2/2F$ (c.f. eq. (7.43)), where R is the radius of the lens. If the conditions for minimum beam radius are fulfilled then $\Phi_{max} = (R/r_l)^2$. As calculated by CHRISTIAN et al. [1961], for values of $R/r_l > 1.6$ the attenuation due to diffraction losses for *one lens*, α_{diffr}^L is approximately given by the relation

$$\alpha_{diffr}^L \simeq 95 \times \exp\left[-1.68\,(R/r_l)^2\right] \quad \text{dB}. \tag{7.48}$$

The absorption loss in the lens material depends on the field distribution and the properties of the dielectric. According to Christian et al. the attenuation for one lens due to dielectric loss, α_ε^L is, for the present case, approximately given by

$$\alpha_\varepsilon^L \simeq 4.34\,\frac{[(R/r_l)^2-1]}{\sqrt{\varepsilon_r-1}}\tan\delta \quad \text{dB}, \tag{7.49}$$

ε_r and $\tan\delta$ being the relative dielectric constant and loss tangent respectively.

The attenuation due to reflections at the surfaces is difficult to calculate since between the surfaces of the lens multiple reflections may occur. As an order of magnitude the attenuation for one lens, due to reflection at one surface can be approximated by:

$$\alpha_{refl}^L \simeq -8.68 \log(1-\Gamma) \quad \text{dB}, \tag{7.50}$$

where Γ is the power reflection coefficient of one surface of the lens. For $\varepsilon_r \geq 1.2$, Γ becomes approximately

$$\Gamma \approx \left(\frac{\sqrt{\varepsilon_r}-1}{\sqrt{\varepsilon_r}+1}\right)^2 + \frac{(4\sqrt{\varepsilon_r}-\varepsilon_r-1)\,[1-[1+(R/r_l)^2+\frac{1}{2}(R/r_l)^4]\exp[-(R/r_l)^2]]}{4\varepsilon_r^{\frac{3}{2}}(\varepsilon_r-1)^2(2ka)^2[1-\exp[-(R/r_l)^2]]}.$$

If $2a/\lambda_0 > 50$, i.e. if the distance between the lenses is longer than 50 wavelengths, the second term in this expression is negligable in comparison to the first and then

$$\alpha_{\text{refl}}^{L} \approx 8.68 \left(\frac{\sqrt{\varepsilon_r} - 1}{\sqrt{\varepsilon_r} + 1} \right)^2 \quad \text{dB}.$$

There exist several methods by which the undesired reflection losses at the surfaces of the lenses can be avoided or reduced by coating the surface of the lens with a non-reflecting layer. These methods will be discussed later on in this section.

In order to determine the attenuation *per metre*, α, we have to calculate $\alpha_{\text{tot}}^{L}/L$, where $\alpha_{\text{tot}}^{L} = \alpha_{\text{diffr}}^{L} + \alpha_{\varepsilon}^{L} + \alpha_{\text{refl}}^{L}$ and $L = 2a$ is the distance between two lenses. From eqs. (7.48), (7.49) and (7.50) we know α_{tot}^{L} as a function of $(R/r_l)^2 = 2\pi R^2/\lambda_0 L$, and therefore we know $(\alpha_{\text{tot}}^{L}/L)(R^2/\lambda_0) = \alpha R^2/\lambda_0$ as a function of $R^2/\lambda_0 L$. This function has been plotted in fig. 7.19 for different values of the dielectric constant of the lens material, where the loss tangent has been assumed to be $\tan \delta = 10^{-4}$. For constant lens radius R and wavelength λ_0, the attenuation per metre passes through a minimum at an optimum value of L. These minimum values are interconnected by the dotted line in fig. 7.19. For a given wavelength the lowest attenuation of the system is obtained at a lens separation L, which can be derived from the optimum value of $R^2/\lambda_0 L$. The choice of lens material and lens radius thus determines the lens separation and attenuation.

A representative example is a system for a wavelength of 1 mm, with lens radius $R = 50$ mm and $\varepsilon_r = 2.56$ (uncoated polystyrene lens). Fig. 7.19 shows that minimum attenuation for $\varepsilon_r = 2.56$ is achieved for $R^2/\lambda_0 L = 0.683$, from which in this case $L = 3.65$ metres. The minimum value of $\alpha R^2/\lambda_0$ for $\varepsilon_r = 2.56$ is equal to 0.365 dB and so in our case $\alpha \simeq 0.15$ dB/m. The same lenses used at 2 mm wavelength require $L = 1.83$ metres and give an attenuation of $\alpha \simeq 0.3$ dB/m. In general the minimum attenuation *per wavelength*, $\alpha\lambda_0$, depends only on the ε_r of the lens material and on the "reduced size" of the beam guide R/λ_0. The curves in fig. 7.19 can be regarded as representing the variation of $\alpha\lambda_0(R/\lambda_0^2)$ as a function of $(\lambda_0/L)(R/\lambda_0)^2$. For our present example

$$\alpha\lambda_0 = 0.365/(R/\lambda_0)^2 \quad \text{dB}.$$

In practice the radius of the lens is determined by the available space and by the problems of manufacture, so that the maximum size of R/λ_0 is fixed for a given wavelength.

The reflection losses can be reduced by applying a coating on the lens surface. The simplest method is the application of a layer of a material with a dielectric constant equal to the square root of that of the lens material and of thickness $\frac{1}{4} \lambda_0$. If such a coating material does not exist a double layer, consisting of a layer having a higher dielectric constant and a layer with a lower dielectric constant, can be used instead (KOTT [1962]). Another method, described by TAUB et al. [1963] uses slits on the surface of the dielectric, thus lowering artificially the dielectric constant at the interface. These means for reduction of the reflections give appreciable lowering of the attenuation constant, but this is effective only close to one wavelength and therefore the attenuation is strongly frequency-dependent.

A type of beam-waveguide which uses appropriately shaped metal reflec-

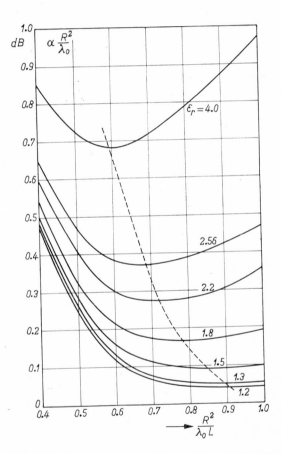

Fig. 7.19. Attenuation function $\alpha R^2/\lambda_0$ for uncoated lenses as a function of $R^2/\lambda_0 L$ for different values of ε_r and for tan $\delta = 10^{-4}$. The dotted line passes through the minimum values. At these minima the optimum lens separation L, for given R and λ_0 can be found. The attenuation per metre is derived by multiplication of the value of the ordinate by λ_0/R^2.

tors as phasecorrecting devices instead of dielectric lenses has been described by DEGENFORD et al. [1964]. Here the beam propagates in zigzag fashion between two rows of reflectors. A measured loss per reflector of approximately 0.015 dB is obtained at 4 mm wavelength. The mirrors were placed 20 cm apart, so that the overall loss was 0.075 dB/metre.

8. Components used in conjunction with guides

In the preceding sections the propagation of electromagnetic radiation through different types of waveguiding structures has been discussed. In order to perform measurements on or with this radiation there is a need for various ancillary components or instruments suitably adapted to the wave guiding system. As remarked in the introduction, the propagation systems for millimetre and submillimetre wavelengths involve a combination of microwave and geometrical optical techniques and this combination also appears in the components. A bend in an oversized waveguide shows some resemblance to an optical plane mirror, a directional coupler looks like a semi-transparent mirror and a resonant cavity shows some similarity to a Fabry-Perot interferometer.

In this section we shall give a survey of devices which have been constructed for application in the millimetre and submillimetre ranges. As far as possible we shall describe the methods of excitation, bends, directional couplers, mode filters, attenuators, and phase shifters for each of the propagation techniques discussed in the preceding sections. Though this survey has no claim to being complete, it should give a general impression of the several possibilities and some limitations of the techniques used in this field.

The field is, however, still rather new and it is not possible to give final recommendations for choosing the most efficient, convenient or simplest device for any application.

8.1. COMPONENTS FOR STANDARD WAVEGUIDES

Since the attenuation of standard waveguides becomes high at very short wavelengths this propagation technique is suitable only for wavelengths in excess of about 2 mm. A large number of components have been constructed (VAN ES et al. [1960], MEREDITH [1963]) for this range and are commercially available. They are in principle scaled-down versions of the components used for cm waves and we will not describe them here in detail. Fig. 7.20 shows an experimental set-up incorporating a number of components for use at 4 mm and 2 mm wavelengths. New methods have had to be used to avoid some of the difficulties of manufacture.

8.2. Components for oversized waveguides

With oversized waveguides (section 4) the techniques for component design, appropriate for conventional waveguides can no longer be used. It is an essential requirement that components in oversized waveguides interact with the wave in a similar fashion over the entire cross-section of the wave front if the generation of higher order modes is to be avoided. Normal microwave equipment, designed for the conventional use of a waveguide, is therefore not suitable when that guide is used as an oversized waveguide for shorter wavelengths. They contain pins or stubs which readily excite modes higher than the desired low loss TE_{10} mode (section 4). We shall now describe some components designed for specifically oversized guides.

8.2.1. *Excitation*

Most sources of coherent millimetre and submillimetre radiation (chapters 5 and 6) have conventional rectangular waveguide outputs which have to be adapted to the oversized guide by means of a tapered section. In order to ensure the conservation of the proper TE_{10} mode a gentle tapering is necessary. In a straight taper the wave front is curved somewhat, since the path length in the centre is shorter than that at the boundaries. This curvature results in a phase lag at the boundaries of the wave front with respect to the centre. If the width of the rectangular oversized guide is a and the length of the taper L this phase lag for a sufficiently large degree of oversizing, is approximately given by

$$\Delta\varphi = \pi a^2 / 4\lambda_0 L.$$

The smaller the slope of the taper, the smaller the phase lag. An acceptable compromise between phase error and the taperlength for rectangular guides is obtained by using a slope not steeper than 10°. As an example, a taper of 200 mm length, tapering to a 3 cm oversized guide gives, for a wavelength of 1 mm, a phase error of about $\frac{2}{3}\pi$ radians, i.e. about 120°.

A correction of this phase error may be effected by reducing the phase velocity in the centre of the taper, e.g. by inserting a dielectric rod, or for a smoother correction a dielectric lens, in the taper (cf. section 7). TAUB [1963] recommends linear tapers about 50 wavelengths long, although non-linear tapers may in principle be shorter and better. For the excitation of the low-loss TE_{01} mode in *circular* waveguides UNGER [1958] employed a "raised

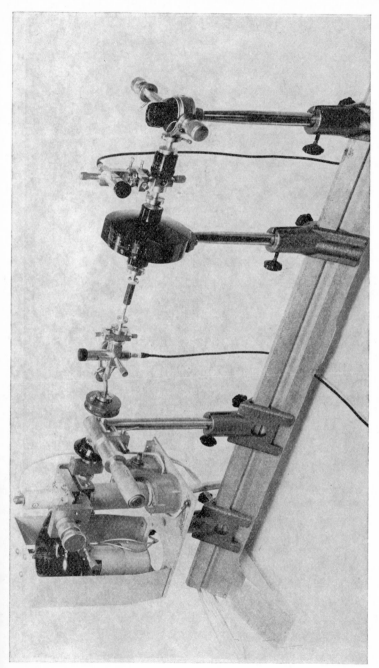

Fig. 7.20. Components for 4 mm and 2 mm in standard waveguide. From left to right: 4 mm; isolator, vane attenuator, wavemeter, sliding-screw tuner. 2 mm; 4 → 2 mm frequency multiplier, pivoting screw, isolator, rotary vane attenuator, directional coupler, waveguide-switch with two short-circuiting plungers (from VAN ES et al. [1960/61]).

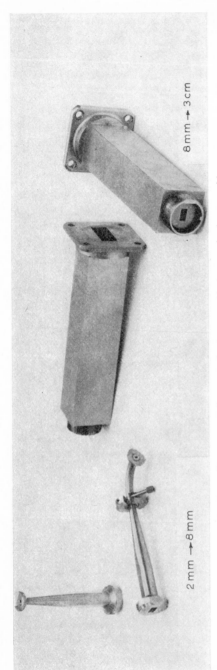

Fig. 7.21. Some tapers from standard waveguide to oversized waveguide.
Left: tapers from 2 mm-conventional guide to 8 mm tall-guide.   Right: tapers from 8 mm-guide to 3 cm-guide.

Fig. 7.22. Two bends and a directional coupler in 8 mm waveguide. The directional coupler contains a thin sheet of mica at the inter-

cosine" taper 250 wavelengths long. A linear taper for this purpose would have required a length of nearly 5000 wavelengths. The reason for this extremely long taper is that the low-loss TE_{01} mode is not the dominant mode, and it is therefore very difficult to suppress spurious modes.

Tapers are most easily constructed by an electroforming process. Insertion losses at 4 mm wavelength of about 0.2-0.3 dB have been reported for suitably designed and constructed tapers (BLED et al. [1964]). In fig. 7.21 several tapers are shown. The 8 mm → 3 cm tapers are milled in two parts out of copper the two halves being soldered together and subsequently gold-plated. The 2 mm → 8 mm tall-guide tapers were constructed by electroforming. Combination of these two tapers makes it possible to use 3 cm standard waveguide as a tall-guide for 2 mm wavelength.

8.2.2. Bends

Bends in oversized waveguide are effectively designed as if the behaviour of the wave were purely optical. 90° bends are therefore constructed from two waveguides set perpendicularly to each other. At the intersection a conducting plane is placed at 45° to the axes of the waveguides. In this case low loss bends can be obtained and BLED et al. [1964] observed attenuations of about 0.3 dB for H bends in 3 cm oversized waveguides with wavelengths between 1 and 4 mm. E bends were somewhat poorer, giving an attenuation of 0.6 dB at $\lambda_0 = $ 2 mm, but even at 1 mm wavelength the attenuation remained under 1 dB per bend.

In fig. 7.22 an E and an H bend are shown. The intersection was milled out of a brass block, as can be seen in the picture. For conventional waveguides the location of the joint between two parts of the guide is of great importance as regards disturbance of the wall-currents. However, in the case of oversized waveguides the field intensities at the walls, and therefore the wall-currents also, are much smaller, which means that the location of the joints is less critical.

It goes without saying that E bends for oversized waveguides may be used as H bends in tall-guides and conversely. If the construction is made so that the reflector can be turned a so-called waveguide switch is obtained. An exploded view is shown in fig. 7.23.

8.2.3. Directional couplers

If the conducting sheets in the bends described above (see fig. 7.22) were replaced by one or more dielectric sheets (for instance mica) they could be used as directional couplers. Fig. 7.24a shows a cross-section of such a

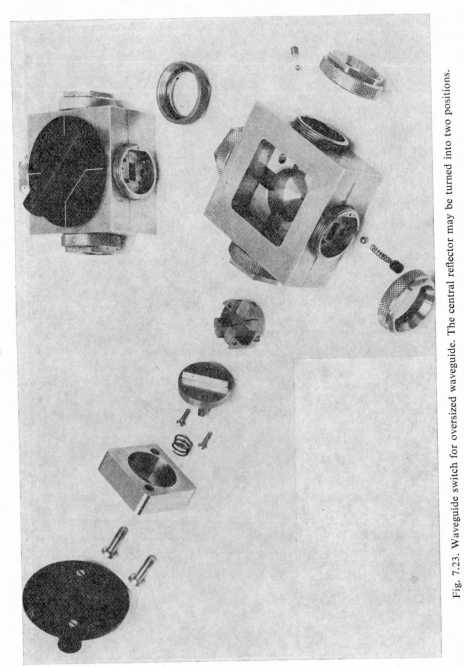

Fig. 7.23. Waveguide switch for oversized waveguide. The central reflector may be turned into two positions.

directional coupler. Of the incident wave, i, a part is reflected into arm 3 and part is transmitted into arm 2. Arm 4 is decoupled from the incident wave. For the same reason arms 3 and 2 are decoupled from each other. Measurements by WORT [1962], at 4.2 mm wavelength, using 3 cm waveguide and a single sheet of mica, about 0.2 mm thick, indicated a 20 dB decoupling of arm 4 from arm 1, whereas in arms 2 and 3 about equal powers were transmitted. In total the loss in the coupler was about 0.6 dB.

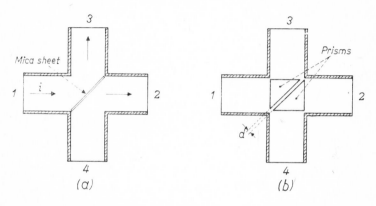

Fig. 7.24. Fixed and variable directional couplers in oversized waveguide. In (a) the incident wave, i, is split at the mica sheet and transmitted into arms 2 and 3. In device (b) the ratio of the emerging powers can be varied with the distance, d, of the two prisms.

BLED et al. [1964] report a directivity of 30 dB at 2 mm wavelength for a similar device. TAUB et al. [1963, 1964a] constructed and assessed several variable directional couplers. Here the mica sheet was replaced by two rectangular prisms or by quartz slabs, the distance between which could be varied (fig. 7.24b). Experiments at 0.9 mm wavelength on such a double-prism device showed a directivity of at least 10 dB, which was improved to 20 dB on applying a dielectric coating to the prisms to reduce the surface reflection (cf. section 7).

8.2.4. Attenuators

One of the arms 2 or 3 in the directional coupler of the preceding paragraph (fig. 7.24) could be loaded with a non-reflecting load and then it would act as a fixed or variable attenuator.

If both arm 2 and arm 3 are closed by a movable reflector another configuration (fig. 7.25) is obtained which can also be used as a variable attenuator, as can be seen from the following calculation. If the lengths of arms 2 and 3 are respectively $l_2 = l_0 + \delta$ and $l_3 = l_0 - \delta$, the signal emerging from arm 4 is proportional to

$$\exp\left(-2\pi\, \mathrm{j} l_2/\lambda_0\right) + \exp\left(-2\pi\, \mathrm{j} l_3/\lambda_0\right) = 2\exp\left(-2\pi\, \mathrm{j} l_0\lambda_0\right)\cos\left(2\pi\delta/\lambda_0\right).$$

This means that for constant l_0 and varying δ the amplitude of the emerging wave varies as $\cos(2\pi\delta/\lambda_0)$. Moreover a constant phase shift, depending on l_0, occurs but can be made zero by a proper choice of l_0. Therefore in the case

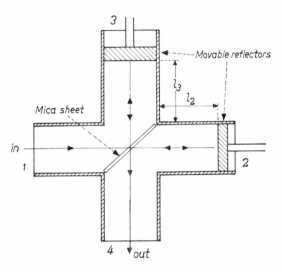

Fig. 7.25. Cross-section of variable attenuator, phase-shifter. For anti-ganged motion of the reflectors the device operates as a variable attenuator. A ganged motion results in a variable phase shift of the emerging wave.

of *anti-ganged* plungers, a variable attenuator is obtained. A different construction using two directional couplers, described by BLED et al. [1964], has a similar performance.

The same authors also describe a flap attenuator, which consists of a cylinder of absorbing material as long as the width of the waveguide, which can be inserted partially into the 3 cm oversized guide through a hole in the broad side. An important point is that the attenuator should act over the whole width of the guide, to avoid the excitation of spurious modes. Insertion losses of about 1 dB were measured while the attenuation could be increased to 35 dB at 1 mm wavelength.

8.2.5. Phase shifters

The device shown in fig. 7.25 can also be used as a phase shifter. If $l_2 = l_3 + n\lambda$ the emerging wave in arm 4 is proportional to $2 \exp(-2\pi j l_2/\lambda)$ which means a phase shift depending on l_2, the amplitude of the output being constant. With *ganged* plungers a variable phase shifter is thus obtained (TAUB et al. [1964a]). Another type of phase shifter, described by BLED et al. [1964] artificially lengthens the waveguide, as illustrated in fig. 7.26.

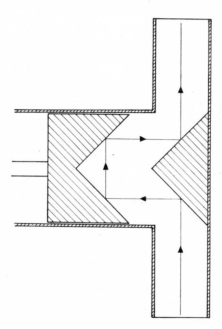

Fig. 7.26. Phase shifter based upon artificial lengthening of the waveguide (after BLED et al. [1964]).

8.2.6. Filters

As is noted in section 4.1, the number of possible modes in oversized waveguides is considerable. For this reason it may be desirable to have sections in the guide where the unwanted modes are suppressed. These mode filters are based upon the special field configuration of the spurious mode in question and have therefore to be designed specifically for this mode. Usually absorbing materials are inserted at places where there is high field concentration for the spurious mode. We will not discuss the many possible solutions in more detail but refer to the literature (e.g. GRIEMSMANN [1963]).

Frequency-selective filters for oversized waveguides are described by TAUB et al. [1964b]. A two-port band-pass filter is obtained by placing a number of resonators, each resonator being several half wavelengths long, in an oversized waveguide. The uniform operation necessary in oversized waveguides is possible if the coupling is distributed over the surface which connects two resonators, e.g. by using perforated metallic plates.

A low-pass/high-pass filter may be obtained by using a four-port multiple slab structure of the kind used for the directional couplers or variable attenuator (fig. 7.24a). The power transmitted from port 1 to port 2 is a function of the distance between the slabs and the wavelength. Numerical results are given by TAUB et al. [1964b].

8.2.7. Crystal detector

A crystal detector-mount for an oversized waveguide is described by BLOM-FIELD [1964]. Here a standard crystal diode is placed in the oversized waveguide off-centre. The radiation is concentrated at the crystal by a parabolic reflector, thus avoiding a tapered transition; at the stage of detection maintenance of mode-purity is of less importance. Comparing this detector with the same crystal mounted in standard waveguide connected to the oversized guide by a 60 cm long taper, the oversized detector mount showed a slight improvement at 0.9 mm wavelength, but was somewhat inferior at 2 mm wavelength.

8.3 COMPONENTS FOR H-GUIDES

Components for the H-guides have to be designed, as do components for oversized waveguides, in such a way that they interact with the wave uniformly over the entire cross-section of the guide. Few precautions are needed to prevent the excitation of higher modes but care has to be taken to avoid radiation loss (cf. section 5.1).

The specific construction of the H-guide, being two metallic plates with a dielectric slab in between, makes it difficult to construct movable parts such as movable reflectors over the entire cross-section of the guide. If, however, the width of the dielectric slab is very small the difficulties are reduced.

A number of components have been described by GRIEMSMANN [1959].

8.3.1. Excitation

The excitation of propagation in the H-guide from standard conventional waveguide is performed by tapers, but in this case there is a need for tapering only in one direction, because the distance between the plates of the H-guide is equal to the width of the standard waveguide. This transition is partially filled with a tapered dielectric, as indicated in fig. 7.27. For a taper 20 wavelengths long, an insertion loss less than 1 dB was estimated at 8 mm wavelength.

In order to eliminate the TM_s asym and the TE_s sym modes a metallic or resistive septum perpendicular to the plates may be inserted in the centre of the guide as is indicated in section 5.1. Because all TE_s modes have longitu-

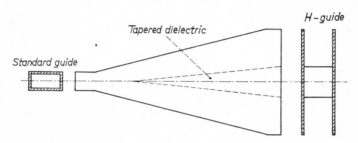

Fig. 7.27. Standard waveguide to H-guide tapered transition.

dinal currents they may be eliminated by making transverse cuts in the metallic plates of the guide with an absorbing material placed over them, outside of the guide. The combination of the central septum and the transverse absorbing strips leaves only the low-loss TM_s sym mode.

8.3.2. Bends and couplers

For gradual H bends only few difficulties may be expected, since no H_y components exist and so the excitation of the TE_s modes is improbable. For a bend perpendicular to the metallic plates (E bend) precautions have to be taken to avoid TE_s modes, such as the above-mentioned absorbing cuts in the metallic plates. The 90° reflecting bends as described for oversized waveguides may be used here as well.

A very simple coupler can be constructed by placing a central septum in the H-guide and using both halves as trough lines. Cross couplers like those used in oversized waveguides are also applicable here.

8.4 COMPONENTS FOR DIELECTRIC ROD LINES AND IMAGE LINES

For dielectric rod and image lines a number of components has been described by KING [1955b]. The components for the image line are easily mounted on the guiding structure, but in the former case no supports can be inserted in the beam without disturbances, and this gives rise to difficulties.

8.4.1. *Excitation*

Starting again from the conventional rectangular guide, a taper or horn is to be used to couple to the dielectric rod or the image line. As has been mentioned in section 7.1, the field configuration of the HE_{11} mode is somewhat similar to that of the TE mode in circular waveguide, apart from the fact that the HE_{11} mode possesses a longitudinal E component as well as an H component. Therefore the transition part between standard rectangular

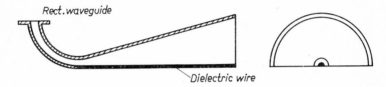

Fig. 7.28. Launching horn for dielectric image line.

waveguide and the dielectric rod or image line contains first a transition from rectangular to circular waveguide. The latter part is succeeded by a circular taper. The dielectric rod penetrates through the tapered horn into the circular waveguide-section and is fastened to the waveguide-wall. For image lines the lower half of both horn and circular waveguide is omitted, the bottom plate of the rectangular waveguide vanishes with a sharp edge (fig. 7.28). For a horn of this type the authors have obtained an attenuation of 1.3 dB at 4 mm wavelength. If the dielectric rod is sufficiently thin (radius $a/\lambda_0 < 0.383/(\varepsilon - 1)^{\frac{1}{2}}$) the dipole mode is the only possible mode and hence no means for spurious mode suppression are necessary.

8.4.2. *Bends, directional couplers*

If possible, bends in dielectric rod lines and image lines should be avoided since they give rise to radiation loss. To guide a wave the velocity of propagation of the electromagnetic waves inside the dielectric rod must be lower than the velocity in the surrounding medium, but at bends, directional couplers and other such discontinuities, there commonly exists a dielectric rod perpendicular to the guiding rod and in the neighbourhood of this the above requirement is no longer fulfilled. This results in a considerable radiation loss. From general geometric considerations one may deduce that this loss is at least 3 dB. One might imagine that bends having only a weak curvature should

Fig. 7.29. Some components for a 4 mm image line. (1) Launching horn, (2) movable reflector, (3) mica sheet directional coupler, (4) point-contact diode-detector with movable parabolic mirror, (5) variable attenuator, (6) matched load, (7) E bend. Another E bend is shown in front. The image line itself consists of an aluminium plate of 7 cm width whereon a strip of "Cellophane" adhesive tape is stuck.

be preferred, but measurements indicate (KING [1955b]), that no improvement can be expected in this way. The simplest and most effective bend is that formed by crossing two dielectric or image lines at 90° and placing a reflector of sufficient size symmetrically at the intersection.

Directional couplers can be similarly made by replacing the reflector by a dielectric sheet, or by two dielectric prisms, as indicated in section 8.1.

In the case of image lines H bends are the more simply constructed. An H bend can be formed from the directional coupler shown in fig. 7.29 (3) replacing the mica by a conducting sheet. E bends are less simple especially if the bends are to be such that the wave has to pass through the image plane. In fig. 7.29 two of these "convex E bends" are shown, consisting of two perpendicular image lines and a plane reflector. The attenuation is of the same order as the attenuation of H bends.

8.4.3. *Attenuators*

If an absorbing material is placed in the neighbourhood of the dielectric rod some of the energy travelling outside the wire will be dissipated. The difficulty with such types of attenuators is how to achieve satisfactory performance without radiation loss. If the shape of the absorbing material is such that the dielectric rod is approached gradually, no measurable radiation loss occurs. As absorbing material wood has excellent properties and a matched load can be made by placing an inside-tapered tube of wood on the dielectric rod (see fig. 7.29 (6)).

8.4.4. *Detection mount*

A detector that fits immediately into an image line is shown in fig. 7.29 (4). The detector itself is located under the parabolic, movable mirror and consists of a 2 mm point-contact diode of the type used in conventional 2 mm waveguides. Compared to a conventional crystal detector in a 4 mm waveguide, tapered to the image line, the sensitivity of this construction was slightly but not significantly better.

8.5. COMPONENTS FOR BEAM GUIDES

Many components based upon optical techniques may be used in the beam guide. As a first order approximation in many calculations the wave fronts may be taken as plane wave fronts and therefore optical calculation methods may be used. Here too it is of importance, in order to avoid higher mode generation, that the components operate uniformly over the cross-section of the beam.

A directional coupler may be constructed by using a semi-transparent mirror or a double prism at the intersection of two crossing beam waveguides. By appropriately closing the arms with reflectors or absorbers, phase-shifters or variable attenuators may be obtained as described in the section on over-sized waveguide components.

Instead of a dielectric sheet at the intersection, a wire or strip grating may be used. In this case it is important that the periodicity of the grating should be smaller than the wavelength in order to avoid sidewards radiation. These gratings reflect waves having the electric field component parallel to the wires or strips, while the component perpendicular to the strips is trans-mitted.

The reflection of these gratings can thus be varied by changing the angle between the direction of polarization of the wave and the wires.

A variable attenuator may be obtained by cascading two such gratings, one of which is rotatable (VAN NIE [1965]).

9. Closing remarks

In the preceding sections a survey has been given of the methods suitable for propagation of millimetre and submillimetre waves. It may be asked which method looks most promising. The answer to this question depends upon the type of experiment involved. For plasma research the beam waveguide seems to be the obvious choice but for solid state spectroscopy at low temperatures, where the waves have to be brought in and out of a cryostat, the oversized waveguide may be more suitable.

In order to facilitate a proper choice of a propagating technique the pro-perties of the different methods are summarized in table 7.3. Here, for every guiding structure discussed in this chapter, the theoretical attenuation at four different wavelengths is given for representative values of the design param-eters. To make a comparison possible, the effective cross-section of the guide is also given. The table contains a review of the specific advantages of the several guiding structures and shows clearly that the problem of the propagation of millimetre and submillimetre waves has no unique solu-tion. The conventional microwave transmission methods fail in this region because the losses become prohibitivily high; on the other hand the optical methods such as the beam waveguide are not yet suited to replace them com-pletely. The single mode operated oversized microwave structures seem to be most promising for the near future, but numerous technical difficulties in component design and mode control are encountered.

TAB

GUIDING STRUCTURE		Theoretical attenuation in dB/m at $\lambda_0 =$			
		4mm	2mm	1mm	0.5
Standard guide		2	4.6	17	48
10 times oversized waveguide		0.11	0.24	0.88	2
Same guide used as tall guide		0.057	0.12	0.46	1
15 times oversized waveguide		0.057	0.2	0.6	1
Same guide used as tall guide		0.04	0.1	0.3	0
H-guide		0.75	1.7	5.5	15
oversized H-guide		0.15	0.3	0.6	1
dielectric rod $\varepsilon \simeq 2.5$; $\tan \delta = 4 \times 10^{-4}$	$2a/\lambda_0 = 0.3$	0.34	0.68	1.36	2
	$2a/\lambda_0 = 0.5$	3.4	6.8	13.6	27
Image line $\varepsilon \simeq 2.5$; $\tan \delta = 4 \times 10^{-4}$ $\sigma = 5.8 \times 10^7$ S/m	$2a/\lambda_0 = 0.3$	0.9	2.3	5.7	15
	$2a/\lambda_0 = 0.5$	5.3	12.1	28.5	69
Beam waveguide	$R/\lambda_0 = 5$	3.7	7.5	14.5	29
	$R/\lambda_0 = 50$	0.04	0.07	0.15	0

Note added in the proof

After completion of this manuscript new investigations on oversized wave-guides and components have been carried out by BUTTERWECK and DE RONDE [1967]. They developed a range of components such as modefilters and transducers, tapers, bends, directional couplers, variable attenuators, phase shifters, variable impedances, plungers and loads. A feature of their design is that they use a "waveguide-approach", rather than an "optical approach", such as TAUB and HINDTN [1964]. Much attention is paid to mode-purity. All components prove to be effective over a frequency decade.

ive guide section	Modes	Advantages	Disadvantages	Components
$0.28 \lambda_0^2$	Single mode	Design flexible and well known	High attenuation; small size	Standard components
$3 \lambda_0^2$ $3 \lambda_0^2$	Many modes possible	Low attenuation, adequate size	Pure mode feeding required; accurate construction of guide and components	Simple but precisely made components
$5 \lambda_0^2$	Single mode	Improved attenuation, flexible design	Small size in one direction	Not many components known
λ_0^2	Several modes possible	Low attenuation	Pure mode feeding required	Constructions may be complicated
λ_0^2 λ_0^2	Single mode	Very low attenuation	May radiate; supports and components may cause difficulty	
λ_0^2 λ_0^2	Single mode	Supports and components easily applicable	Higher attenuation than diel. rod	Simple constructions
λ_0^2 λ_0^2	Many beam modes possible	Open structure, easily accessible; for large lenses improved attenuation	For moderate size lenses, high attenuation; large structure	Simple constructions based upon optical techniques

References

F. A. BENSON and D. H. STEVEN, Proc. IEE **110** (1963) 1008.

G. BIERNSON and D. J. KINSLEY, IEEE Trans. on Microwave Theory and Techniques MTT **13** (1965) 345.

J. BLED, A. BRESSON, R. PAPOULAR and J. G. WEGROWE, Onde Elect. **44** (1964) 26.

D. L. H. BLOMFIELD, J. Sci. Instr. **41** (1964) 517.

H. J. BUTTERWECK and F. C. DE RONDE, Oversized rectangular waveguide components for mm waves, Philips Technical Review (1967) in the press.

J. R. CARSON, S. P. MEAD and S. A. SCHELKUNOFF, Bell Syst. Techn. J. **15** (1936) 310.

C. H. CHANDLER, J. Appl. Phys. **20** (1949) 1188.

J. R. CHRISTIAN and G. GOUBAU, IRE Trans. on Antennas and Propagation AP **9** (1961) 256.

M. COHN, IRE Trans. on Microwave Theory and Techniques MTT **7** (1959) 202.

M. COHN, IRE Trans. on Microwave Theory and Techniques MTT 8 (1960) 449.

R. E. COLLIN, Field Theory of Guided Waves (McGraw-Hill Book Comp. Inc., New York, 1960).

A. L. CULLEN and E. F. F. GILLESPIE, Proc. Symp. on Millimeter Waves, New York 1959 (Polytechnic Press of the Polytechnic Inst. of Brooklyn) p. 109.

J. E. DEGENFORD, M. O. SIRKIS and W. H. STEIER, IEEE Trans. on Microwave Theory and Techniques MTT 12 (1964) 445.

P. DIAMENT, S. P. SCHLESINGER and A. VIGANTS, IRE Trans. on Microwave Theory and Techniques MTT 9 (1961) 332.

W. M. ELSASSER, J. Appl. Phys. 20 (1949) 1193.

C. W. VAN ES, M. GEVERS and F. C. DE RONDE, Philips Tech. Rev. 22 (1960/61) 181.

J. W. E. GRIEMSMANN and L. BIRENBAUM, Proc. Symp. on Millimeter Waves, New York 1959 (Polytechnic Press of Polytechnic Inst. of Brooklyn) p. 543.

J. W. E. GRIEMSMANN, Microwaves 2 (1963) 20.

G. GOUBAU and F. SCHWERING, IRE Trans. on Antennas and Propagation AP 9 (1961) 248.

D. HONDROS and P. DEBEYE, Ann. d. Physik 32 (1910) 462.

A. E. KARBOWIAK, Proc. IRE 46 (1958) 1706.

D. D. KING, J. Appl. Phys. 23 (1952) 699.

D. D. KING, IRE Trans. on Microwave Theory and Techniques MTT 3 (1955) 75.

D. D. KING, IRE Trans. on Microwave Theory and Techniques MTT 3 (1955b) 35.

D. D. KING and S. P. SCHLESINGER, IRE Trans. on Microwave Theory and Techniques MTT 5 (1957) 31.

M. J. KING, J. D. RODGERS, F. SOBEL, F. L. WENTHWORTH and J. C. WILTSE, Electronic Communications, Scientific Rep. no. 2 (1960) p. 15.

M. A. KOTT, IRE Trans. on Microwave Theory and Techniques MTT 10 (1962) 401.

P. MALLACH, Fernm. Techn. Zeitschrift 1 (1955) 8.

N. MARCUVITZ, Waveguide Handbook (McGraw-Hill Book Comp. Inc., New York, 1951).

C. H. MARTIN, Proc. IRE 48 (1960) 250.

R. MEREDITH and J. H. PREECE, IEEE Trans. on Microwave Theory and Techniques MTT 11 (1963) 332.

R. A. MORSE and R. E. BEAM, Proc. of the National Electronics Conference 1956 (The National Electronics Conference Inc., Chicago).

A. G. VAN NIE, Philips Res. Reports 19 (1964) 378.

A. G. VAN NIE, Nachr. Techn. Z. 1 (1965) 17.

S. A. SCHELKUNOFF, Electromagnetic Waves (D. van Nostrand Comp. Inc., New York, 1943) p. 425.

S. P. SCHLESINGER and D. D. KING, IRE Trans. on Microwave Theory and Techniques MTT 6 (1958) 291.

S. P. SCHLESINGER, P. DIAMENT and A. VIGANTS, IRE Trans. on Microwave Theory and Techniques MTT 8 (1960) 252.

G. SCHULTEN, Arch. Electr. Uebertr. 14 (1960) 163.

J. A. STRATTON, Electromagnetic Theory (McGraw-Hill Book Comp. Inc., New York, 1941).

K. TAKIYAMA and H. SHIGESAWA, Sci. Eng. Rev. Doshisha Univ. 2 (1962) 139.

J. J. TAUB, H. J. HINDIN, O. F. HINCKELMANN and M. L. WRIGHT, IEEE Trans. on Microwave Theory and Techniques, MTT 11 (1963) 338.

J. J. TAUB and H. J. HINDIN, Microwaves 3 (1964a) 20.

J. J. TAUB, H. J. HINDIN and G. P. KURPIS, IEEE Trans. on Microwave Theory and Techniques MTT 12 (1964b) 618.

F. J. TISCHER, Proc. IEE 106 (1959).

F. J. TISCHER, IEEE Trans. on Microwave Theory and Techniques MTT 11 (1963) 291.

H. G. UNGER, Bell Syst. Techn. J. 37 (1958) 899.

D. J. H. WORT, J. Sci. Instr. 39 (1962) 317.

Author index

Subject index

P. 132